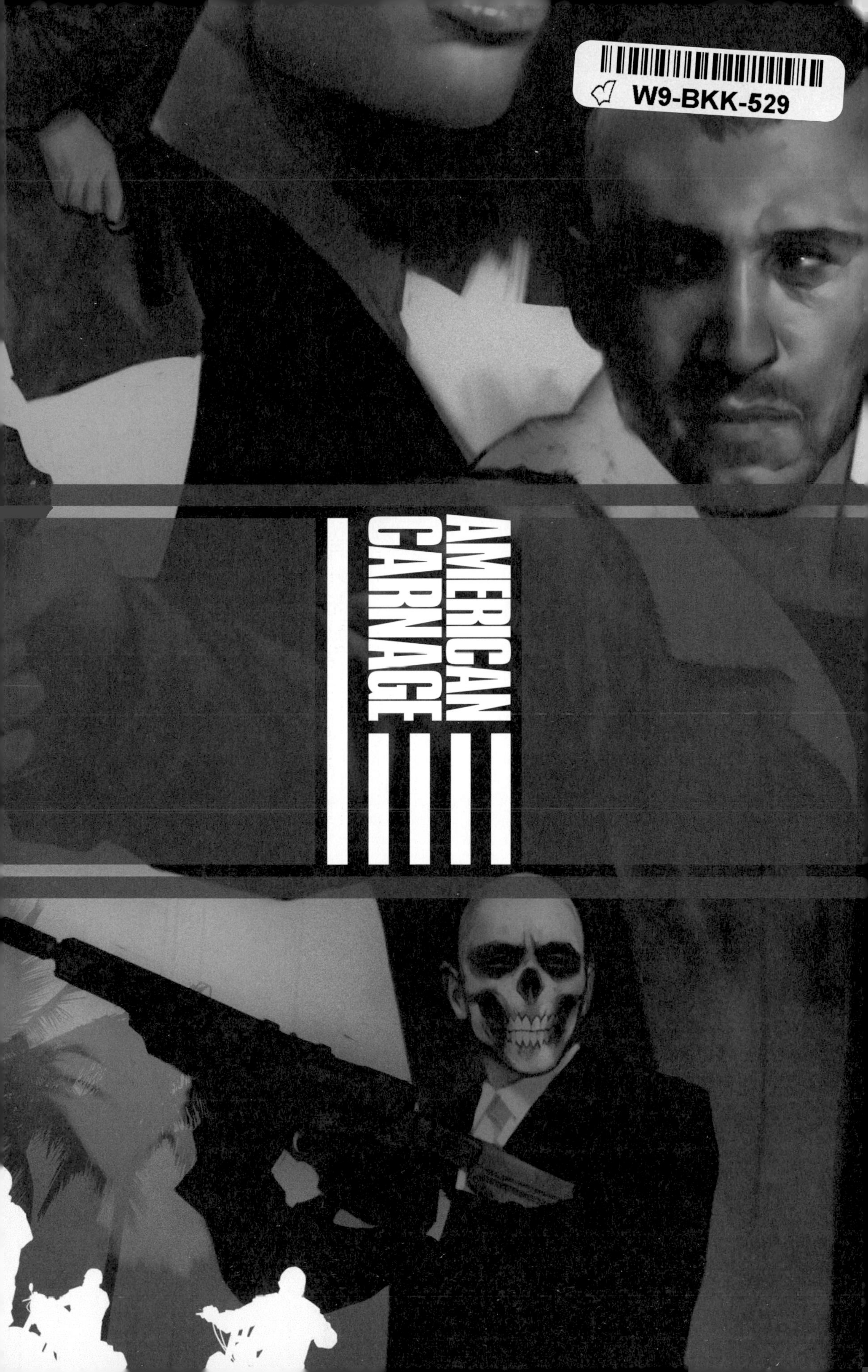
AMERICAN
CARNAGE

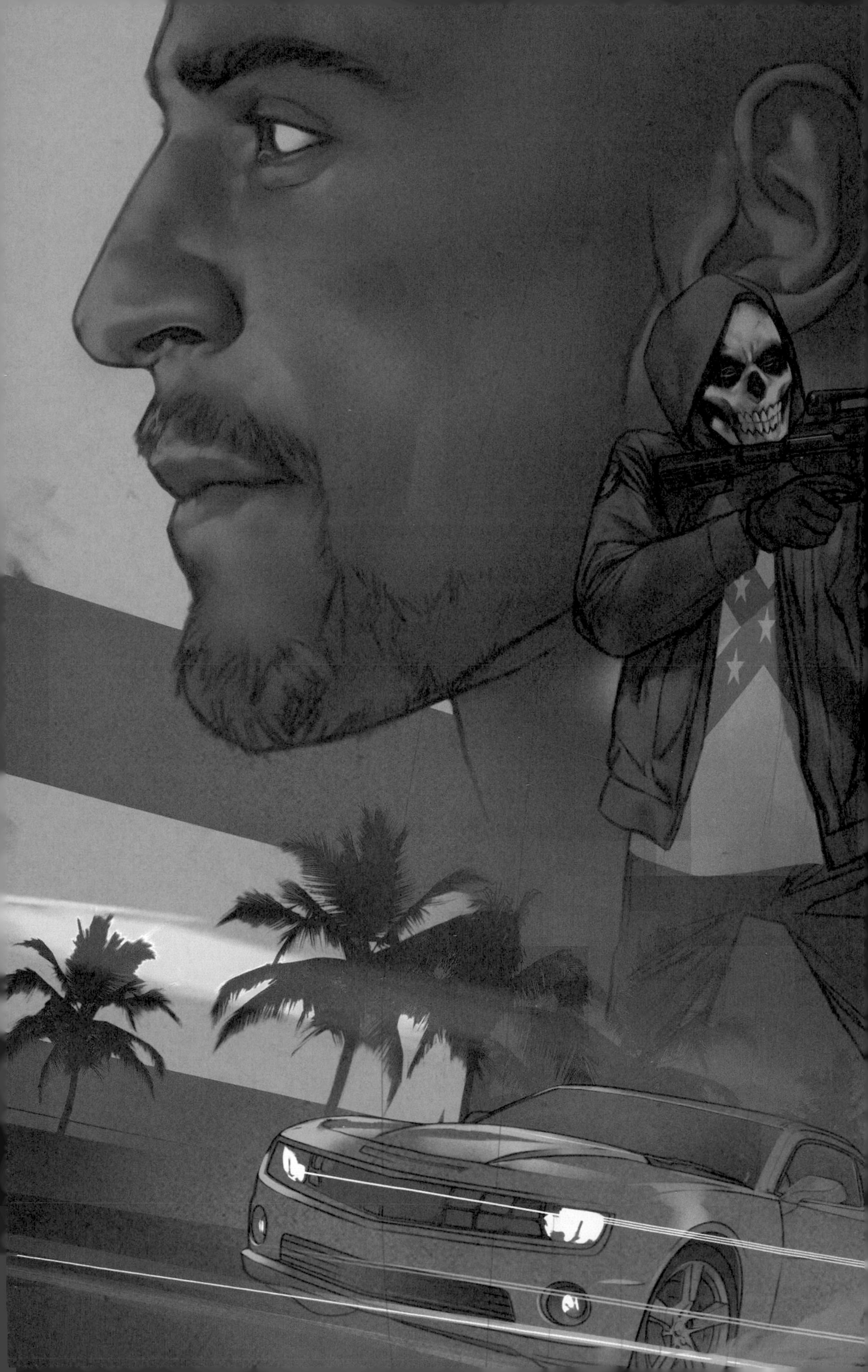

AMERICAN CARNAGE

Written by
BRYAN HILL

Art by
LEANDRO FERNANDEZ

Colors by
DEAN WHITE

Letters by
PAT BROSSEAU

Collection Cover Art and
Original Series Covers by
BEN OLIVER

AMERICAN CARNAGE created by
BRYAN HILL and **LEANDRO FERNANDEZ**

ANDY KHOURI Editor – Original Series MAGGIE HOWELL Assistant Editor – Original Series
JEB WOODARD Group Editor – Collected Editions SCOTT NYBAKKEN Editor – Collected Edition
STEVE COOK Design Director – Books DAMIAN RYLAND Publication Design ADAM RADO Publication Production

BOB HARRAS Senior VP – Editor-in-Chief, DC Comics MARK DOYLE Executive Editor, Vertigo & Black Label

DAN DiDIO Publisher JIM LEE Publisher & Chief Creative Officer BOBBIE CHASE VP – New Publishing Initiatives & Talent Development
DON FALLETTI VP – Manufacturing Operations & Workflow Management LAWRENCE GANEM VP – Talent Services
ALISON GILL Senior VP – Manufacturing & Operations HANK KANALZ Senior VP – Publishing Strategy & Support Services
DAN MIRON VP – Publishing Operations NICK J. NAPOLITANO VP – Manufacturing Administration & Design
NANCY SPEARS VP – Sales MICHELE R. WELLS VP & Executive Editor, Young Reader

AMERICAN CARNAGE

DC Comics, 2900 West Alameda Ave., Burbank, CA 91505
Printed by LSC Communications, Kendallville, IN, USA. 9/20/19. First Printing.
ISBN: 978-1-4012-9145-7

Library of Congress Cataloging-in-Publication Data is available.

PEFC Certified

This product is from
sustainably managed
forests and controlled
sources

PEFC

PEFC/29-31-337   www.pefc.org

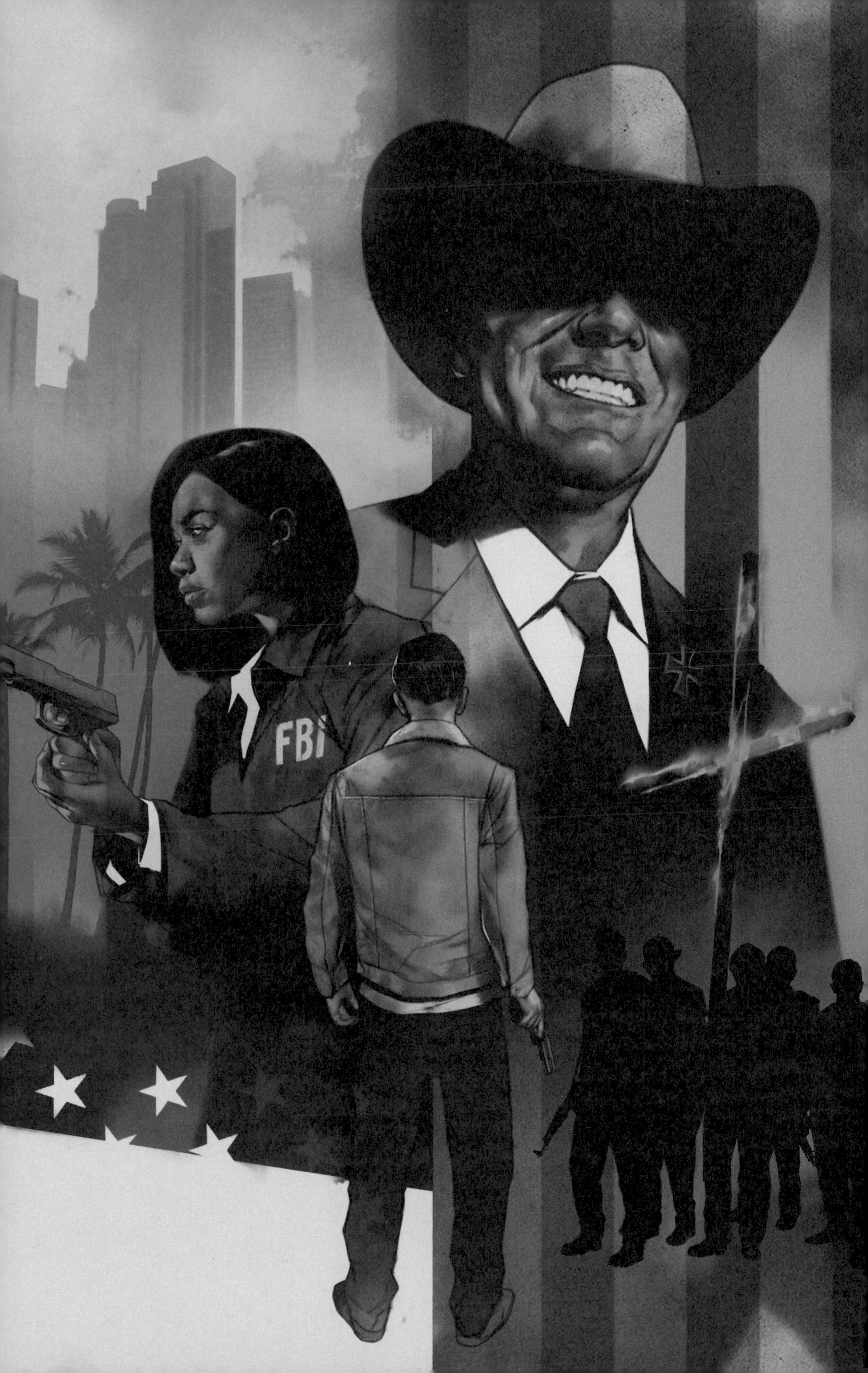
FBI

CHAPTER ONE: FREEDOM

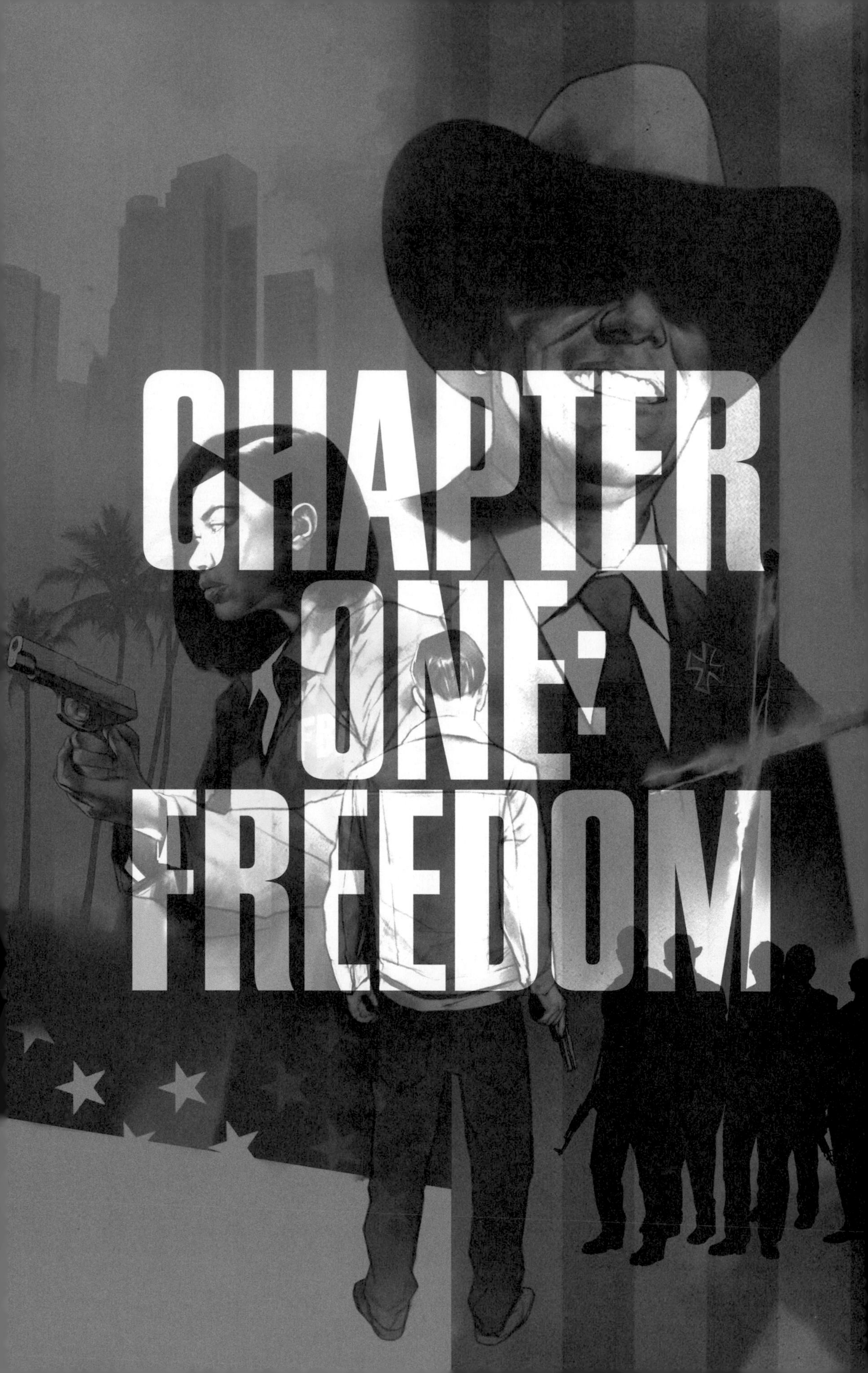

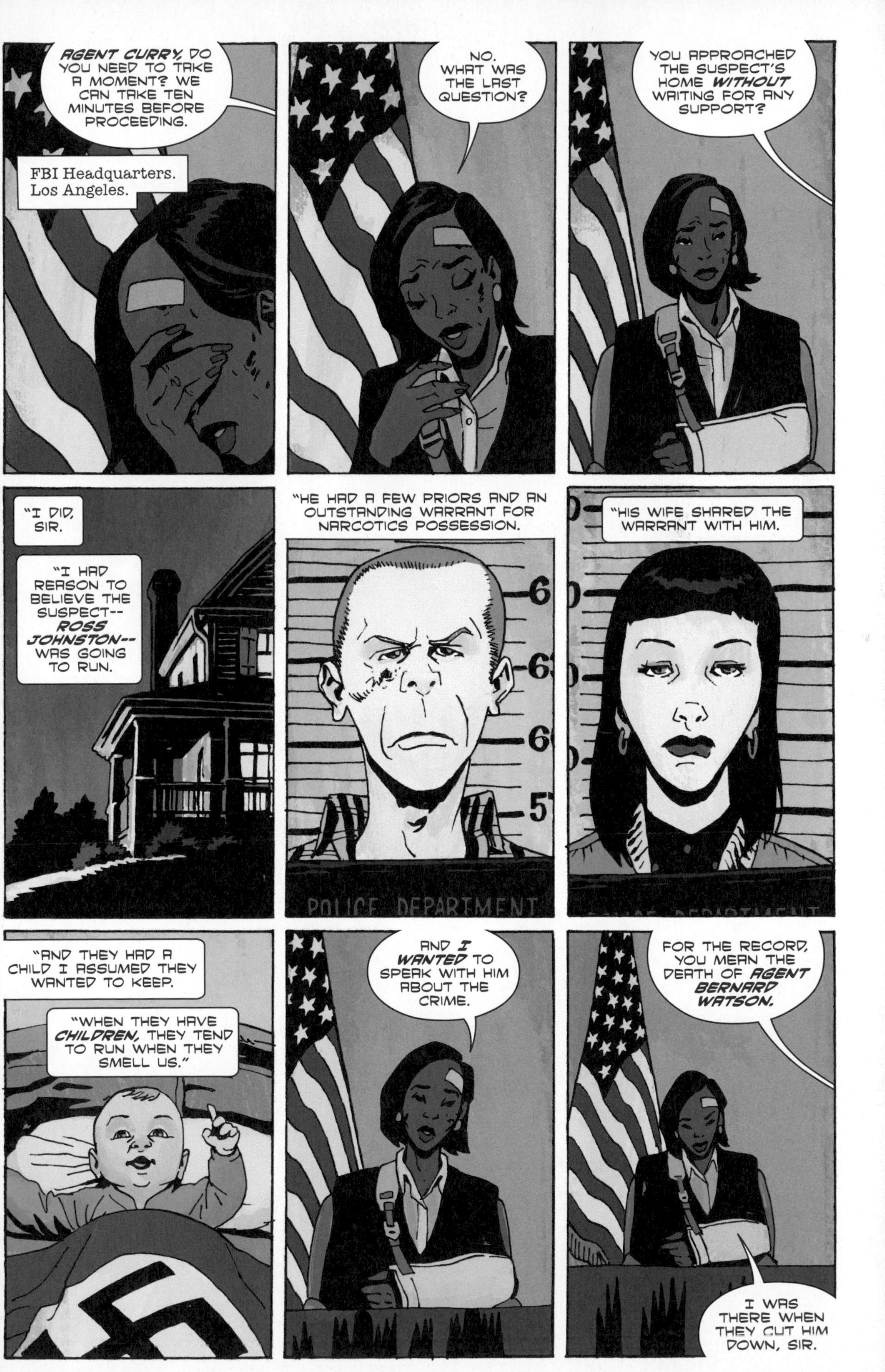
AGENT CURRY, DO YOU NEED TO TAKE A MOMENT? WE CAN TAKE TEN MINUTES BEFORE PROCEEDING.
FBI Headquarters. Los Angeles.
NO. WHAT WAS THE LAST QUESTION?
YOU APPROACHED THE SUSPECT'S HOME WITHOUT WAITING FOR ANY SUPPORT?
"I DID, SIR.
"I HAD REASON TO BELIEVE THE SUSPECT-- ROSS JOHNSTON-- WAS GOING TO RUN.
"HE HAD A FEW PRIORS AND AN OUTSTANDING WARRANT FOR NARCOTICS POSSESSION.
POLICE DEPARTMENT
"HIS WIFE SHARED THE WARRANT WITH HIM.
"AND THEY HAD A CHILD I ASSUMED THEY WANTED TO KEEP.
"WHEN THEY HAVE CHILDREN, THEY TEND TO RUN WHEN THEY SMELL US."
AND I WANTED TO SPEAK WITH HIM ABOUT THE CRIME.
FOR THE RECORD, YOU MEAN THE DEATH OF AGENT BERNARD WATSON.
I WAS THERE WHEN THEY CUT HIM DOWN, SIR.

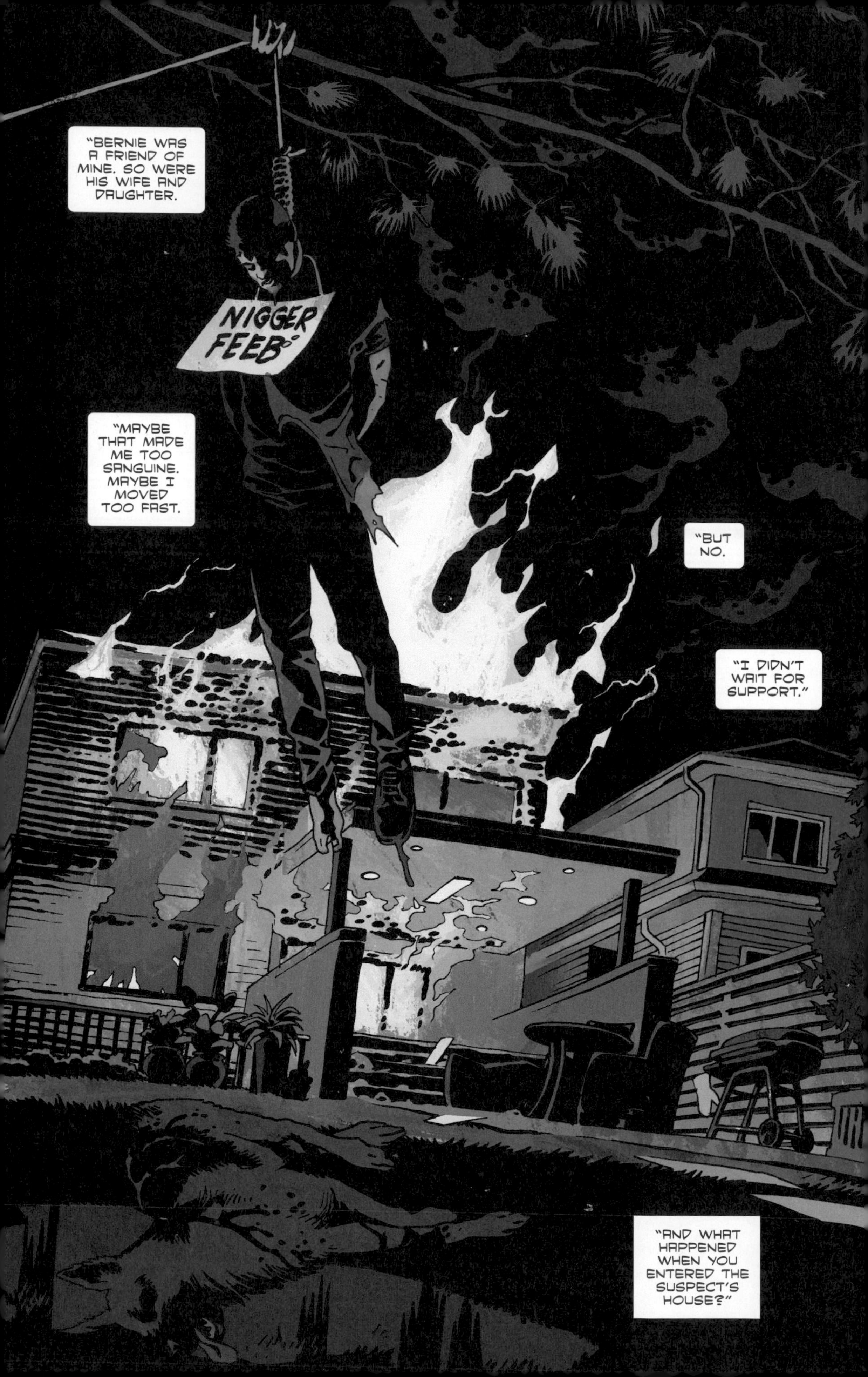
"BERNIE WAS A FRIEND OF MINE. SO WERE HIS WIFE AND DAUGHTER.
NIGGER FEEB
"MAYBE THAT MADE ME TOO SANGUINE. MAYBE I MOVED TOO FAST.
"BUT NO.
"I DIDN'T WAIT FOR SUPPORT."
"AND WHAT HAPPENED WHEN YOU ENTERED THE SUSPECT'S HOUSE?"

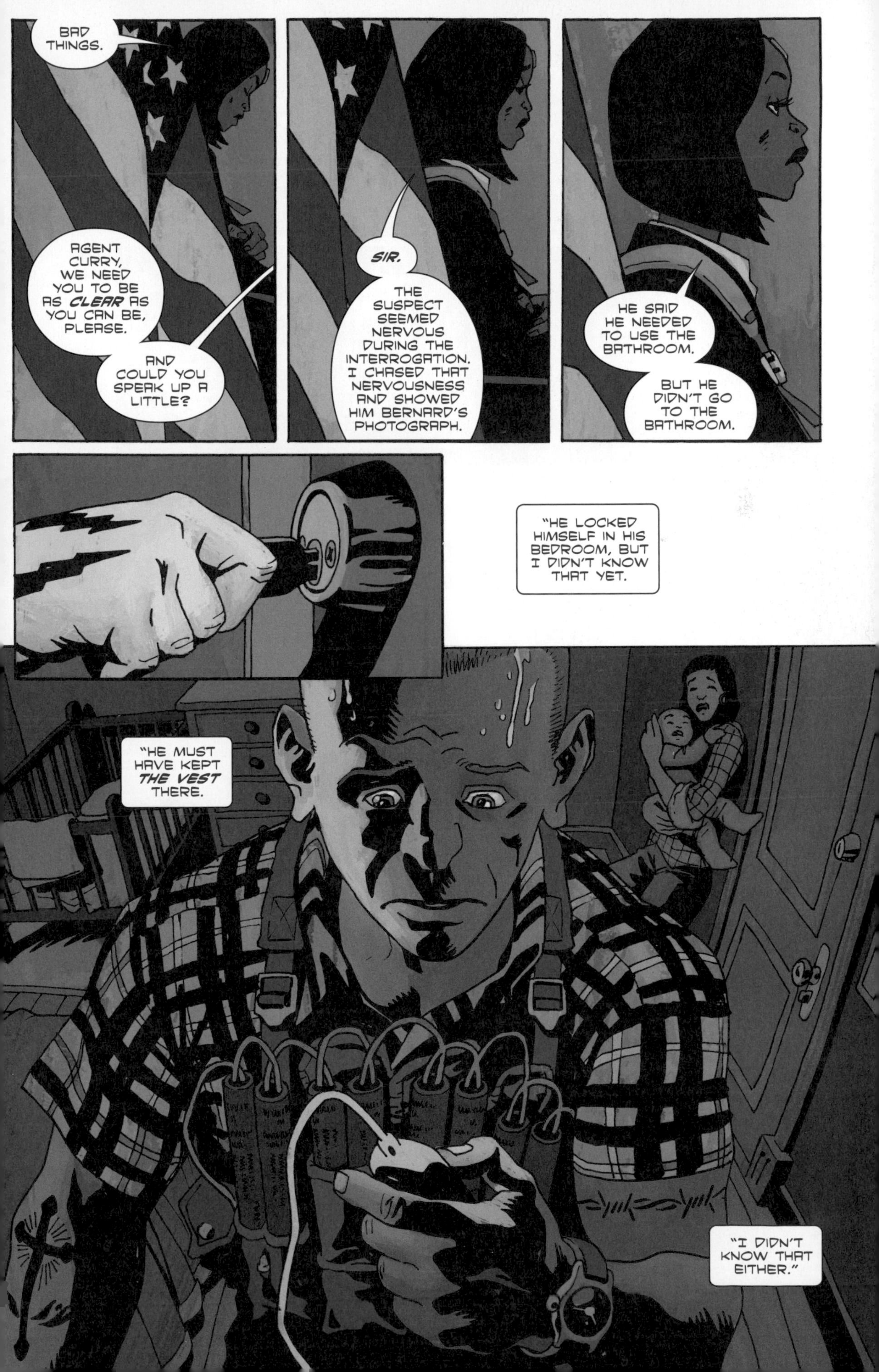
BAD THINGS.
AGENT CURRY, WE NEED YOU TO BE AS CLEAR AS YOU CAN BE, PLEASE.
AND COULD YOU SPEAK UP A LITTLE?
SIR.
THE SUSPECT SEEMED NERVOUS DURING THE INTERROGATION. I CHASED THAT NERVOUSNESS AND SHOWED HIM BERNARD'S PHOTOGRAPH.
HE SAID HE NEEDED TO USE THE BATHROOM.
BUT HE DIDN'T GO TO THE BATHROOM.
"HE LOCKED HIMSELF IN HIS BEDROOM, BUT I DIDN'T KNOW THAT YET.
"HE MUST HAVE KEPT THE VEST THERE.
"I DIDN'T KNOW THAT EITHER."

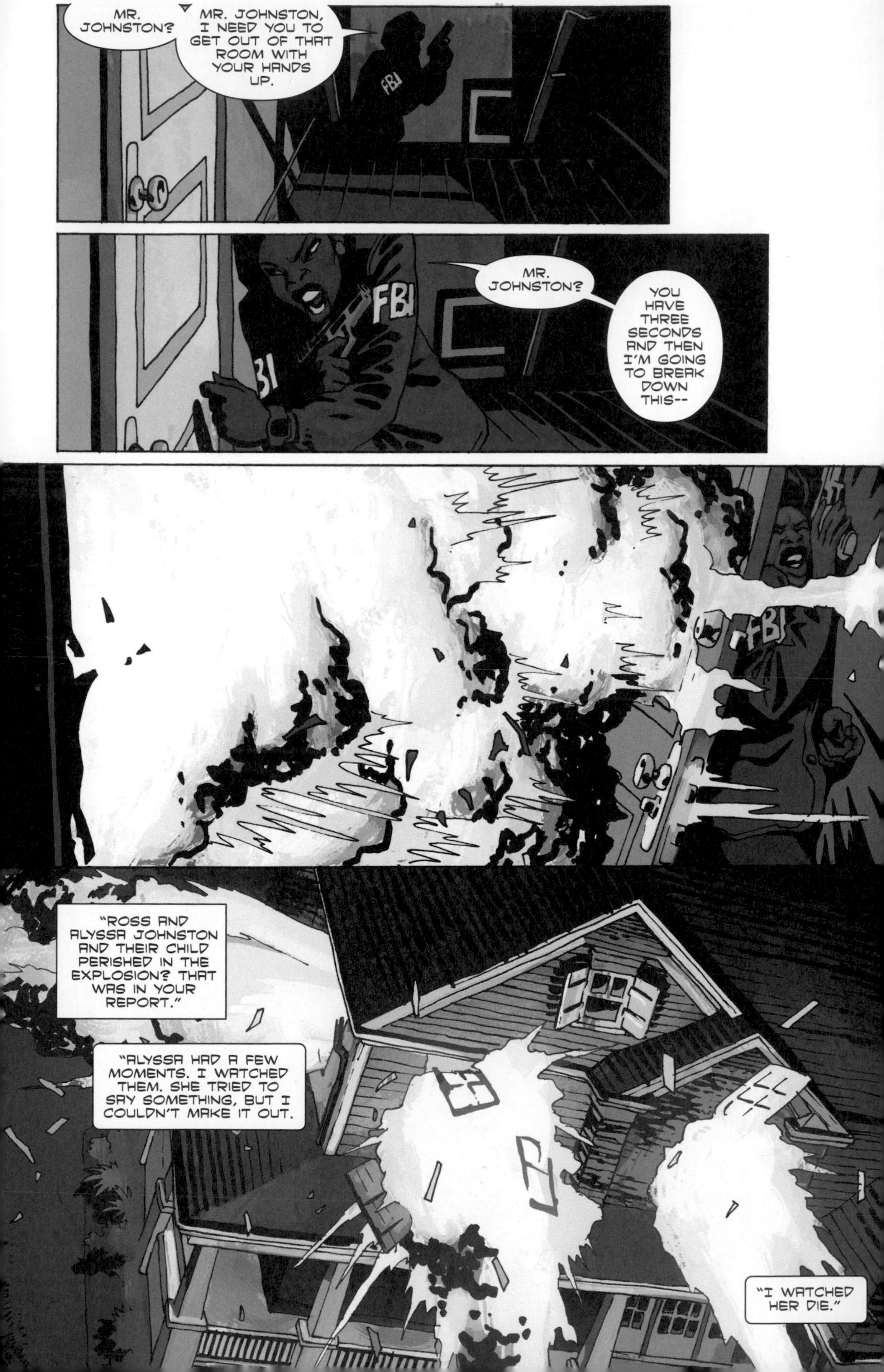

MR. JOHNSTON?
MR. JOHNSTON, I NEED YOU TO GET OUT OF THAT ROOM WITH YOUR HANDS UP.
MR. JOHNSTON?
YOU HAVE THREE SECONDS AND THEN I'M GOING TO BREAK DOWN THIS--
"ROSS AND ALYSSA JOHNSTON AND THEIR CHILD PERISHED IN THE EXPLOSION? THAT WAS IN YOUR REPORT."
"ALYSSA HAD A FEW MOMENTS. I WATCHED THEM. SHE TRIED TO SAY SOMETHING, BUT I COULDN'T MAKE IT OUT.
"I WATCHED HER DIE."

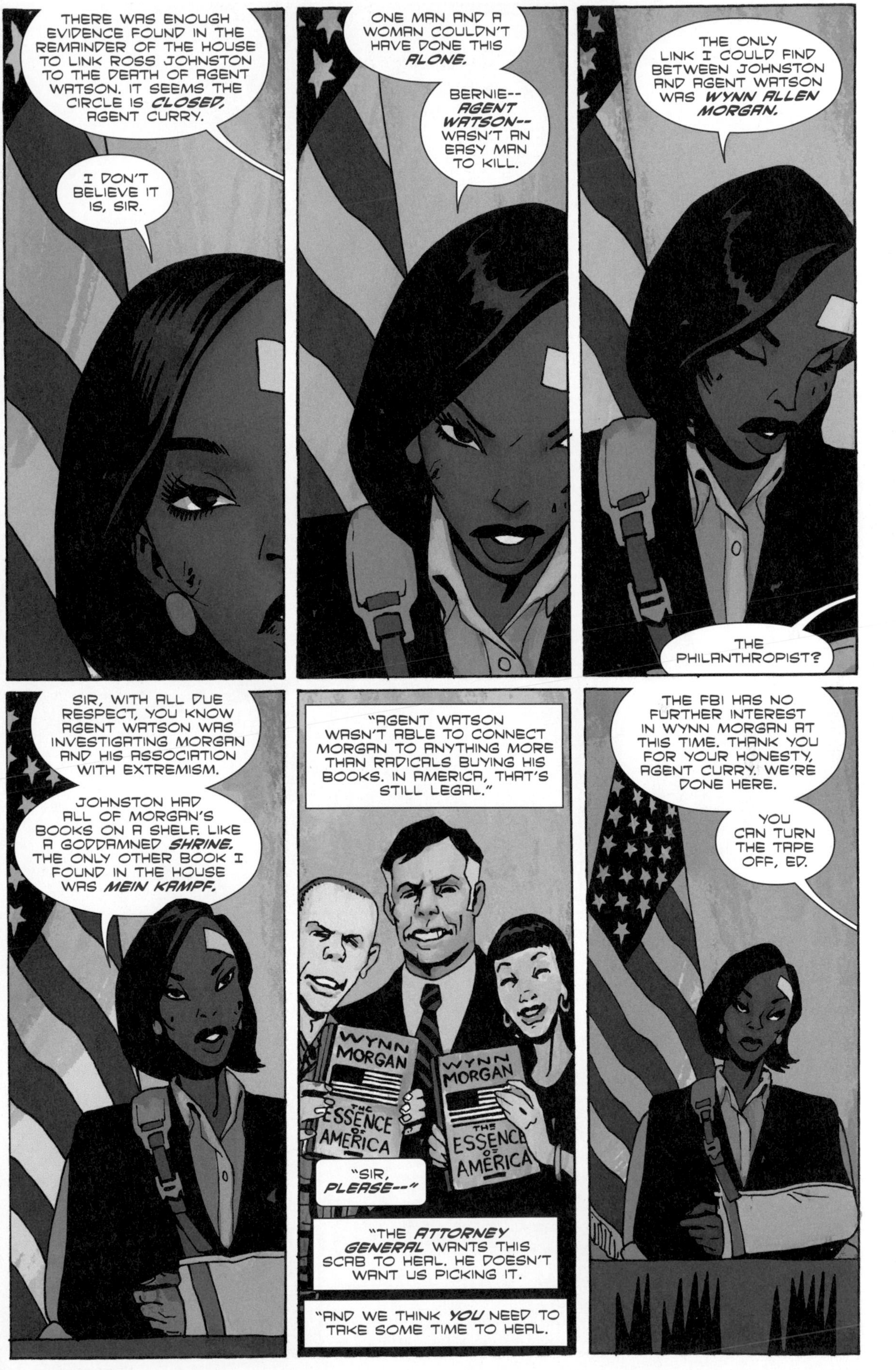
THERE WAS ENOUGH EVIDENCE FOUND IN THE REMAINDER OF THE HOUSE TO LINK ROSS JOHNSTON TO THE DEATH OF AGENT WATSON. IT SEEMS THE CIRCLE IS CLOSED, AGENT CURRY.
I DON'T BELIEVE IT IS, SIR.
ONE MAN AND A WOMAN COULDN'T HAVE DONE THIS ALONE.
BERNIE-- AGENT WATSON-- WASN'T AN EASY MAN TO KILL.
THE ONLY LINK I COULD FIND BETWEEN JOHNSTON AND AGENT WATSON WAS WYNN ALLEN MORGAN.
THE PHILANTHROPIST?
SIR, WITH ALL DUE RESPECT, YOU KNOW AGENT WATSON WAS INVESTIGATING MORGAN AND HIS ASSOCIATION WITH EXTREMISM.
JOHNSTON HAD ALL OF MORGAN'S BOOKS ON A SHELF. LIKE A GODDAMNED SHRINE. THE ONLY OTHER BOOK I FOUND IN THE HOUSE WAS MEIN KAMPF.
"AGENT WATSON WASN'T ABLE TO CONNECT MORGAN TO ANYTHING MORE THAN RADICALS BUYING HIS BOOKS. IN AMERICA, THAT'S STILL LEGAL."
WYNN MORGAN THE ESSENCE OF AMERICA
WYNN MORGAN THE ESSENCE OF AMERICA
"SIR, PLEASE--"
"THE ATTORNEY GENERAL WANTS THIS SCAB TO HEAL. HE DOESN'T WANT US PICKING IT.
"AND WE THINK YOU NEED TO TAKE SOME TIME TO HEAL.
THE FBI HAS NO FURTHER INTEREST IN WYNN MORGAN AT THIS TIME. THANK YOU FOR YOUR HONESTY, AGENT CURRY. WE'RE DONE HERE.
YOU CAN TURN THE TAPE OFF, ED.

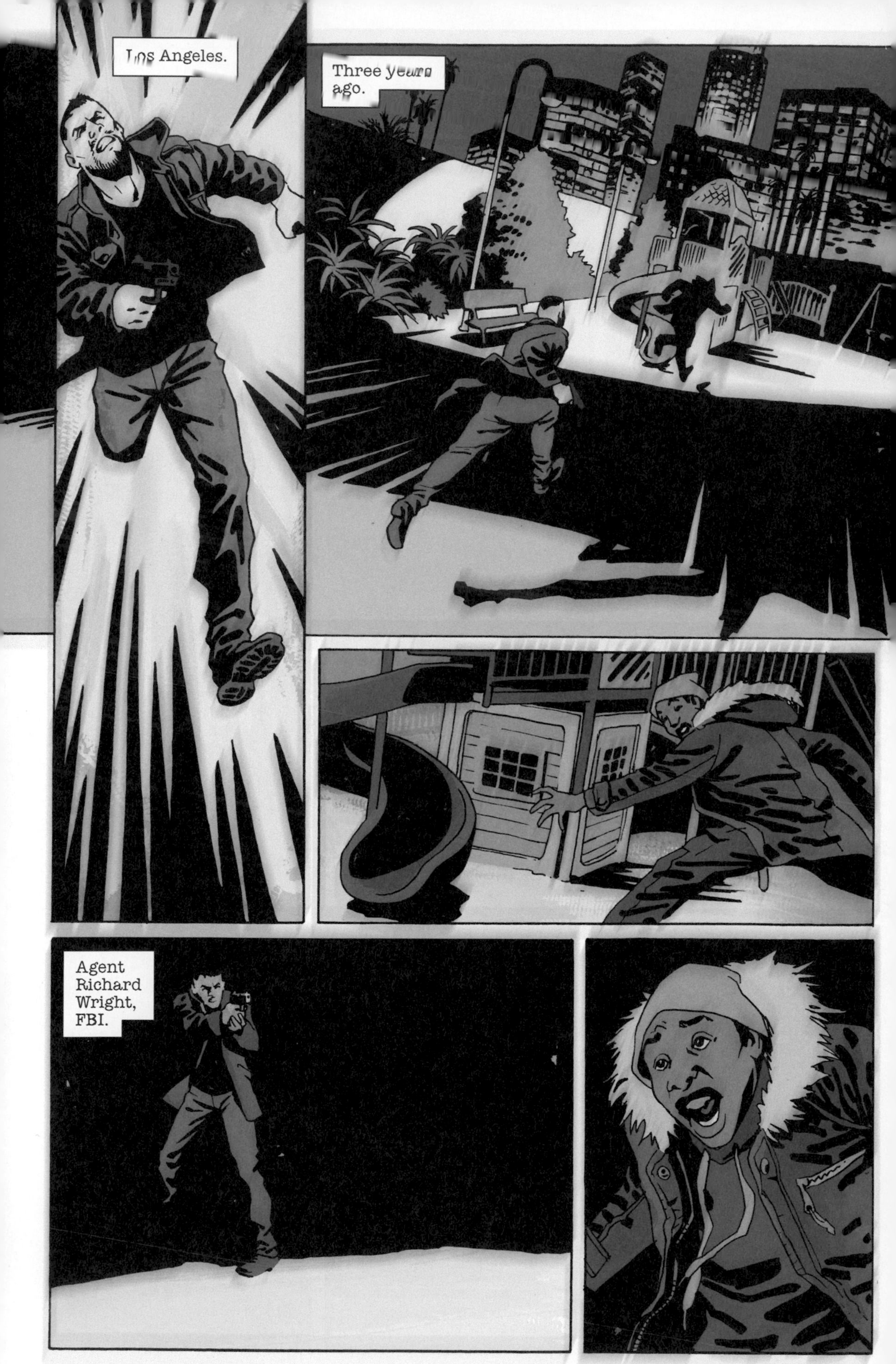
Los Angeles.
Three years ago.
Agent Richard Wright, FBI.

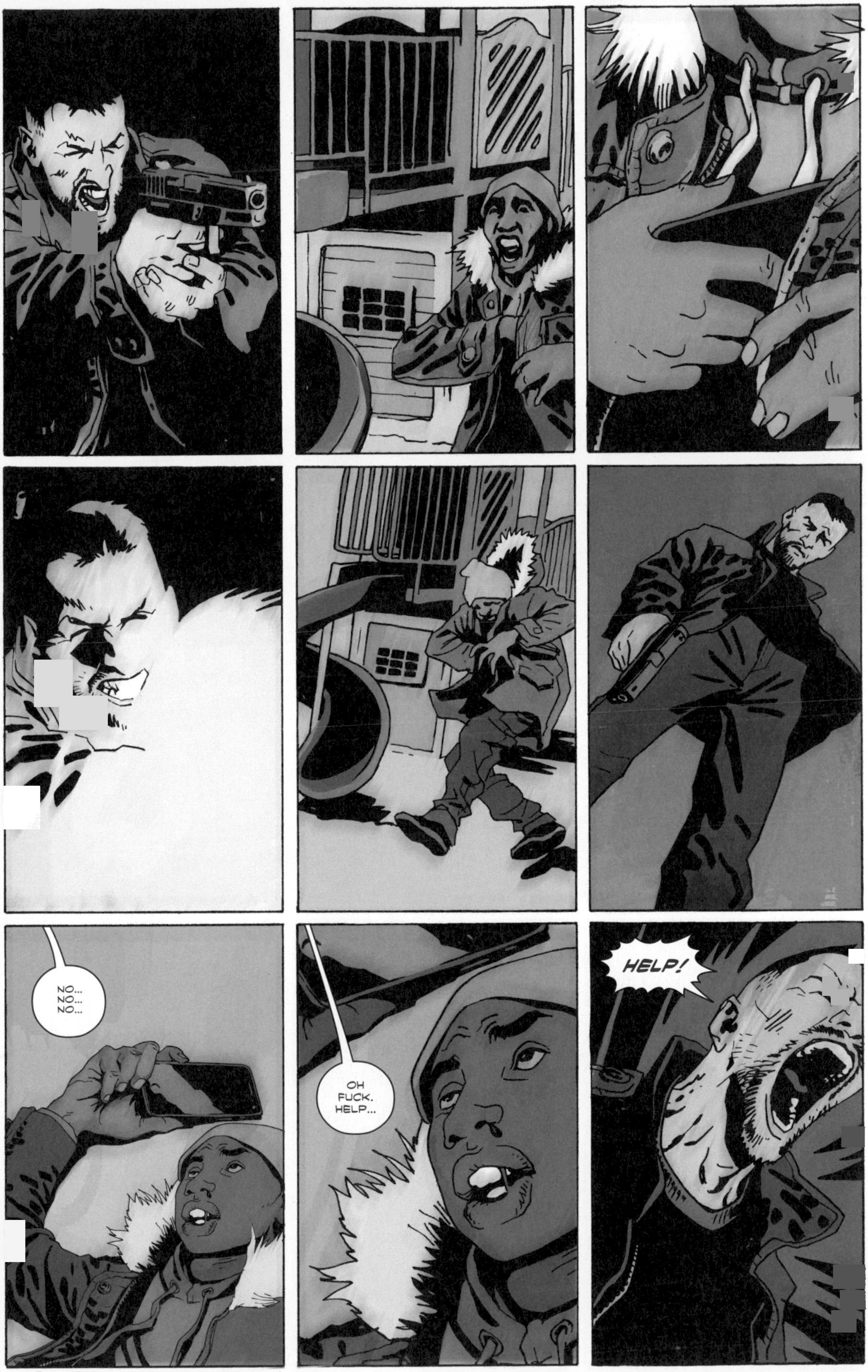

NO... NO... NO...
OH FUCK. HELP...
HELP!

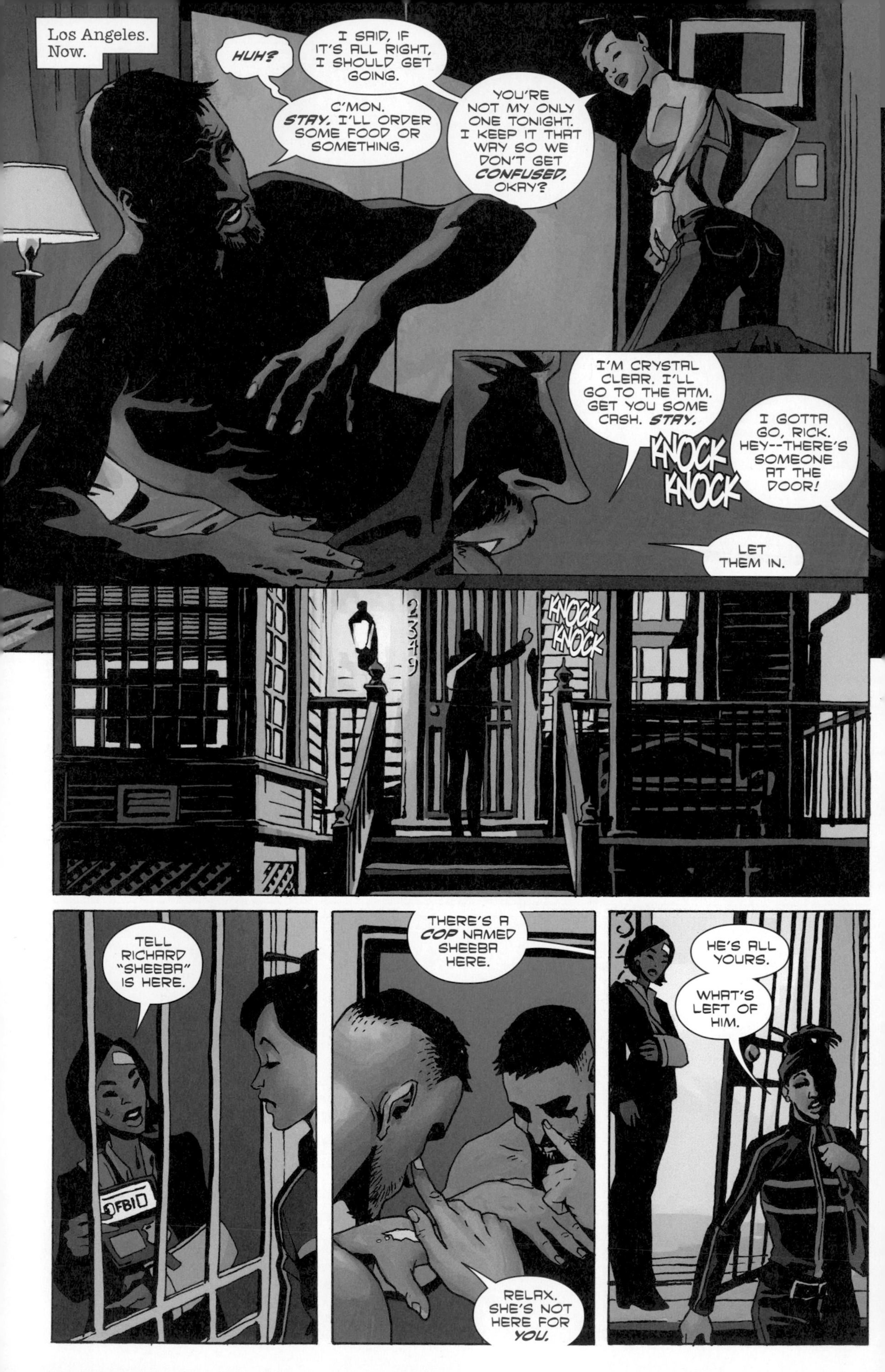
Los Angeles. Now.
HUH?
I SAID, IF IT'S ALL RIGHT, I SHOULD GET GOING.
C'MON. STAY. I'LL ORDER SOME FOOD OR SOMETHING.
YOU'RE NOT MY ONLY ONE TONIGHT. I KEEP IT THAT WAY SO WE DON'T GET CONFUSED, OKAY?
I'M CRYSTAL CLEAR. I'LL GO TO THE ATM. GET YOU SOME CASH. STAY.
KNOCK KNOCK
I GOTTA GO, RICK. HEY--THERE'S SOMEONE AT THE DOOR!
LET THEM IN.
KNOCK KNOCK
TELL RICHARD "SHEEBA" IS HERE.
THERE'S A COP NAMED SHEEBA HERE.
RELAX. SHE'S NOT HERE FOR YOU.
HE'S ALL YOURS.
WHAT'S LEFT OF HIM.

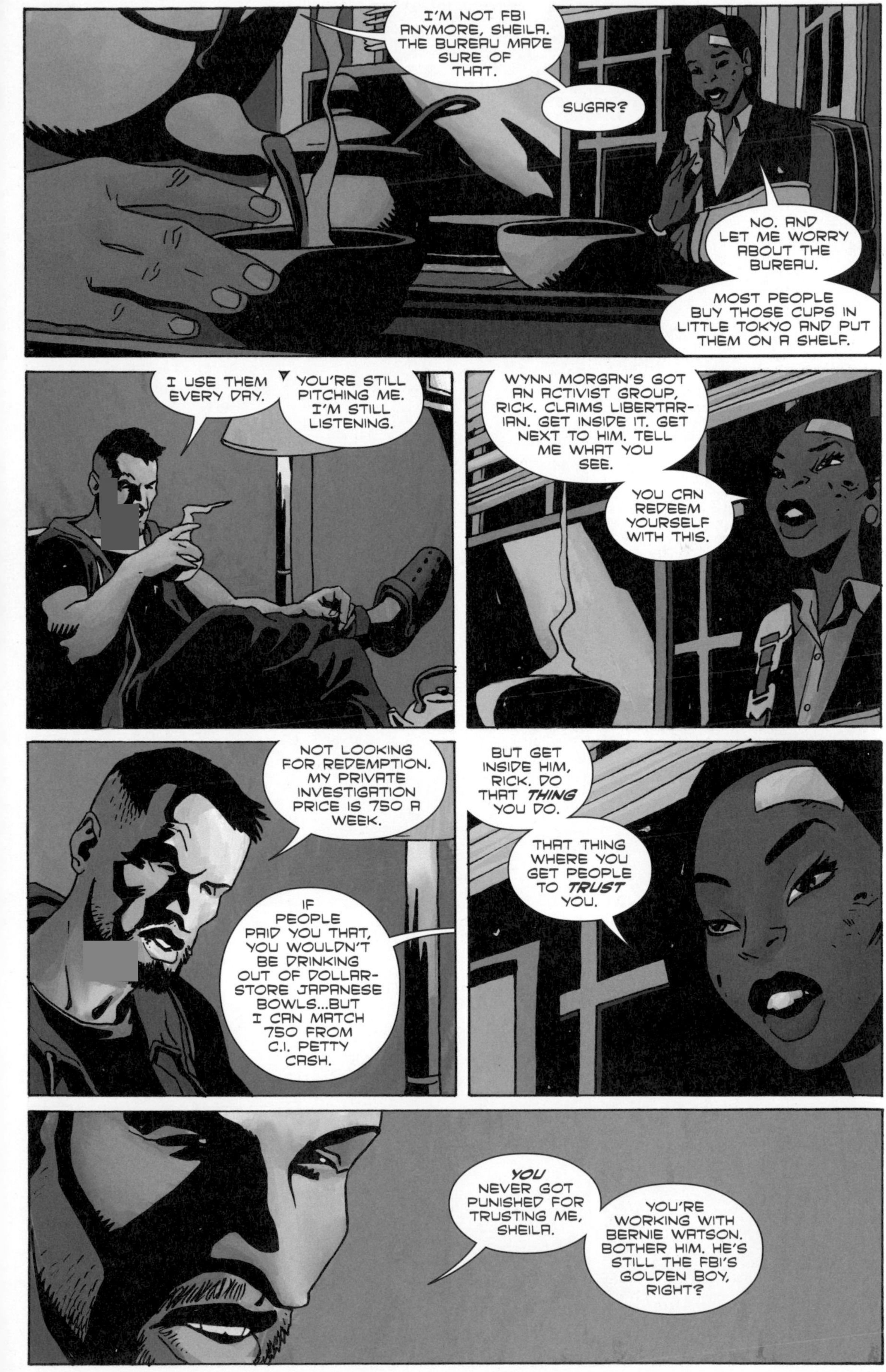
I'M NOT FBI ANYMORE, SHEILA. THE BUREAU MADE SURE OF THAT.
SUGAR?
NO. AND LET ME WORRY ABOUT THE BUREAU.
MOST PEOPLE BUY THOSE CUPS IN LITTLE TOKYO AND PUT THEM ON A SHELF.
I USE THEM EVERY DAY.
YOU'RE STILL PITCHING ME. I'M STILL LISTENING.
WYNN MORGAN'S GOT AN ACTIVIST GROUP, RICK. CLAIMS LIBERTARIAN. GET INSIDE IT. GET NEXT TO HIM. TELL ME WHAT YOU SEE.
YOU CAN REDEEM YOURSELF WITH THIS.
NOT LOOKING FOR REDEMPTION. MY PRIVATE INVESTIGATION PRICE IS 750 A WEEK.
IF PEOPLE PAID YOU THAT, YOU WOULDN'T BE DRINKING OUT OF DOLLAR-STORE JAPANESE BOWLS...BUT I CAN MATCH 750 FROM C.I. PETTY CASH.
BUT GET INSIDE HIM, RICK. DO THAT *THING* YOU DO.
THAT THING WHERE YOU GET PEOPLE TO *TRUST* YOU.
YOU NEVER GOT PUNISHED FOR TRUSTING ME, SHEILA.
YOU'RE WORKING WITH BERNIE WATSON. BOTHER HIM. HE'S STILL THE FBI'S GOLDEN BOY, RIGHT?

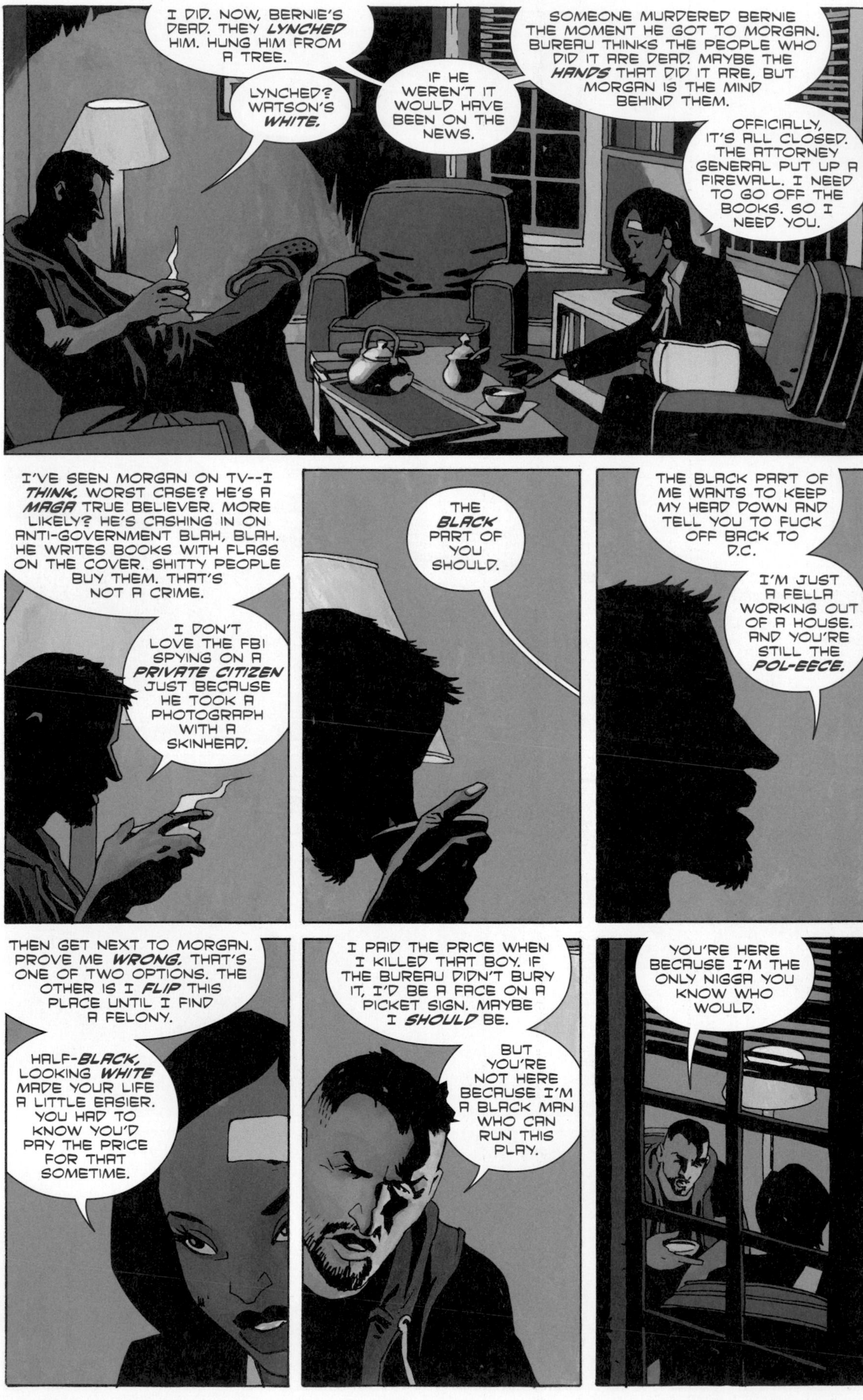

I DID. NOW, BERNIE'S DEAD. THEY *LYNCHED* HIM. HUNG HIM FROM A TREE.
LYNCHED? WATSON'S *WHITE.*
IF HE WEREN'T IT WOULD HAVE BEEN ON THE NEWS.
SOMEONE MURDERED BERNIE THE MOMENT HE GOT TO MORGAN. BUREAU THINKS THE PEOPLE WHO DID IT ARE DEAD. MAYBE THE *HANDS* THAT DID IT ARE, BUT MORGAN IS THE MIND BEHIND THEM.
OFFICIALLY, IT'S ALL CLOSED. THE ATTORNEY GENERAL PUT UP A FIREWALL. I NEED TO GO OFF THE BOOKS. SO I NEED YOU.
I'VE SEEN MORGAN ON TV--I *THINK.* WORST CASE? HE'S A *MAGA* TRUE BELIEVER. MORE LIKELY? HE'S CASHING IN ON ANTI-GOVERNMENT BLAH, BLAH. HE WRITES BOOKS WITH FLAGS ON THE COVER. SHITTY PEOPLE BUY THEM. THAT'S NOT A CRIME.
I DON'T LOVE THE FBI SPYING ON A *PRIVATE CITIZEN* JUST BECAUSE HE TOOK A PHOTOGRAPH WITH A SKINHEAD.
THE *BLACK* PART OF YOU SHOULD.
THE BLACK PART OF ME WANTS TO KEEP MY HEAD DOWN AND TELL YOU TO FUCK OFF BACK TO D.C.
I'M JUST A FELLA WORKING OUT OF A HOUSE. AND YOU'RE STILL THE *POL-EECE.*
THEN GET NEXT TO MORGAN. PROVE ME *WRONG.* THAT'S ONE OF TWO OPTIONS. THE OTHER IS I *FLIP* THIS PLACE UNTIL I FIND A FELONY.
HALF-*BLACK,* LOOKING *WHITE* MADE YOUR LIFE A LITTLE EASIER. YOU HAD TO KNOW YOU'D PAY THE PRICE FOR THAT SOMETIME.
I PAID THE PRICE WHEN I KILLED THAT BOY. IF THE BUREAU DIDN'T BURY IT, I'D BE A FACE ON A PICKET SIGN. MAYBE I *SHOULD* BE.
BUT YOU'RE NOT HERE BECAUSE I'M A BLACK MAN WHO CAN RUN THIS PLAY.
YOU'RE HERE BECAUSE I'M THE ONLY NIGGA YOU KNOW WHO WOULD.

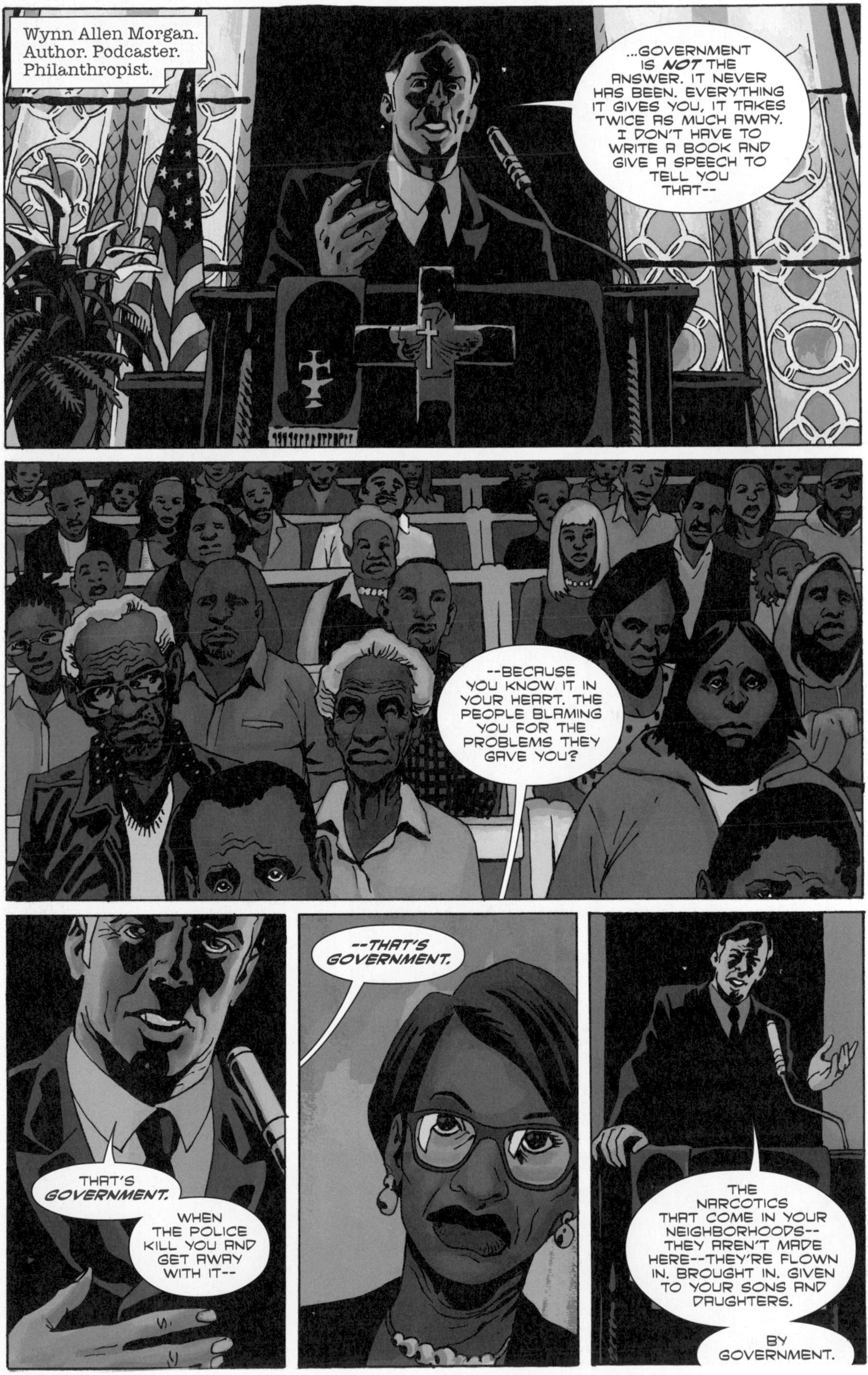
Wynn Allen Morgan. Author. Podcaster. Philanthropist.
...GOVERNMENT IS NOT THE ANSWER. IT NEVER HAS BEEN. EVERYTHING IT GIVES YOU, IT TAKES TWICE AS MUCH AWAY. I DON'T HAVE TO WRITE A BOOK AND GIVE A SPEECH TO TELL YOU THAT--
--BECAUSE YOU KNOW IT IN YOUR HEART. THE PEOPLE BLAMING YOU FOR THE PROBLEMS THEY GAVE YOU?
THAT'S GOVERNMENT.
WHEN THE POLICE KILL YOU AND GET AWAY WITH IT--
--THAT'S GOVERNMENT.
THE NARCOTICS THAT COME IN YOUR NEIGHBORHOODS--THEY AREN'T MADE HERE--THEY'RE FLOWN IN. BROUGHT IN. GIVEN TO YOUR SONS AND DAUGHTERS.
BY GOVERNMENT.

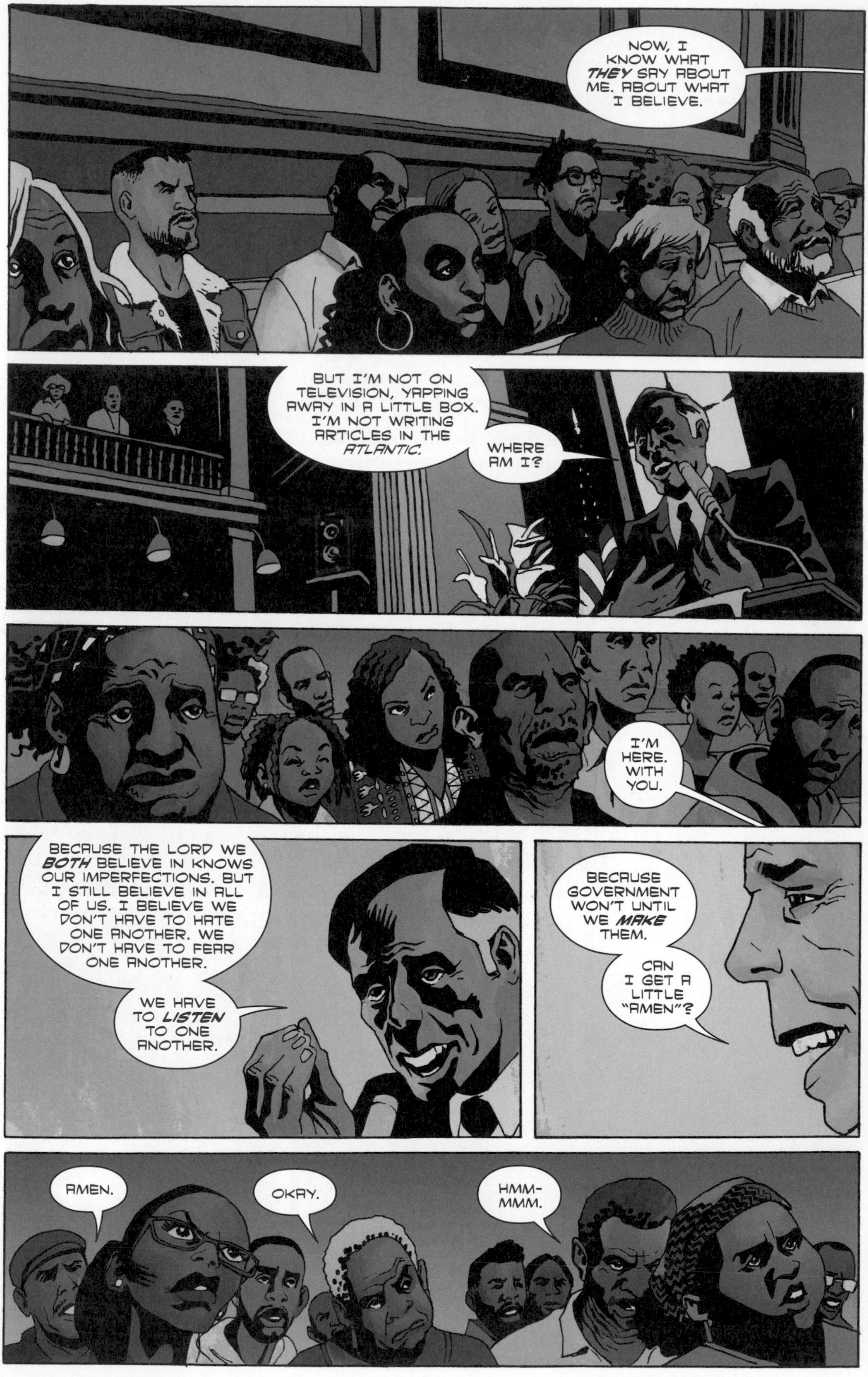
NOW, I KNOW WHAT *THEY* SAY ABOUT ME. ABOUT WHAT I BELIEVE.
BUT I'M NOT ON TELEVISION, YAPPING AWAY IN A LITTLE BOX. I'M NOT WRITING ARTICLES IN THE *ATLANTIC.*
WHERE AM I?
I'M HERE. WITH YOU.
BECAUSE THE LORD WE *BOTH* BELIEVE IN KNOWS OUR IMPERFECTIONS. BUT I STILL BELIEVE IN ALL OF US. I BELIEVE WE DON'T HAVE TO HATE ONE ANOTHER. WE DON'T HAVE TO FEAR ONE ANOTHER.
WE HAVE TO *LISTEN* TO ONE ANOTHER.
BECAUSE GOVERNMENT WON'T UNTIL WE *MAKE* THEM.
CAN I GET A LITTLE "AMEN"?
AMEN.
OKAY.
HMM-MMM.

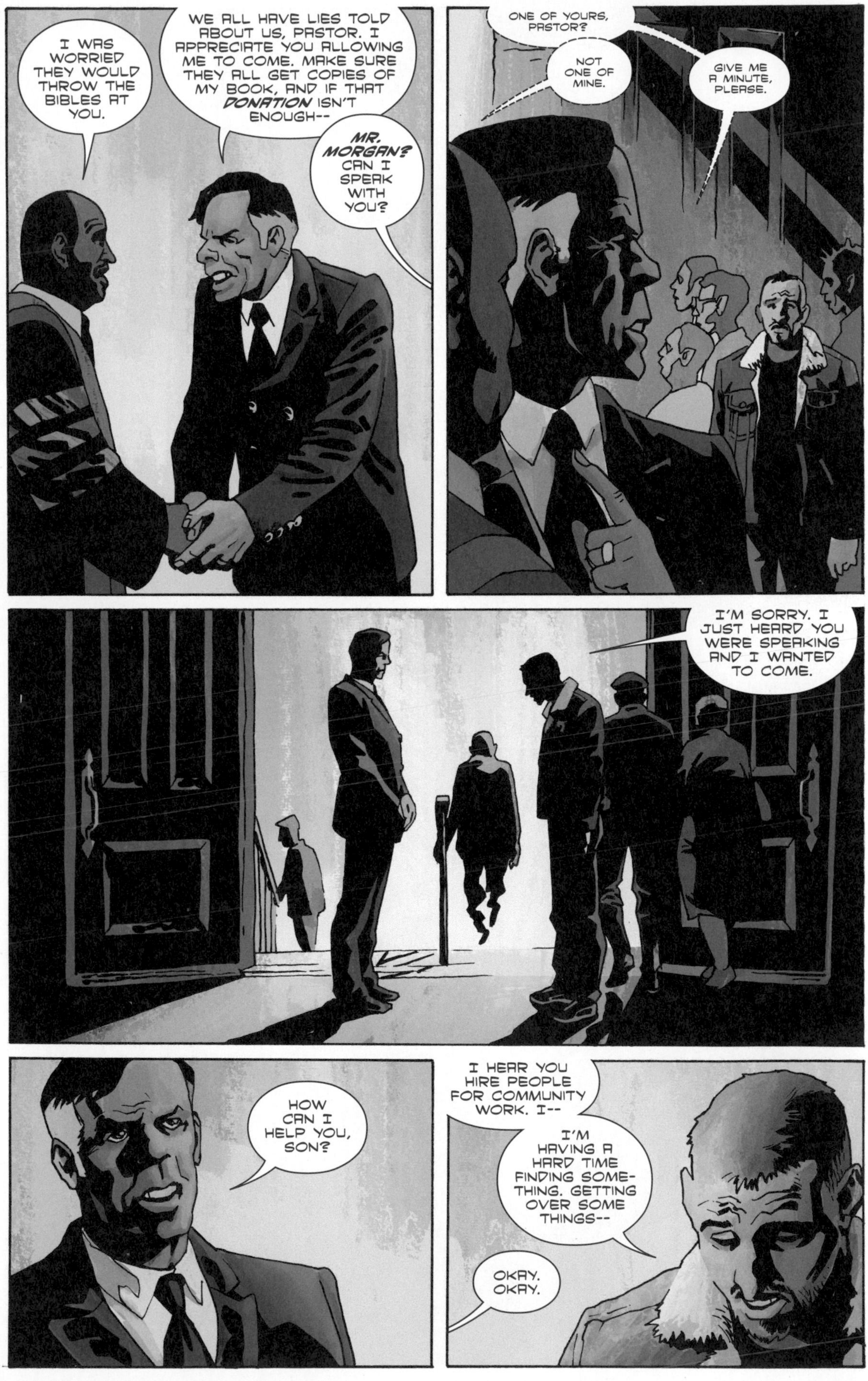
I WAS WORRIED THEY WOULD THROW THE BIBLES AT YOU.
WE ALL HAVE LIES TOLD ABOUT US, PASTOR. I APPRECIATE YOU ALLOWING ME TO COME. MAKE SURE THEY ALL GET COPIES OF MY BOOK, AND IF THAT DONATION ISN'T ENOUGH--
MR. MORGAN? CAN I SPEAK WITH YOU?
ONE OF YOURS, PASTOR?
NOT ONE OF MINE.
GIVE ME A MINUTE, PLEASE.
I'M SORRY. I JUST HEARD YOU WERE SPEAKING AND I WANTED TO COME.
HOW CAN I HELP YOU, SON?
I HEAR YOU HIRE PEOPLE FOR COMMUNITY WORK. I--
I'M HAVING A HARD TIME FINDING SOMETHING. GETTING OVER SOME THINGS--
OKAY. OKAY.

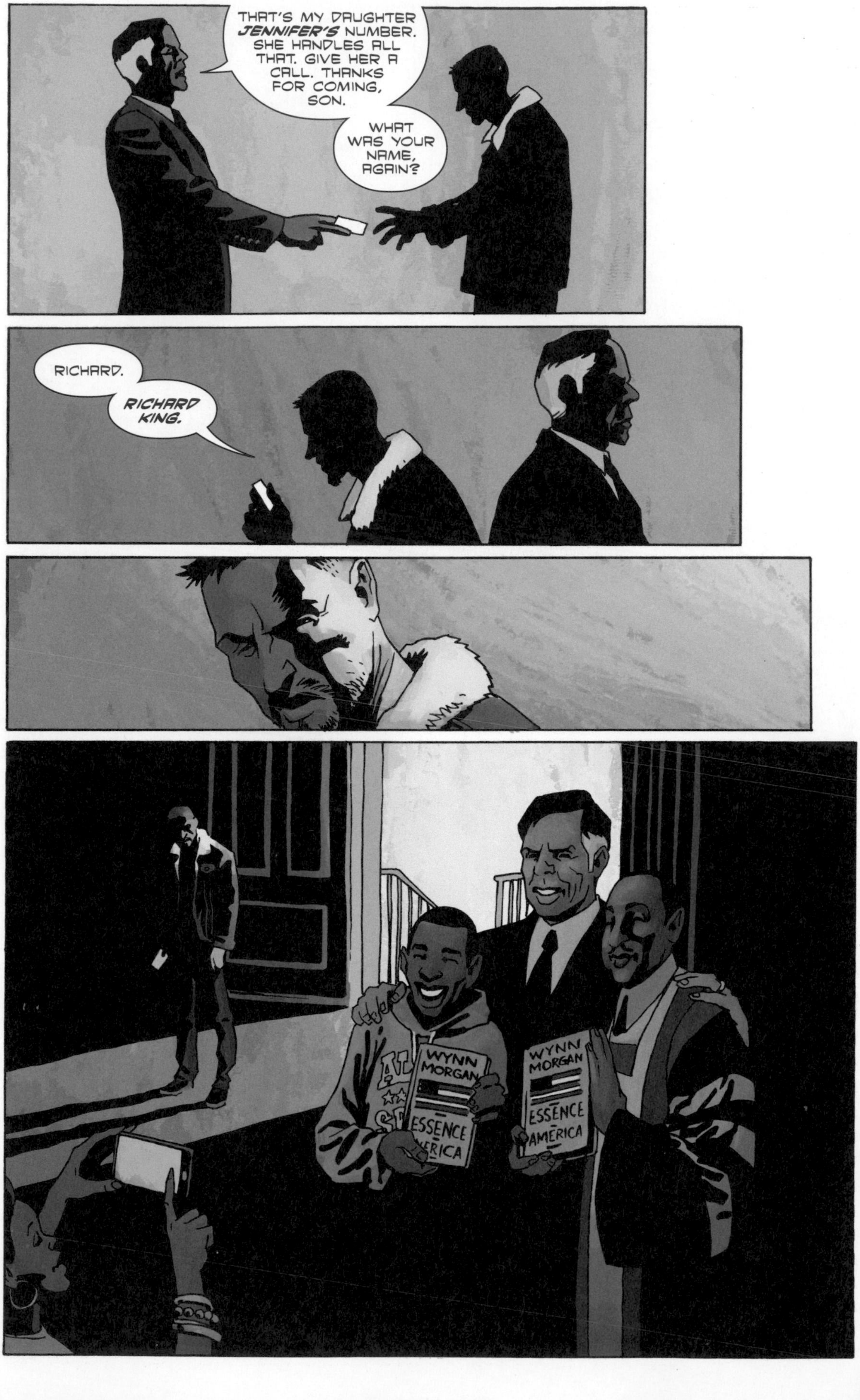
THAT'S MY DAUGHTER *JENNIFER'S* NUMBER. SHE HANDLES ALL THAT. GIVE HER A CALL. THANKS FOR COMING, SON.
WHAT WAS YOUR NAME, AGAIN?
RICHARD.
RICHARD KING.
WYNN MORGAN
ESSENCE AMERICA
WYNN MORGAN
ESSENCE AMERICA

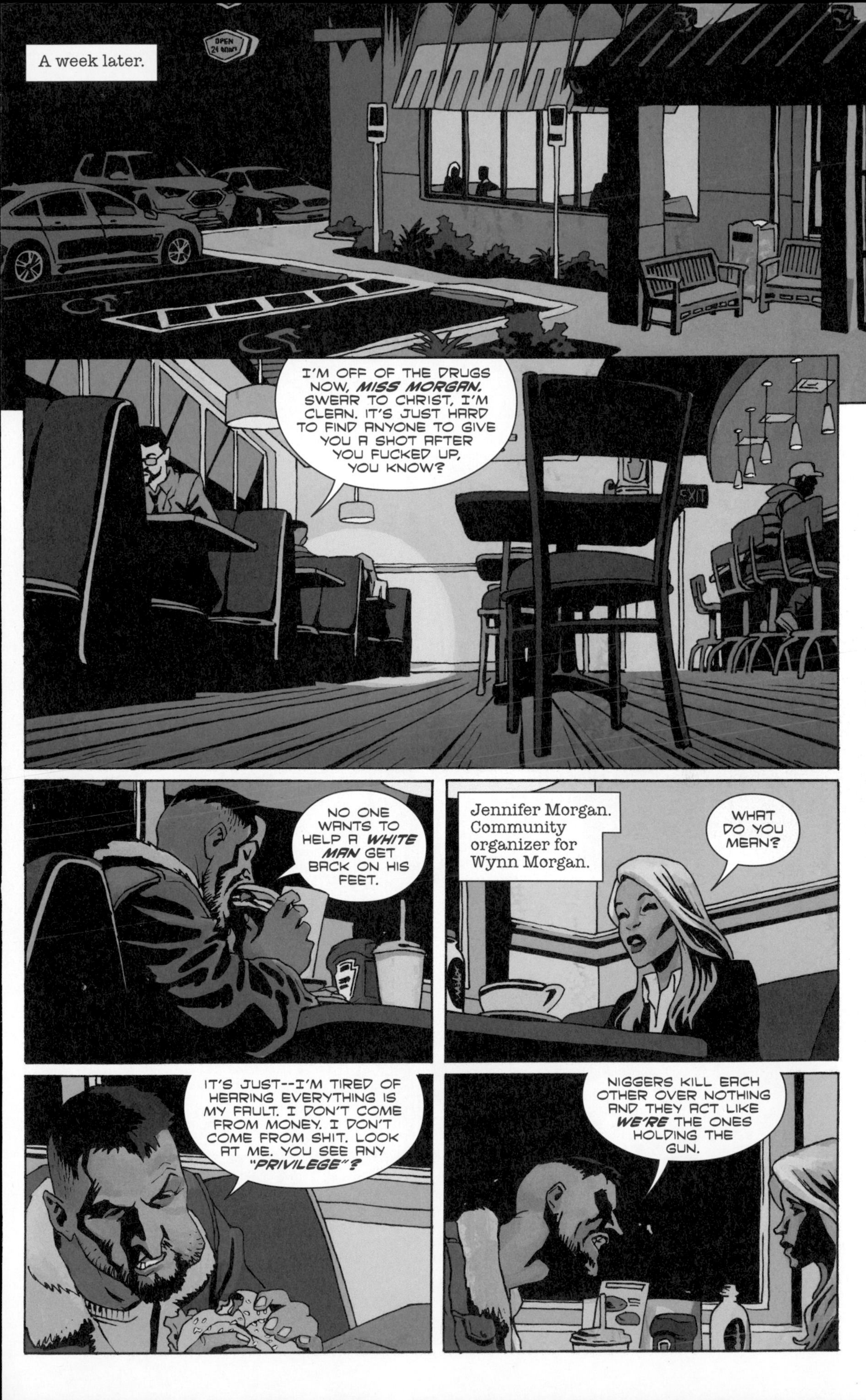
A week later.
I'M OFF OF THE DRUGS NOW, MISS MORGAN. SWEAR TO CHRIST, I'M CLEAN. IT'S JUST HARD TO FIND ANYONE TO GIVE YOU A SHOT AFTER YOU FUCKED UP, YOU KNOW?
NO ONE WANTS TO HELP A WHITE MAN GET BACK ON HIS FEET.
Jennifer Morgan. Community organizer for Wynn Morgan.
WHAT DO YOU MEAN?
IT'S JUST--I'M TIRED OF HEARING EVERYTHING IS MY FAULT. I DON'T COME FROM MONEY. I DON'T COME FROM SHIT. LOOK AT ME. YOU SEE ANY "PRIVILEGE"?
NIGGERS KILL EACH OTHER OVER NOTHING AND THEY ACT LIKE WE'RE THE ONES HOLDING THE GUN.

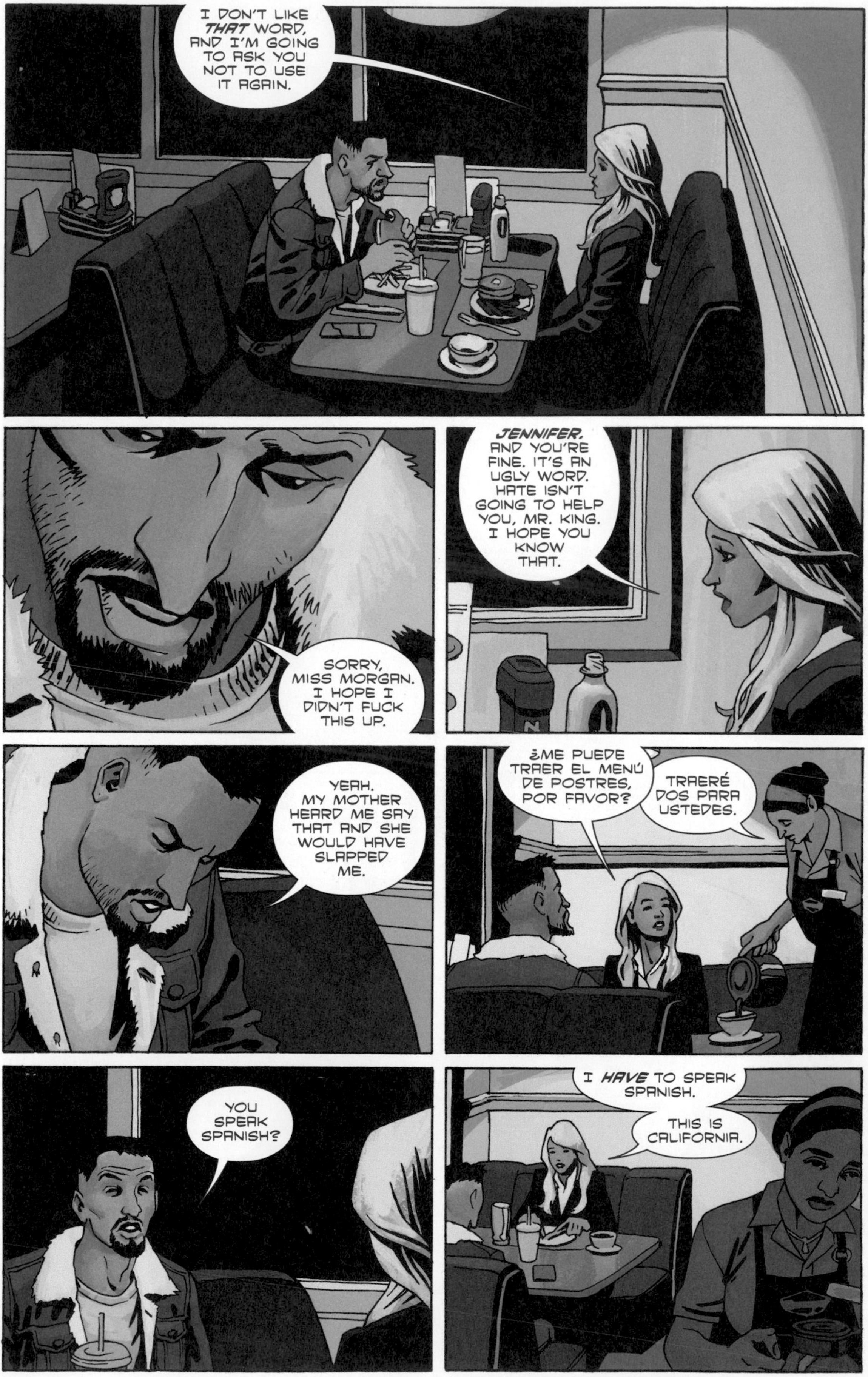
I DON'T LIKE *THAT* WORD, AND I'M GOING TO ASK YOU NOT TO USE IT AGAIN.
SORRY, MISS MORGAN. I HOPE I DIDN'T FUCK THIS UP.
JENNIFER. AND YOU'RE FINE. IT'S AN UGLY WORD. HATE ISN'T GOING TO HELP YOU, MR. KING. I HOPE YOU KNOW THAT.
YEAH. MY MOTHER HEARD ME SAY THAT AND SHE WOULD HAVE SLAPPED ME.
¿ME PUEDE TRAER EL MENÚ DE POSTRES, POR FAVOR?
TRAERÉ DOS PARA USTEDES.
YOU SPEAK SPANISH?
I *HAVE* TO SPEAK SPANISH.
THIS IS CALIFORNIA.

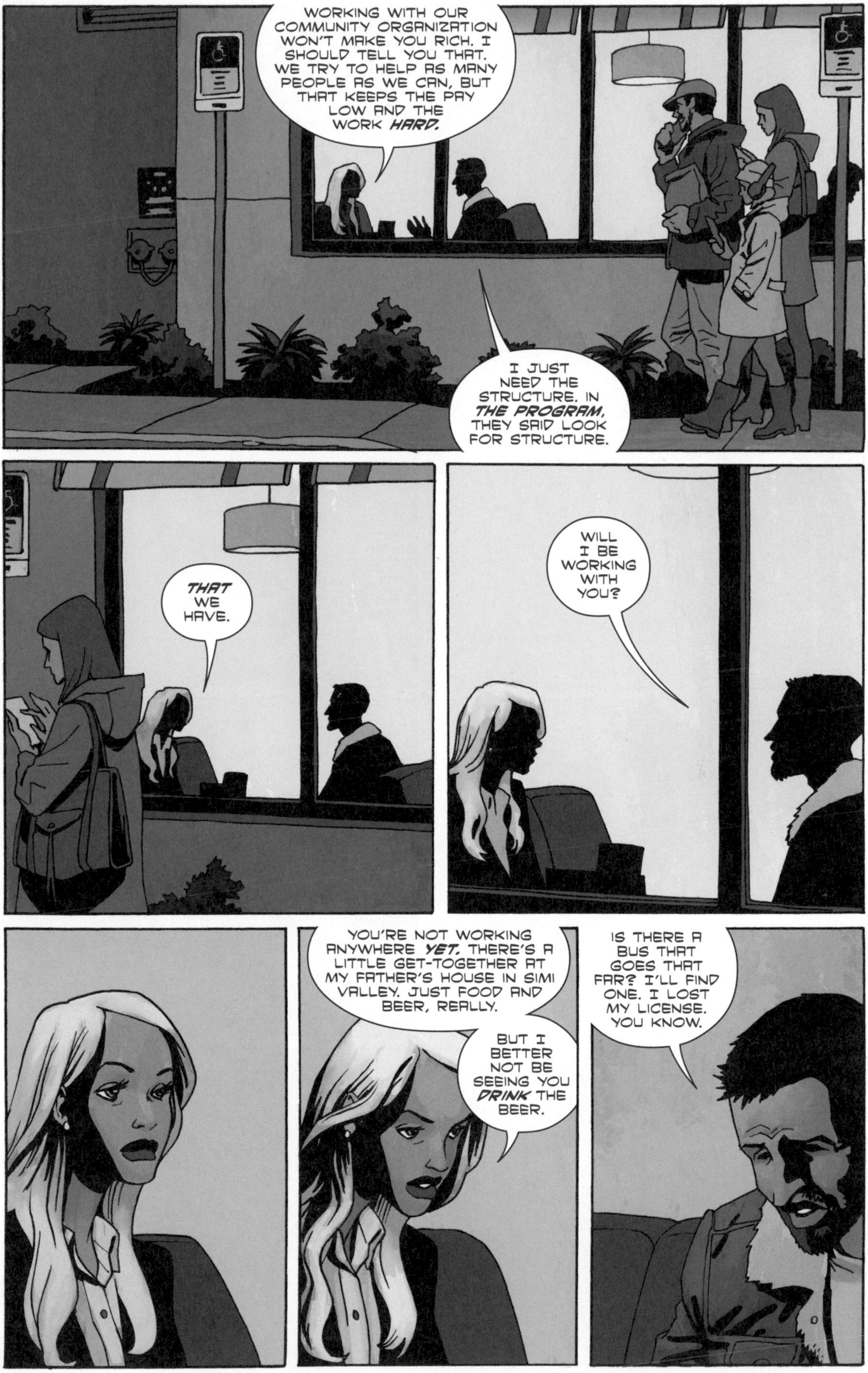
WORKING WITH OUR COMMUNITY ORGANIZATION WON'T MAKE YOU RICH. I SHOULD TELL YOU THAT. WE TRY TO HELP AS MANY PEOPLE AS WE CAN, BUT THAT KEEPS THE PAY LOW AND THE WORK *HARD.*
I JUST NEED THE STRUCTURE. IN *THE PROGRAM,* THEY SAID LOOK FOR STRUCTURE.
THAT WE HAVE.
WILL I BE WORKING WITH YOU?
YOU'RE NOT WORKING ANYWHERE *YET.* THERE'S A LITTLE GET-TOGETHER AT MY FATHER'S HOUSE IN SIMI VALLEY. JUST FOOD AND BEER, REALLY.
BUT I BETTER NOT BE SEEING YOU *DRINK* THE BEER.
IS THERE A BUS THAT GOES THAT FAR? I'LL FIND ONE. I LOST MY LICENSE. YOU KNOW.

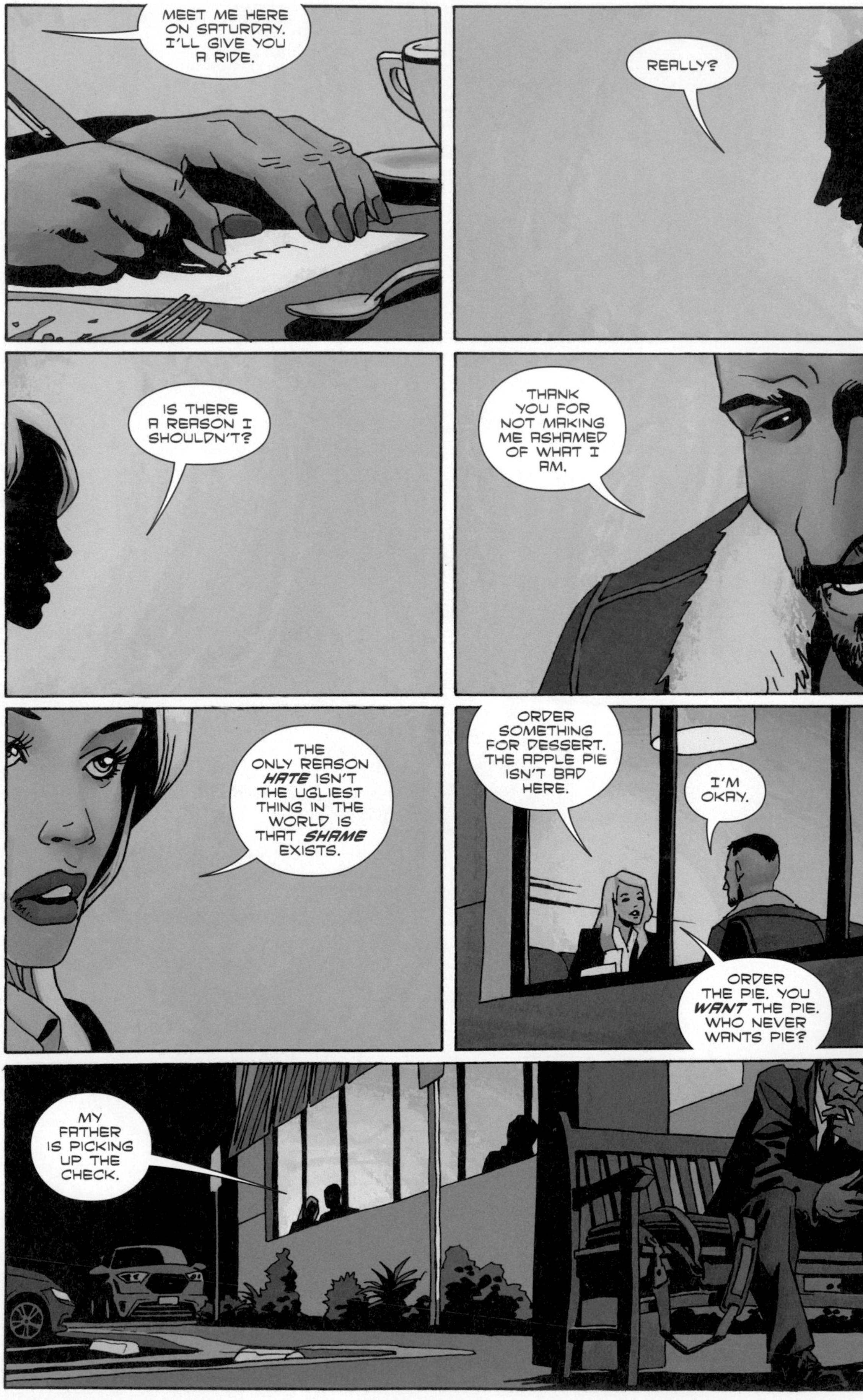
MEET ME HERE ON SATURDAY. I'LL GIVE YOU A RIDE.
REALLY?
IS THERE A REASON I SHOULDN'T?
THANK YOU FOR NOT MAKING ME ASHAMED OF WHAT I AM.
THE ONLY REASON HATE ISN'T THE UGLIEST THING IN THE WORLD IS THAT SHAME EXISTS.
ORDER SOMETHING FOR DESSERT. THE APPLE PIE ISN'T BAD HERE.
I'M OKAY.
ORDER THE PIE. YOU WANT THE PIE. WHO NEVER WANTS PIE?
MY FATHER IS PICKING UP THE CHECK.

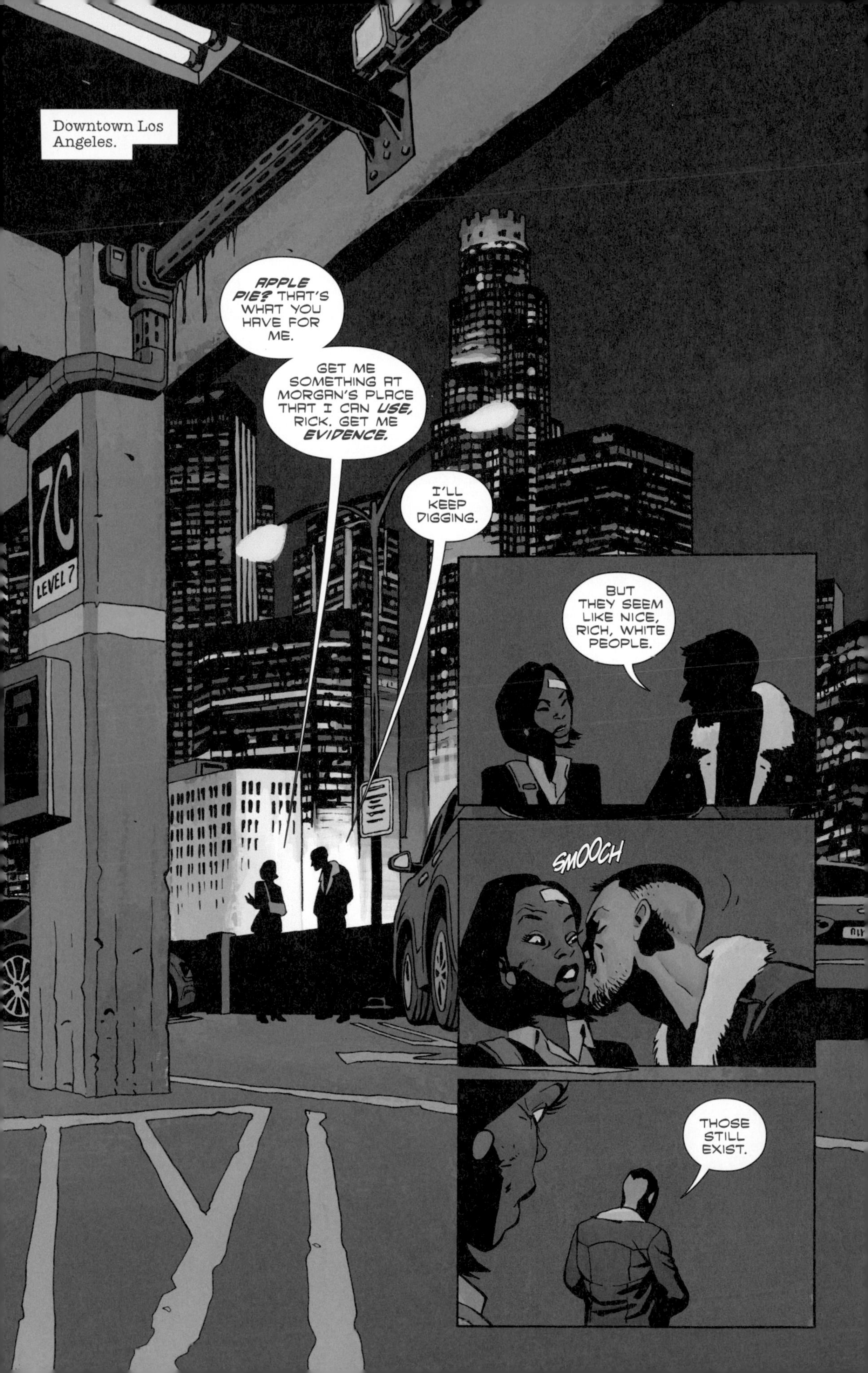
Downtown Los Angeles.
7C
LEVEL 7
APPLE PIE? THAT'S WHAT YOU HAVE FOR ME.
GET ME SOMETHING AT MORGAN'S PLACE THAT I CAN USE, RICK. GET ME EVIDENCE.
I'LL KEEP DIGGING.
BUT THEY SEEM LIKE NICE, RICH, WHITE PEOPLE.
SMOOCH
THOSE STILL EXIST.

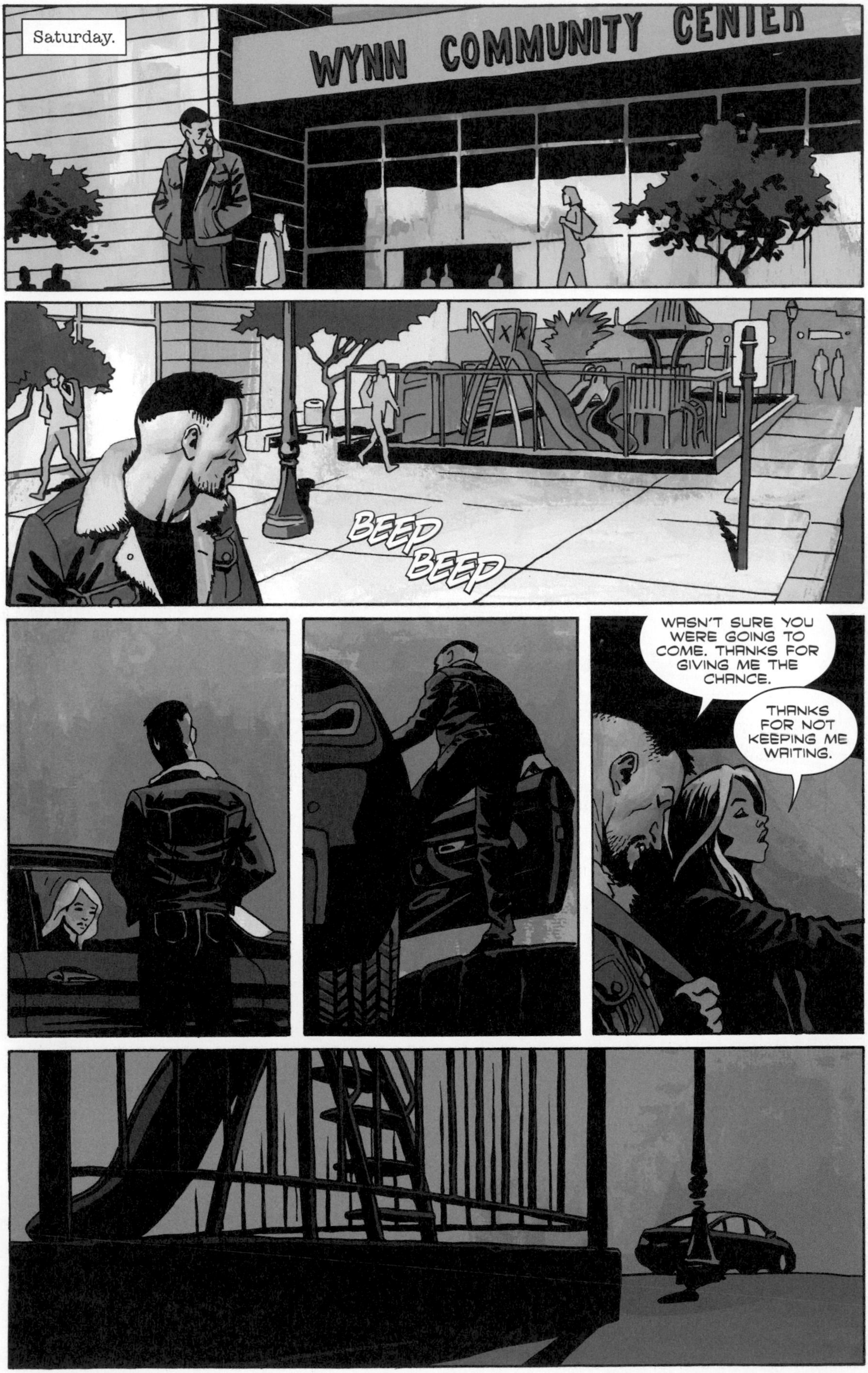
Saturday.
WYNN COMMUNITY CENTER
BEEP BEEP
WASN'T SURE YOU WERE GOING TO COME. THANKS FOR GIVING ME THE CHANCE.
THANKS FOR NOT KEEPING ME WAITING.

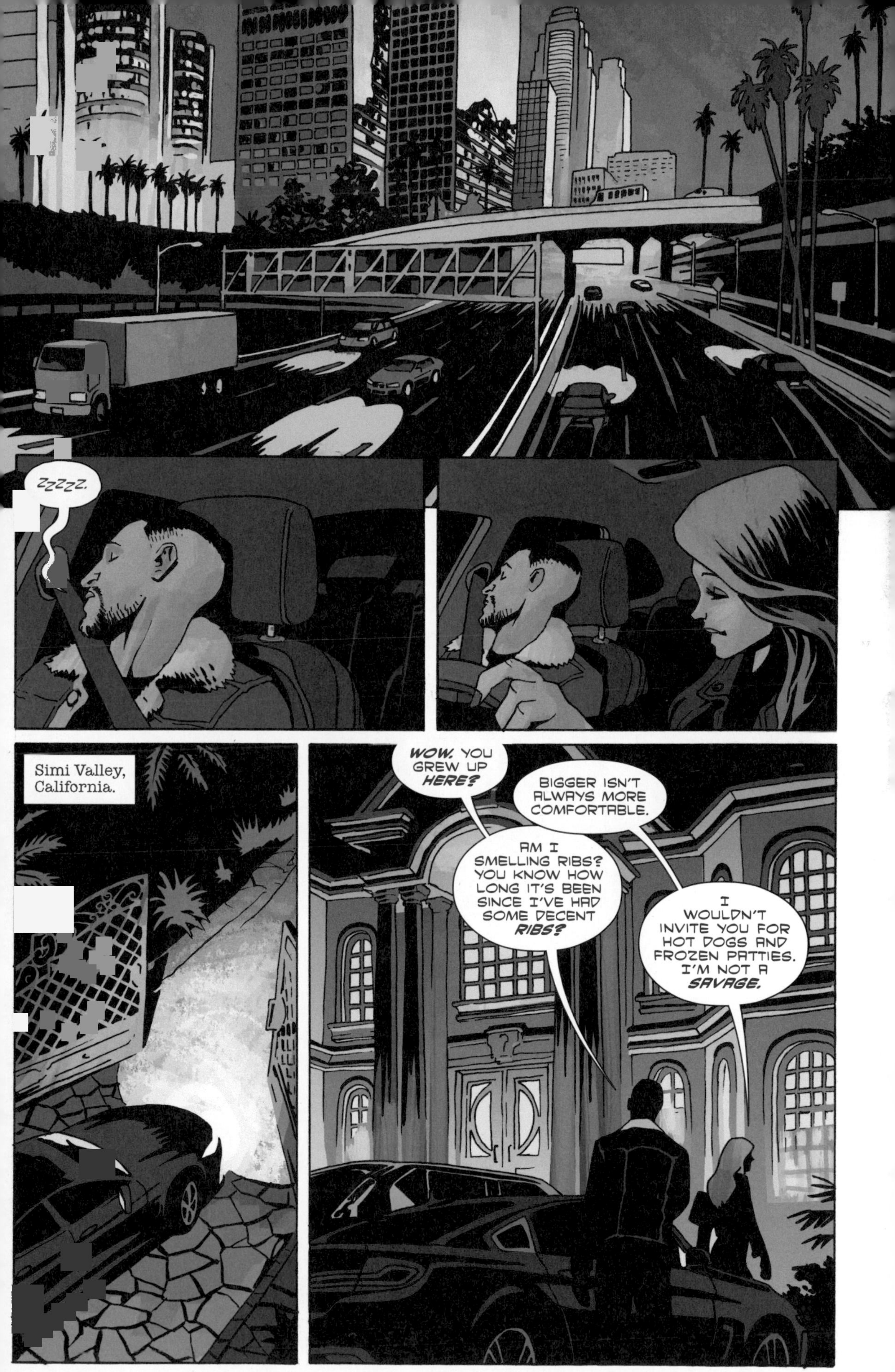
ZZZZZ.
Simi Valley, California.
WOW. YOU GREW UP HERE?
BIGGER ISN'T ALWAYS MORE COMFORTABLE.
AM I SMELLING RIBS? YOU KNOW HOW LONG IT'S BEEN SINCE I'VE HAD SOME DECENT RIBS?
I WOULDN'T INVITE YOU FOR HOT DOGS AND FROZEN PATTIES. I'M NOT A SAVAGE.

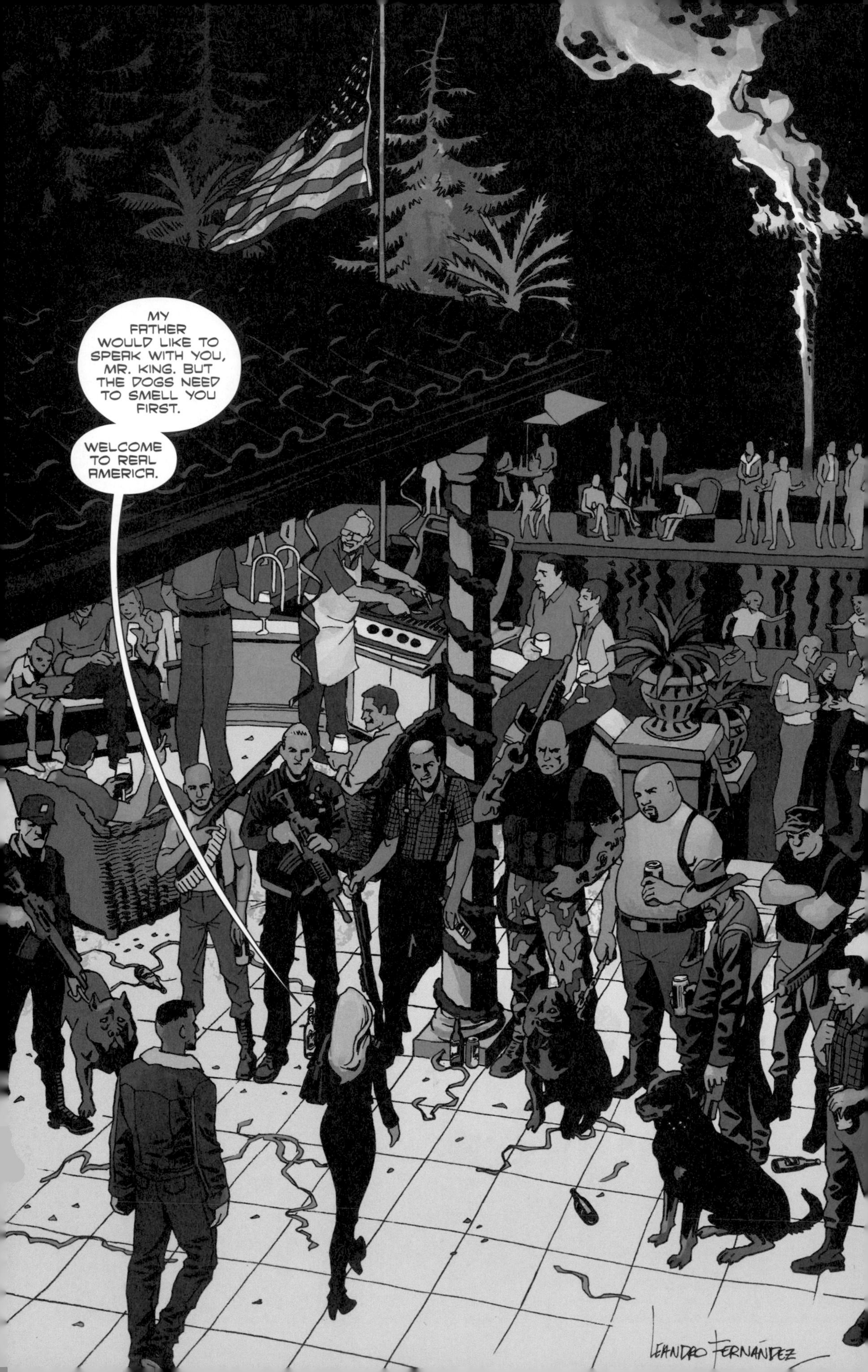
MY FATHER WOULD LIKE TO SPEAK WITH YOU, MR. KING. BUT THE DOGS NEED TO SMELL YOU FIRST.
WELCOME TO REAL AMERICA.
LEANDRO FERNANDEZ

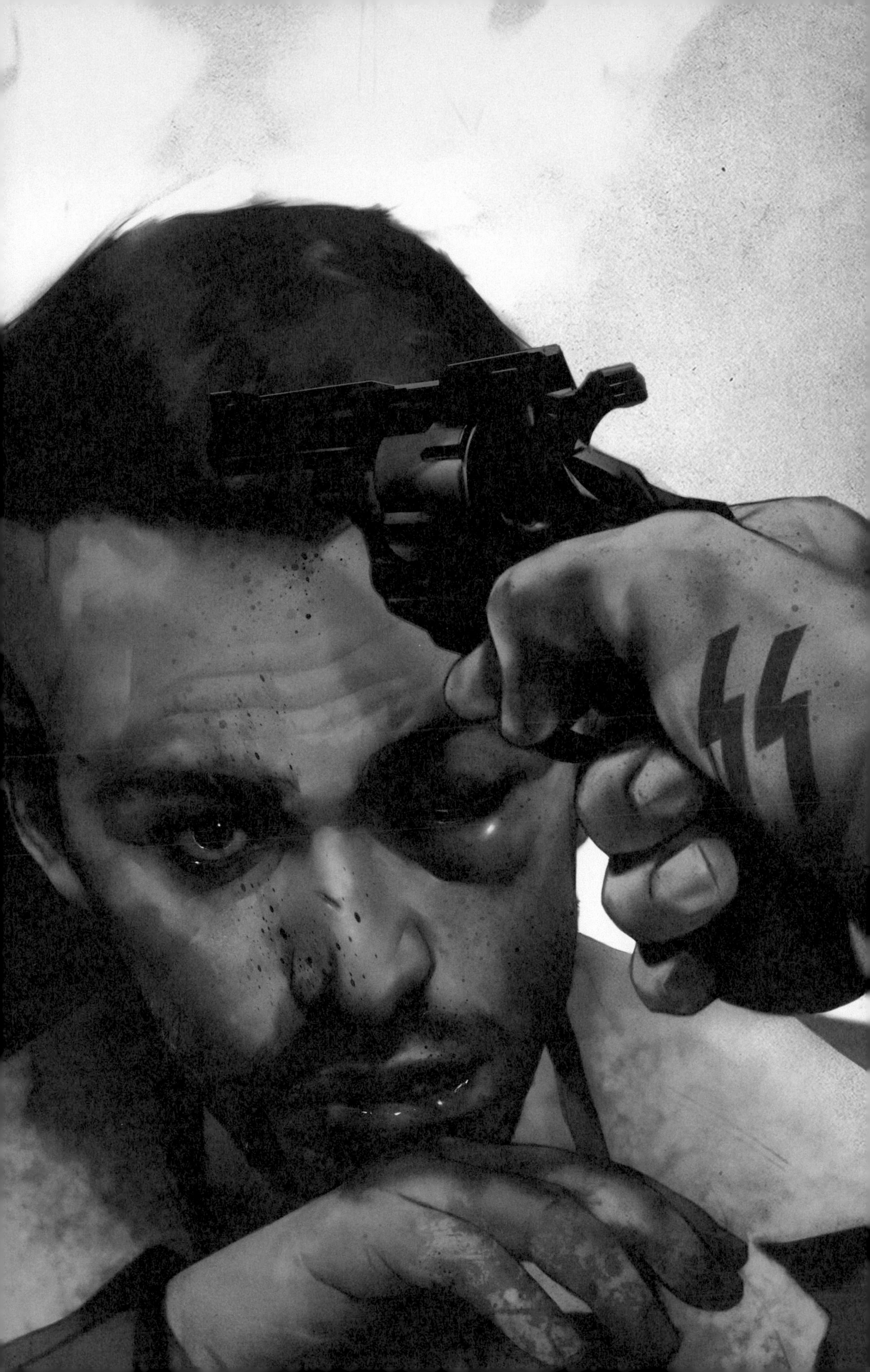

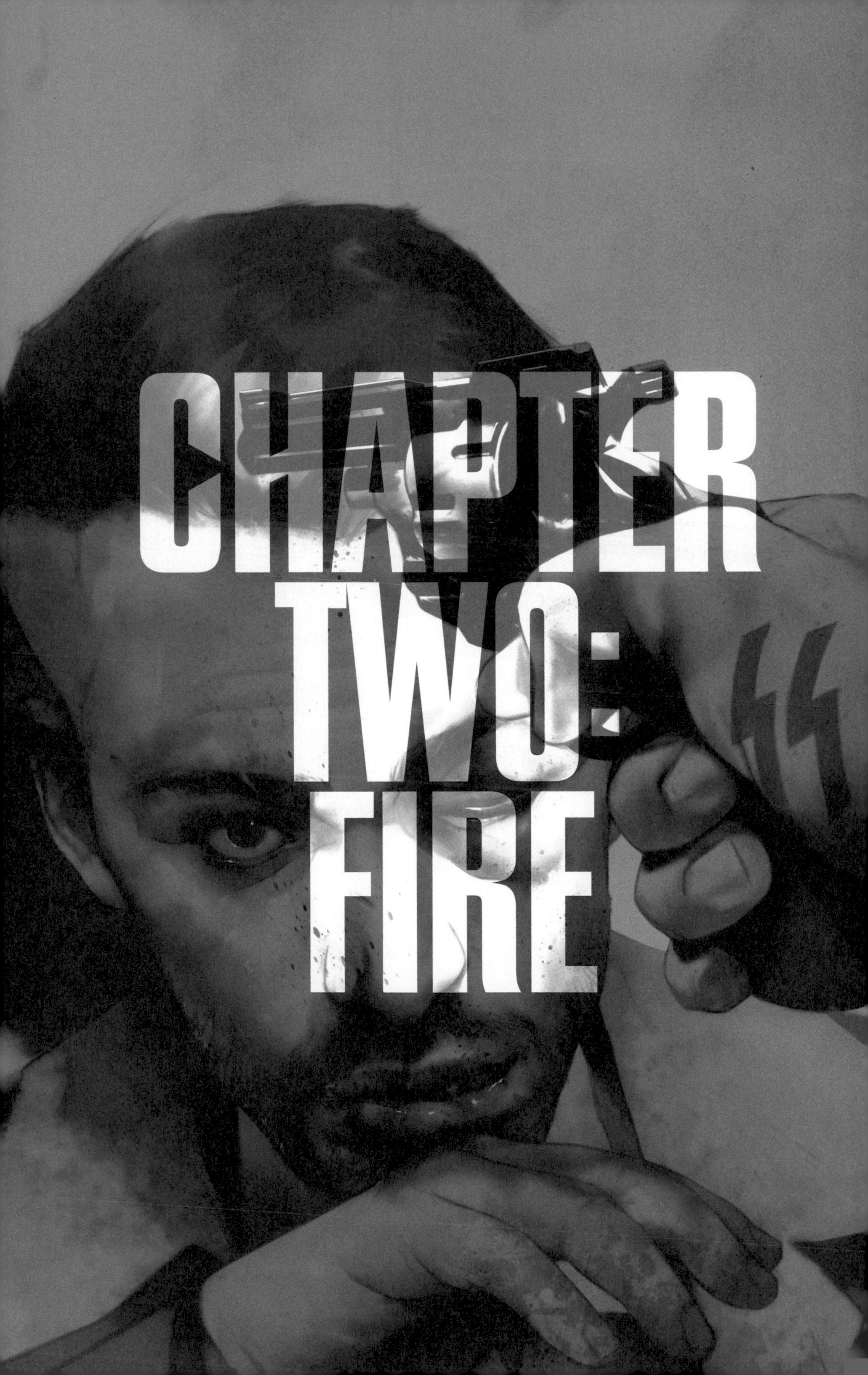
CHAPTER
TWO:
FIRE

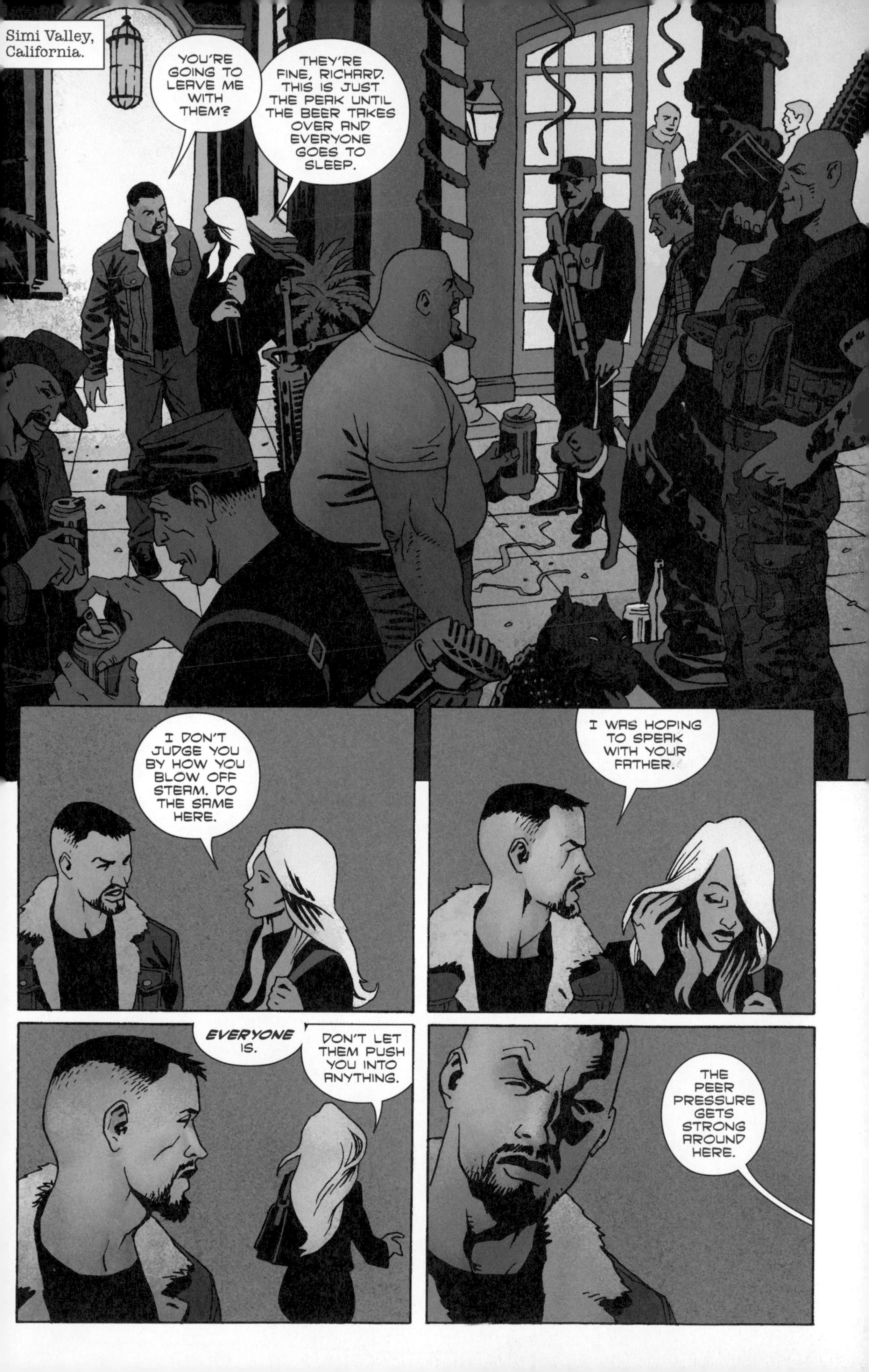
Simi Valley, California.
YOU'RE GOING TO LEAVE ME WITH THEM?
THEY'RE FINE, RICHARD. THIS IS JUST THE PEAK UNTIL THE BEER TAKES OVER AND EVERYONE GOES TO SLEEP.
I DON'T JUDGE YOU BY HOW YOU BLOW OFF STEAM. DO THE SAME HERE.
I WAS HOPING TO SPEAK WITH YOUR FATHER.
EVERYONE IS.
DON'T LET THEM PUSH YOU INTO ANYTHING.
THE PEER PRESSURE GETS STRONG AROUND HERE.

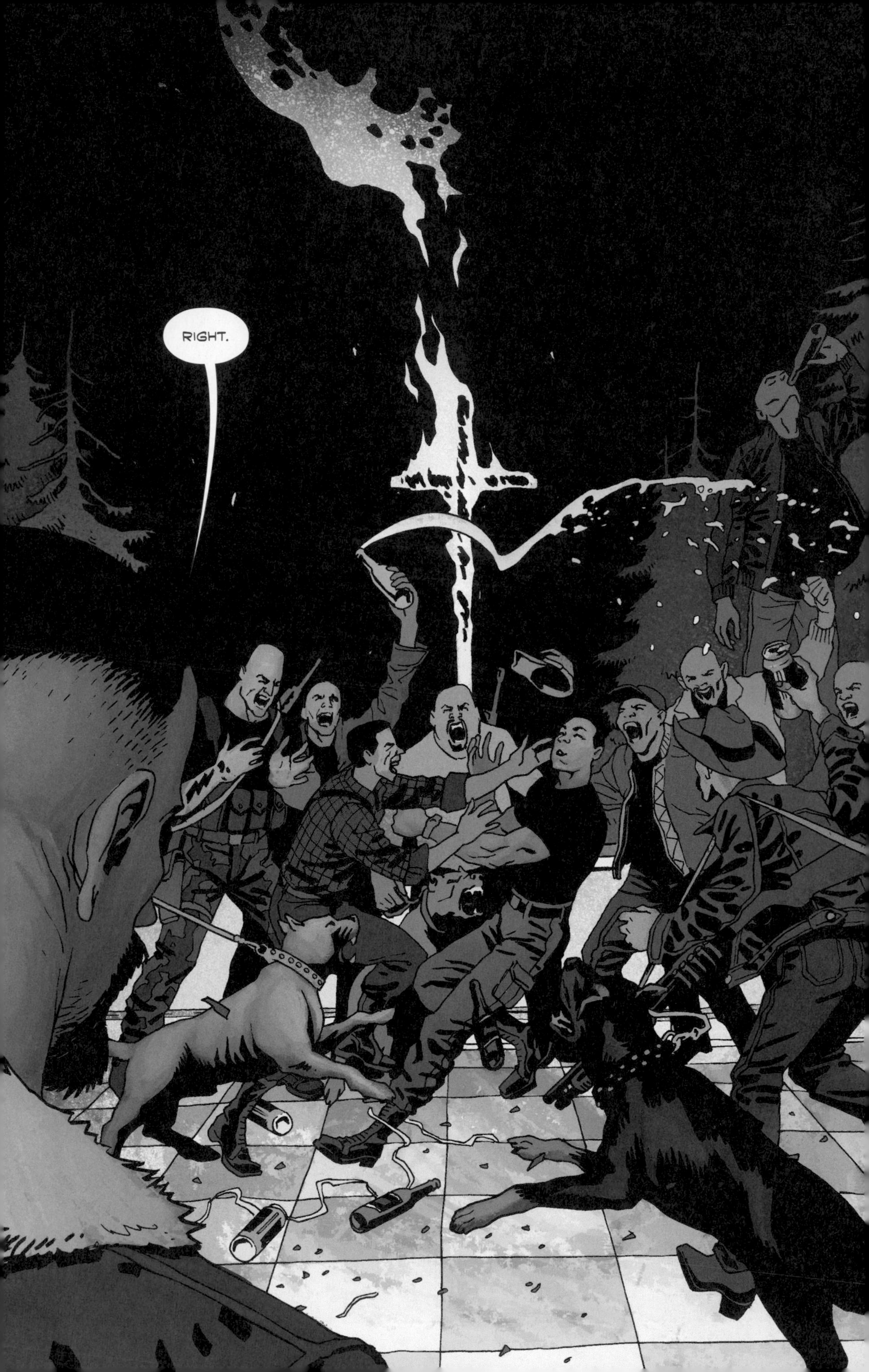
RIGHT.

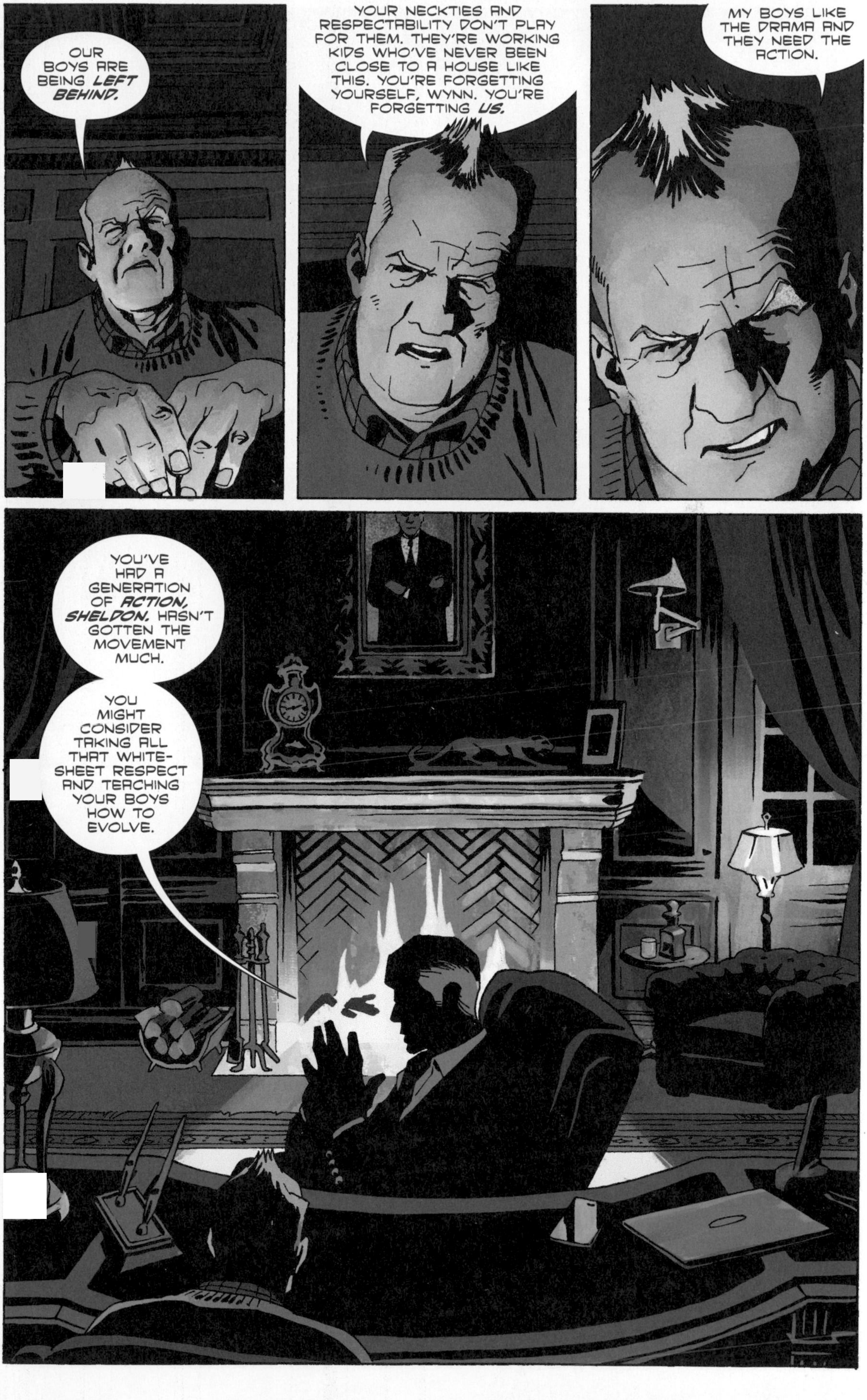
OUR BOYS ARE BEING LEFT BEHIND.
YOUR NECKTIES AND RESPECTABILITY DON'T PLAY FOR THEM. THEY'RE WORKING KIDS WHO'VE NEVER BEEN CLOSE TO A HOUSE LIKE THIS. YOU'RE FORGETTING YOURSELF, WYNN. YOU'RE FORGETTING US.
MY BOYS LIKE THE DRAMA AND THEY NEED THE ACTION.
YOU'VE HAD A GENERATION OF ACTION, SHELDON. HASN'T GOTTEN THE MOVEMENT MUCH.
YOU MIGHT CONSIDER TAKING ALL THAT WHITE-SHEET RESPECT AND TEACHING YOUR BOYS HOW TO EVOLVE.

YOU NEED US. YOU'RE NOT BUILDING ANYTHING ON *BOOK TOURS* AND *NIGGER CHURCHES.*

I *NEED* YOU?

GODDAMN RIGHT, YOU DO.

PEOPLE SEE THOSE BALD HEADS AND THAT INK AND IT *SCARES* THEM. IF YOU WANT TO BE THE CURE FOR MONSTERS, YOU NEED MONSTERS TO MAKE THE WORLD CALL OUT FOR YOU.

WHEN THEY STOP BEING AFRAID, THAT'S WHEN WE ALL FADE AWAY.

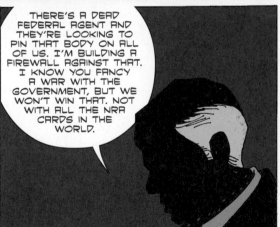

THERE'S A DEAD FEDERAL AGENT AND THEY'RE LOOKING TO PIN THAT BODY ON ALL OF US. I'M BUILDING A FIREWALL AGAINST THAT. I KNOW YOU FANCY A WAR WITH THE GOVERNMENT, BUT WE WON'T WIN THAT. NOT WITH ALL THE NRA CARDS IN THE WORLD.

STAND DOWN. NO VIOLENCE. LET THIS STORM PASS.

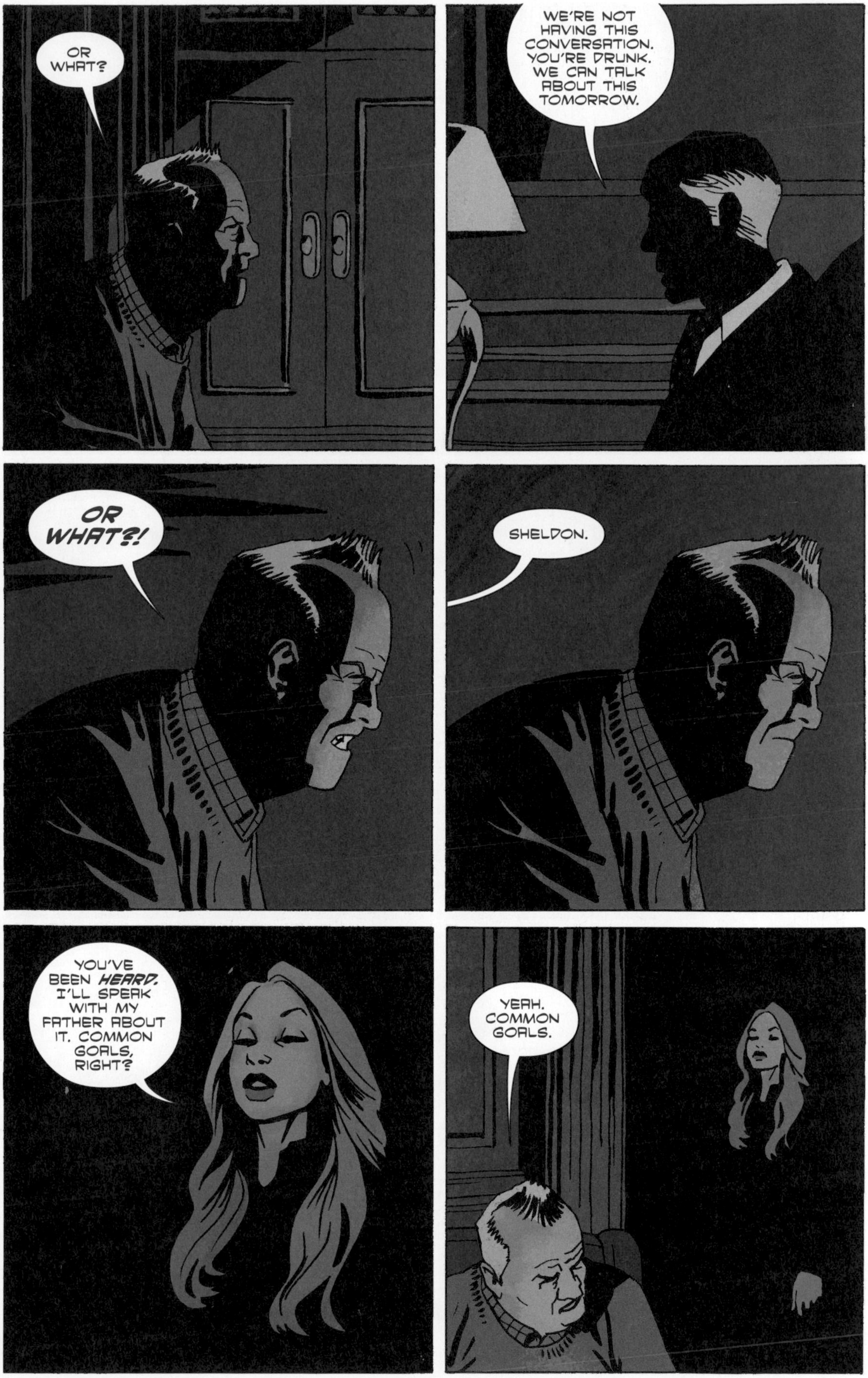
OR WHAT?
WE'RE NOT HAVING THIS CONVERSATION. YOU'RE DRUNK. WE CAN TALK ABOUT THIS TOMORROW.
OR WHAT?!
SHELDON.
YOU'VE BEEN HEARD. I'LL SPEAK WITH MY FATHER ABOUT IT. COMMON GOALS, RIGHT?
YEAH. COMMON GOALS.

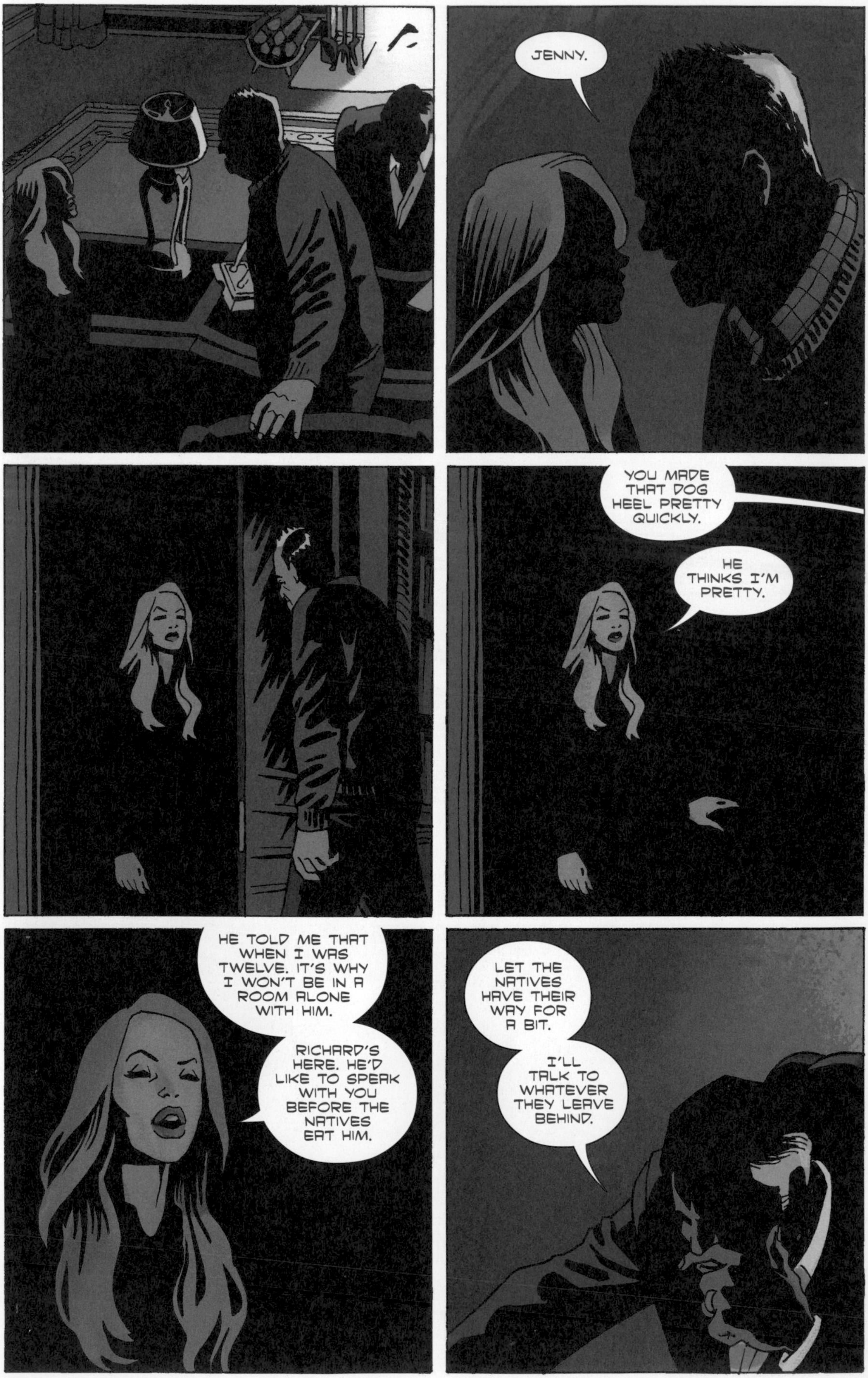
JENNY.
YOU MADE THAT DOG HEEL PRETTY QUICKLY.
HE THINKS I'M PRETTY.
HE TOLD ME THAT WHEN I WAS TWELVE. IT'S WHY I WON'T BE IN A ROOM ALONE WITH HIM.
RICHARD'S HERE. HE'D LIKE TO SPEAK WITH YOU BEFORE THE NATIVES EAT HIM.
LET THE NATIVES HAVE THEIR WAY FOR A BIT.
I'LL TALK TO WHATEVER THEY LEAVE BEHIND.

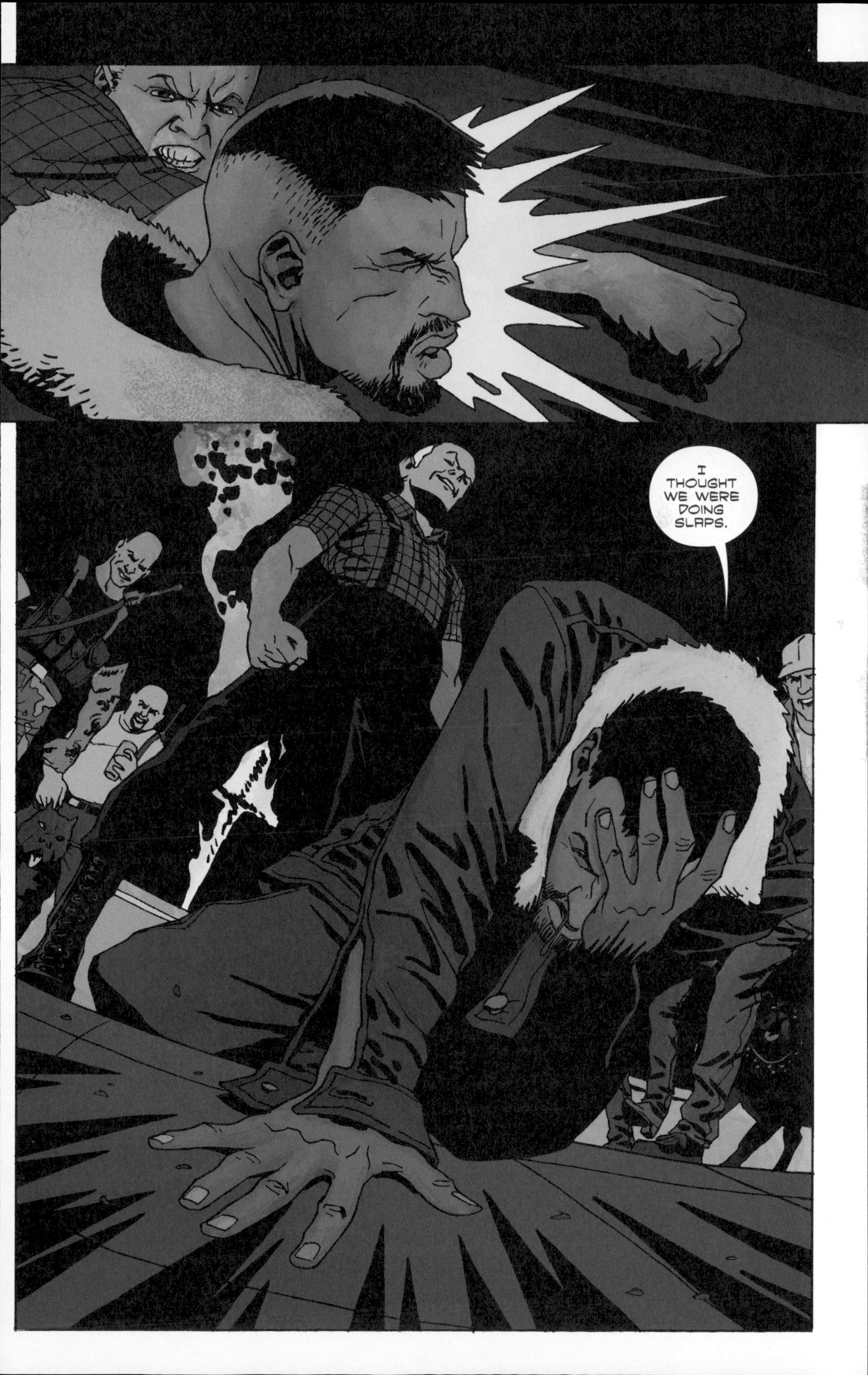
I THOUGHT WE WERE DOING SLAPS.

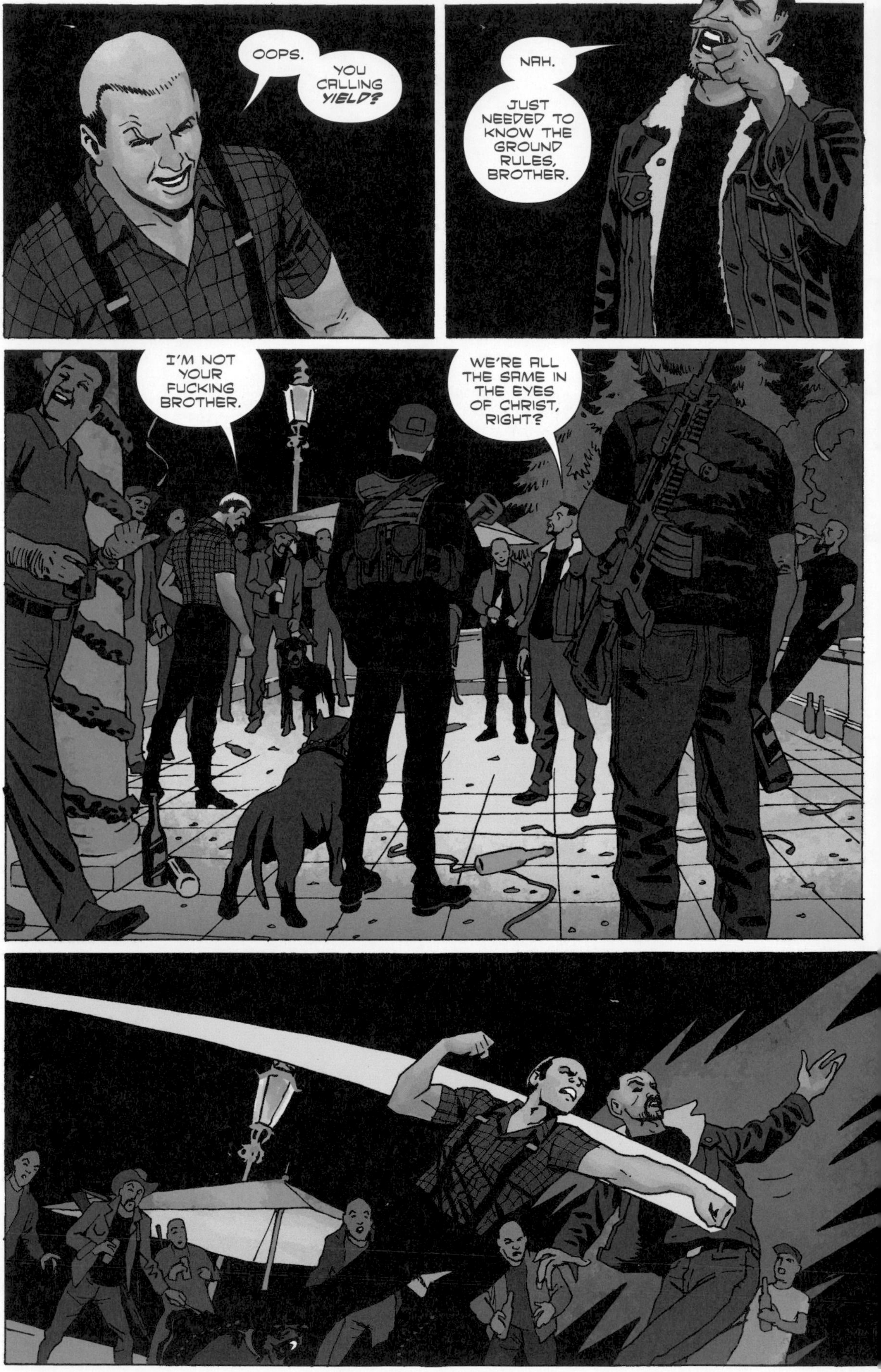
OOPS.
YOU CALLING YIELD?
NAH.
JUST NEEDED TO KNOW THE GROUND RULES, BROTHER.
I'M NOT YOUR FUCKING BROTHER.
WE'RE ALL THE SAME IN THE EYES OF CHRIST, RIGHT?

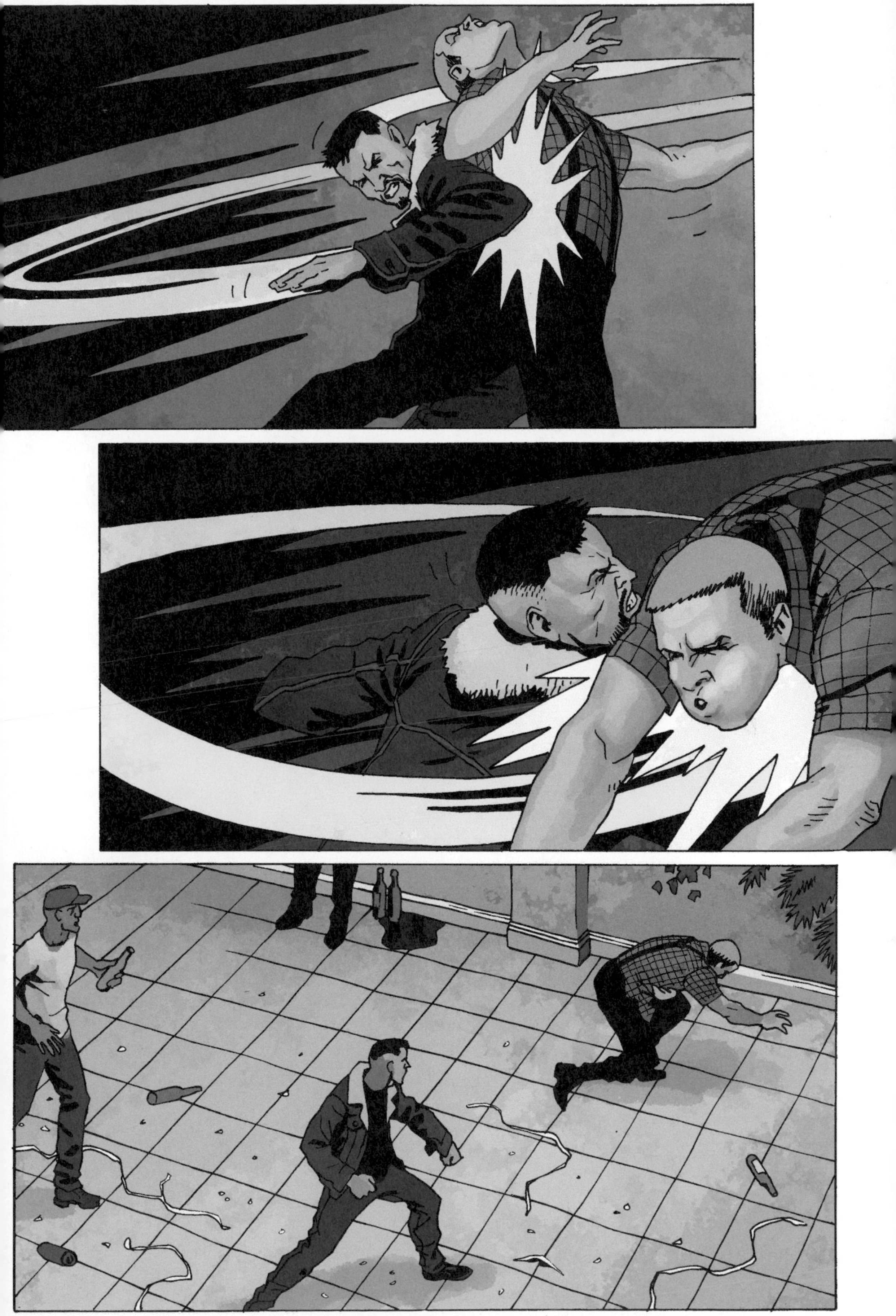

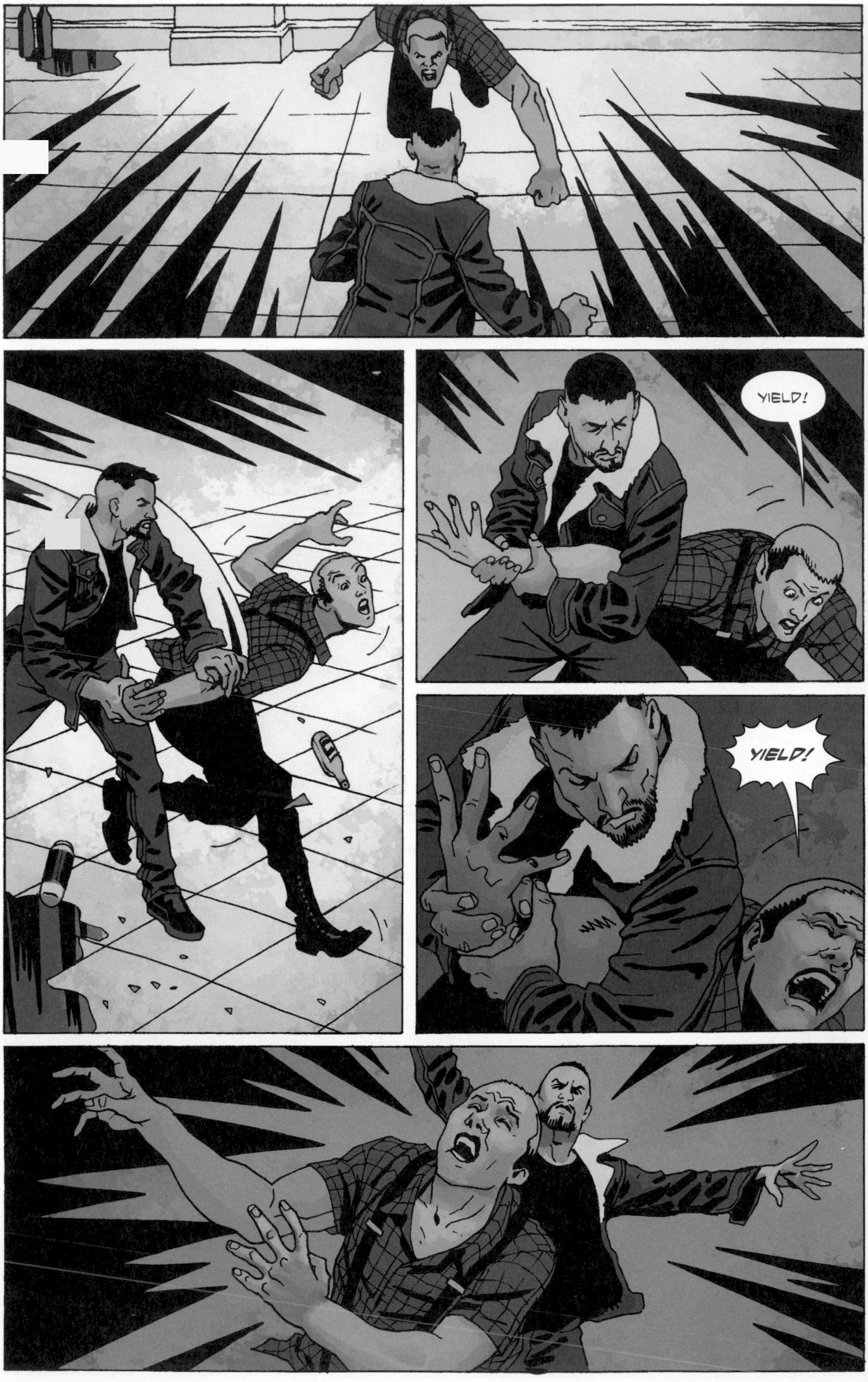
YIELD!
YIELD!

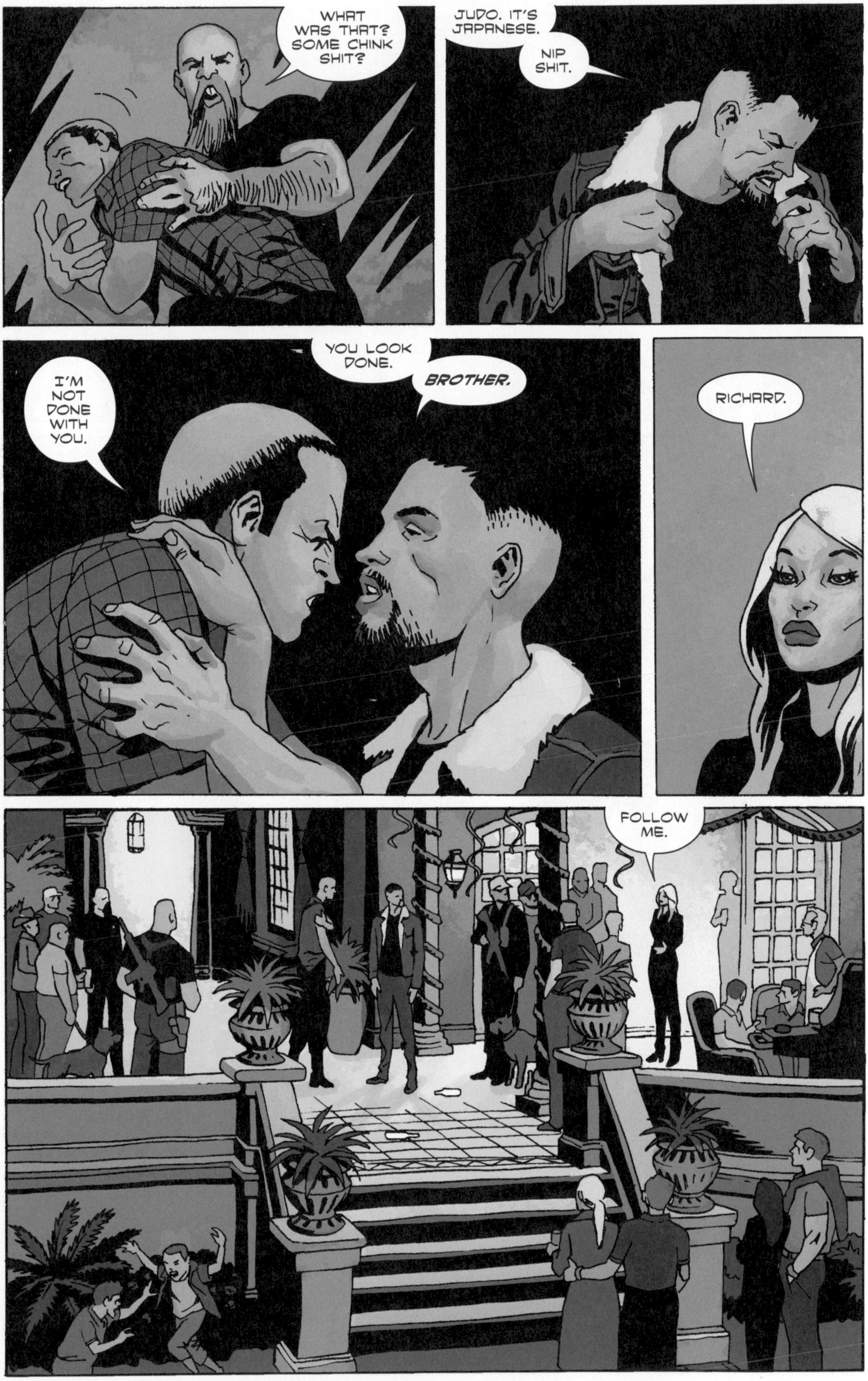
WHAT WAS THAT? SOME CHINK SHIT?
JUDO. IT'S JAPANESE.
NIP SHIT.
I'M NOT DONE WITH YOU.
YOU LOOK DONE.
BROTHER.
RICHARD.
FOLLOW ME.

WANNA TELL ME WHAT *THAT* WAS?

JUST A CONVERSATION IN A LANGUAGE HE COULD UNDERSTAND.

YOU HUMILIATED HIM.

SOMETIMES THAT HAPPENS IN A BACK-YARD.

BILLY AND HIS BROTHER WERE *ARMY.* MIDDLE EAST. RIGHT IN THE CENTER. BILLY IS THE ONE WHO CAME BACK AND HE BROUGHT *PTSD* WITH HIM.

HE'S GOT MORE PRIDE THAN COMMON SENSE, BUT THAT'S *ALL* HE HAS. AND YOU JUST TOOK THAT FROM HIM IN FRONT OF THE ONLY FAMILY HE'S GOT.

HOW DOES *ANY* OF THAT MAKE BRINGING YOU IN EASIER?

I'M SORRY.

WIPE YOUR NOSE.

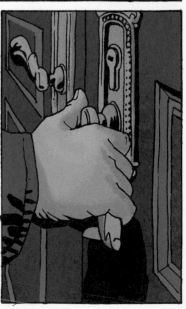

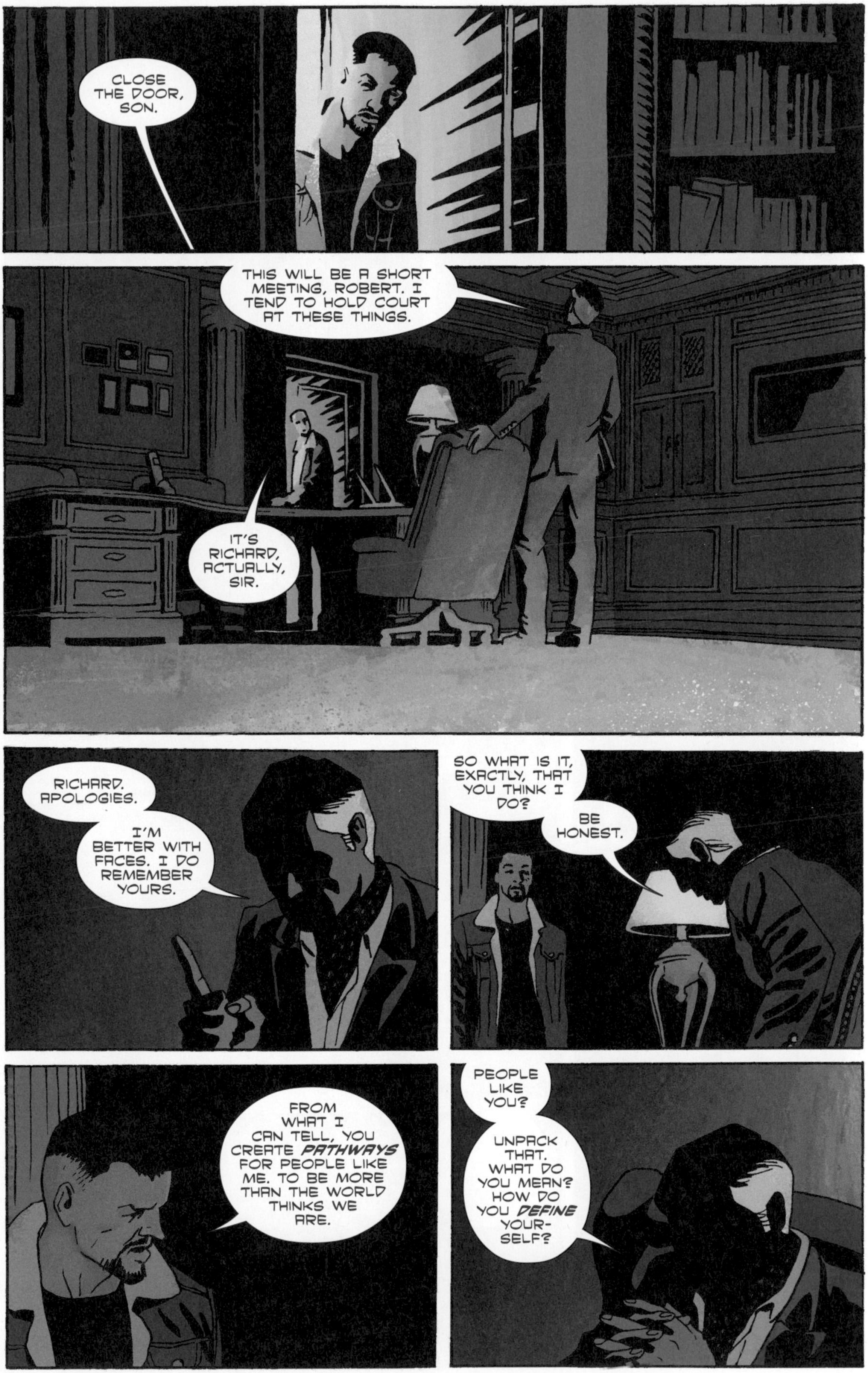
CLOSE THE DOOR, SON.
THIS WILL BE A SHORT MEETING, ROBERT. I TEND TO HOLD COURT AT THESE THINGS.
IT'S RICHARD, ACTUALLY, SIR.
RICHARD. APOLOGIES.
I'M BETTER WITH FACES. I DO REMEMBER YOURS.
SO WHAT IS IT, EXACTLY, THAT YOU THINK I DO?
BE HONEST.
FROM WHAT I CAN TELL, YOU CREATE *PATHWAYS* FOR PEOPLE LIKE ME. TO BE MORE THAN THE WORLD THINKS WE ARE.
PEOPLE LIKE YOU?
UNPACK THAT. WHAT DO YOU MEAN? HOW DO YOU *DEFINE* YOURSELF?

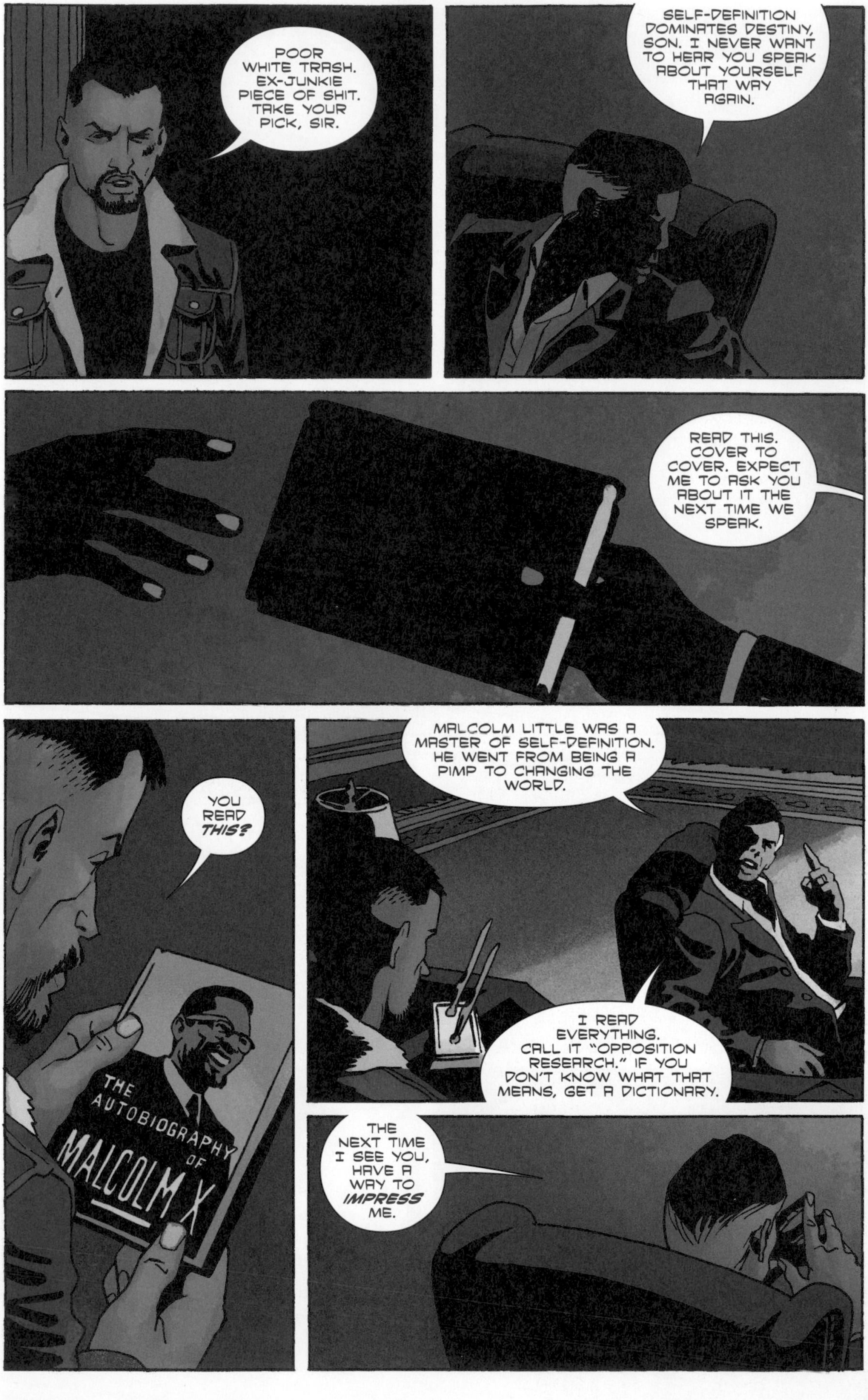
POOR WHITE TRASH. EX-JUNKIE PIECE OF SHIT. TAKE YOUR PICK, SIR.
SELF-DEFINITION DOMINATES DESTINY, SON. I NEVER WANT TO HEAR YOU SPEAK ABOUT YOURSELF THAT WAY AGAIN.
READ THIS. COVER TO COVER. EXPECT ME TO ASK YOU ABOUT IT THE NEXT TIME WE SPEAK.
YOU READ *THIS?*
THE AUTOBIOGRAPHY OF MALCOLM X
MALCOLM LITTLE WAS A MASTER OF SELF-DEFINITION. HE WENT FROM BEING A PIMP TO CHANGING THE WORLD.
I READ EVERYTHING. CALL IT "OPPOSITION RESEARCH." IF YOU DON'T KNOW WHAT THAT MEANS, GET A DICTIONARY.
THE NEXT TIME I SEE YOU, HAVE A WAY TO *IMPRESS* ME.

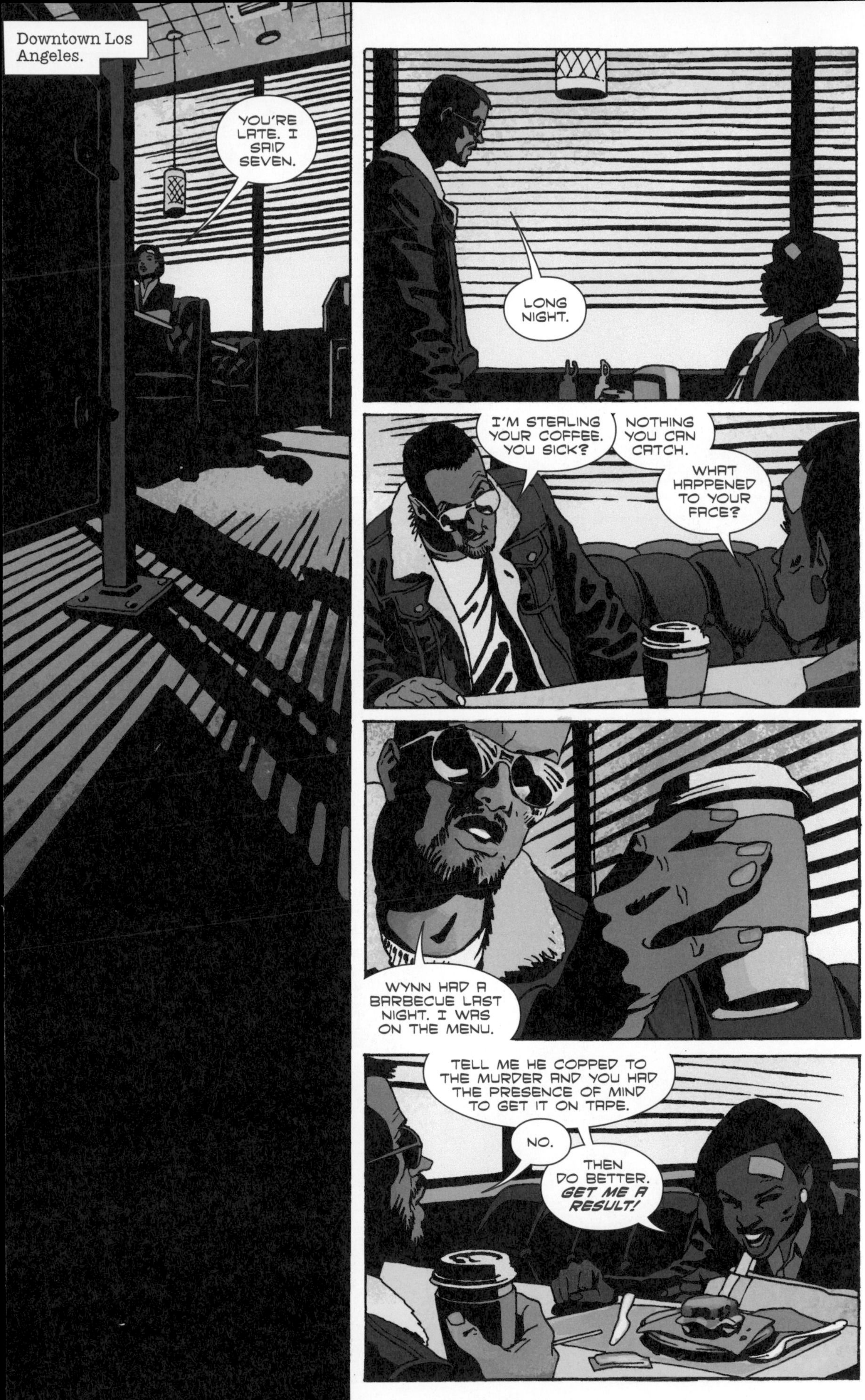
Downtown Los Angeles.
YOU'RE LATE. I SAID SEVEN.
LONG NIGHT.
I'M STEALING YOUR COFFEE. YOU SICK?
NOTHING YOU CAN CATCH.
WHAT HAPPENED TO YOUR FACE?
WYNN HAD A BARBECUE LAST NIGHT. I WAS ON THE MENU.
TELL ME HE COPPED TO THE MURDER AND YOU HAD THE PRESENCE OF MIND TO GET IT ON TAPE.
NO.
THEN DO BETTER. GET ME A RESULT!

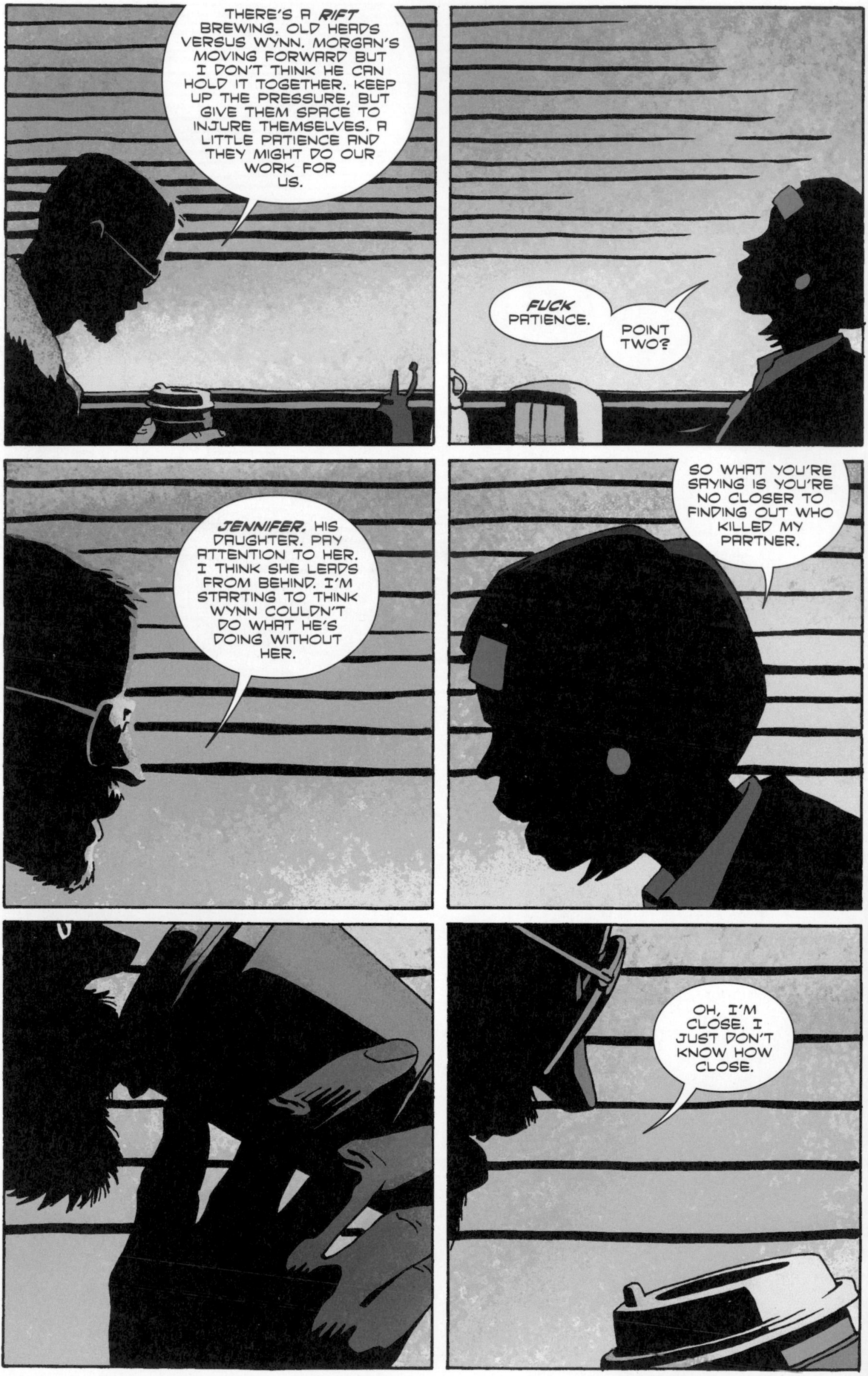
THERE'S A RIFT BREWING. OLD HEADS VERSUS WYNN. MORGAN'S MOVING FORWARD BUT I DON'T THINK HE CAN HOLD IT TOGETHER. KEEP UP THE PRESSURE, BUT GIVE THEM SPACE TO INJURE THEMSELVES. A LITTLE PATIENCE AND THEY MIGHT DO OUR WORK FOR US.
FUCK PATIENCE.
POINT TWO?
JENNIFER. HIS DAUGHTER. PAY ATTENTION TO HER. I THINK SHE LEADS FROM BEHIND. I'M STARTING TO THINK WYNN COULDN'T DO WHAT HE'S DOING WITHOUT HER.
SO WHAT YOU'RE SAYING IS YOU'RE NO CLOSER TO FINDING OUT WHO KILLED MY PARTNER.
OH, I'M CLOSE. I JUST DON'T KNOW HOW CLOSE.

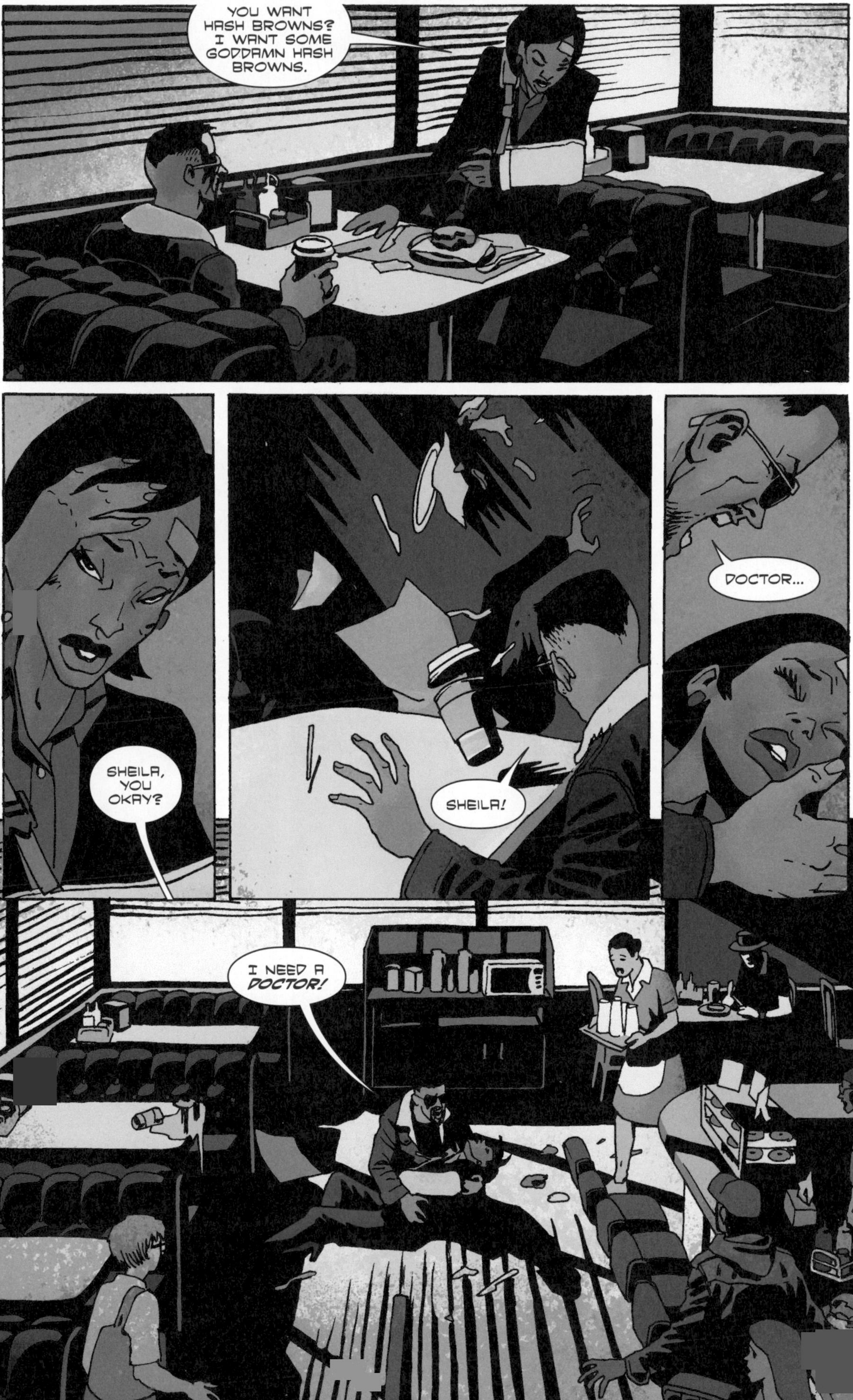
YOU WANT HASH BROWNS? I WANT SOME GODDAMN HASH BROWNS.
SHEILA, YOU OKAY?
SHEILA!
DOCTOR...
I NEED A *DOCTOR!*

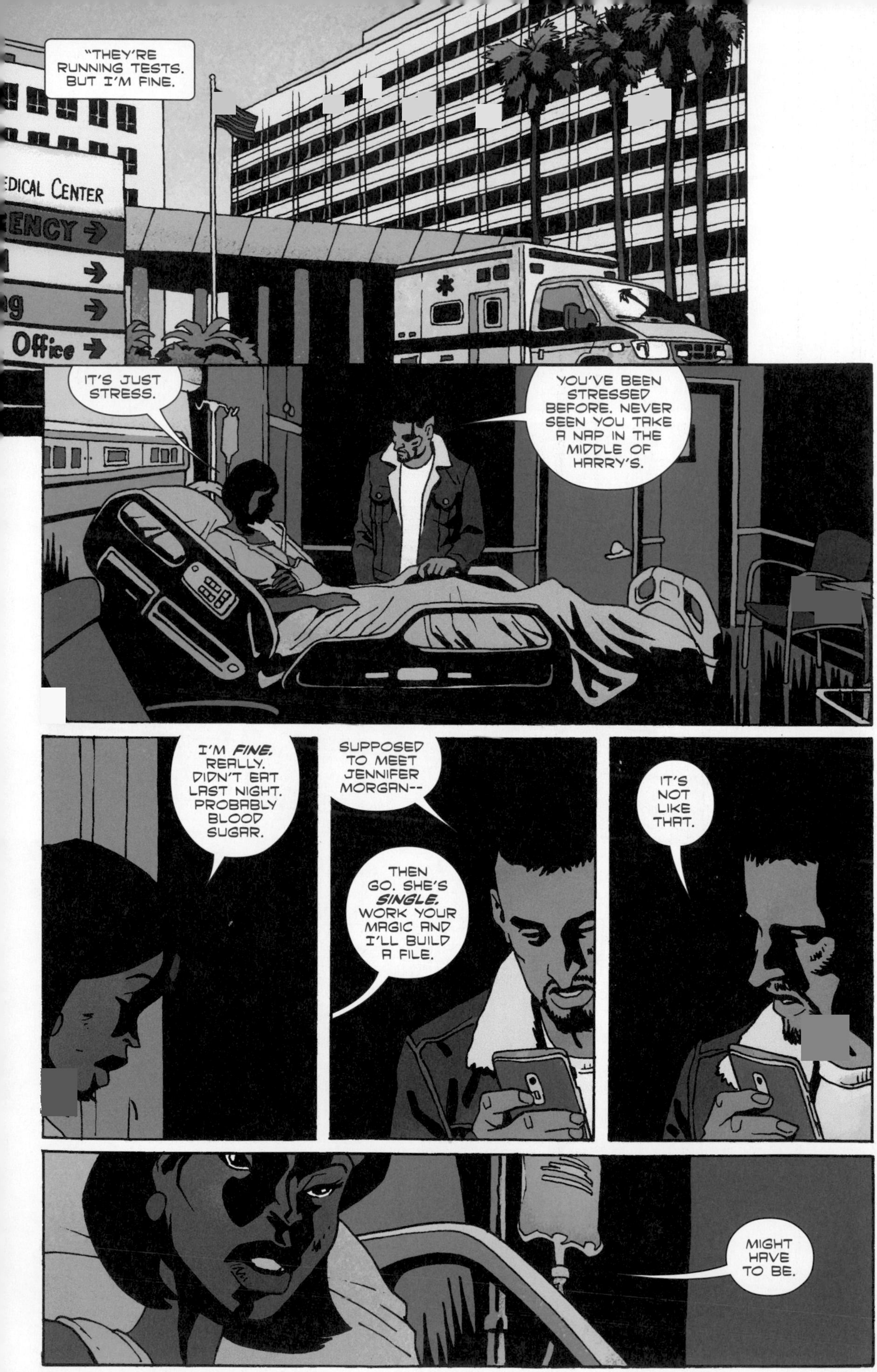
"THEY'RE RUNNING TESTS. BUT I'M FINE.
EDICAL CENTER
ENCY
Office
IT'S JUST STRESS.
YOU'VE BEEN STRESSED BEFORE. NEVER SEEN YOU TAKE A NAP IN THE MIDDLE OF HARRY'S.
I'M *FINE.* REALLY. DIDN'T EAT LAST NIGHT. PROBABLY BLOOD SUGAR.
SUPPOSED TO MEET JENNIFER MORGAN--
THEN GO. SHE'S *SINGLE.* WORK YOUR MAGIC AND I'LL BUILD A FILE.
IT'S NOT LIKE THAT.
MIGHT HAVE TO BE.

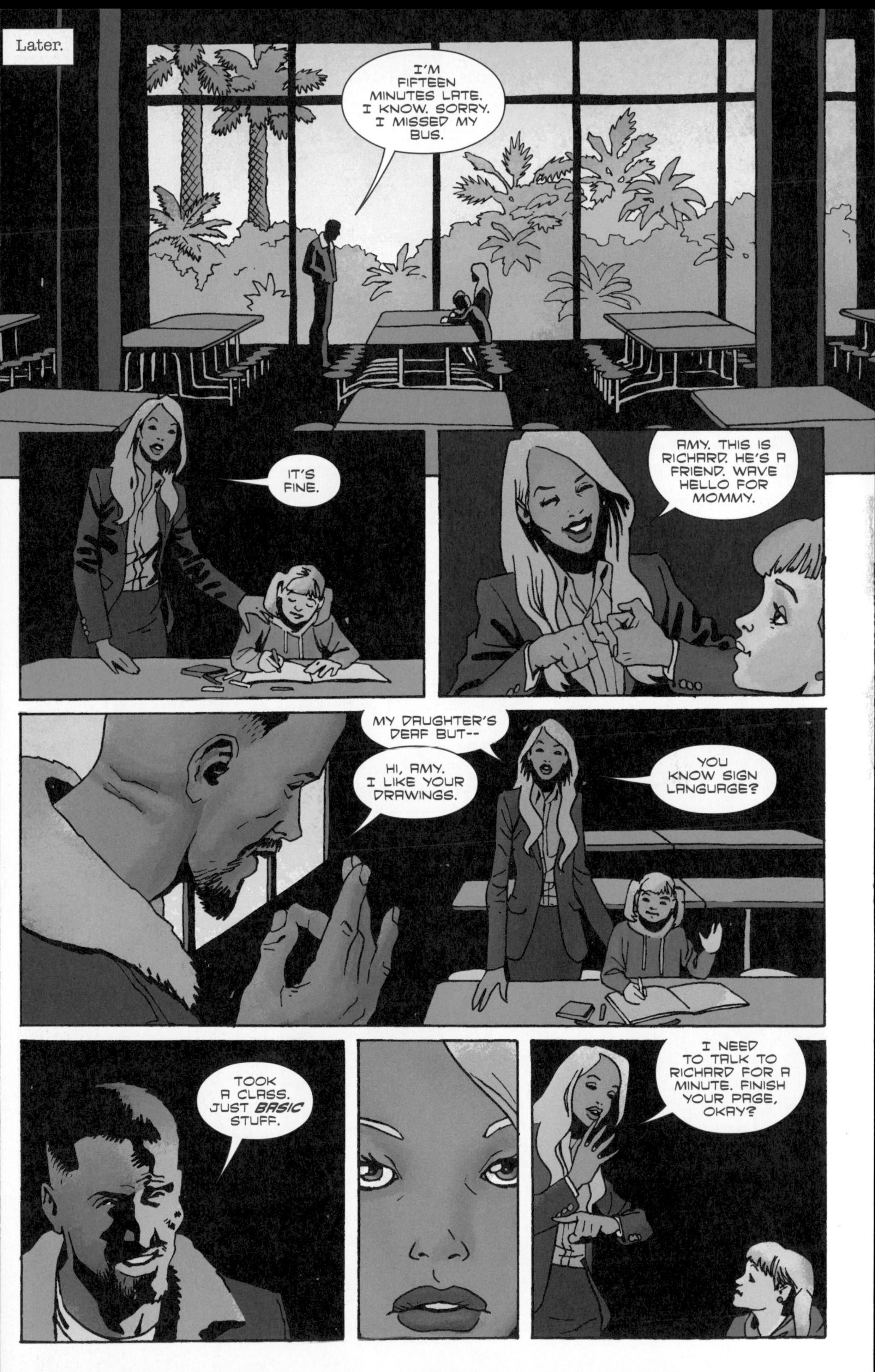
Later.
I'M FIFTEEN MINUTES LATE. I KNOW. SORRY. I MISSED MY BUS.
IT'S FINE.
AMY. THIS IS RICHARD. HE'S A FRIEND. WAVE HELLO FOR MOMMY.
MY DAUGHTER'S DEAF BUT--
HI, AMY. I LIKE YOUR DRAWINGS.
YOU KNOW SIGN LANGUAGE?
TOOK A CLASS. JUST BASIC STUFF.
I NEED TO TALK TO RICHARD FOR A MINUTE. FINISH YOUR PAGE, OKAY?

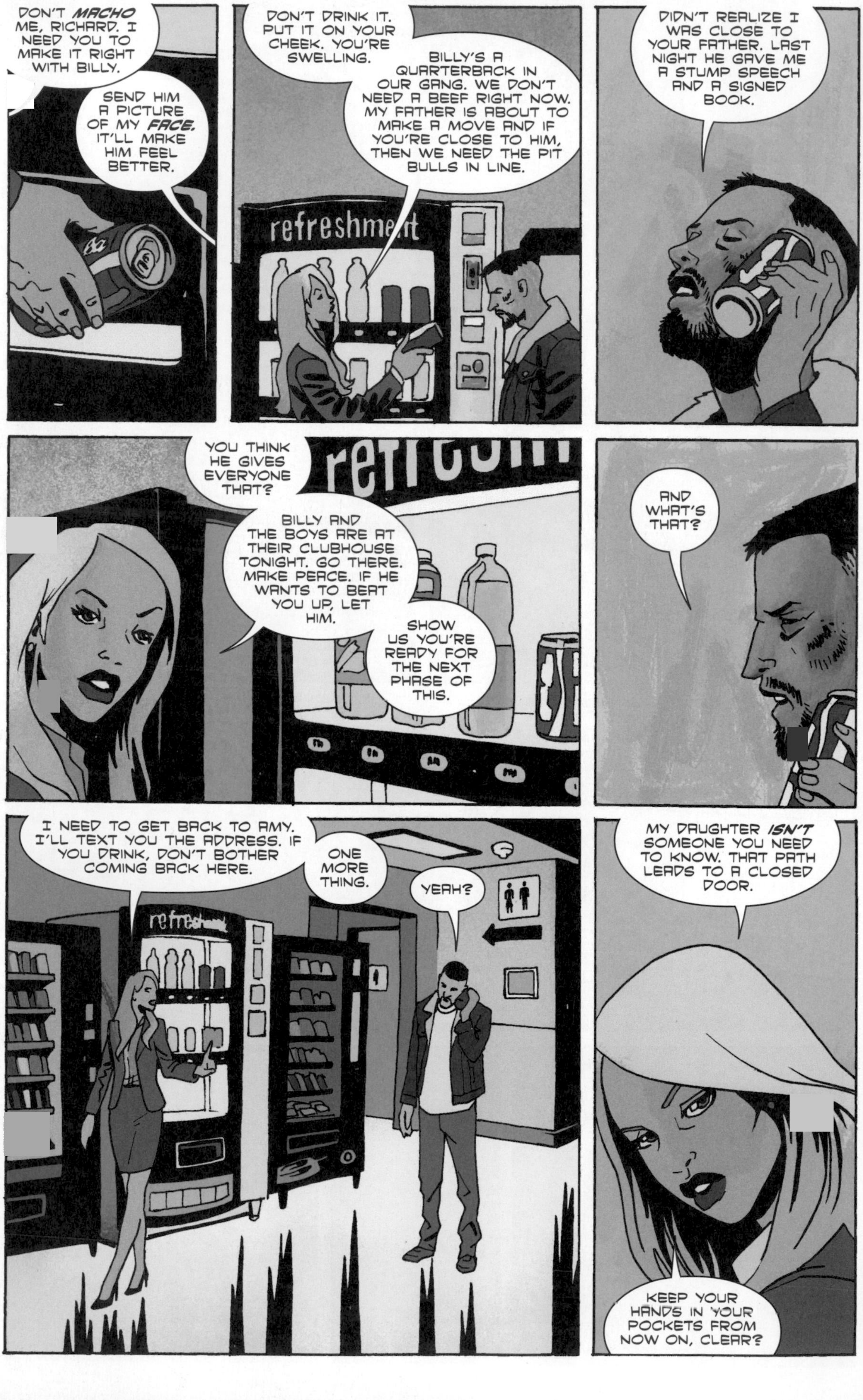
DON'T MACHO ME, RICHARD. I NEED YOU TO MAKE IT RIGHT WITH BILLY.
SEND HIM A PICTURE OF MY FACE. IT'LL MAKE HIM FEEL BETTER.
DON'T DRINK IT. PUT IT ON YOUR CHEEK. YOU'RE SWELLING.
BILLY'S A QUARTERBACK IN OUR GANG. WE DON'T NEED A BEEF RIGHT NOW. MY FATHER IS ABOUT TO MAKE A MOVE AND IF YOU'RE CLOSE TO HIM, THEN WE NEED THE PIT BULLS IN LINE.
refreshment
DIDN'T REALIZE I WAS CLOSE TO YOUR FATHER. LAST NIGHT HE GAVE ME A STUMP SPEECH AND A SIGNED BOOK.
YOU THINK HE GIVES EVERYONE THAT?
BILLY AND THE BOYS ARE AT THEIR CLUBHOUSE TONIGHT. GO THERE. MAKE PEACE. IF HE WANTS TO BEAT YOU UP, LET HIM.
SHOW US YOU'RE READY FOR THE NEXT PHASE OF THIS.
AND WHAT'S THAT?
I NEED TO GET BACK TO AMY. I'LL TEXT YOU THE ADDRESS. IF YOU DRINK, DON'T BOTHER COMING BACK HERE.
ONE MORE THING.
YEAH?
MY DAUGHTER ISN'T SOMEONE YOU NEED TO KNOW. THAT PATH LEADS TO A CLOSED DOOR.
KEEP YOUR HANDS IN YOUR POCKETS FROM NOW ON, CLEAR?

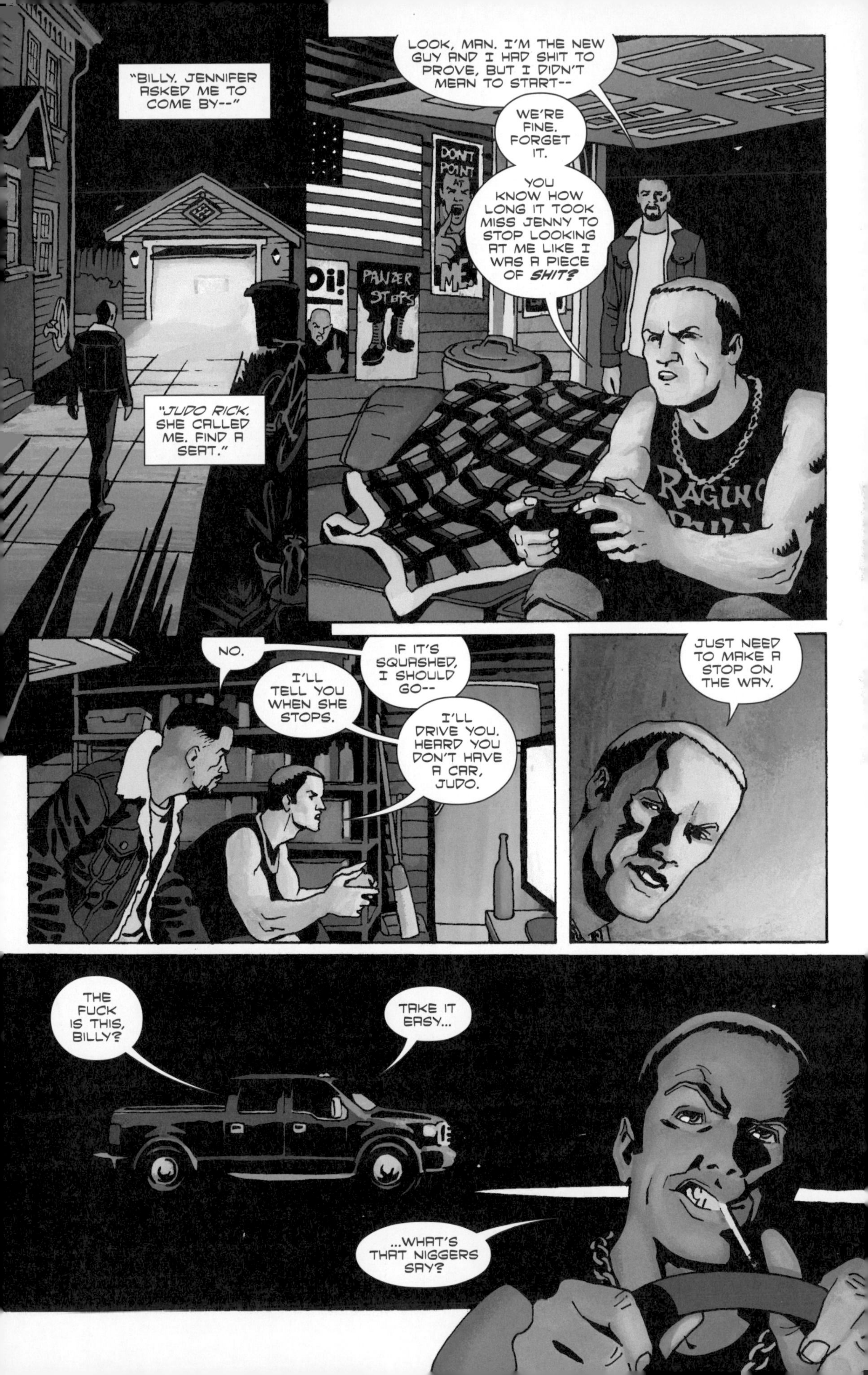
"BILLY. JENNIFER ASKED ME TO COME BY--"
"JUDO RICK. SHE CALLED ME. FIND A SEAT."
LOOK, MAN. I'M THE NEW GUY AND I HAD SHIT TO PROVE, BUT I DIDN'T MEAN TO START--
WE'RE FINE. FORGET IT.
YOU KNOW HOW LONG IT TOOK MISS JENNY TO STOP LOOKING AT ME LIKE I WAS A PIECE OF *SHIT?*
DON'T POINT AT ME
Oi!
PANZER STOPS
NO.
IF IT'S SQUASHED, I SHOULD GO--
I'LL TELL YOU WHEN SHE STOPS.
I'LL DRIVE YOU. HEARD YOU DON'T HAVE A CAR, JUDO.
JUST NEED TO MAKE A STOP ON THE WAY.
THE FUCK IS THIS, BILLY?
TAKE IT EASY...
...WHAT'S THAT NIGGERS SAY?

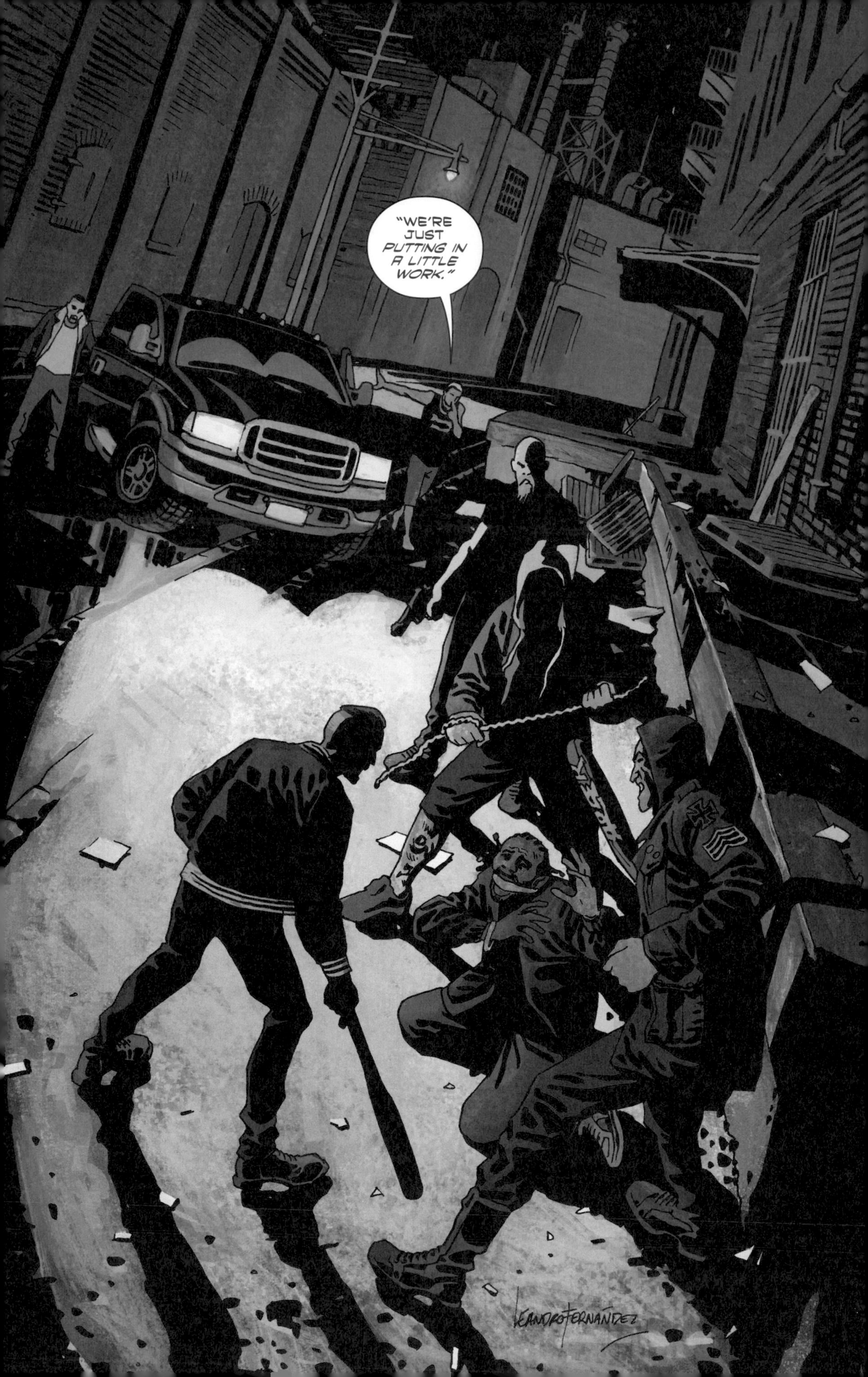
"WE'RE JUST PUTTING IN A LITTLE WORK."
LEANDRO FERNANDEZ

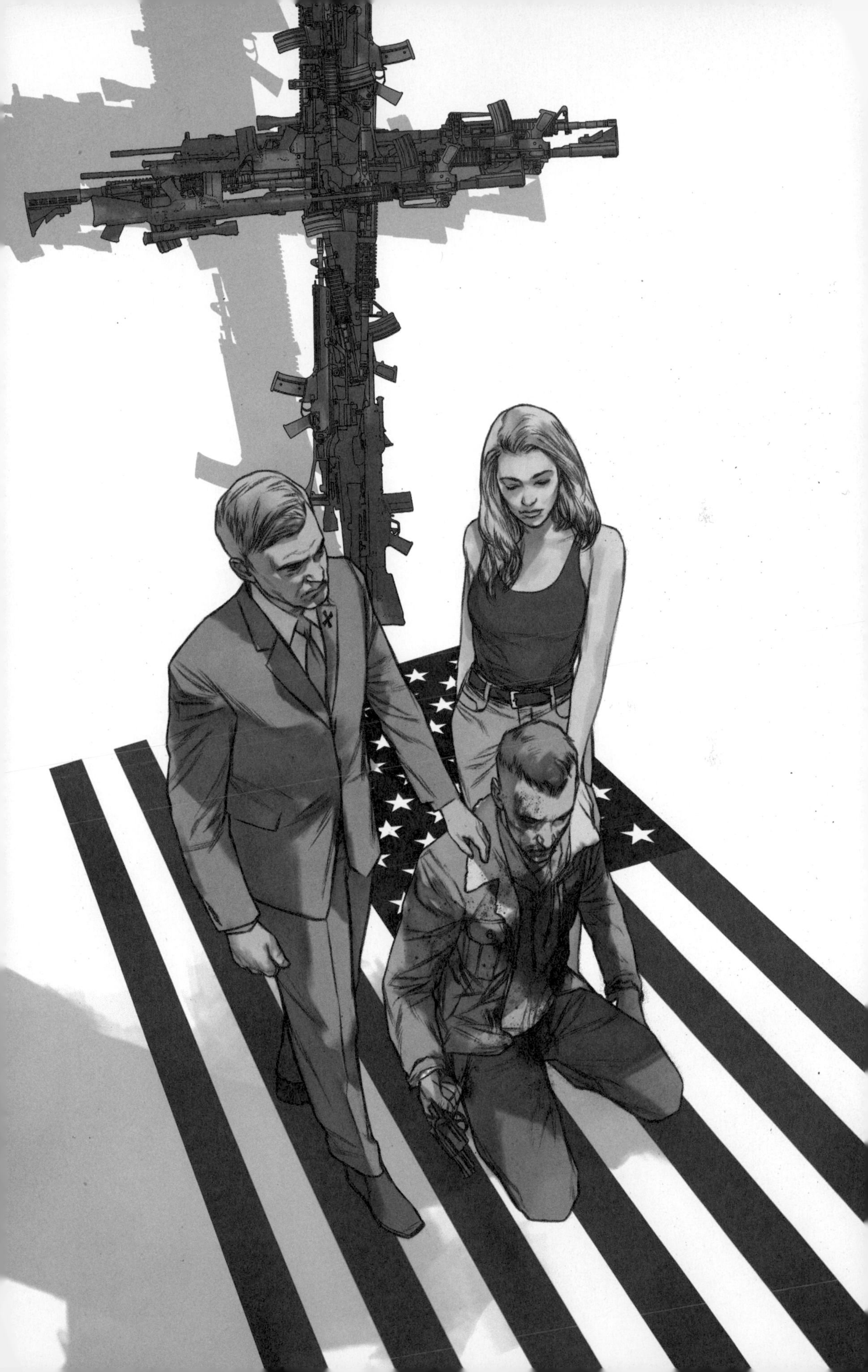

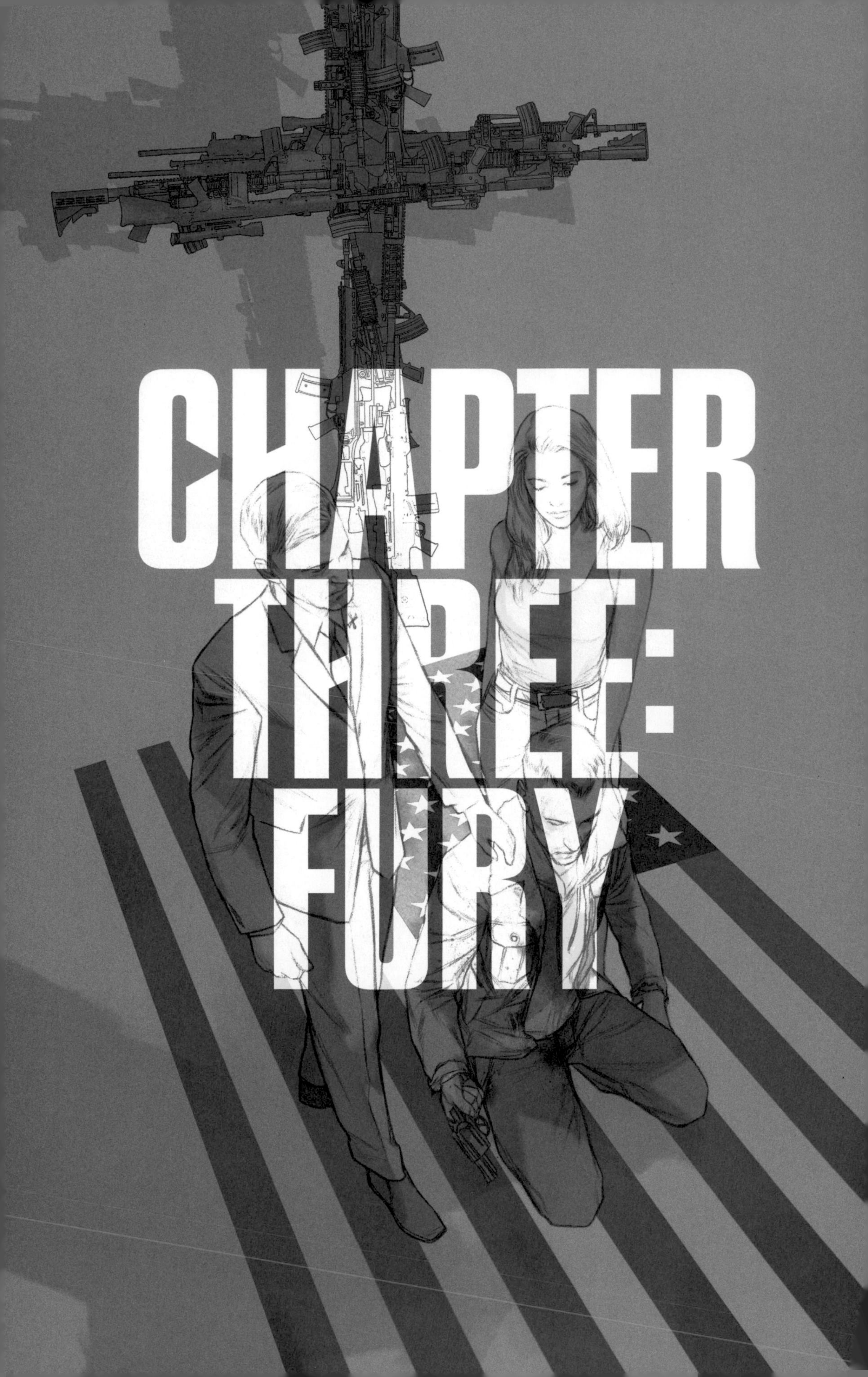
CHAPTER
THREE:
FURY

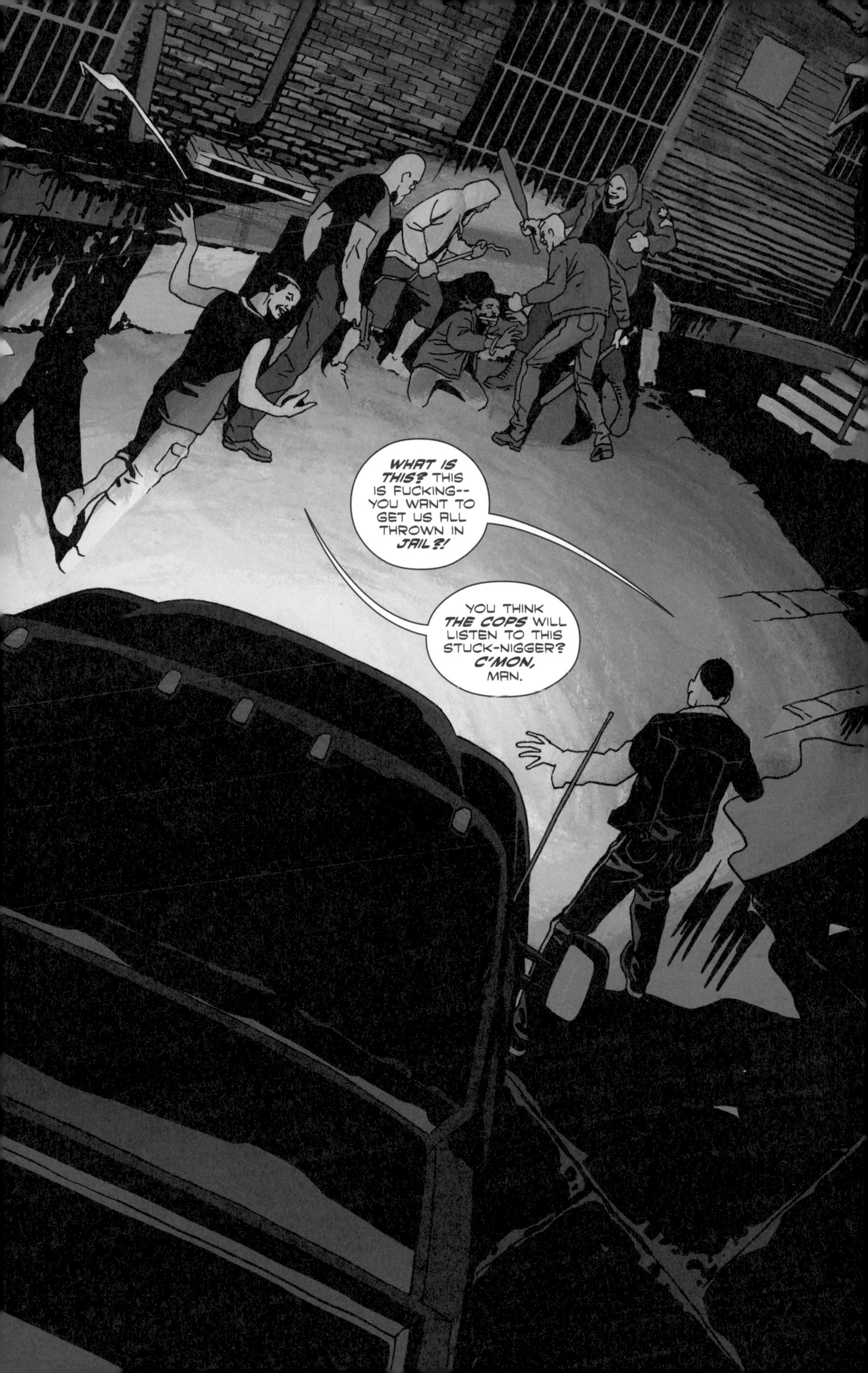
WHAT IS THIS? THIS IS FUCKING-- YOU WANT TO GET US ALL THROWN IN JAIL?!
YOU THINK THE COPS WILL LISTEN TO THIS STUCK-NIGGER? C'MON, MAN.

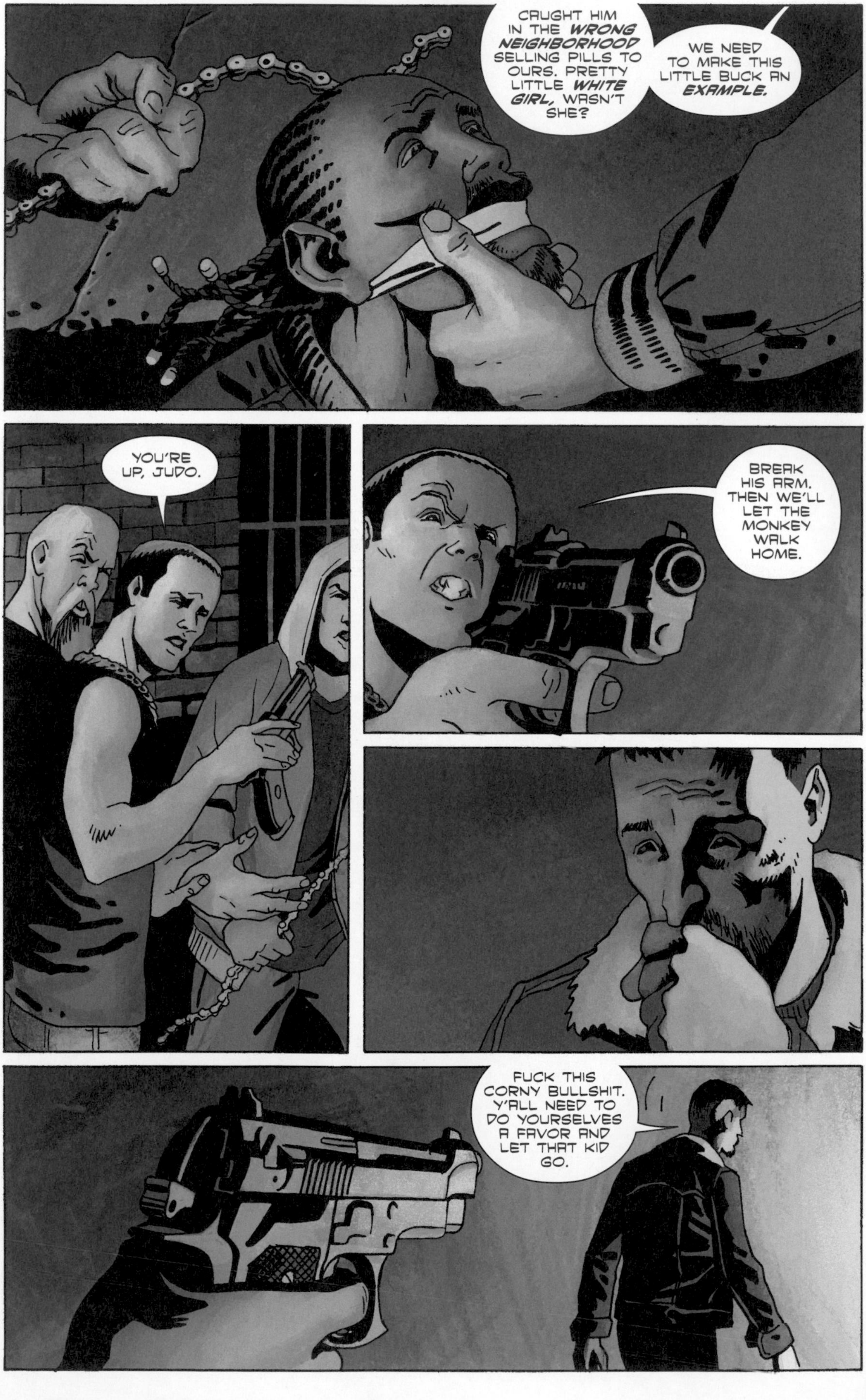
CAUGHT HIM IN THE *WRONG NEIGHBORHOOD* SELLING PILLS TO OURS. PRETTY LITTLE *WHITE GIRL,* WASN'T SHE?
WE NEED TO MAKE THIS LITTLE BUCK AN *EXAMPLE.*
YOU'RE UP, JUDO.
BREAK HIS ARM. THEN WE'LL LET THE MONKEY WALK HOME.
FUCK THIS CORNY BULLSHIT. Y'ALL NEED TO DO YOURSELVES A FAVOR AND LET THAT KID GO.

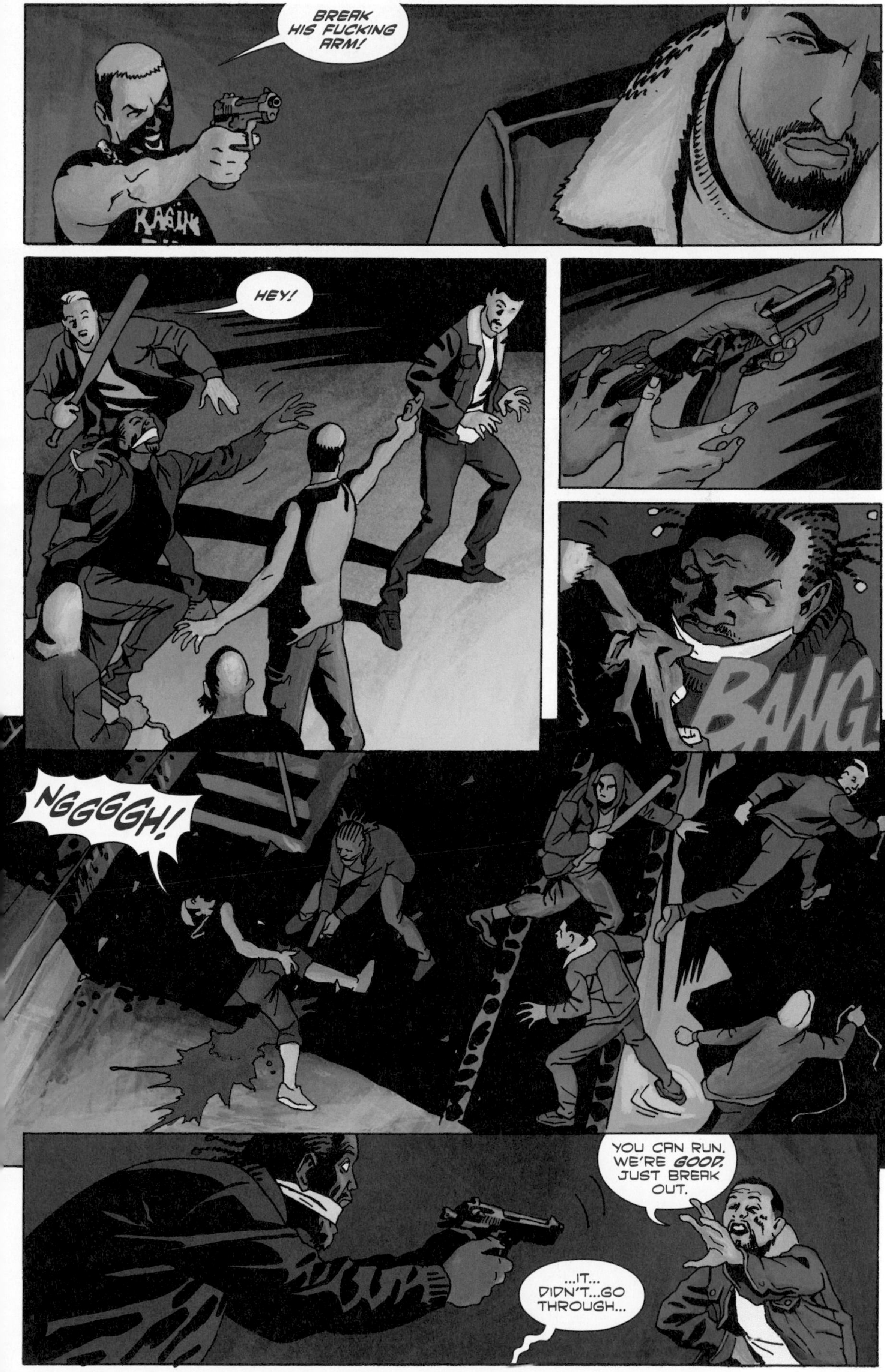
BREAK HIS FUCKING ARM!
HEY!
BANG
NGGGGH!
YOU CAN RUN. WE'RE *GOOD.* JUST BREAK OUT.
...IT... DIDN'T...GO THROUGH...

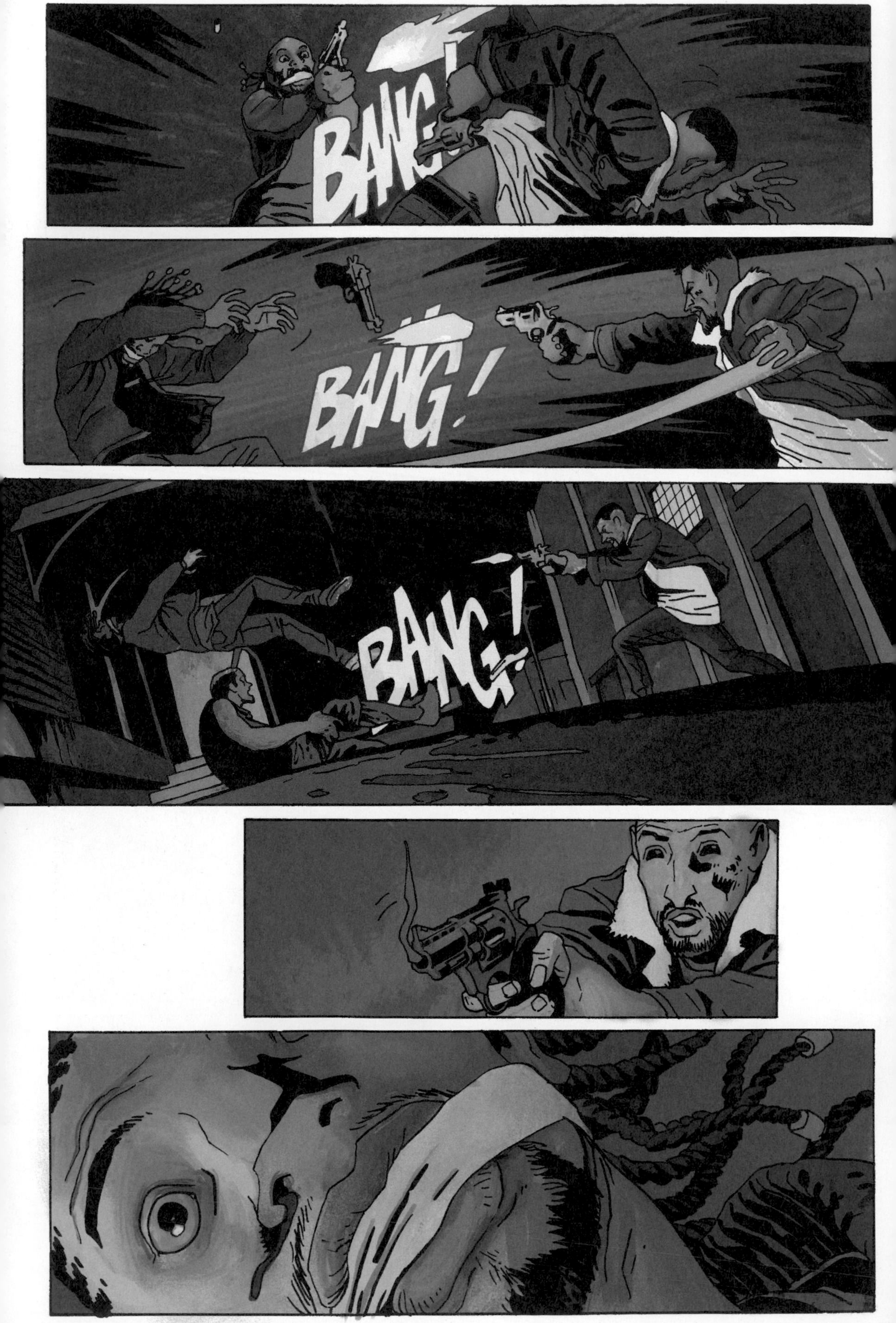
BANG!
BANG!
BANG!

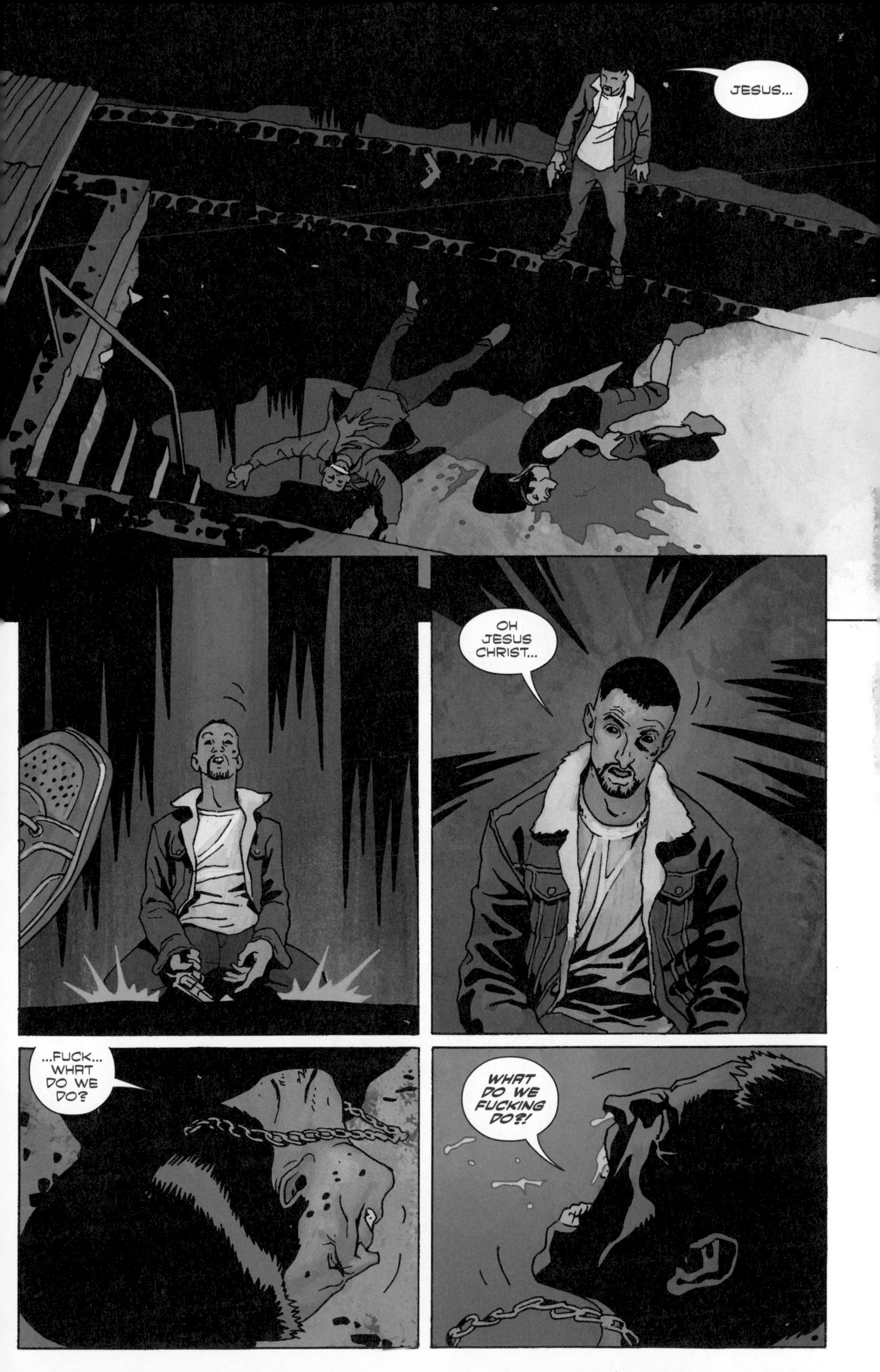
JESUS...
OH JESUS CHRIST...
...FUCK... WHAT DO WE DO?
WHAT DO WE FUCKING DO?!

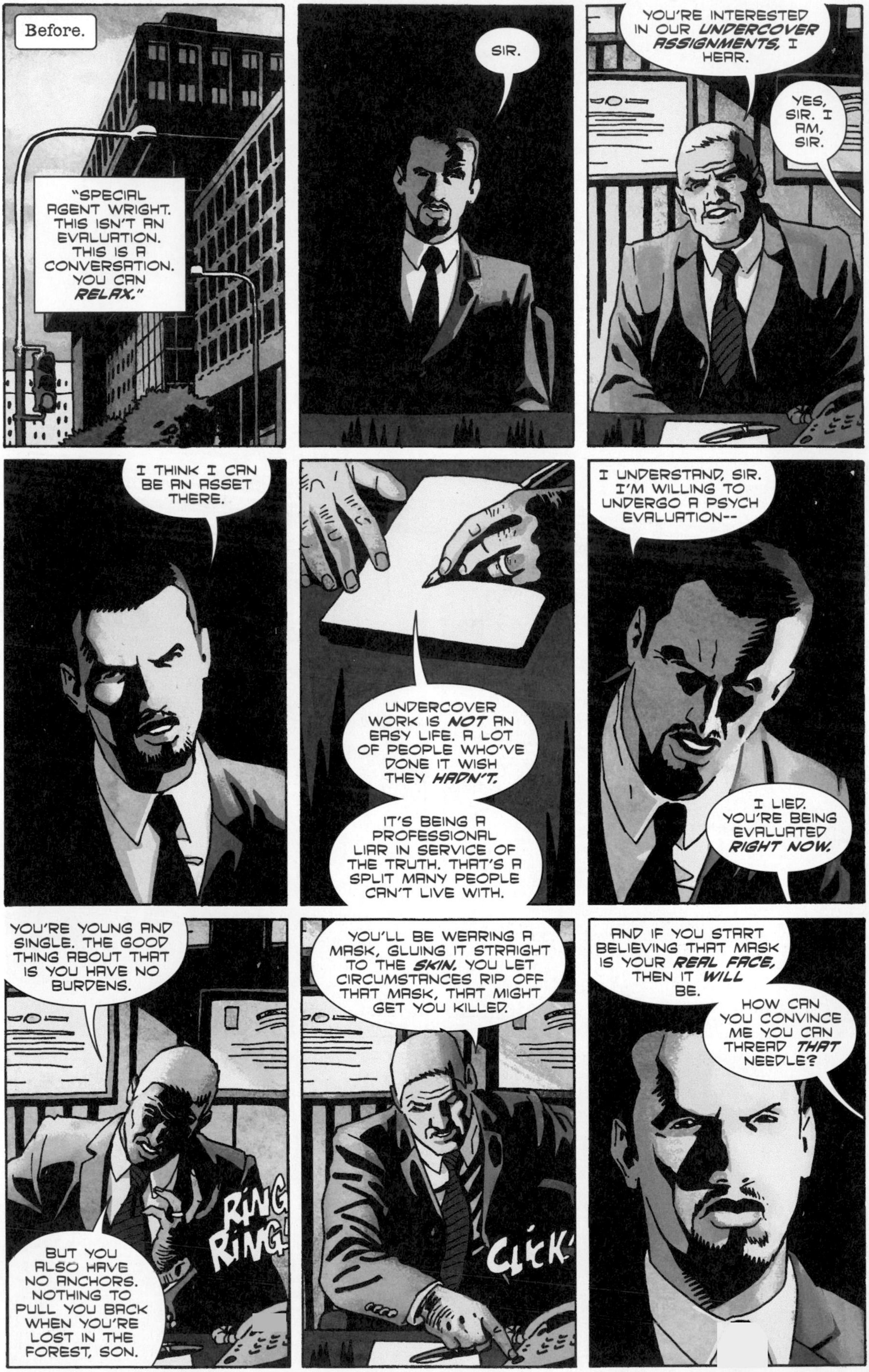
Before.
"SPECIAL AGENT WRIGHT. THIS ISN'T AN EVALUATION. THIS IS A CONVERSATION. YOU CAN RELAX."
SIR.
YOU'RE INTERESTED IN OUR UNDERCOVER ASSIGNMENTS, I HEAR.
YES, SIR. I AM, SIR.
I THINK I CAN BE AN ASSET THERE.
UNDERCOVER WORK IS NOT AN EASY LIFE. A LOT OF PEOPLE WHO'VE DONE IT WISH THEY HADN'T.
IT'S BEING A PROFESSIONAL LIAR IN SERVICE OF THE TRUTH. THAT'S A SPLIT MANY PEOPLE CAN'T LIVE WITH.
I UNDERSTAND, SIR. I'M WILLING TO UNDERGO A PSYCH EVALUATION--
I LIED. YOU'RE BEING EVALUATED RIGHT NOW.
YOU'RE YOUNG AND SINGLE. THE GOOD THING ABOUT THAT IS YOU HAVE NO BURDENS.
RING RING
BUT YOU ALSO HAVE NO ANCHORS. NOTHING TO PULL YOU BACK WHEN YOU'RE LOST IN THE FOREST, SON.
YOU'LL BE WEARING A MASK, GLUING IT STRAIGHT TO THE SKIN. YOU LET CIRCUMSTANCES RIP OFF THAT MASK, THAT MIGHT GET YOU KILLED.
CLICK
AND IF YOU START BELIEVING THAT MASK IS YOUR REAL FACE, THEN IT WILL BE.
HOW CAN YOU CONVINCE ME YOU CAN THREAD THAT NEEDLE?

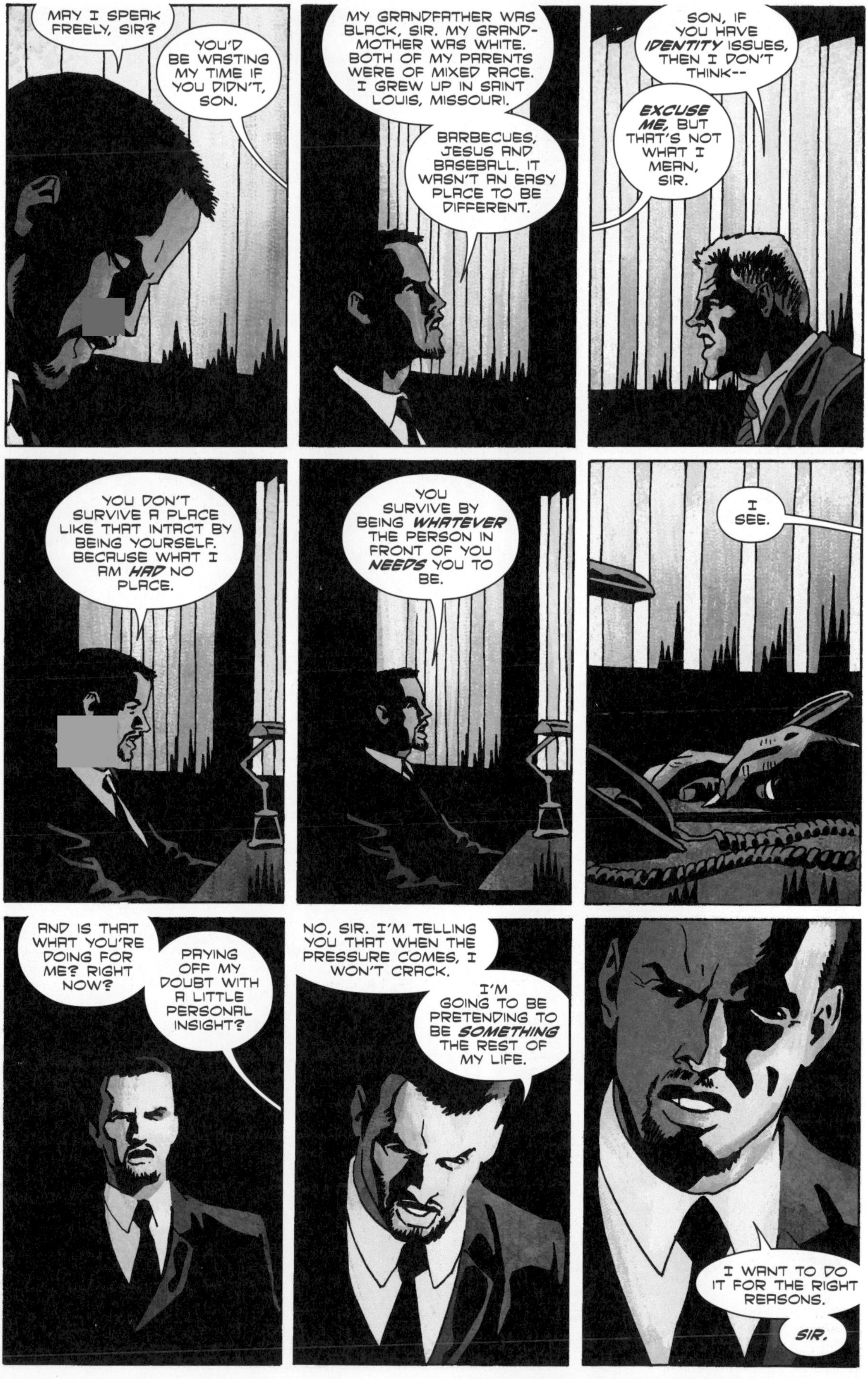
MAY I SPEAK FREELY, SIR?
YOU'D BE WASTING MY TIME IF YOU DIDN'T, SON.
MY GRANDFATHER WAS BLACK, SIR. MY GRAND-MOTHER WAS WHITE. BOTH OF MY PARENTS WERE OF MIXED RACE. I GREW UP IN SAINT LOUIS, MISSOURI.
BARBECUES, JESUS AND BASEBALL. IT WASN'T AN EASY PLACE TO BE DIFFERENT.
SON, IF YOU HAVE *IDENTITY* ISSUES, THEN I DON'T THINK--
EXCUSE ME, BUT THAT'S NOT WHAT I MEAN, SIR.
YOU DON'T SURVIVE A PLACE LIKE THAT INTACT BY BEING YOURSELF. BECAUSE WHAT I AM *HAD* NO PLACE.
YOU SURVIVE BY BEING *WHATEVER* THE PERSON IN FRONT OF YOU *NEEDS* YOU TO BE.
I SEE.
AND IS THAT WHAT YOU'RE DOING FOR ME? RIGHT NOW?
PAYING OFF MY DOUBT WITH A LITTLE PERSONAL INSIGHT?
NO, SIR. I'M TELLING YOU THAT WHEN THE PRESSURE COMES, I WON'T CRACK.
I'M GOING TO BE PRETENDING TO BE *SOMETHING* THE REST OF MY LIFE.
I WANT TO DO IT FOR THE RIGHT REASONS.
SIR.

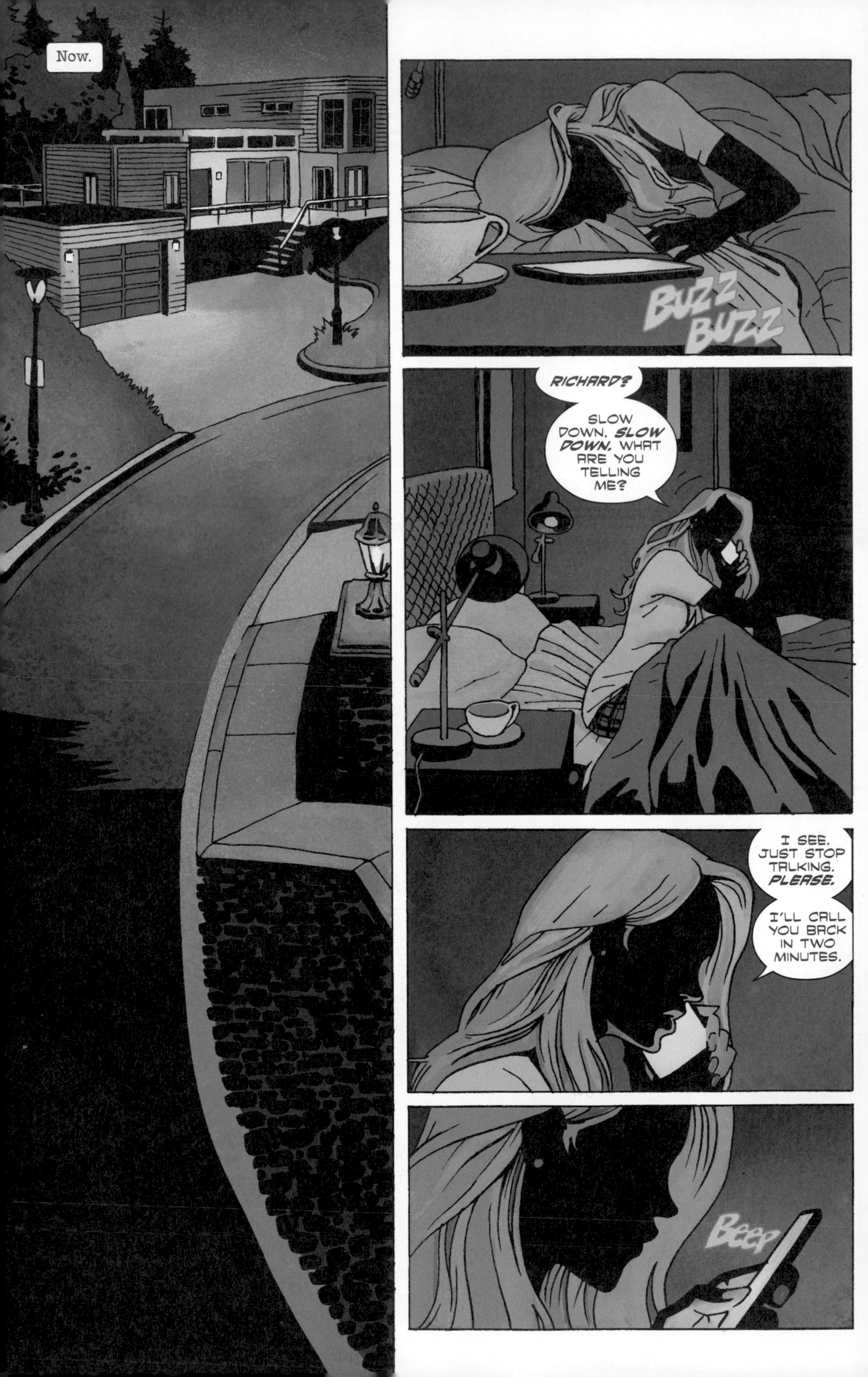
Now.
BUZZ BUZZ
RICHARD?
SLOW DOWN. SLOW DOWN. WHAT ARE YOU TELLING ME?
I SEE. JUST STOP TALKING. PLEASE.
I'LL CALL YOU BACK IN TWO MINUTES.
Beep

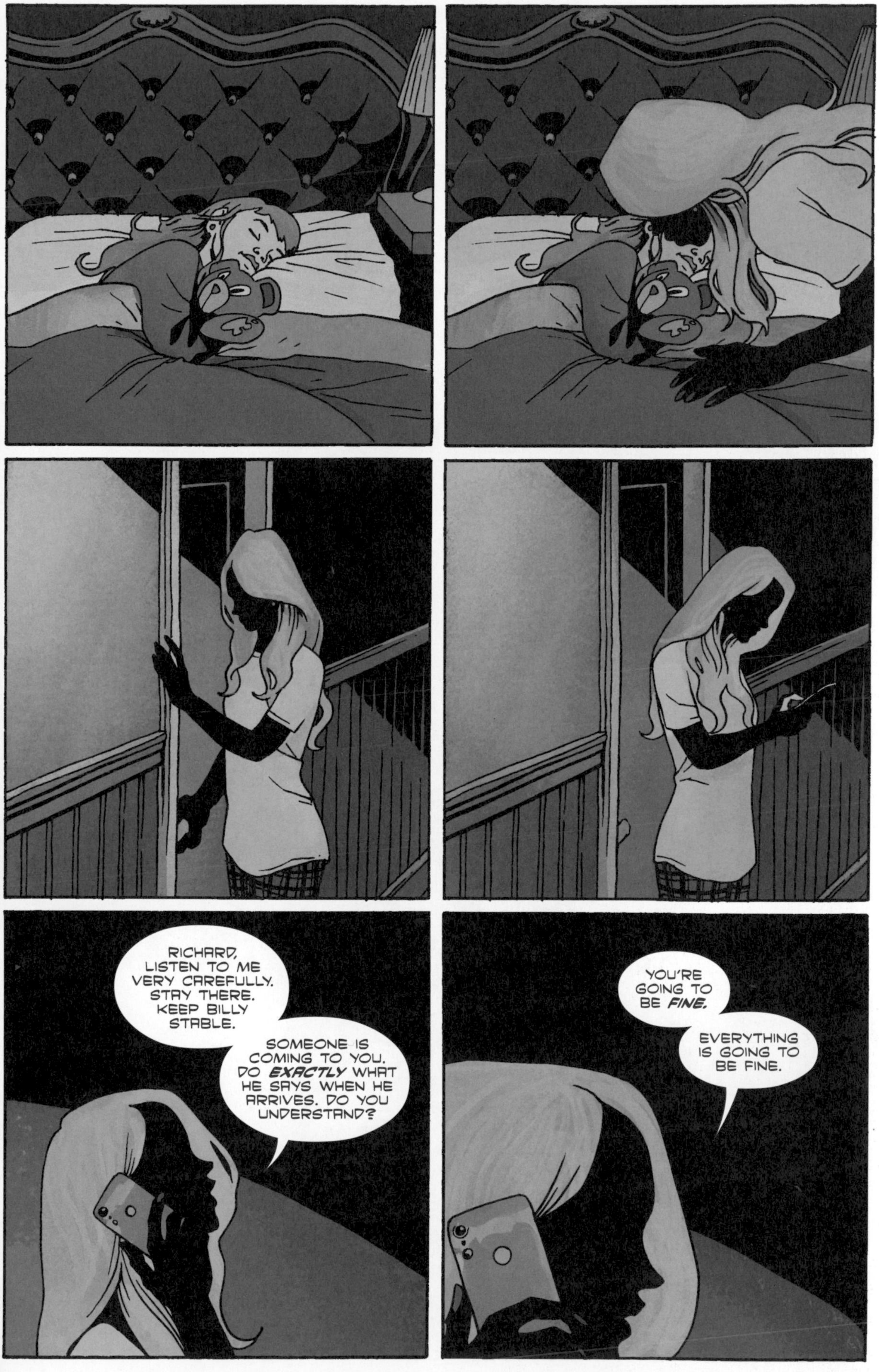
RICHARD, LISTEN TO ME VERY CAREFULLY. STAY THERE. KEEP BILLY STABLE.
SOMEONE IS COMING TO YOU. DO *EXACTLY* WHAT HE SAYS WHEN HE ARRIVES. DO YOU UNDERSTAND?
YOU'RE GOING TO BE *FINE.*
EVERYTHING IS GOING TO BE FINE.

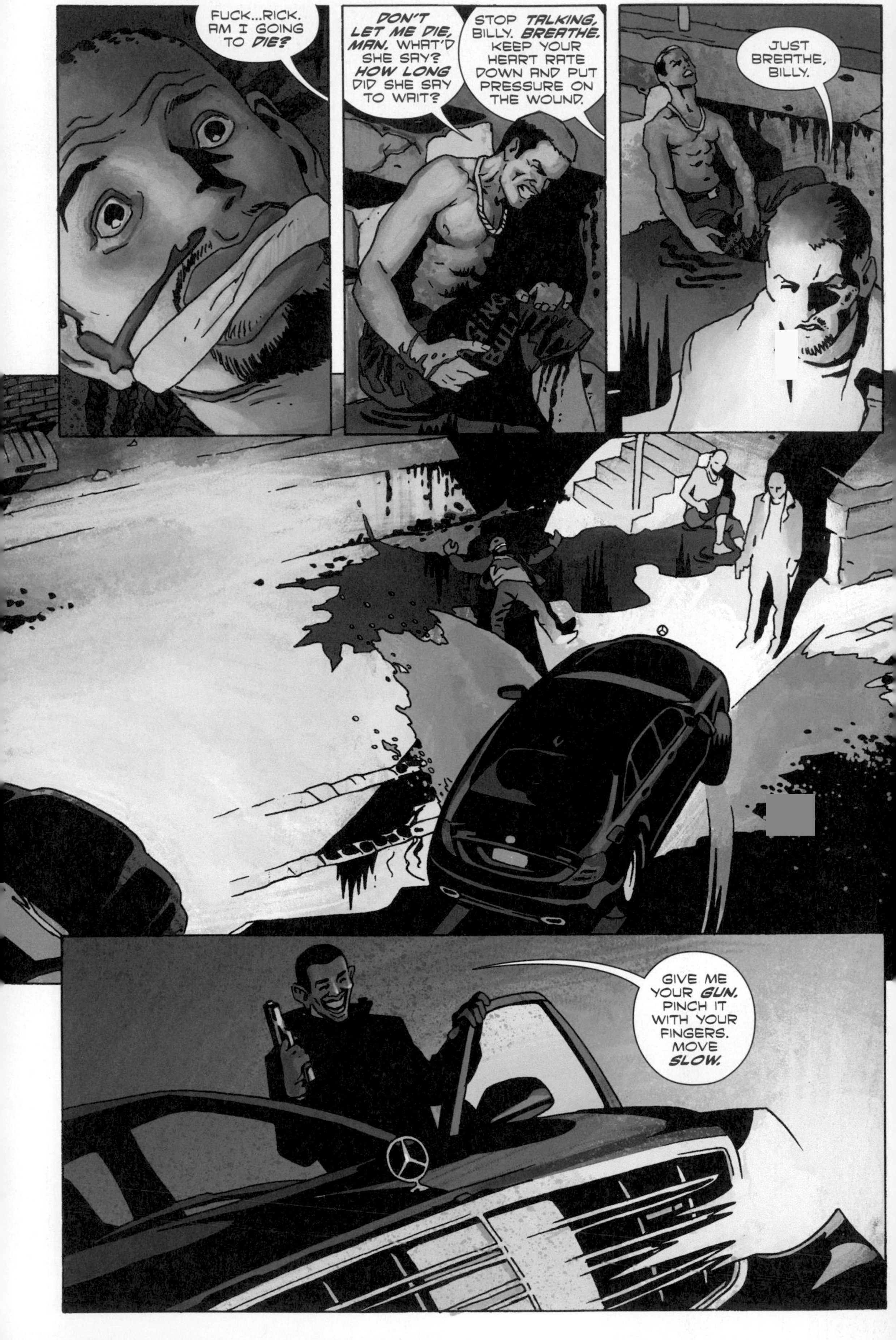

FUCK...RICK. AM I GOING TO DIE?
DON'T LET ME DIE, MAN. WHAT'D SHE SAY? HOW LONG DID SHE SAY TO WAIT?
STOP TALKING, BILLY. BREATHE. KEEP YOUR HEART RATE DOWN AND PUT PRESSURE ON THE WOUND.
JUST BREATHE, BILLY.
GIVE ME YOUR GUN. PINCH IT WITH YOUR FINGERS. MOVE SLOW.

JENNIFER SENT YOU? WHAT'S UP WITH THAT MASK?

YOU *WERE* TOLD TO DO EXACTLY AS I SAY. HAND ME THE GUN. SLOWLY. DO *NOT* SPEAK AGAIN.

NGGGGGH...

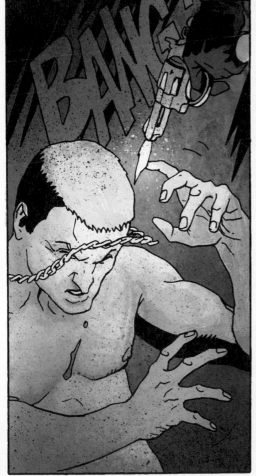

BANG

WAIT--

SPEAK *AGAIN* AND I WILL KILL YOU.

STAND OVER THE WHITE MAN. *NOW.*

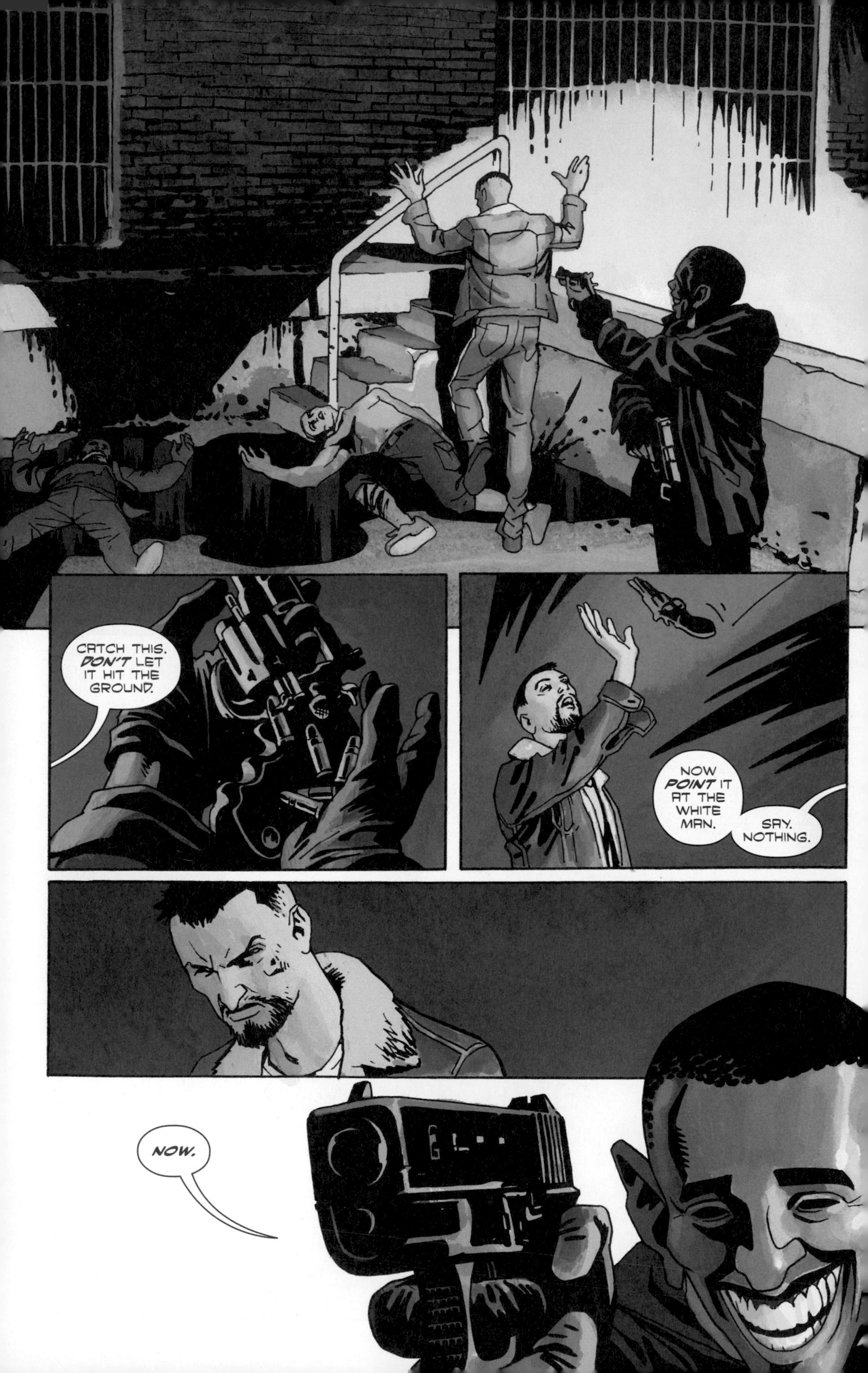
CATCH THIS. DON'T LET IT HIT THE GROUND.
NOW POINT IT AT THE WHITE MAN.
SAY. NOTHING.
NOW.

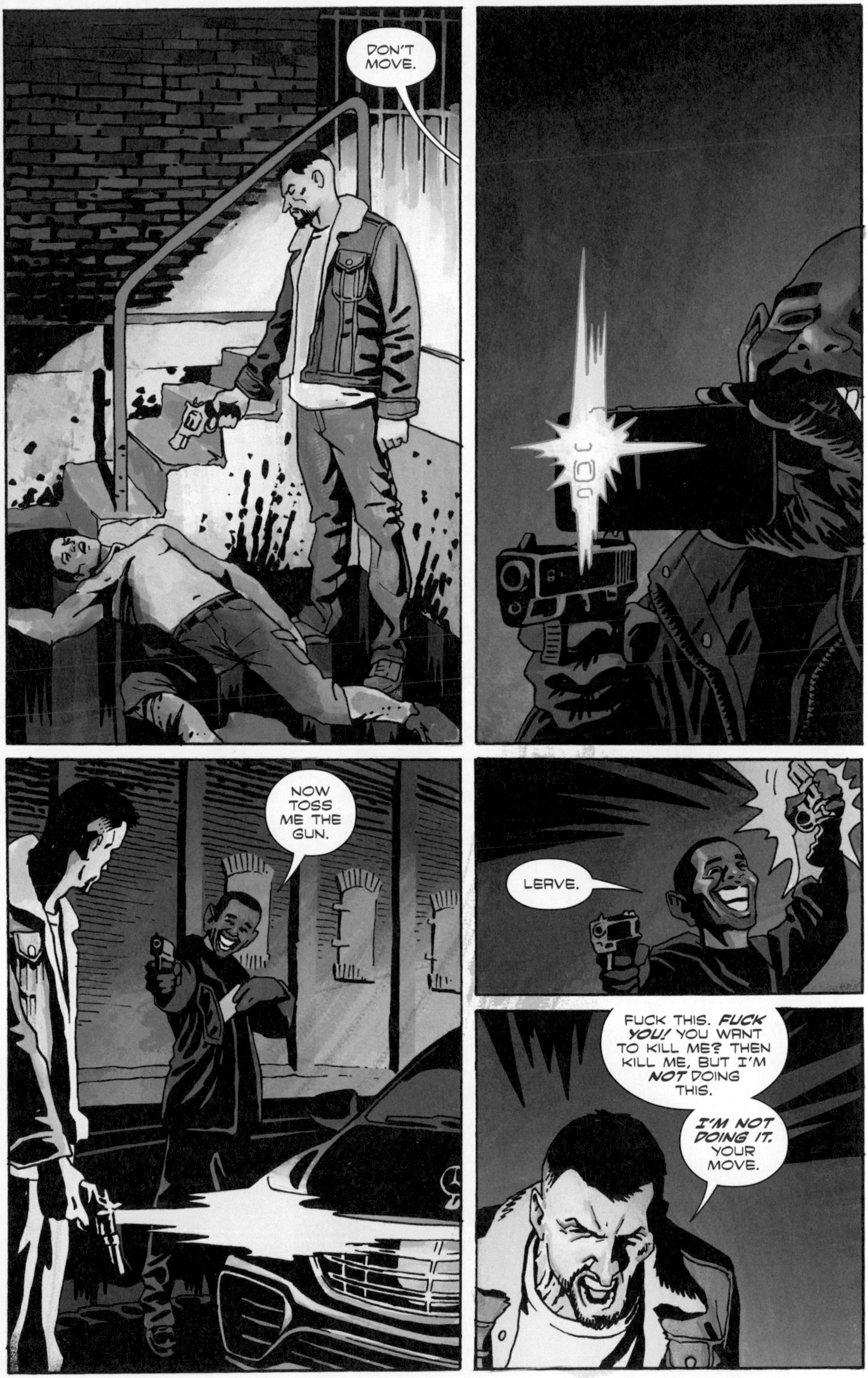
DON'T MOVE.
NOW TOSS ME THE GUN.
LEAVE.
FUCK THIS. *FUCK YOU!* YOU WANT TO KILL ME? THEN KILL ME, BUT I'M *NOT* DOING THIS.
I'M NOT DOING IT. YOUR MOVE.

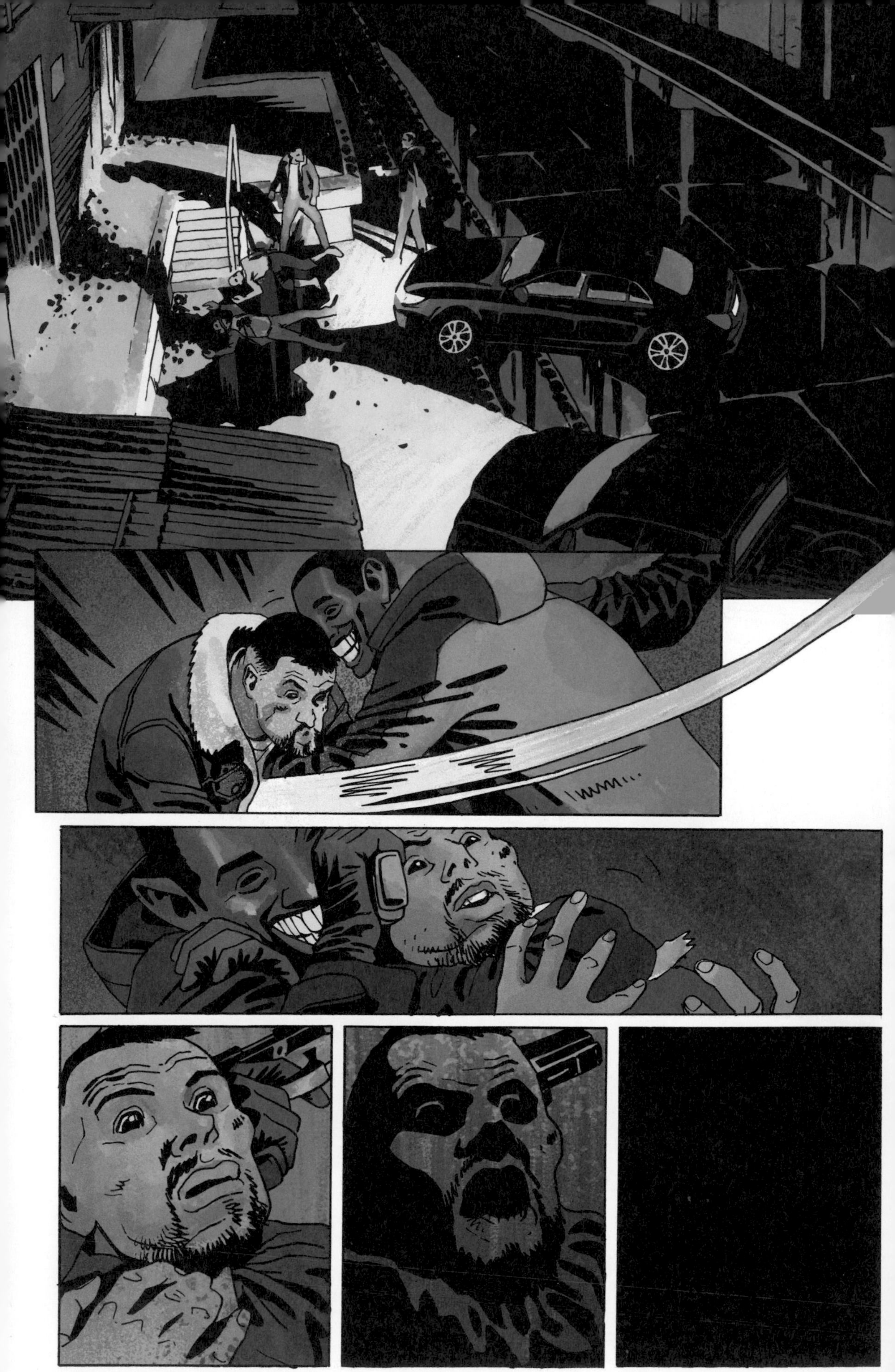

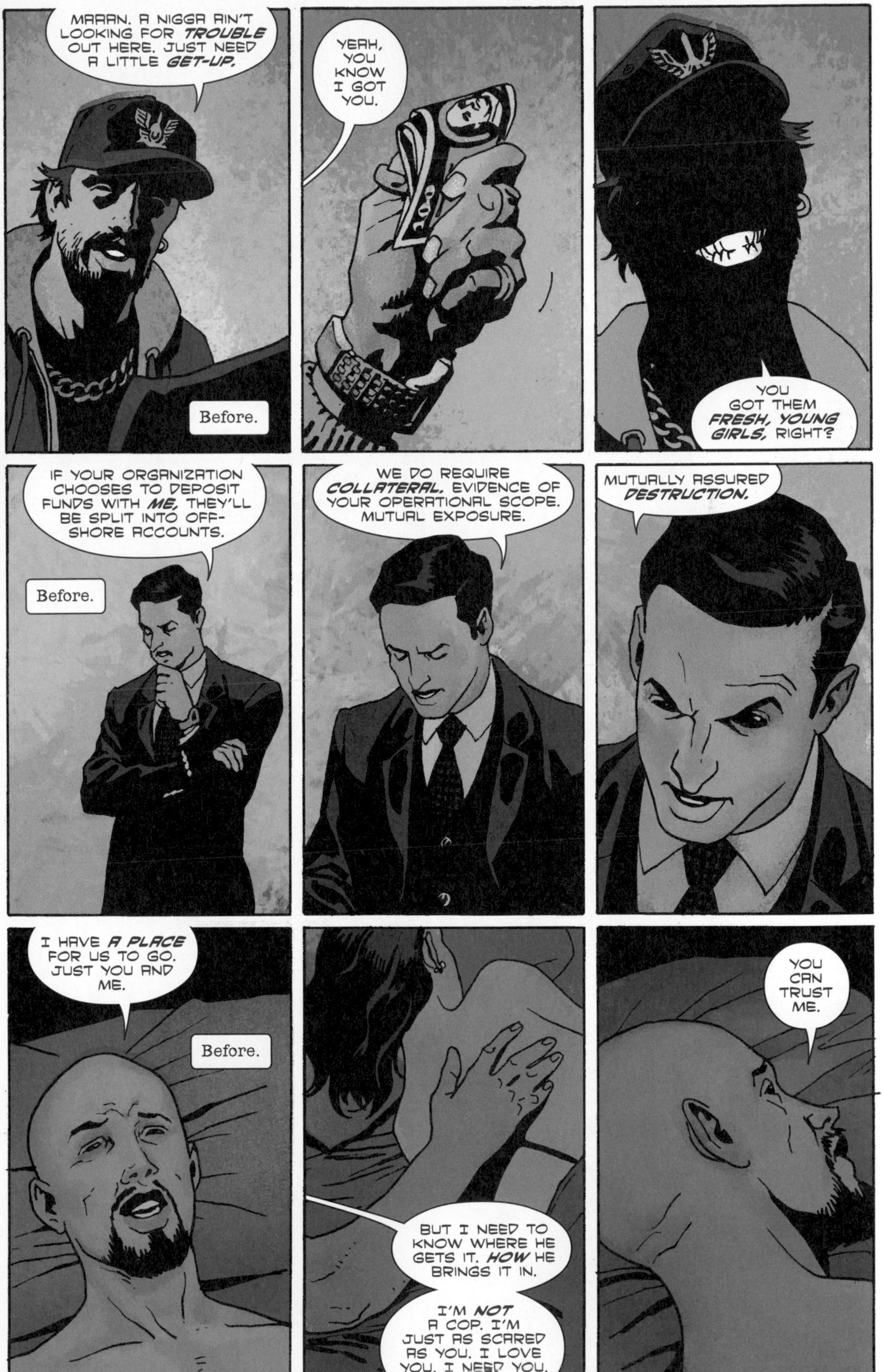

MAAAN. A NIGGA AIN'T LOOKING FOR TROUBLE OUT HERE. JUST NEED A LITTLE GET-UP.
Before.
YEAH, YOU KNOW I GOT YOU.
YOU GOT THEM FRESH, YOUNG GIRLS, RIGHT?
IF YOUR ORGANIZATION CHOOSES TO DEPOSIT FUNDS WITH ME, THEY'LL BE SPLIT INTO OFF-SHORE ACCOUNTS.
Before.
WE DO REQUIRE COLLATERAL. EVIDENCE OF YOUR OPERATIONAL SCOPE. MUTUAL EXPOSURE.
MUTUALLY ASSURED DESTRUCTION.
I HAVE A PLACE FOR US TO GO. JUST YOU AND ME.
Before.
BUT I NEED TO KNOW WHERE HE GETS IT. HOW HE BRINGS IT IN.
I'M NOT A COP. I'M JUST AS SCARED AS YOU. I LOVE YOU. I NEED YOU.
YOU CAN TRUST ME.

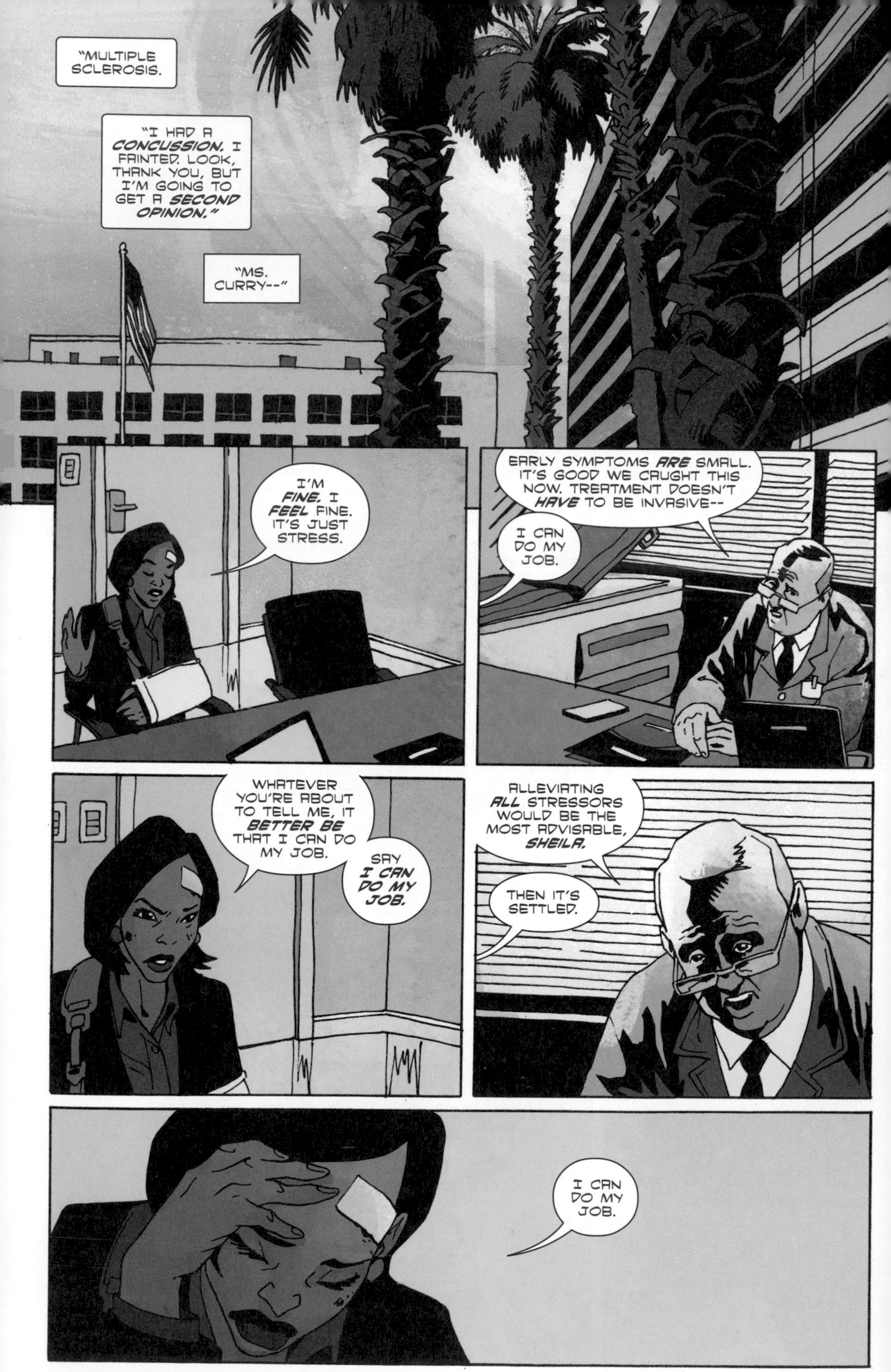
"MULTIPLE SCLEROSIS.
"I HAD A CONCUSSION. I FAINTED. LOOK, THANK YOU, BUT I'M GOING TO GET A SECOND OPINION."
"MS. CURRY--"
I'M FINE. I FEEL FINE. IT'S JUST STRESS.
EARLY SYMPTOMS ARE SMALL. IT'S GOOD WE CAUGHT THIS NOW. TREATMENT DOESN'T HAVE TO BE INVASIVE--
I CAN DO MY JOB.
WHATEVER YOU'RE ABOUT TO TELL ME, IT BETTER BE THAT I CAN DO MY JOB.
SAY I CAN DO MY JOB.
ALLEVIATING ALL STRESSORS WOULD BE THE MOST ADVISABLE, SHEILA.
THEN IT'S SETTLED.
I CAN DO MY JOB.

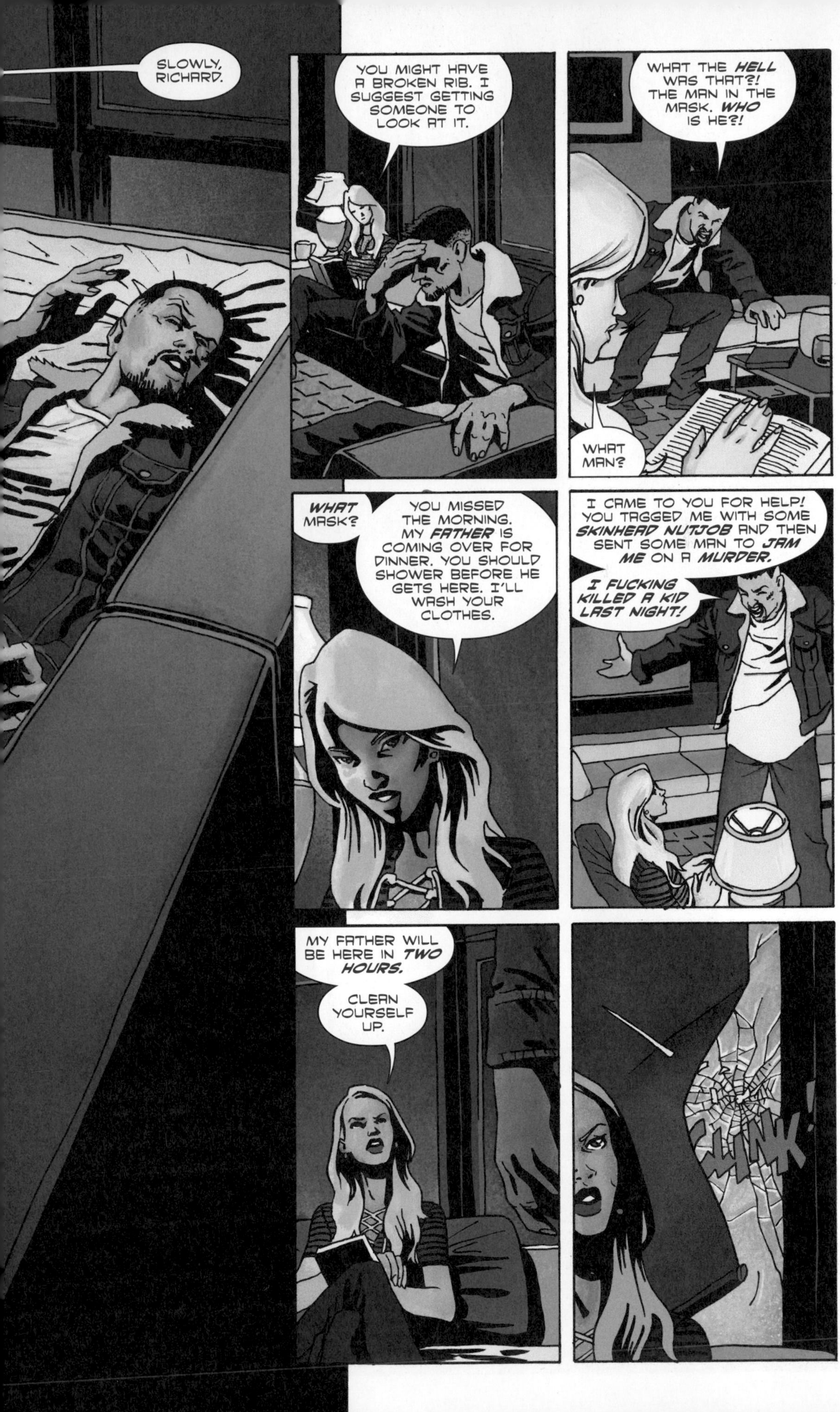
SLOWLY, RICHARD.
YOU MIGHT HAVE A BROKEN RIB. I SUGGEST GETTING SOMEONE TO LOOK AT IT.
WHAT THE HELL WAS THAT?! THE MAN IN THE MASK. WHO IS HE?!
WHAT MAN?
WHAT MASK?
YOU MISSED THE MORNING. MY FATHER IS COMING OVER FOR DINNER. YOU SHOULD SHOWER BEFORE HE GETS HERE. I'LL WASH YOUR CLOTHES.
I CAME TO YOU FOR HELP! YOU TAGGED ME WITH SOME SKINHEAD NUTJOB AND THEN SENT SOME MAN TO JAM ME ON A MURDER.
I FUCKING KILLED A KID LAST NIGHT!
MY FATHER WILL BE HERE IN TWO HOURS.
CLEAN YOURSELF UP.
CHINK!

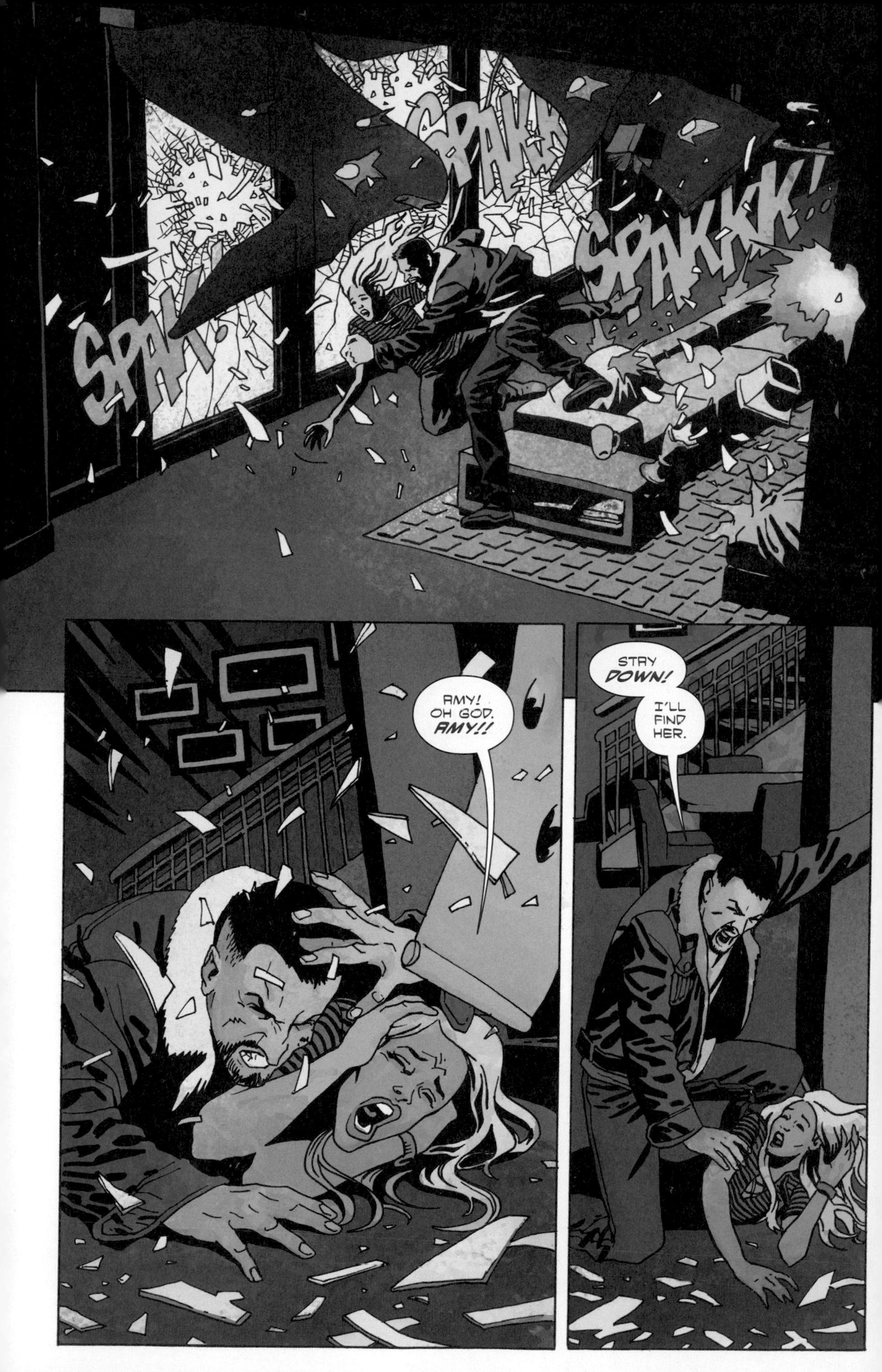
SPAK!
SPAKK
SPAKKK!
AMY! OH GOD. AMY!!
STAY DOWN!
I'LL FIND HER.

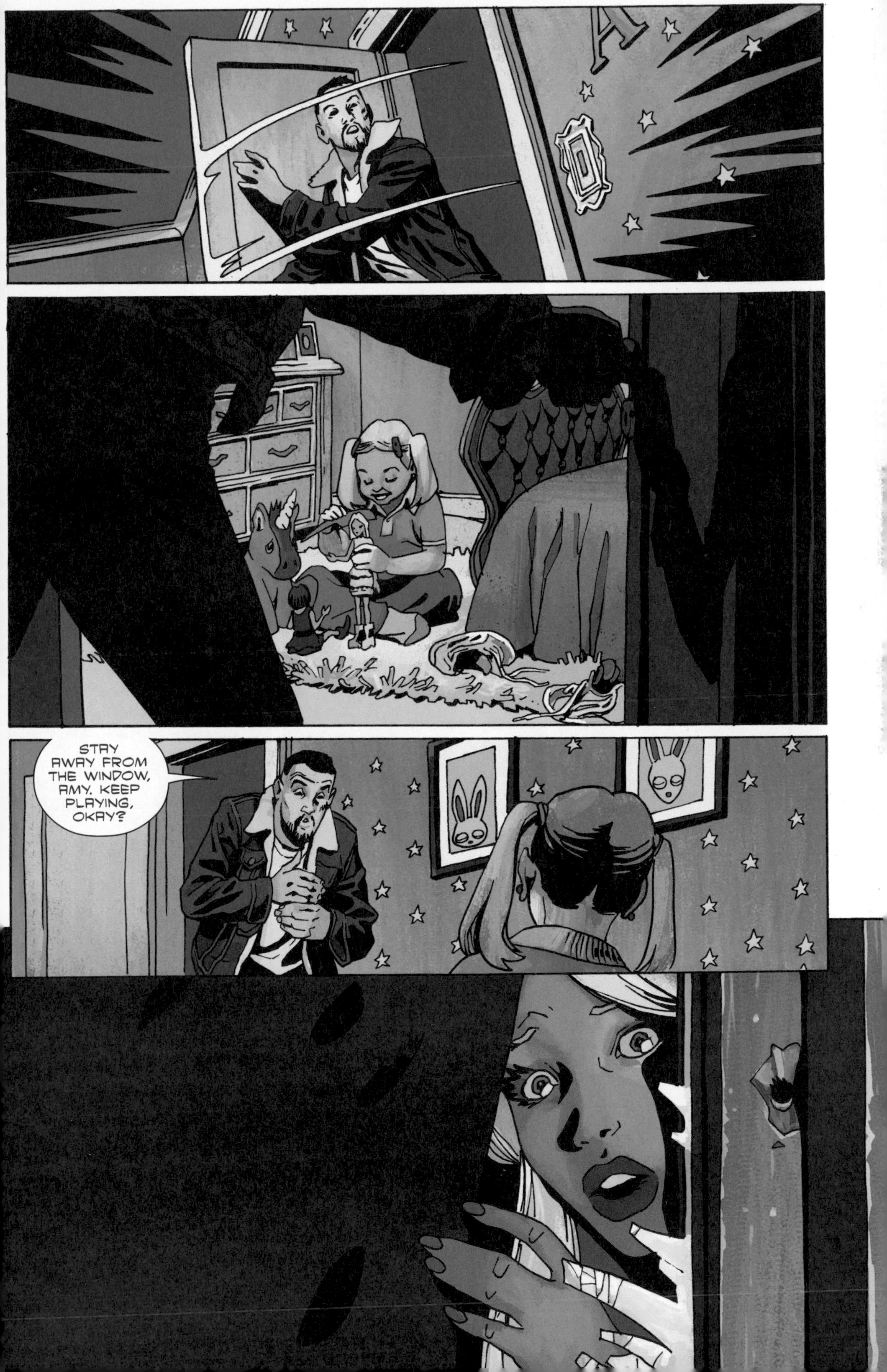
STAY AWAY FROM THE WINDOW, AMY. KEEP PLAYING, OKAY?

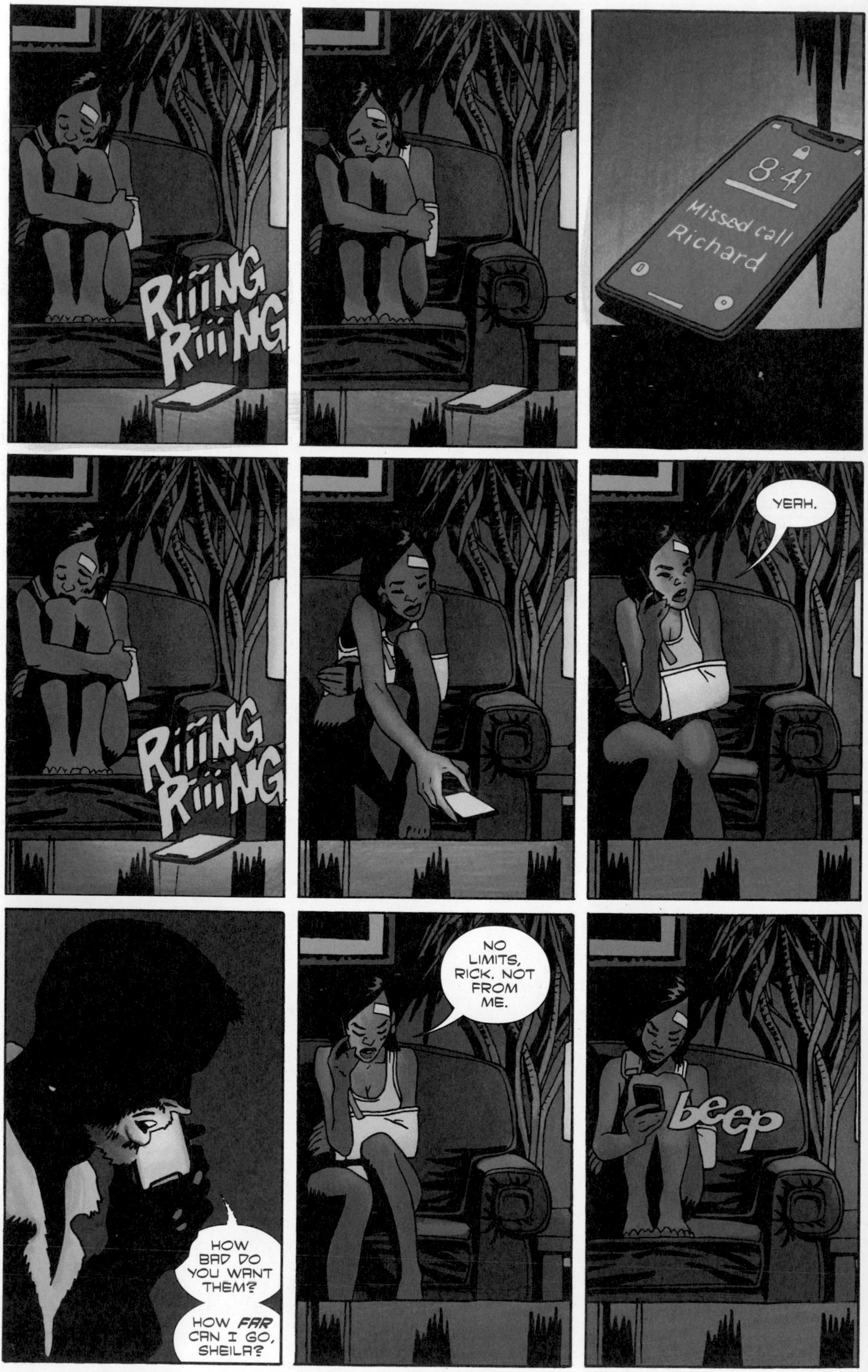
RIIING RIIING
8:41
Missed call
Richard
RIIING RIIING
YEAH.
HOW BAD DO YOU WANT THEM?
HOW FAR CAN I GO, SHEILA?
NO LIMITS, RICK. NOT FROM ME.
beep

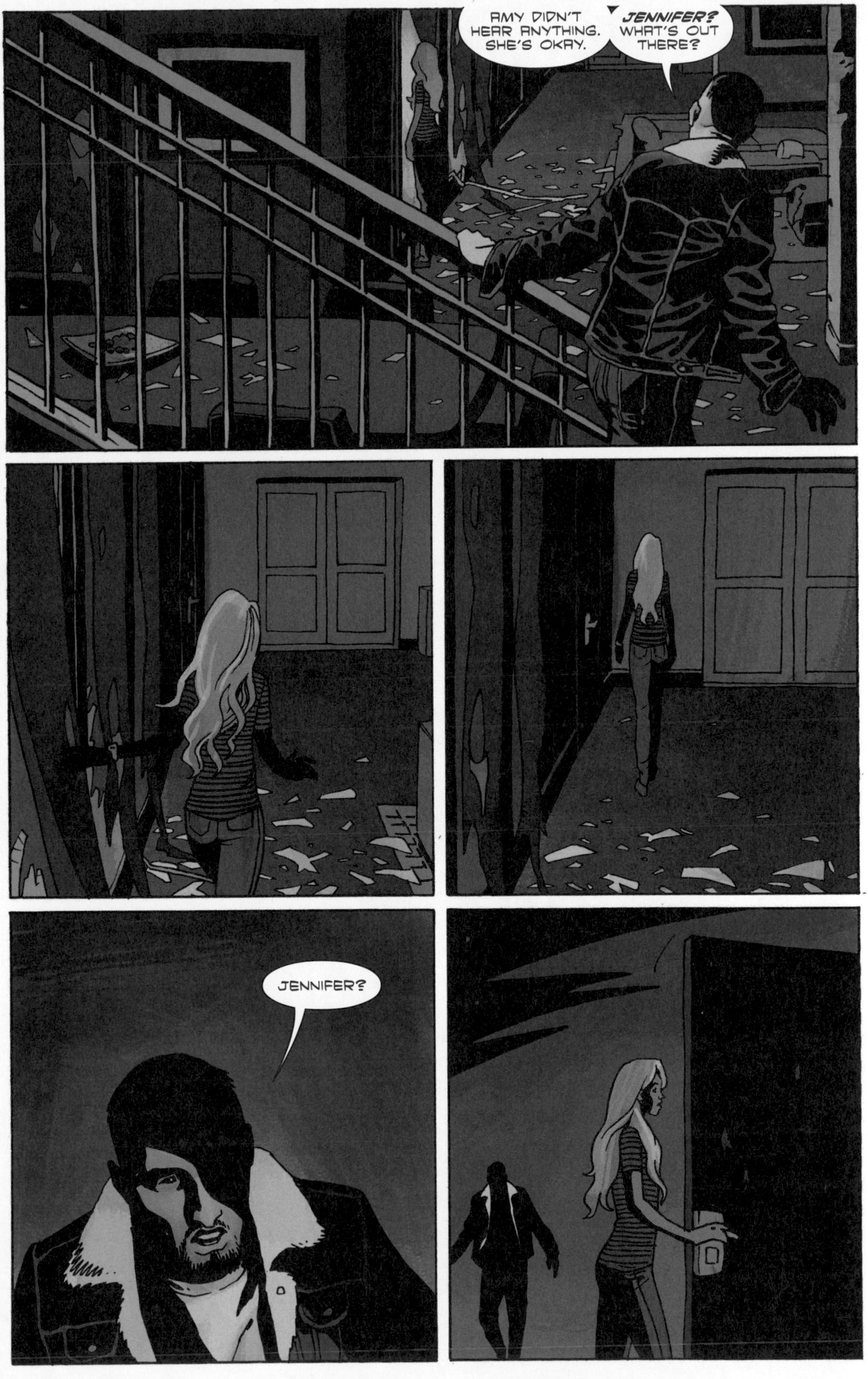
AMY DIDN'T HEAR ANYTHING. SHE'S OKAY.
JENNIFER? WHAT'S OUT THERE?
JENNIFER?

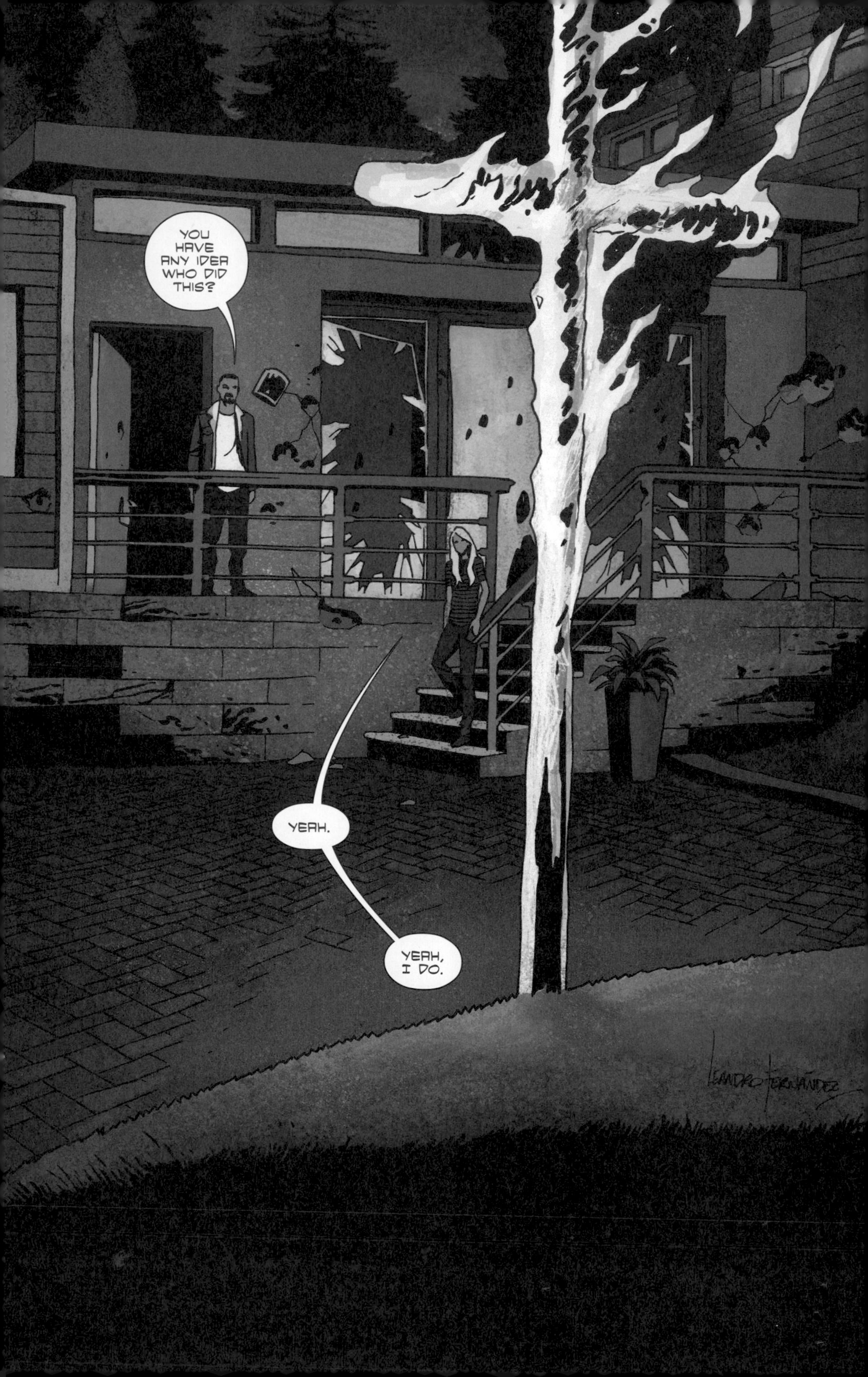
YOU HAVE ANY IDEA WHO DID THIS?
YEAH.
YEAH, I DO.
LEANDRO FERNÁNDEZ

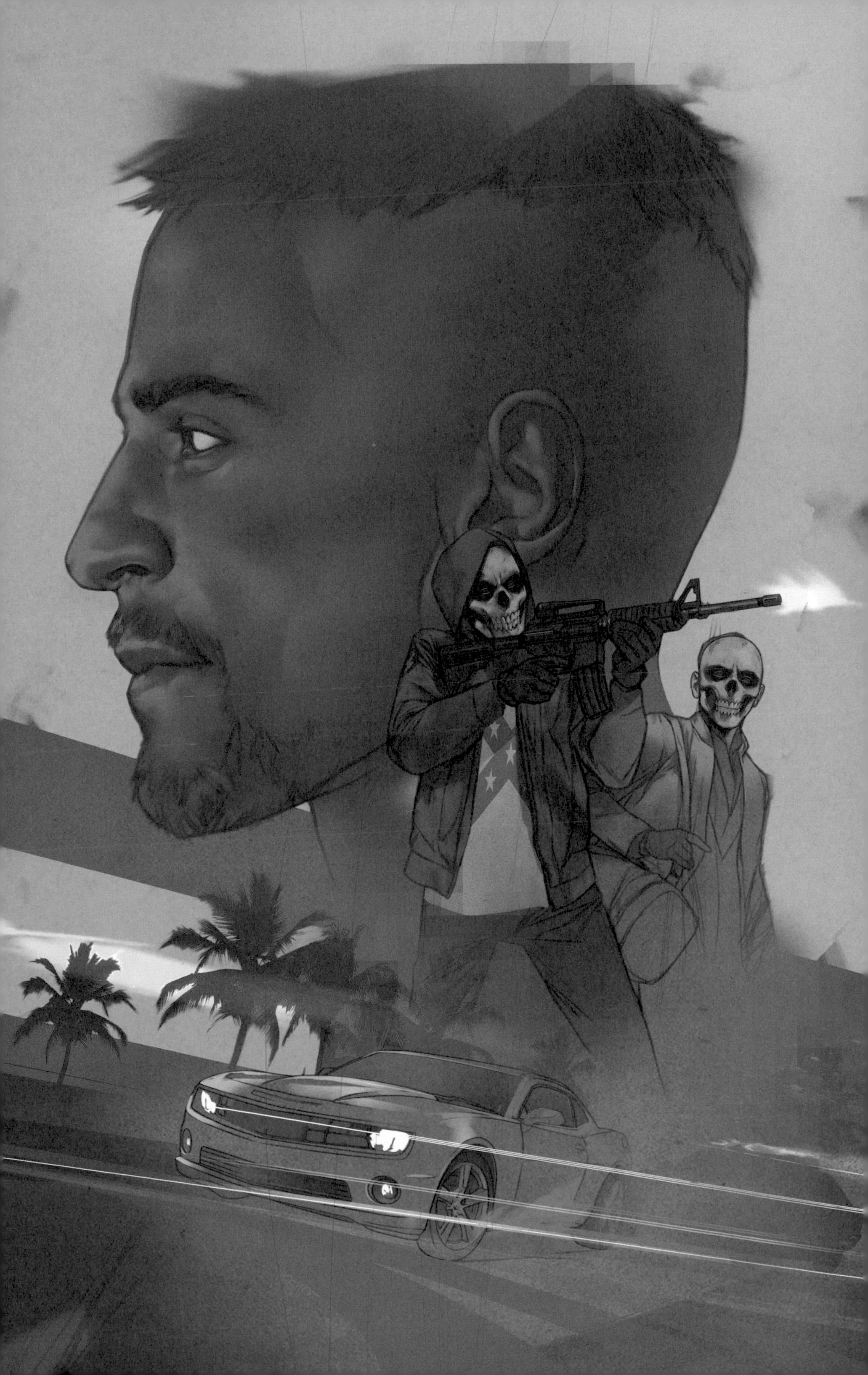

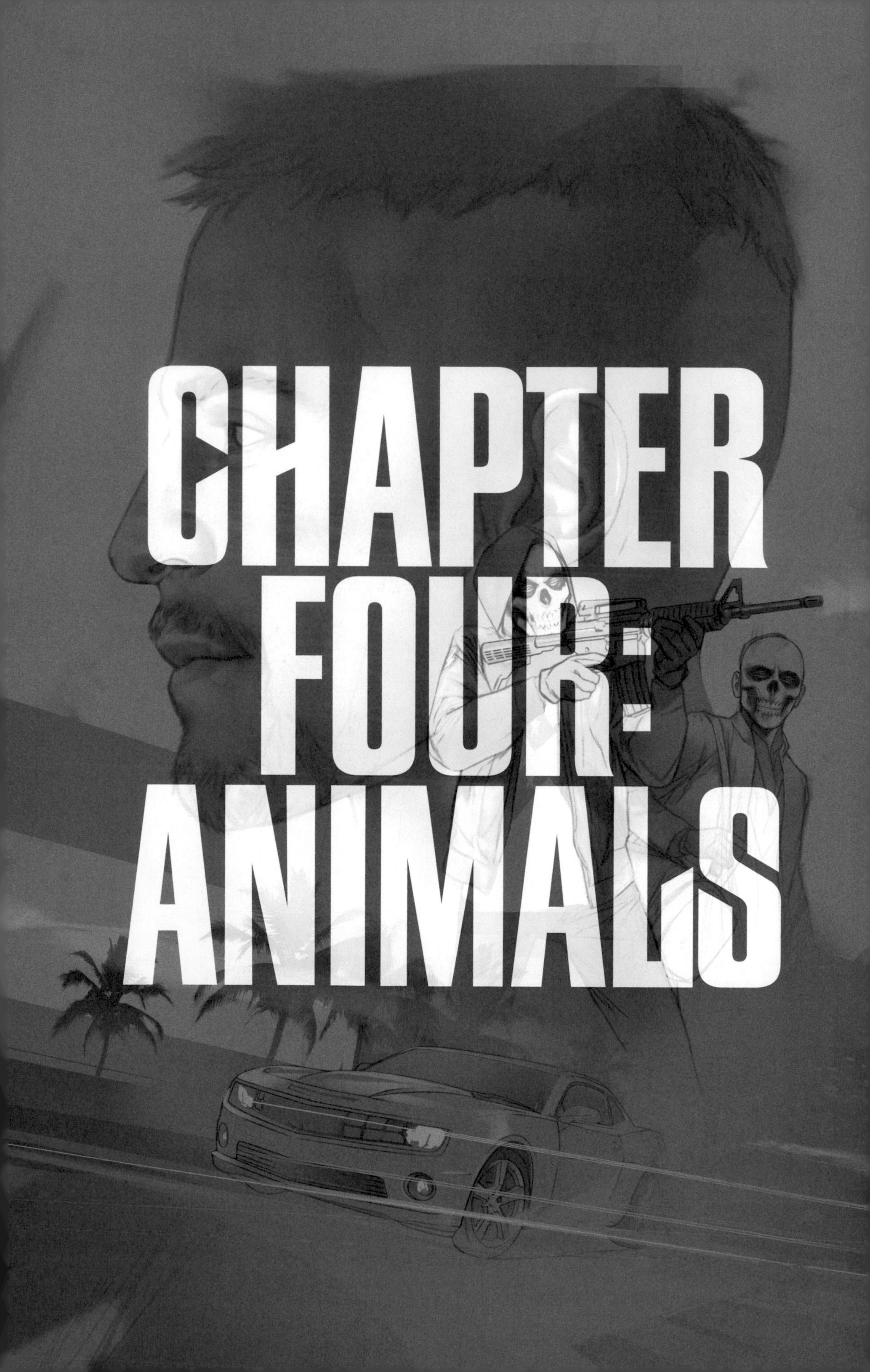
CHAPTER
FOUR:
ANIMALS

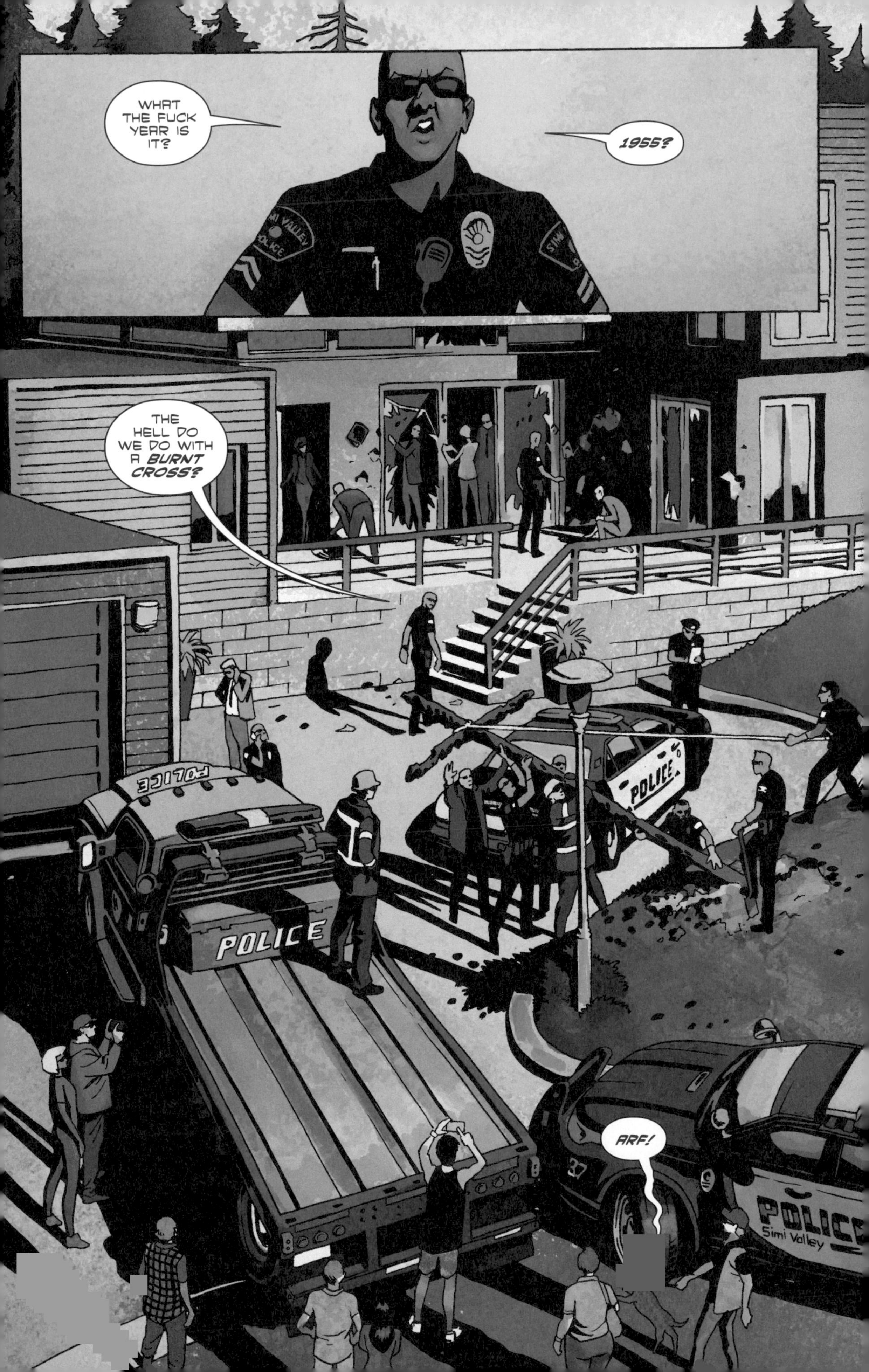

WHAT THE FUCK YEAR IS IT?
1955?
SIMI VALLEY POLICE
THE HELL DO WE DO WITH A BURNT CROSS?
POLICE
POLICE
POLICE
ARF!
POLICE Simi Valley

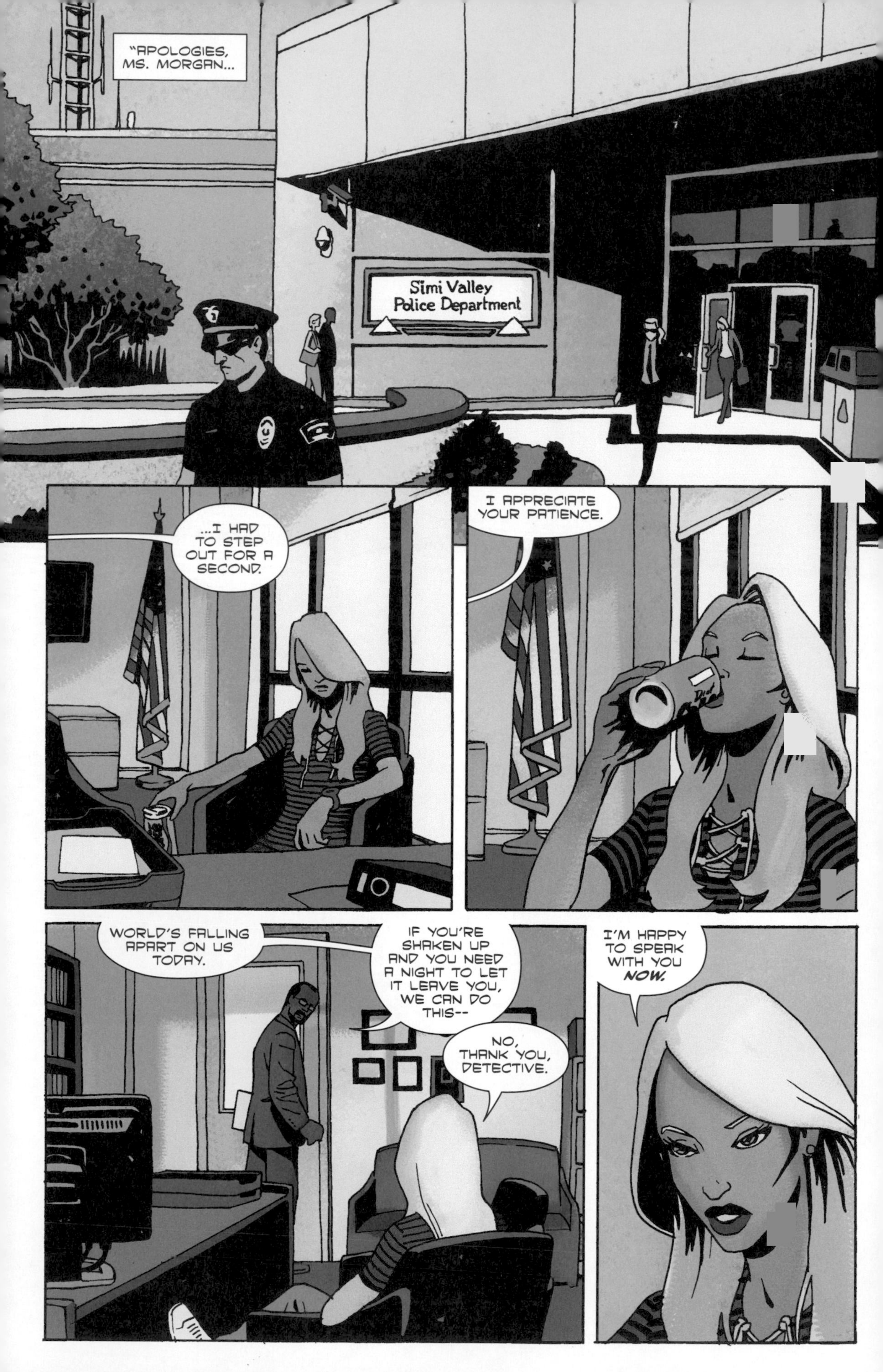
"APOLOGIES, MS. MORGAN...
Simi Valley Police Department
...I HAD TO STEP OUT FOR A SECOND.
I APPRECIATE YOUR PATIENCE.
WORLD'S FALLING APART ON US TODAY.
IF YOU'RE SHAKEN UP AND YOU NEED A NIGHT TO LET IT LEAVE YOU, WE CAN DO THIS--
NO, THANK YOU, DETECTIVE.
I'M HAPPY TO SPEAK WITH YOU *NOW.*

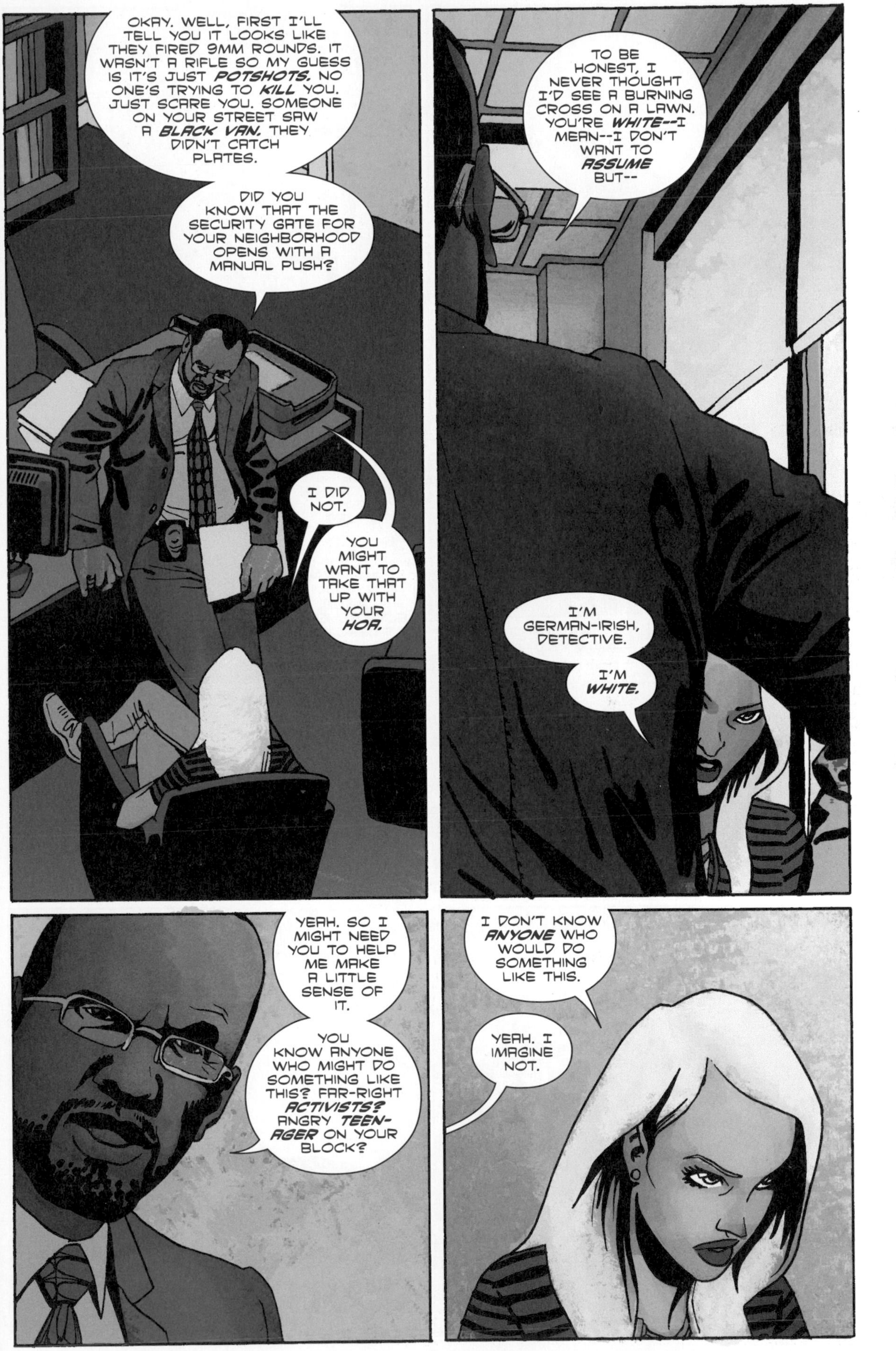
OKAY. WELL, FIRST I'LL TELL YOU IT LOOKS LIKE THEY FIRED 9MM ROUNDS. IT WASN'T A RIFLE SO MY GUESS IS IT'S JUST POTSHOTS. NO ONE'S TRYING TO KILL YOU. JUST SCARE YOU. SOMEONE ON YOUR STREET SAW A BLACK VAN. THEY DIDN'T CATCH PLATES.
DID YOU KNOW THAT THE SECURITY GATE FOR YOUR NEIGHBORHOOD OPENS WITH A MANUAL PUSH?
I DID NOT.
YOU MIGHT WANT TO TAKE THAT UP WITH YOUR HOA.
TO BE HONEST, I NEVER THOUGHT I'D SEE A BURNING CROSS ON A LAWN. YOU'RE WHITE--I MEAN--I DON'T WANT TO ASSUME BUT--
I'M GERMAN-IRISH, DETECTIVE.
I'M WHITE.
YEAH. SO I MIGHT NEED YOU TO HELP ME MAKE A LITTLE SENSE OF IT.
YOU KNOW ANYONE WHO MIGHT DO SOMETHING LIKE THIS? FAR-RIGHT ACTIVISTS? ANGRY TEEN-AGER ON YOUR BLOCK?
I DON'T KNOW ANYONE WHO WOULD DO SOMETHING LIKE THIS.
YEAH. I IMAGINE NOT.

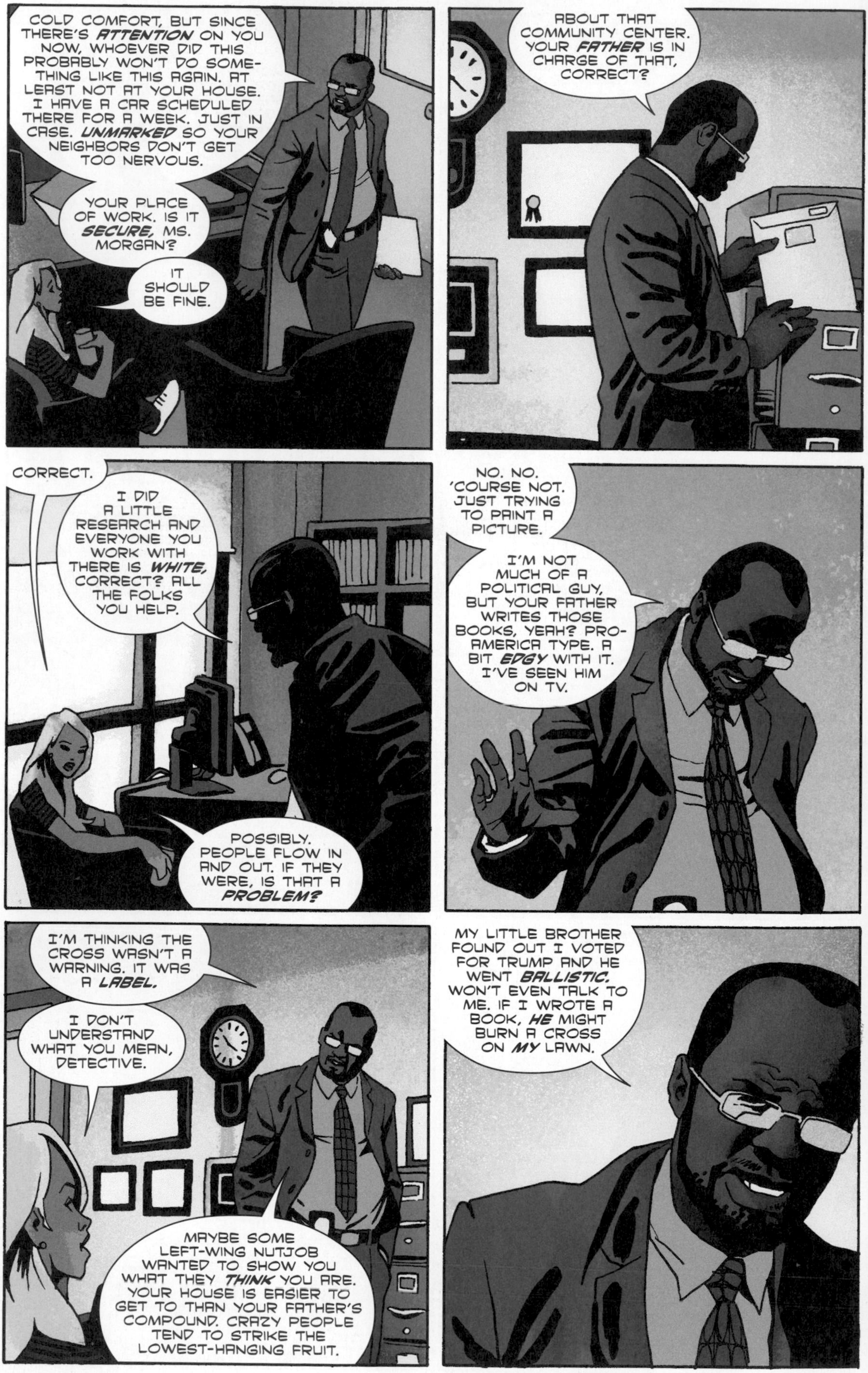
COLD COMFORT, BUT SINCE THERE'S ATTENTION ON YOU NOW, WHOEVER DID THIS PROBABLY WON'T DO SOMETHING LIKE THIS AGAIN. AT LEAST NOT AT YOUR HOUSE. I HAVE A CAR SCHEDULED THERE FOR A WEEK. JUST IN CASE. UNMARKED SO YOUR NEIGHBORS DON'T GET TOO NERVOUS.
YOUR PLACE OF WORK. IS IT SECURE, MS. MORGAN?
IT SHOULD BE FINE.
ABOUT THAT COMMUNITY CENTER. YOUR FATHER IS IN CHARGE OF THAT, CORRECT?
CORRECT.
I DID A LITTLE RESEARCH AND EVERYONE YOU WORK WITH THERE IS WHITE, CORRECT? ALL THE FOLKS YOU HELP.
POSSIBLY. PEOPLE FLOW IN AND OUT. IF THEY WERE, IS THAT A PROBLEM?
NO. NO. 'COURSE NOT. JUST TRYING TO PAINT A PICTURE.
I'M NOT MUCH OF A POLITICAL GUY, BUT YOUR FATHER WRITES THOSE BOOKS, YEAH? PRO-AMERICA TYPE. A BIT EDGY WITH IT. I'VE SEEN HIM ON TV.
I'M THINKING THE CROSS WASN'T A WARNING. IT WAS A LABEL.
I DON'T UNDERSTAND WHAT YOU MEAN, DETECTIVE.
MAYBE SOME LEFT-WING NUTJOB WANTED TO SHOW YOU WHAT THEY THINK YOU ARE. YOUR HOUSE IS EASIER TO GET TO THAN YOUR FATHER'S COMPOUND. CRAZY PEOPLE TEND TO STRIKE THE LOWEST-HANGING FRUIT.
MY LITTLE BROTHER FOUND OUT I VOTED FOR TRUMP AND HE WENT BALLISTIC. WON'T EVEN TALK TO ME. IF I WROTE A BOOK, HE MIGHT BURN A CROSS ON MY LAWN.

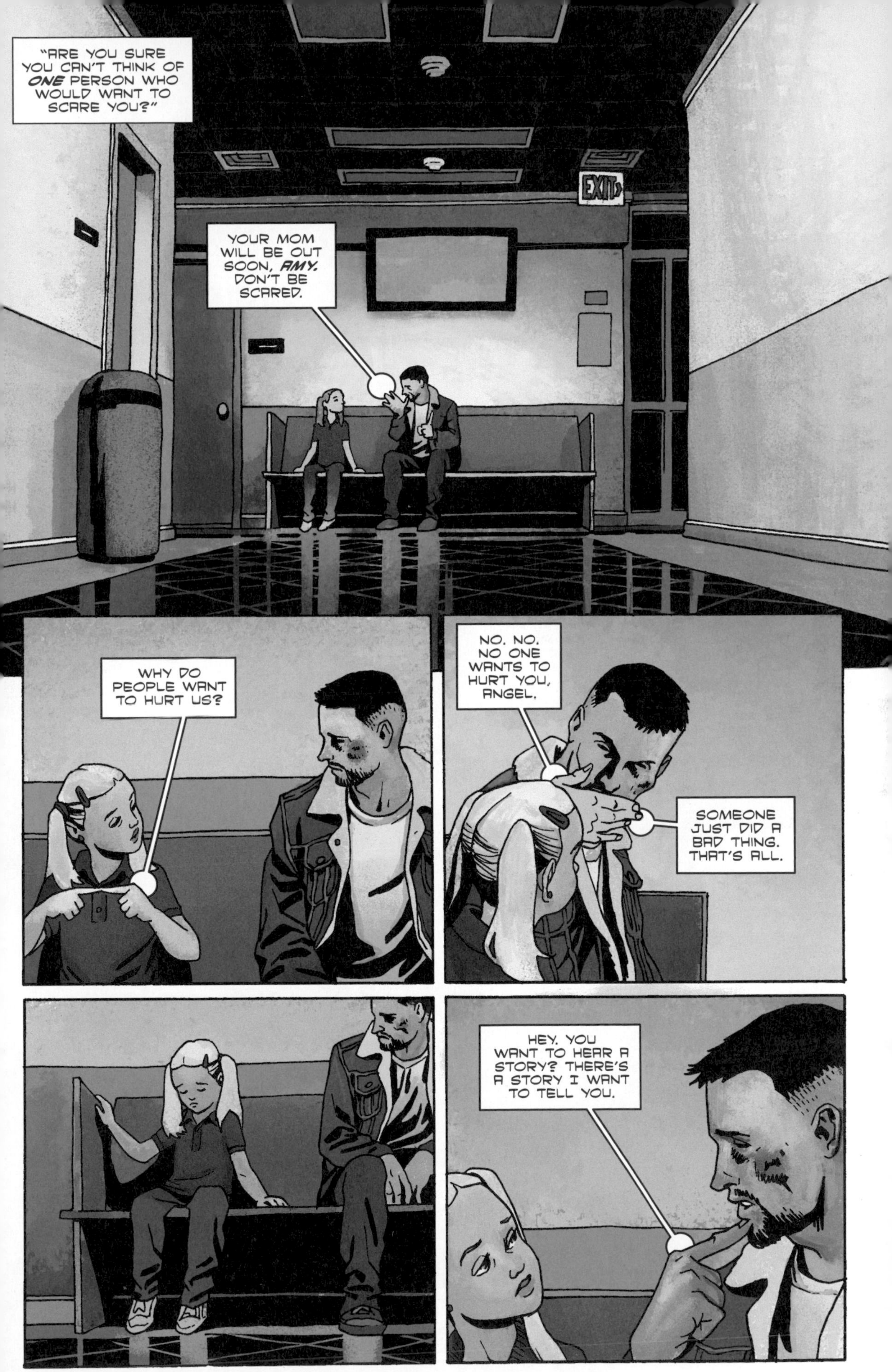
"ARE YOU SURE YOU CAN'T THINK OF ONE PERSON WHO WOULD WANT TO SCARE YOU?"
EXIT
YOUR MOM WILL BE OUT SOON, AMY. DON'T BE SCARED.
WHY DO PEOPLE WANT TO HURT US?
NO. NO. NO ONE WANTS TO HURT YOU, ANGEL.
SOMEONE JUST DID A BAD THING. THAT'S ALL.
HEY. YOU WANT TO HEAR A STORY? THERE'S A STORY I WANT TO TELL YOU.

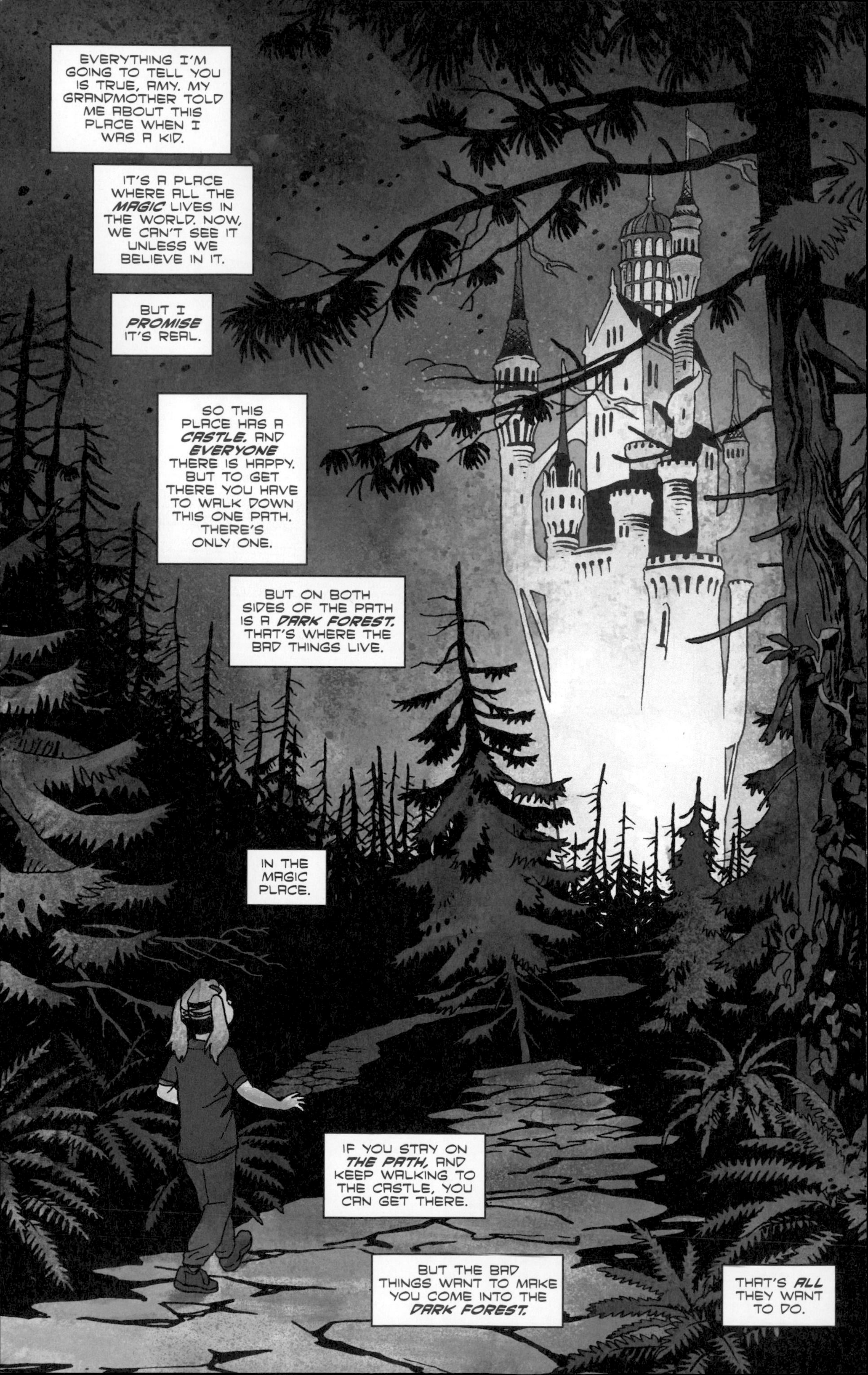
EVERYTHING I'M GOING TO TELL YOU IS TRUE, AMY. MY GRANDMOTHER TOLD ME ABOUT THIS PLACE WHEN I WAS A KID.
IT'S A PLACE WHERE ALL THE MAGIC LIVES IN THE WORLD. NOW, WE CAN'T SEE IT UNLESS WE BELIEVE IN IT.
BUT I PROMISE IT'S REAL.
SO THIS PLACE HAS A CASTLE, AND EVERYONE THERE IS HAPPY. BUT TO GET THERE YOU HAVE TO WALK DOWN THIS ONE PATH. THERE'S ONLY ONE.
BUT ON BOTH SIDES OF THE PATH IS A DARK FOREST. THAT'S WHERE THE BAD THINGS LIVE.
IN THE MAGIC PLACE.
IF YOU STAY ON THE PATH, AND KEEP WALKING TO THE CASTLE, YOU CAN GET THERE.
BUT THE BAD THINGS WANT TO MAKE YOU COME INTO THE DARK FOREST.
THAT'S ALL THEY WANT TO DO.

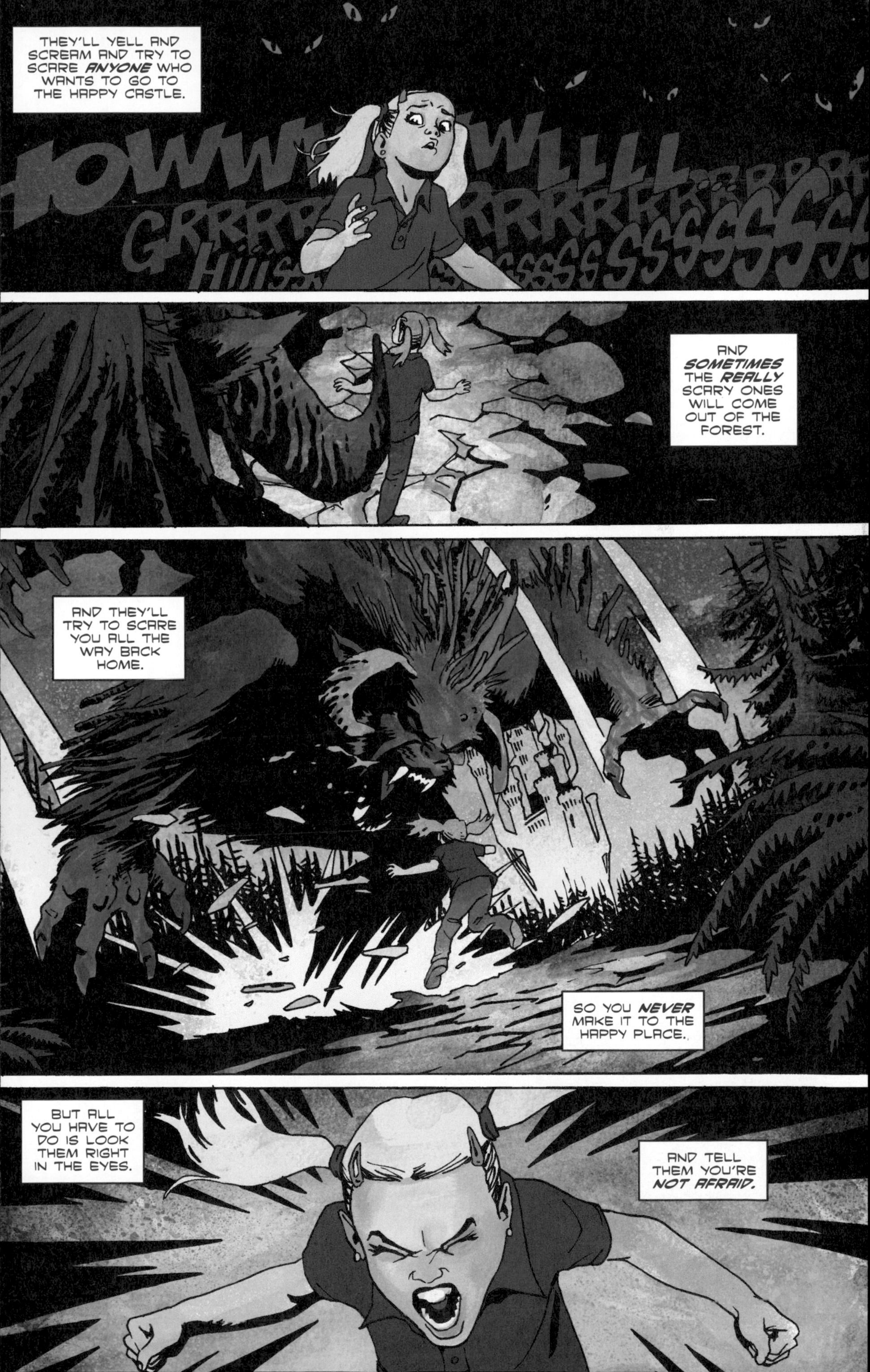
THEY'LL YELL AND SCREAM AND TRY TO SCARE *ANYONE* WHO WANTS TO GO TO THE HAPPY CASTLE.
AND *SOMETIMES* THE *REALLY* SCARY ONES WILL COME OUT OF THE FOREST.
AND THEY'LL TRY TO SCARE YOU ALL THE WAY BACK HOME.
SO YOU *NEVER* MAKE IT TO THE HAPPY PLACE.
BUT ALL YOU HAVE TO DO IS LOOK THEM RIGHT IN THE EYES.
AND TELL THEM YOU'RE *NOT AFRAID.*

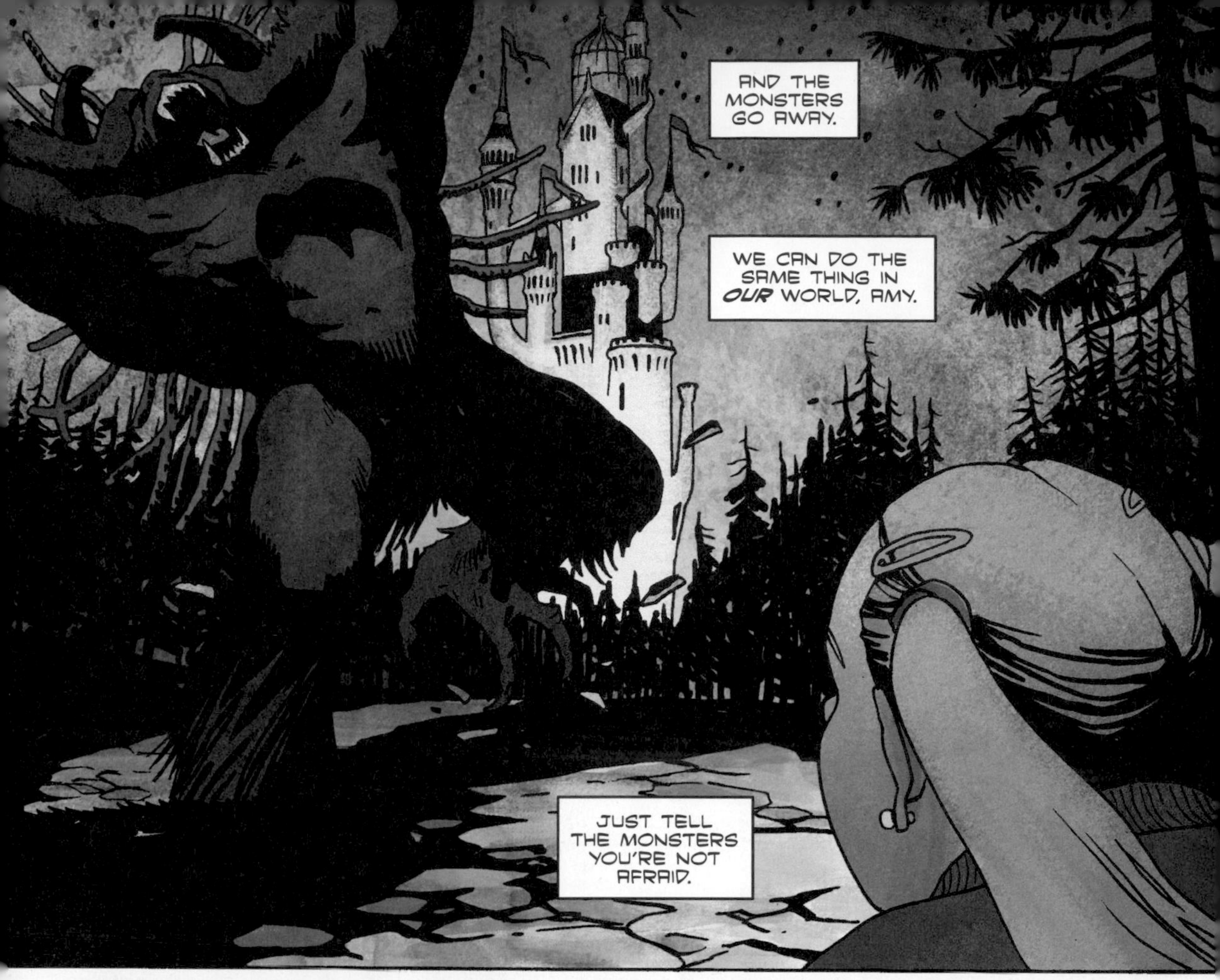
AND THE MONSTERS GO AWAY.
WE CAN DO THE SAME THING IN OUR WORLD, AMY.
JUST TELL THE MONSTERS YOU'RE NOT AFRAID.

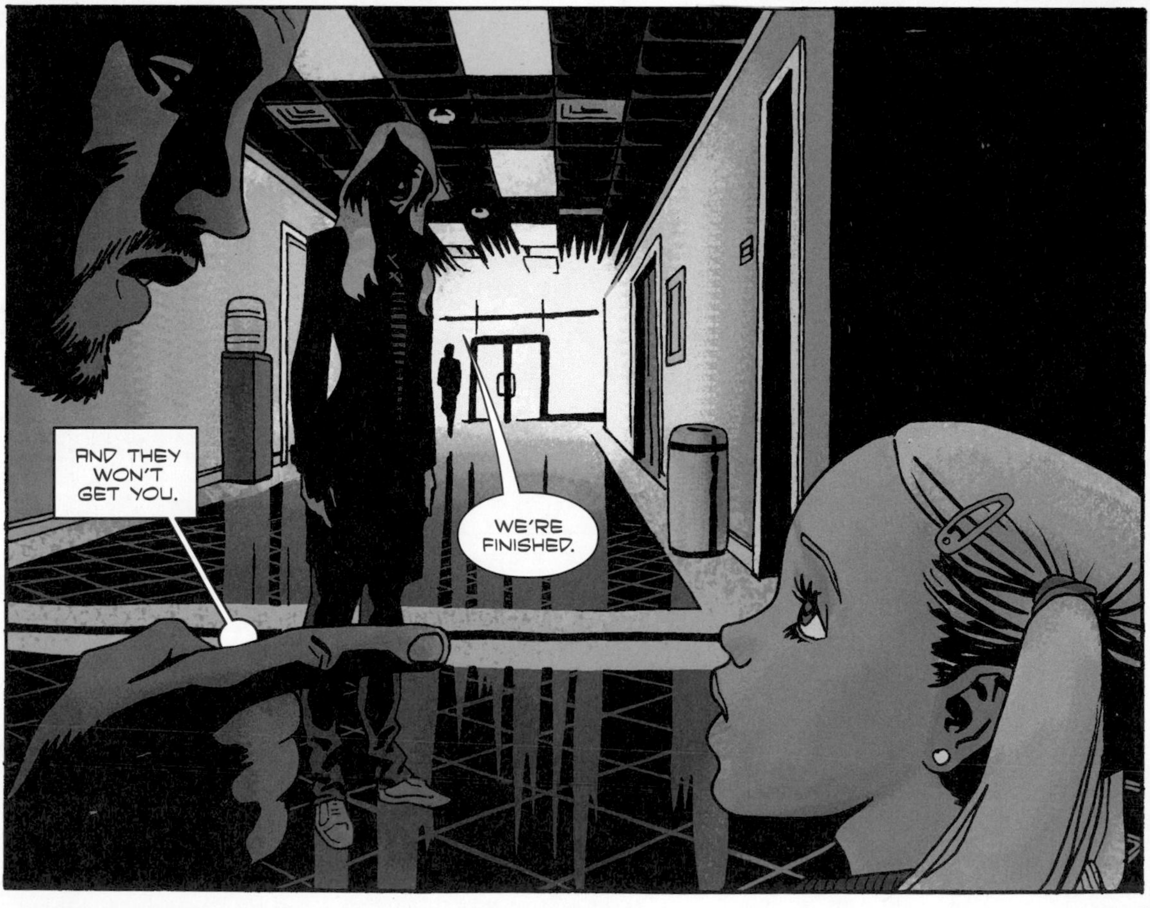
AND THEY WON'T GET YOU.
WE'RE FINISHED.

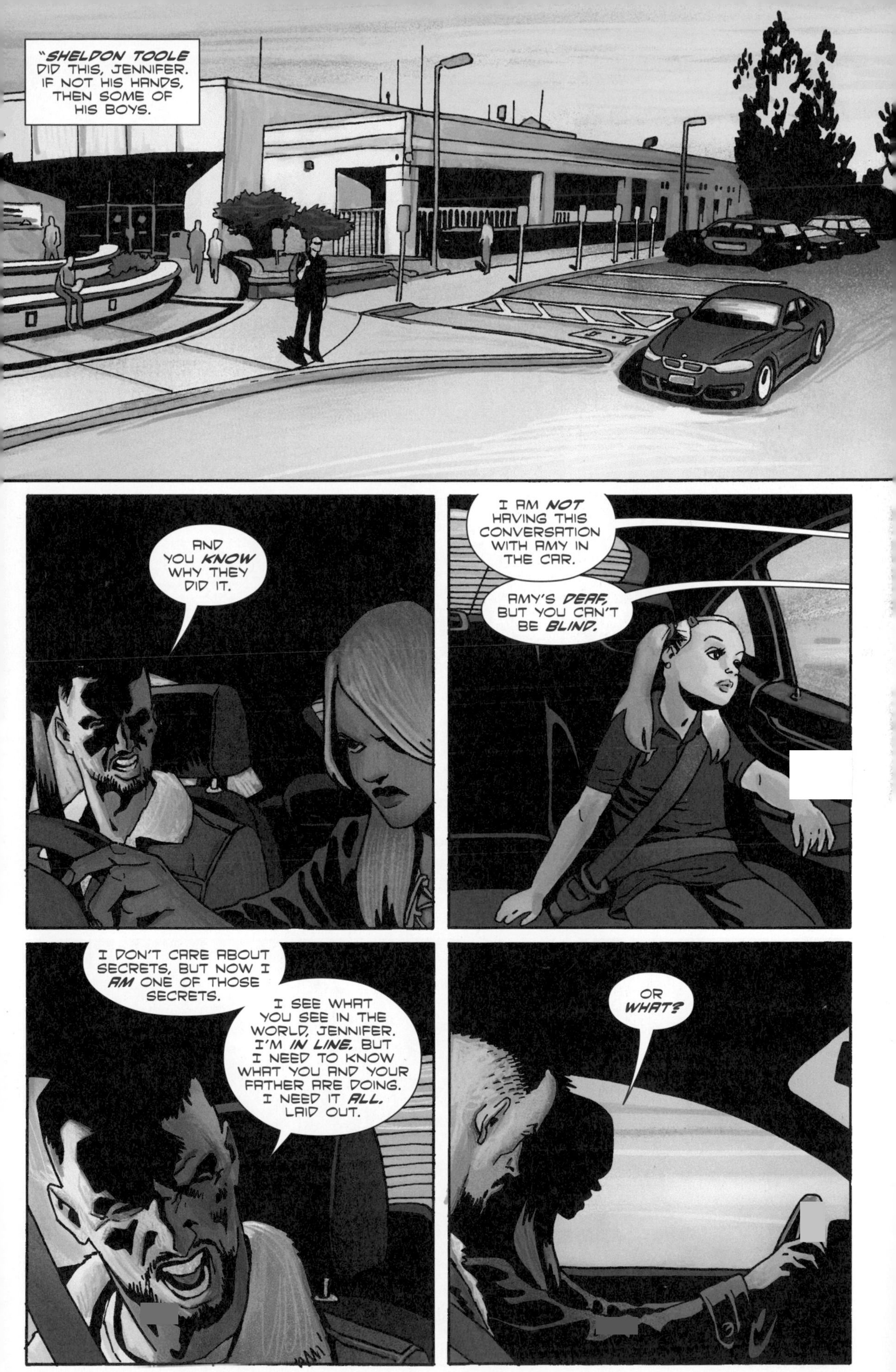
"SHELDON TOOLE DID THIS, JENNIFER. IF NOT HIS HANDS, THEN SOME OF HIS BOYS.
AND YOU KNOW WHY THEY DID IT.
I AM NOT HAVING THIS CONVERSATION WITH AMY IN THE CAR.
AMY'S DEAF, BUT YOU CAN'T BE BLIND.
I DON'T CARE ABOUT SECRETS, BUT NOW I AM ONE OF THOSE SECRETS.
I SEE WHAT YOU SEE IN THE WORLD, JENNIFER. I'M IN LINE, BUT I NEED TO KNOW WHAT YOU AND YOUR FATHER ARE DOING. I NEED IT ALL, LAID OUT.
OR WHAT?

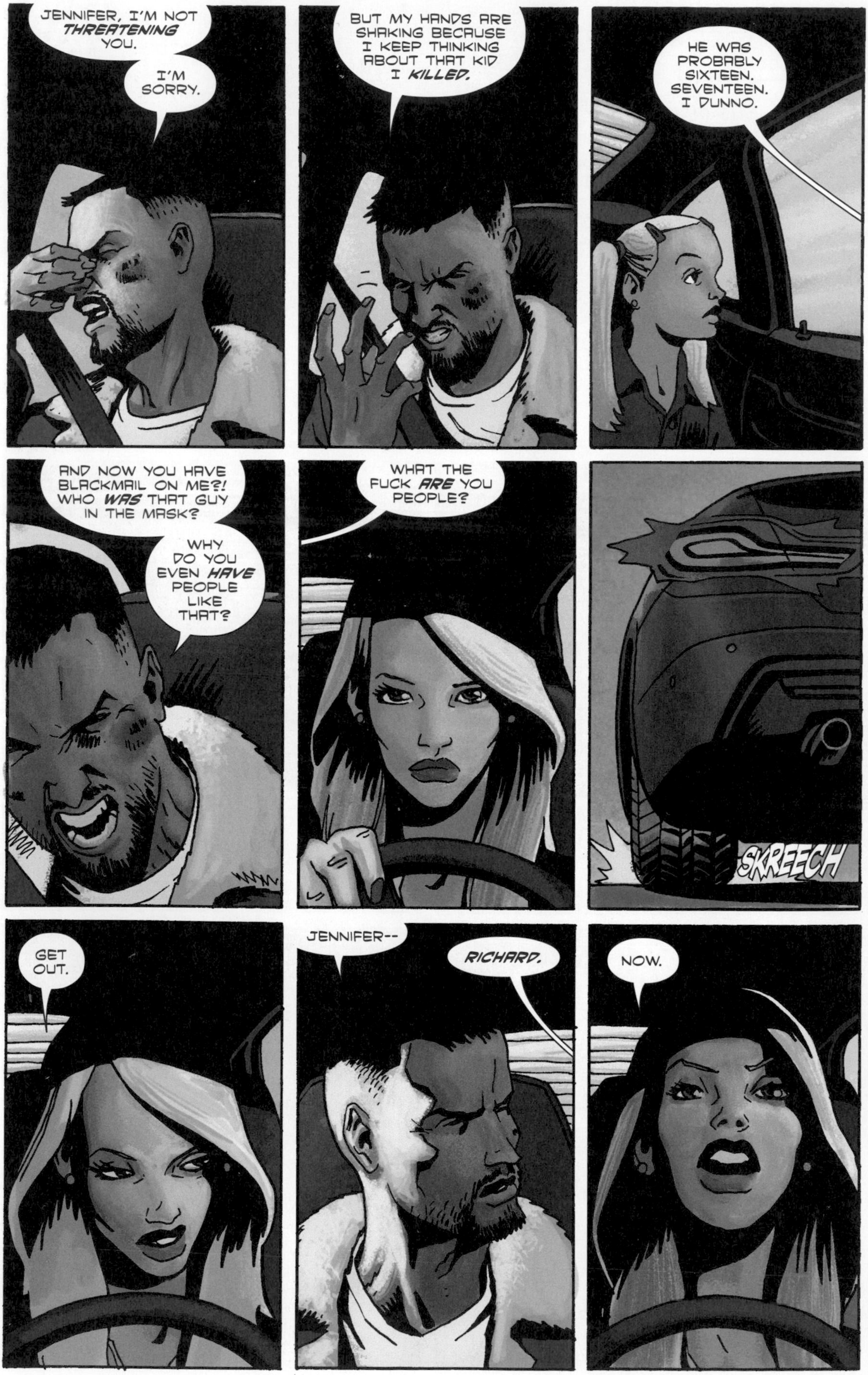
JENNIFER, I'M NOT THREATENING YOU.
I'M SORRY.
BUT MY HANDS ARE SHAKING BECAUSE I KEEP THINKING ABOUT THAT KID I KILLED.
HE WAS PROBABLY SIXTEEN. SEVENTEEN. I DUNNO.
AND NOW YOU HAVE BLACKMAIL ON ME?! WHO WAS THAT GUY IN THE MASK?
WHY DO YOU EVEN HAVE PEOPLE LIKE THAT?
WHAT THE FUCK ARE YOU PEOPLE?
SKREECH
GET OUT.
JENNIFER--
RICHARD.
NOW.

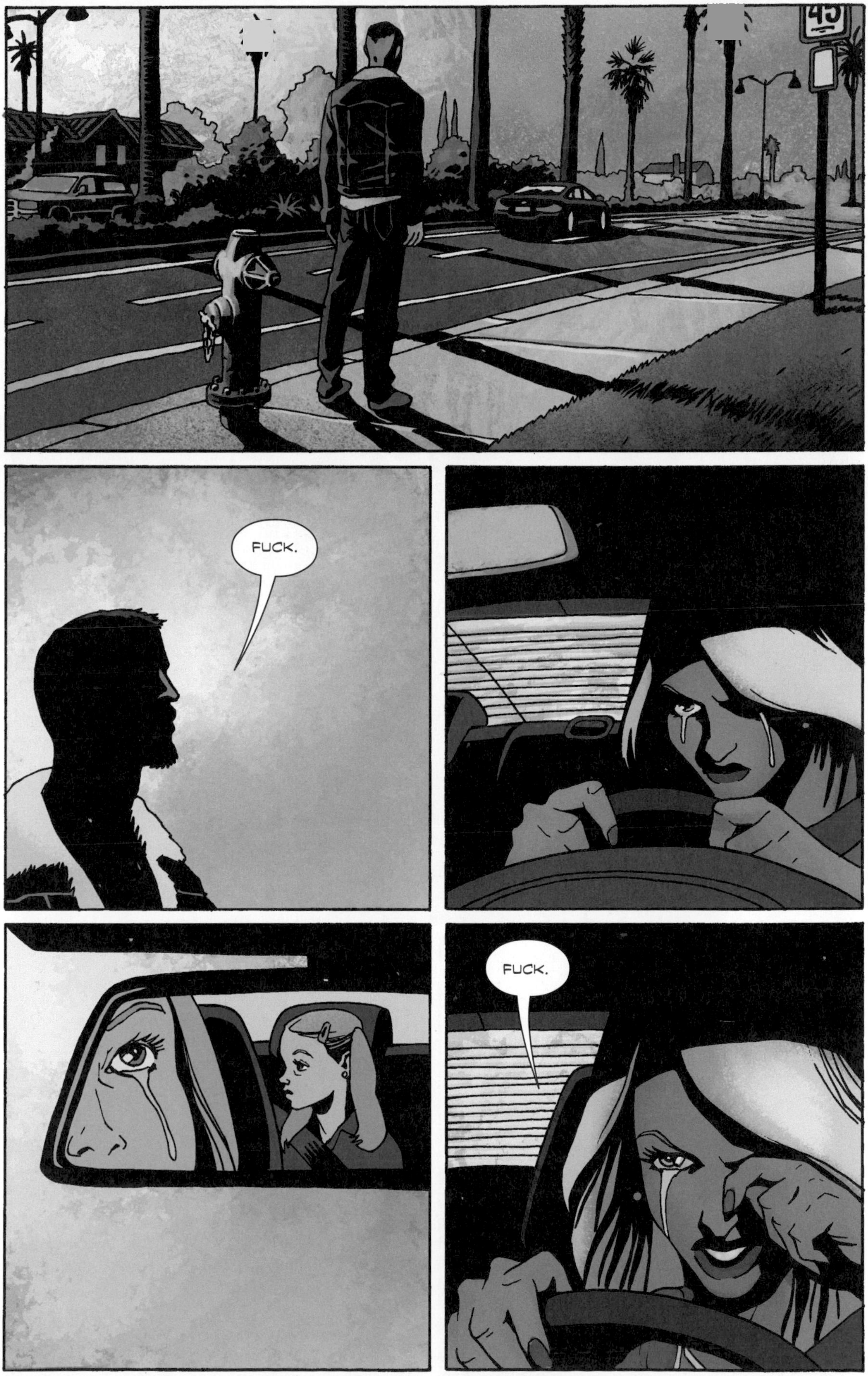
FUCK.
FUCK.

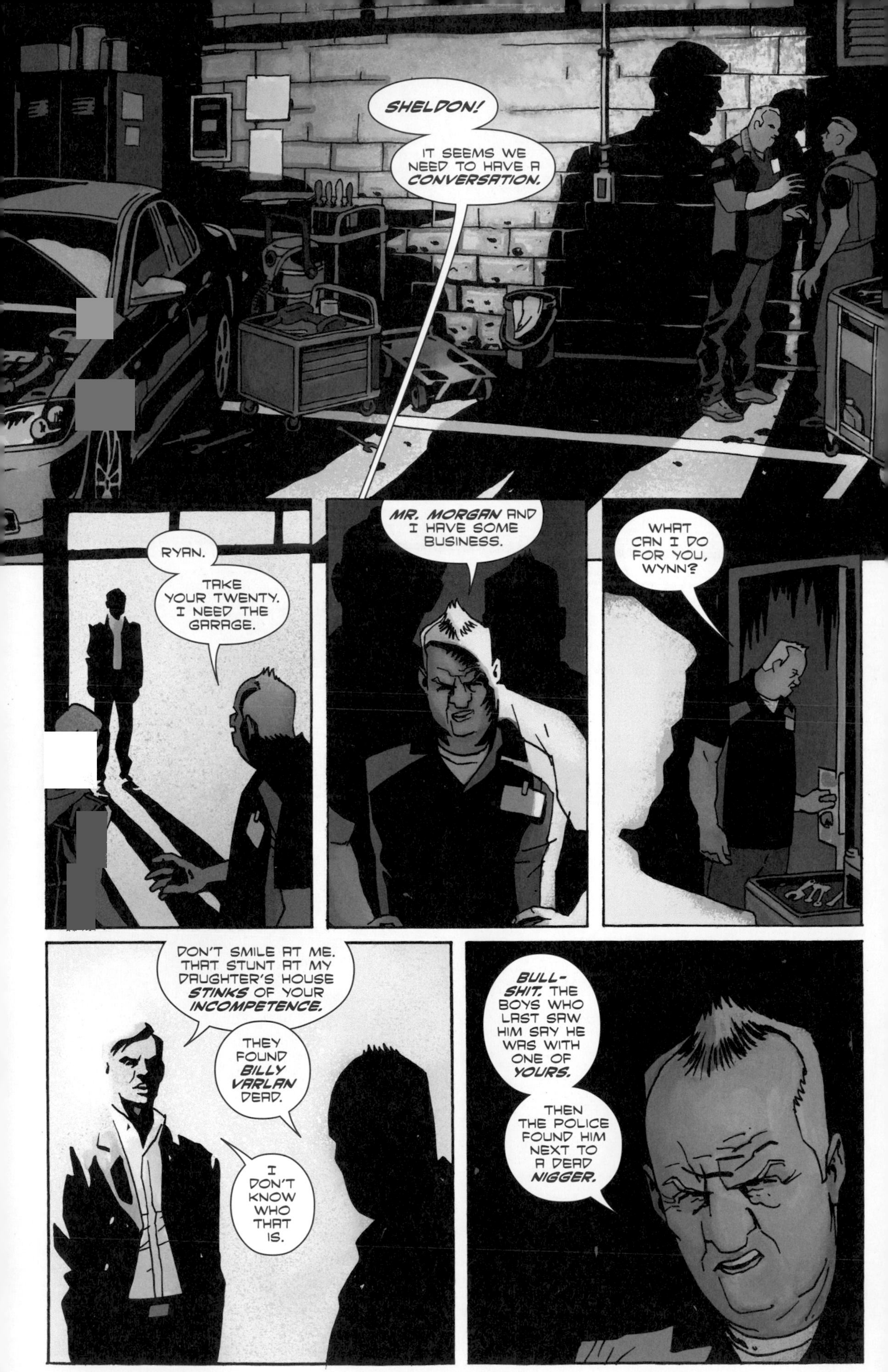
SHELDON!
IT SEEMS WE NEED TO HAVE A CONVERSATION.
RYAN.
TAKE YOUR TWENTY. I NEED THE GARAGE.
MR. MORGAN AND I HAVE SOME BUSINESS.
WHAT CAN I DO FOR YOU, WYNN?
DON'T SMILE AT ME. THAT STUNT AT MY DAUGHTER'S HOUSE STINKS OF YOUR INCOMPETENCE.
THEY FOUND BILLY VARLAN DEAD.
I DON'T KNOW WHO THAT IS.
BULL-SHIT. THE BOYS WHO LAST SAW HIM SAY HE WAS WITH ONE OF YOURS.
THEN THE POLICE FOUND HIM NEXT TO A DEAD NIGGER.

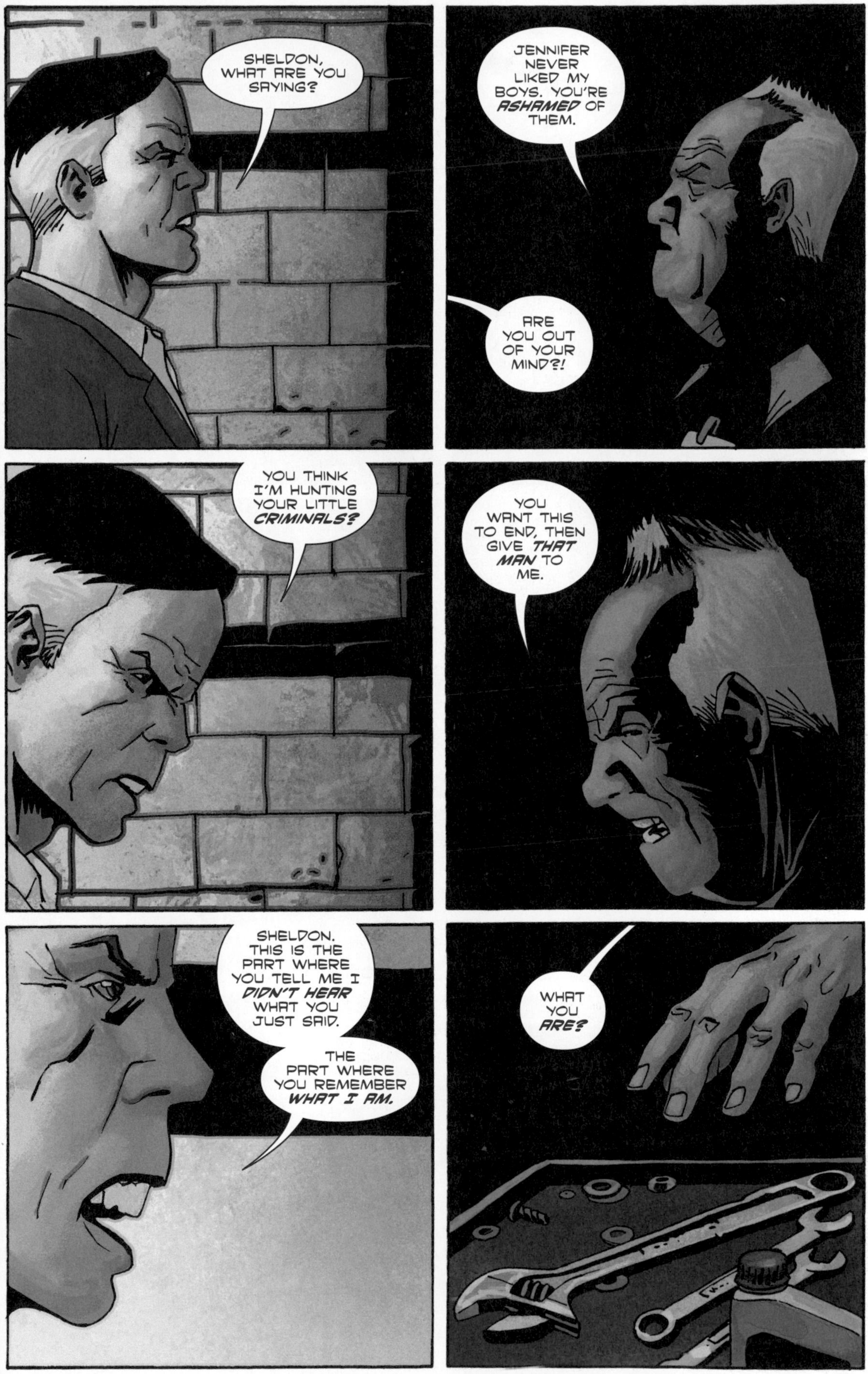
SHELDON, WHAT ARE YOU SAYING?
JENNIFER NEVER LIKED MY BOYS. YOU'RE ASHAMED OF THEM.
ARE YOU OUT OF YOUR MIND?!
YOU THINK I'M HUNTING YOUR LITTLE CRIMINALS?
YOU WANT THIS TO END, THEN GIVE THAT MAN TO ME.
SHELDON. THIS IS THE PART WHERE YOU TELL ME I DIDN'T HEAR WHAT YOU JUST SAID.
THE PART WHERE YOU REMEMBER WHAT I AM.
WHAT YOU ARE?

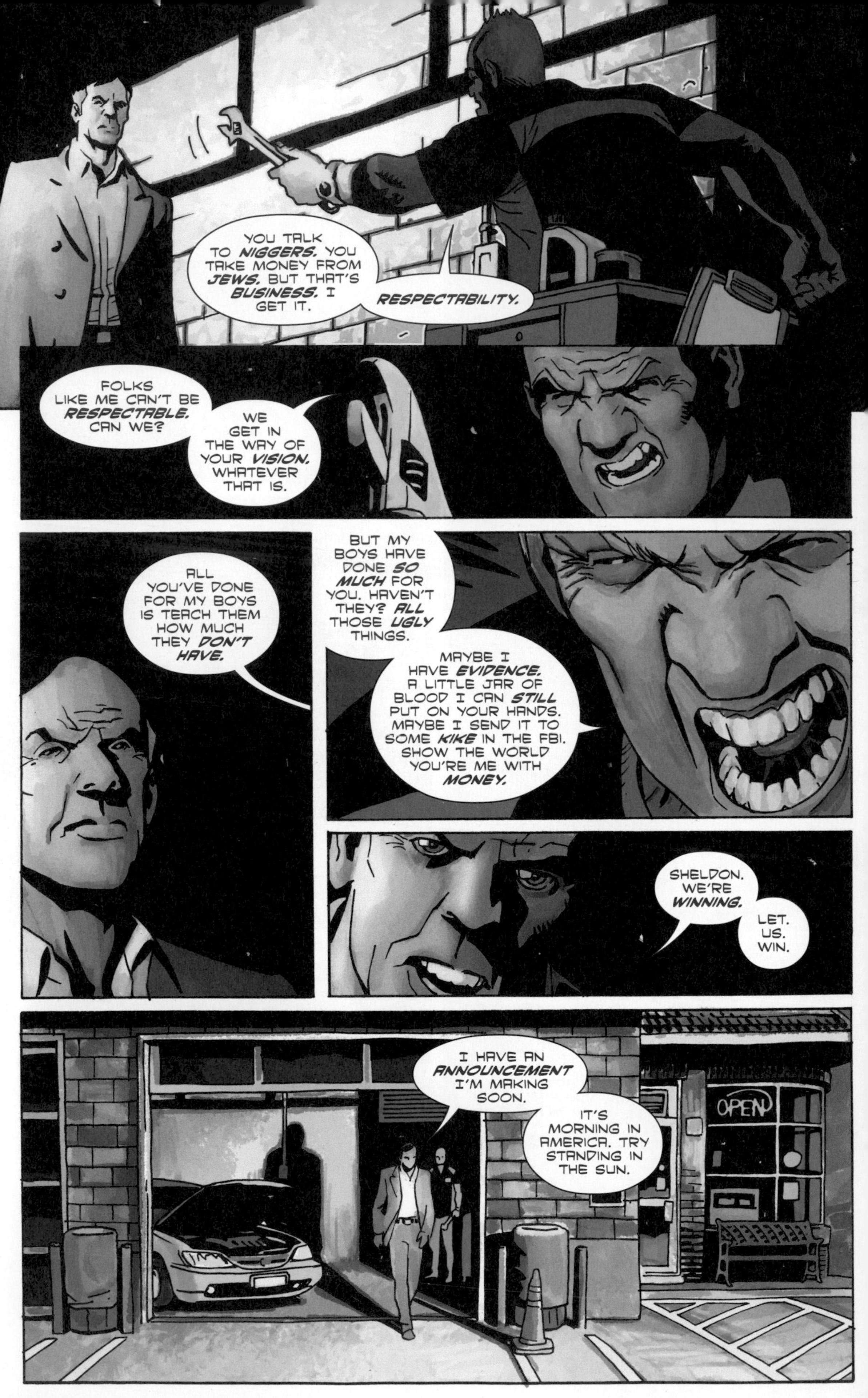
YOU TALK TO NIGGERS. YOU TAKE MONEY FROM JEWS. BUT THAT'S BUSINESS. I GET IT.
RESPECTABILITY.
FOLKS LIKE ME CAN'T BE RESPECTABLE. CAN WE?
WE GET IN THE WAY OF YOUR VISION. WHATEVER THAT IS.
ALL YOU'VE DONE FOR MY BOYS IS TEACH THEM HOW MUCH THEY DON'T HAVE.
BUT MY BOYS HAVE DONE SO MUCH FOR YOU. HAVEN'T THEY? ALL THOSE UGLY THINGS.
MAYBE I HAVE EVIDENCE. A LITTLE JAR OF BLOOD I CAN STILL PUT ON YOUR HANDS. MAYBE I SEND IT TO SOME KIKE IN THE FBI. SHOW THE WORLD YOU'RE ME WITH MONEY.
SHELDON. WE'RE WINNING.
LET. US. WIN.
I HAVE AN ANNOUNCEMENT I'M MAKING SOON.
IT'S MORNING IN AMERICA. TRY STANDING IN THE SUN.
OPEN

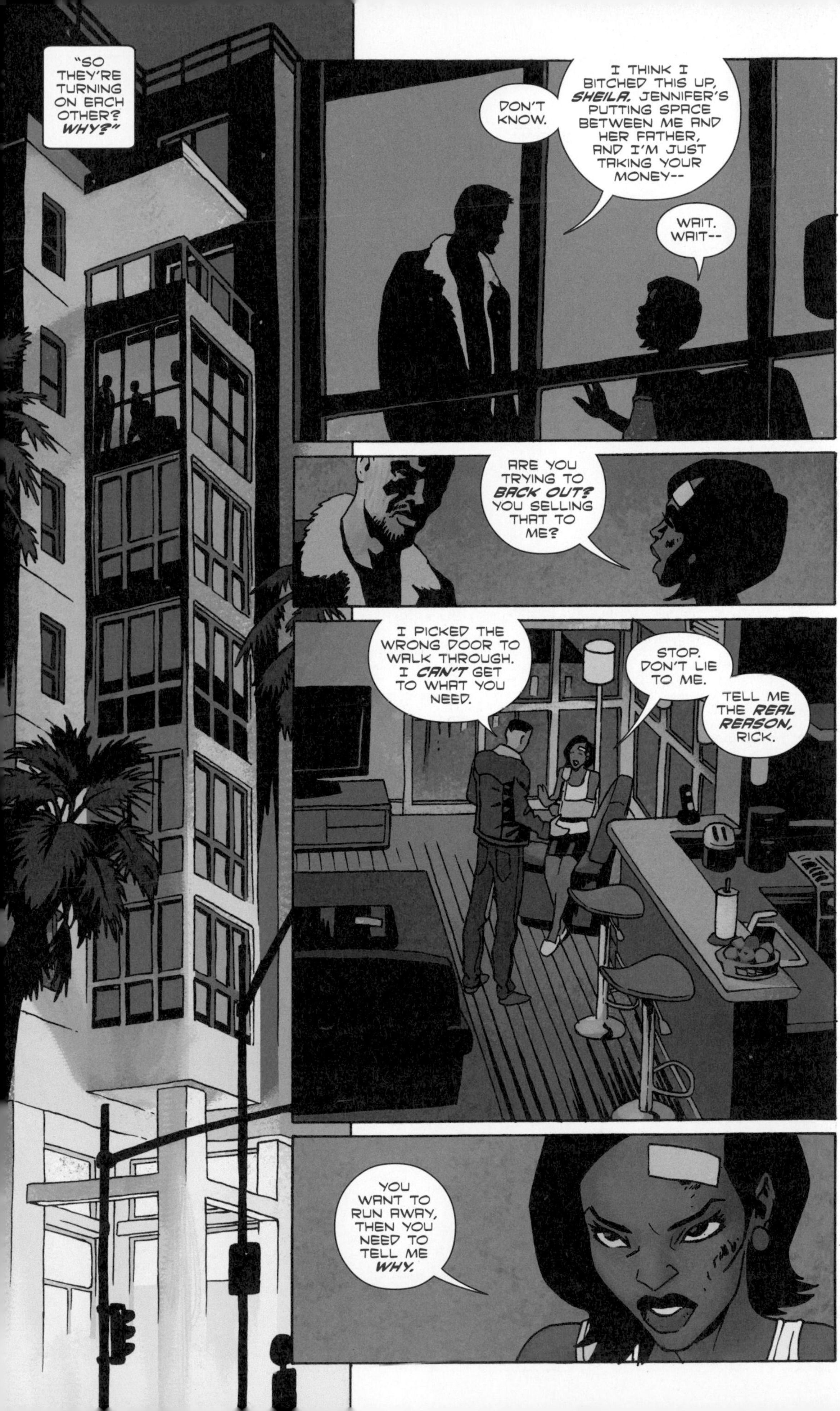
"SO THEY'RE TURNING ON EACH OTHER? WHY?"
DON'T KNOW.
I THINK I BITCHED THIS UP, SHEILA. JENNIFER'S PUTTING SPACE BETWEEN ME AND HER FATHER, AND I'M JUST TAKING YOUR MONEY--
WAIT. WAIT--
ARE YOU TRYING TO BACK OUT? YOU SELLING THAT TO ME?
I PICKED THE WRONG DOOR TO WALK THROUGH. I CAN'T GET TO WHAT YOU NEED.
STOP. DON'T LIE TO ME.
TELL ME THE REAL REASON, RICK.
YOU WANT TO RUN AWAY, THEN YOU NEED TO TELL ME WHY.

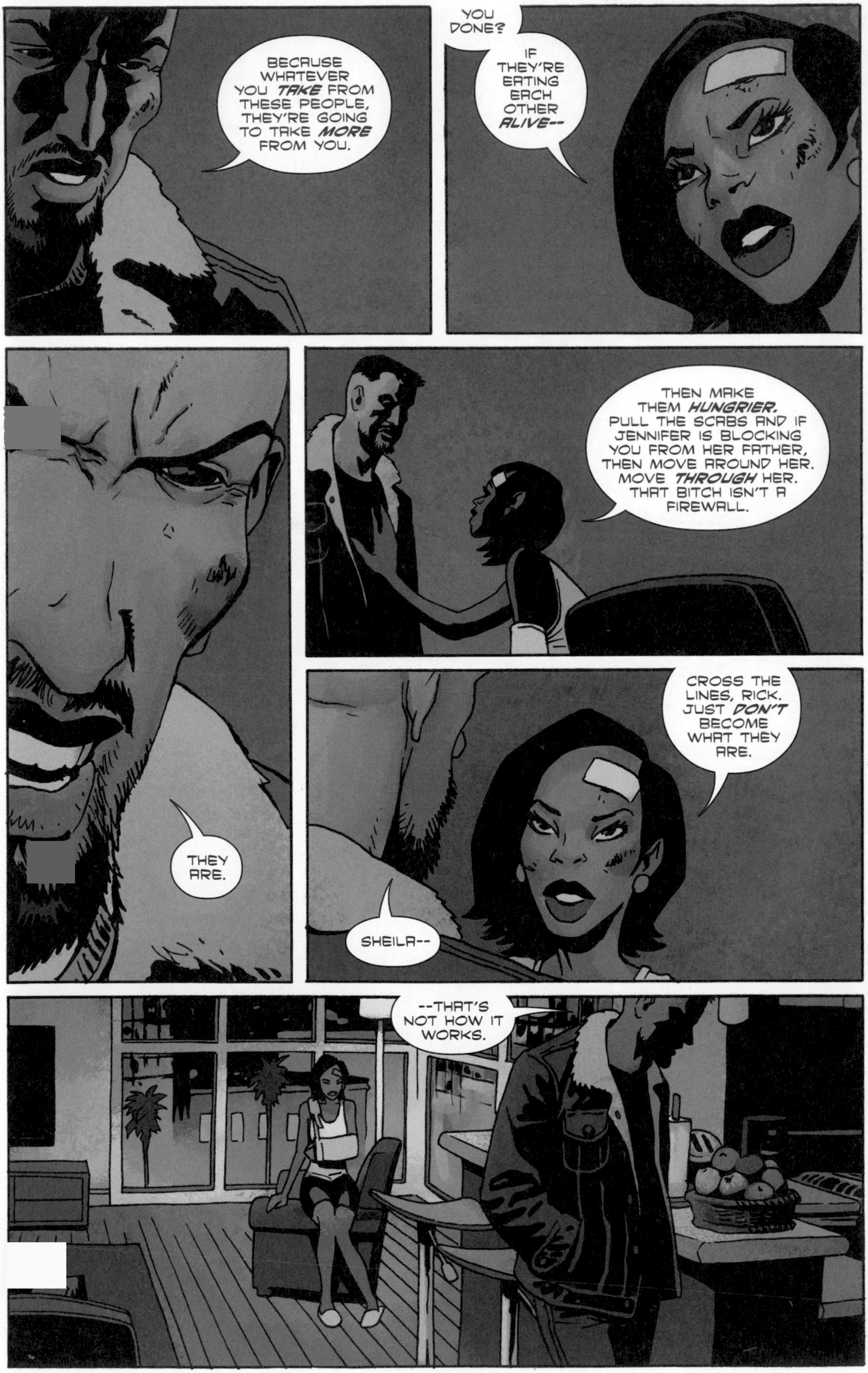
BECAUSE WHATEVER YOU TAKE FROM THESE PEOPLE, THEY'RE GOING TO TAKE MORE FROM YOU.
YOU DONE?
IF THEY'RE EATING EACH OTHER ALIVE--
THEY ARE.
THEN MAKE THEM HUNGRIER. PULL THE SCABS AND IF JENNIFER IS BLOCKING YOU FROM HER FATHER, THEN MOVE AROUND HER. MOVE THROUGH HER. THAT BITCH ISN'T A FIREWALL.
CROSS THE LINES, RICK. JUST DON'T BECOME WHAT THEY ARE.
SHEILA--
--THAT'S NOT HOW IT WORKS.

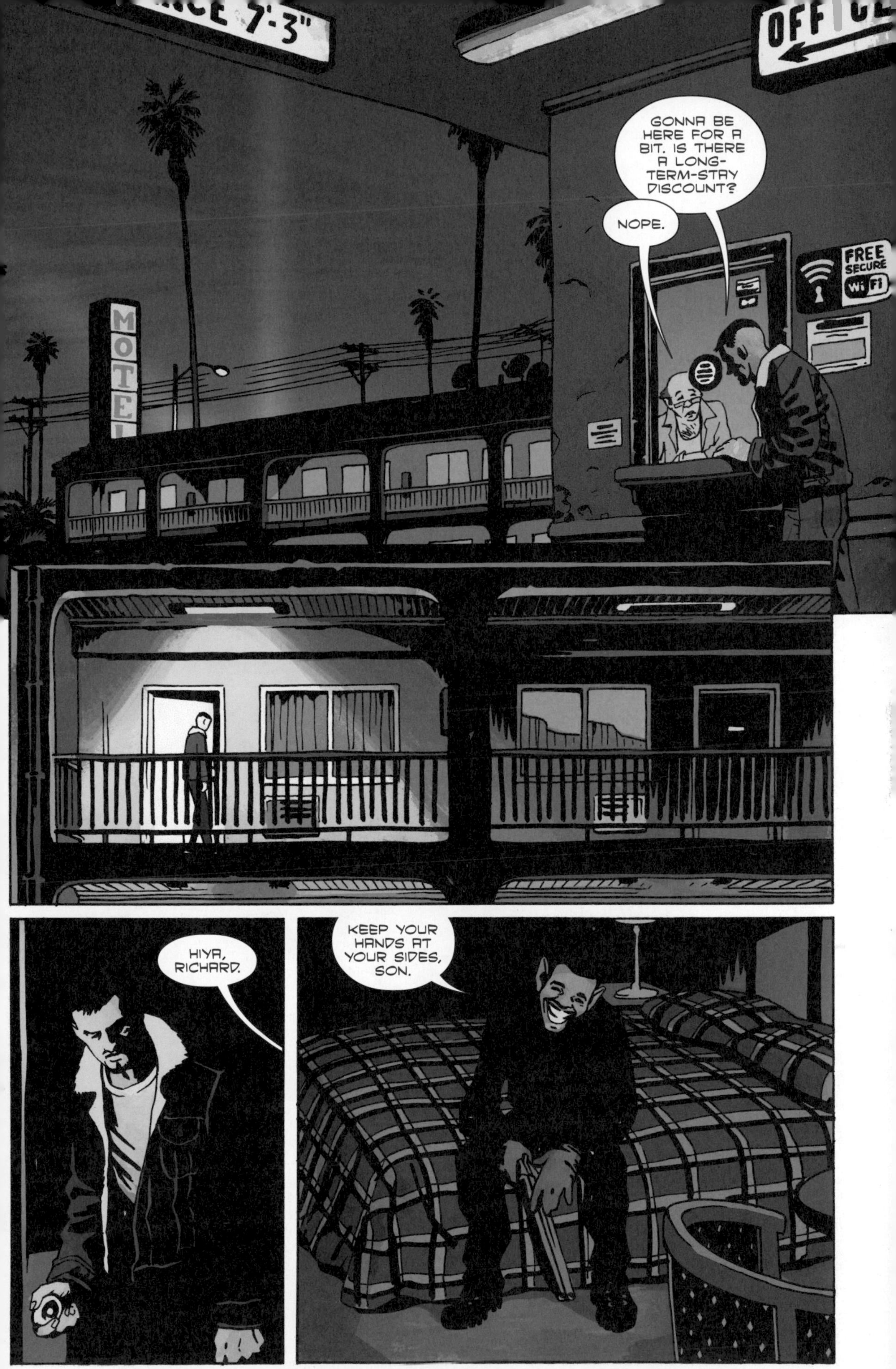

ANCE 7'-3"
OFFICE
MOTEL
FREE SECURE WiFi
GONNA BE HERE FOR A BIT. IS THERE A LONG-TERM-STAY DISCOUNT?
NOPE.
HIYA, RICHARD.
KEEP YOUR HANDS AT YOUR SIDES, SON.

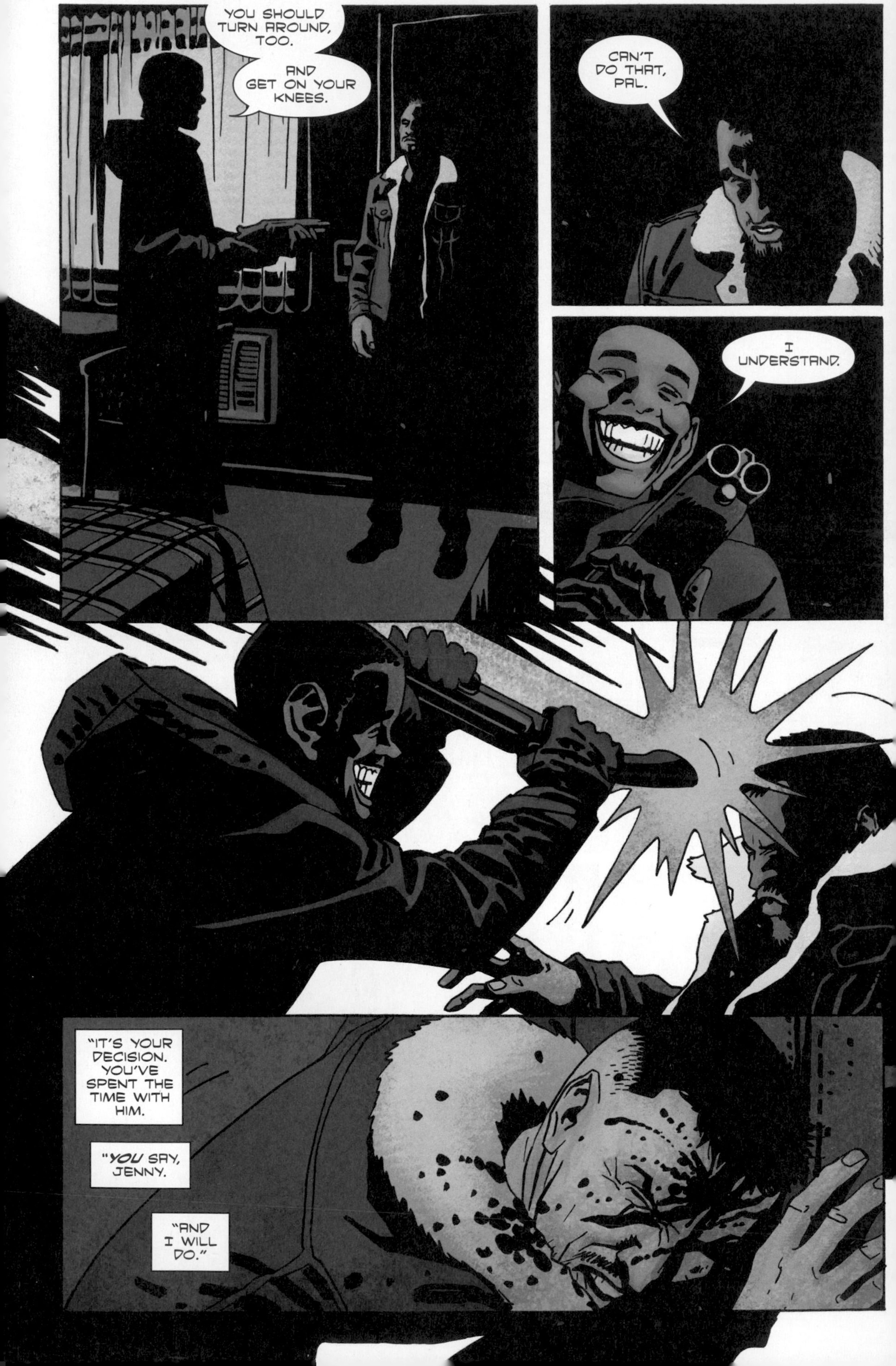
YOU SHOULD TURN AROUND, TOO.
AND GET ON YOUR KNEES.
CAN'T DO THAT, PAL.
I UNDERSTAND.
"IT'S YOUR DECISION. YOU'VE SPENT THE TIME WITH HIM.
"YOU SAY, JENNY.
"AND I WILL DO."

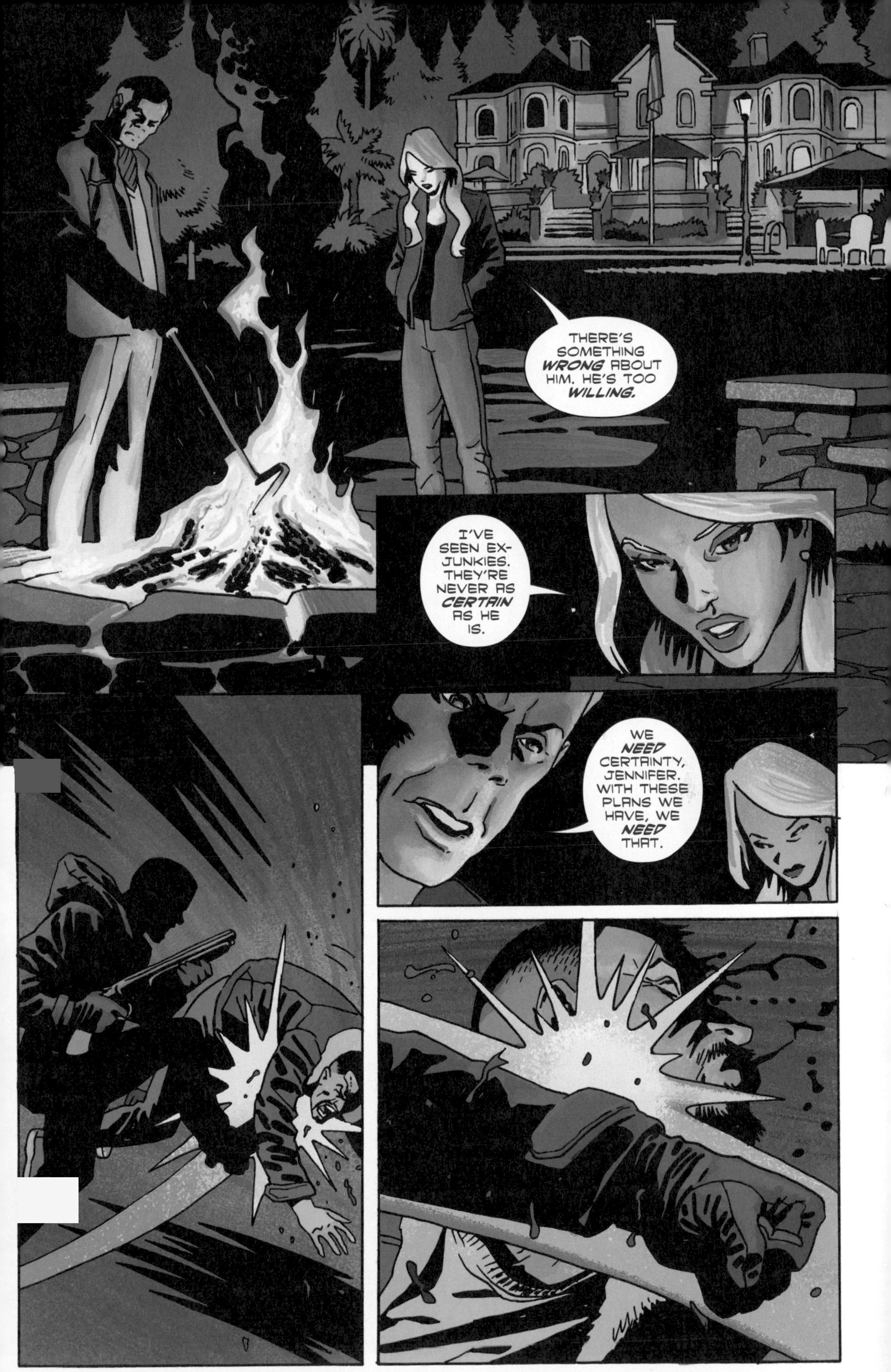

THERE'S SOMETHING WRONG ABOUT HIM. HE'S TOO WILLING.
I'VE SEEN EX-JUNKIES. THEY'RE NEVER AS CERTAIN AS HE IS.
WE NEED CERTAINTY, JENNIFER. WITH THESE PLANS WE HAVE, WE NEED THAT.

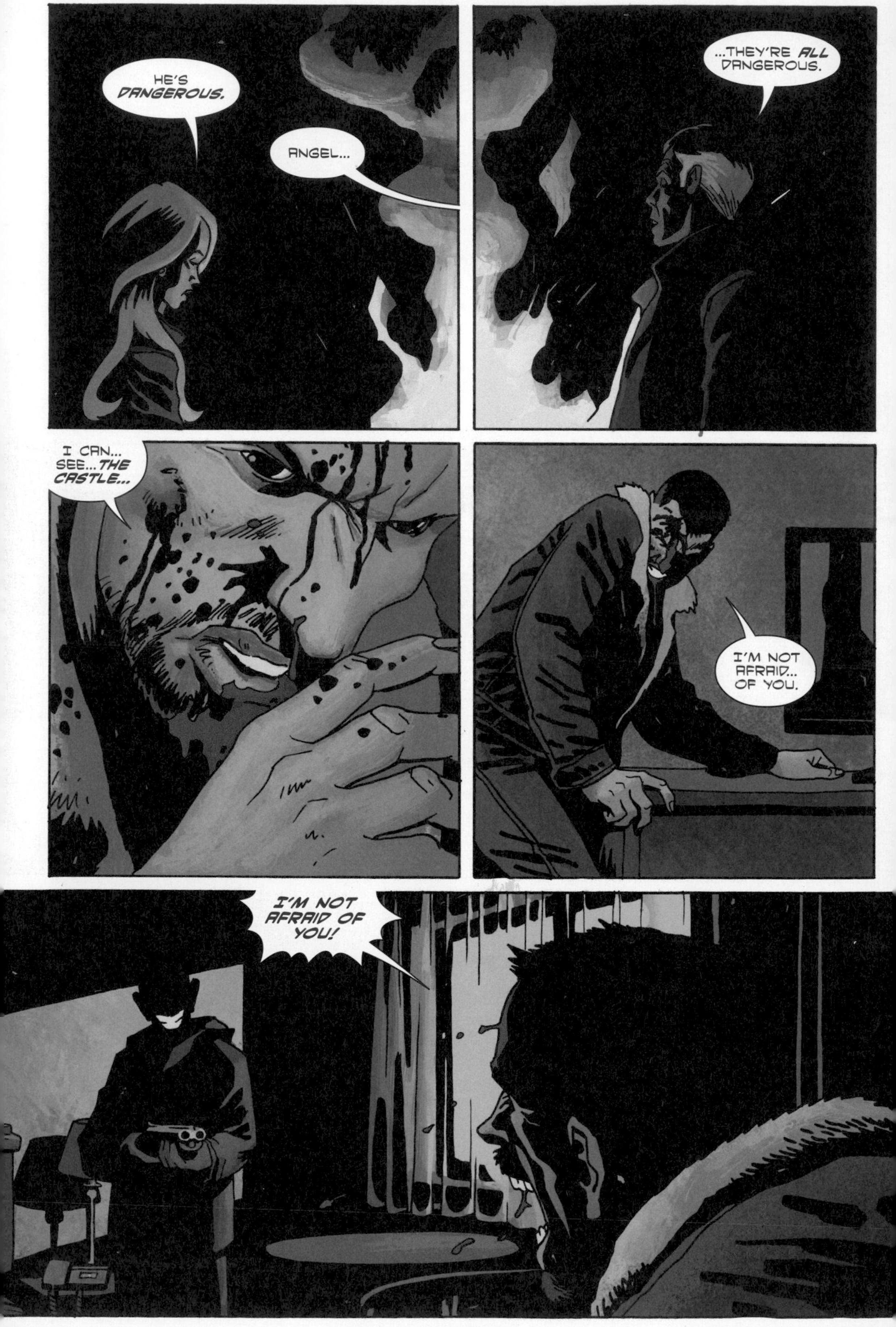
HE'S DANGEROUS.
ANGEL...
...THEY'RE ALL DANGEROUS.
I CAN... SEE... THE CASTLE...
I'M NOT AFRAID... OF YOU.
I'M NOT AFRAID OF YOU!

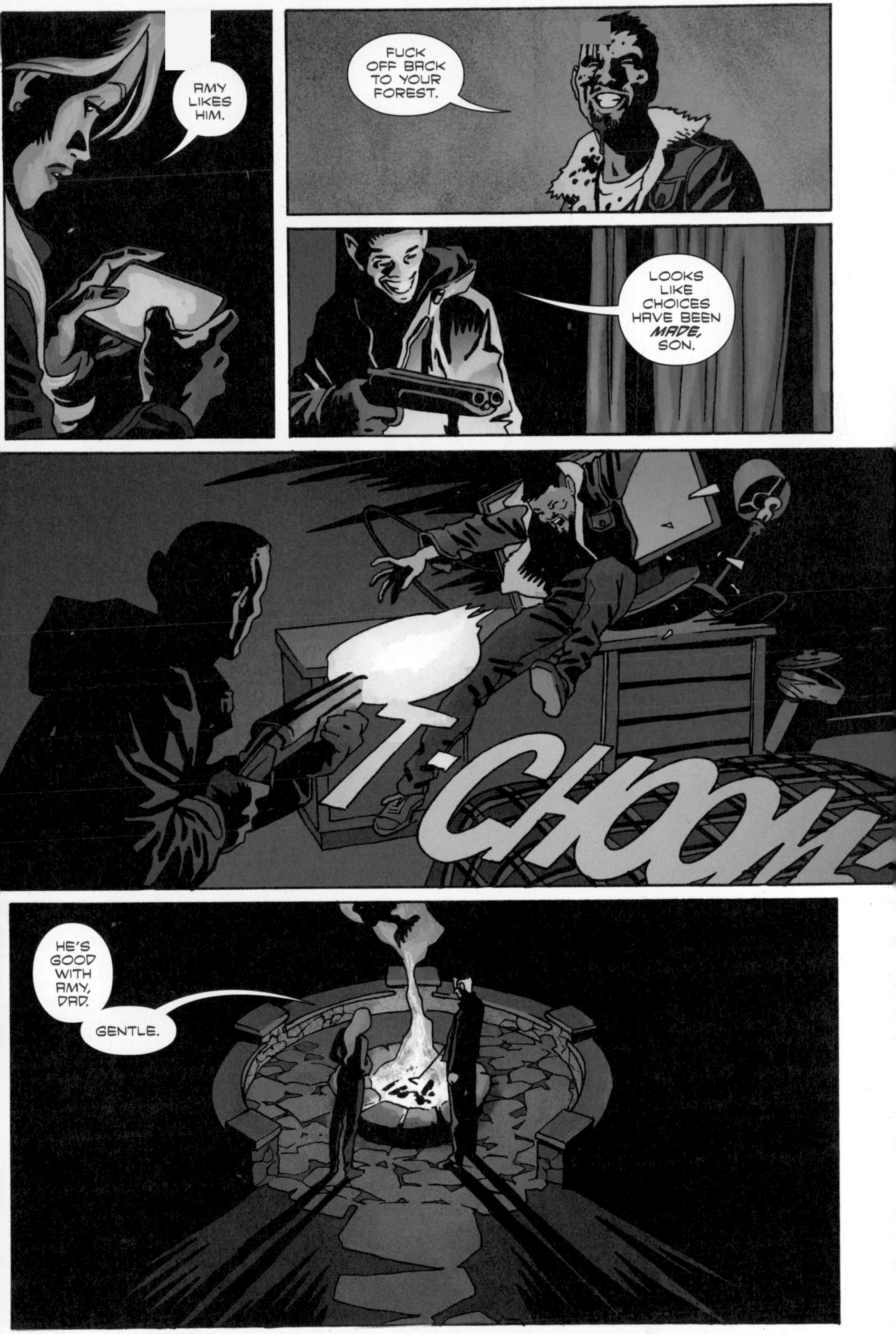
AMY LIKES HIM.
FUCK OFF BACK TO YOUR FOREST.
LOOKS LIKE CHOICES HAVE BEEN *MADE,* SON.
T-CHOOM
HE'S GOOD WITH AMY, DAD.
GENTLE.

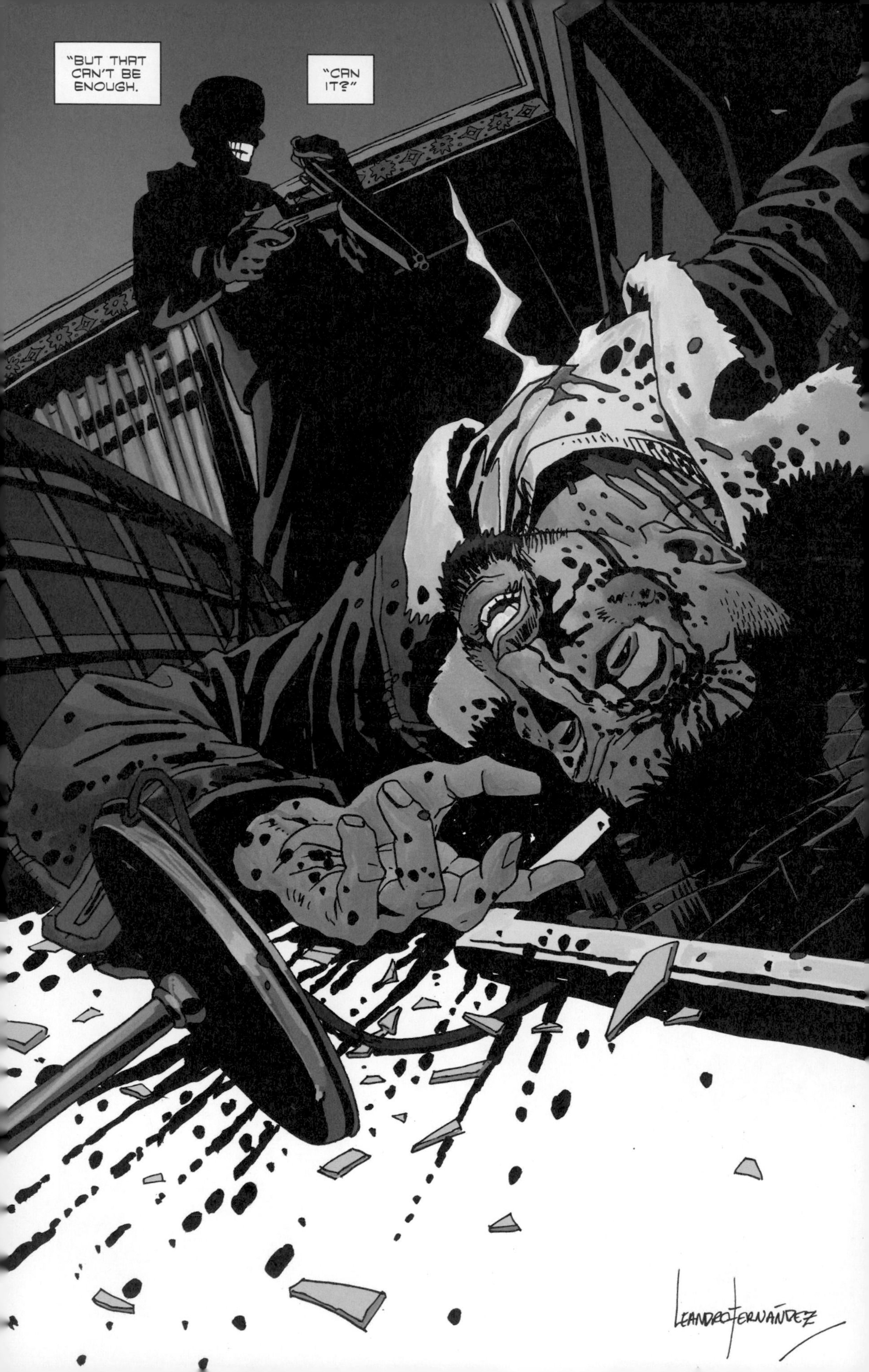
"BUT THAT CAN'T BE ENOUGH.
"CAN IT?"
LEANDRO FERNÁNDEZ

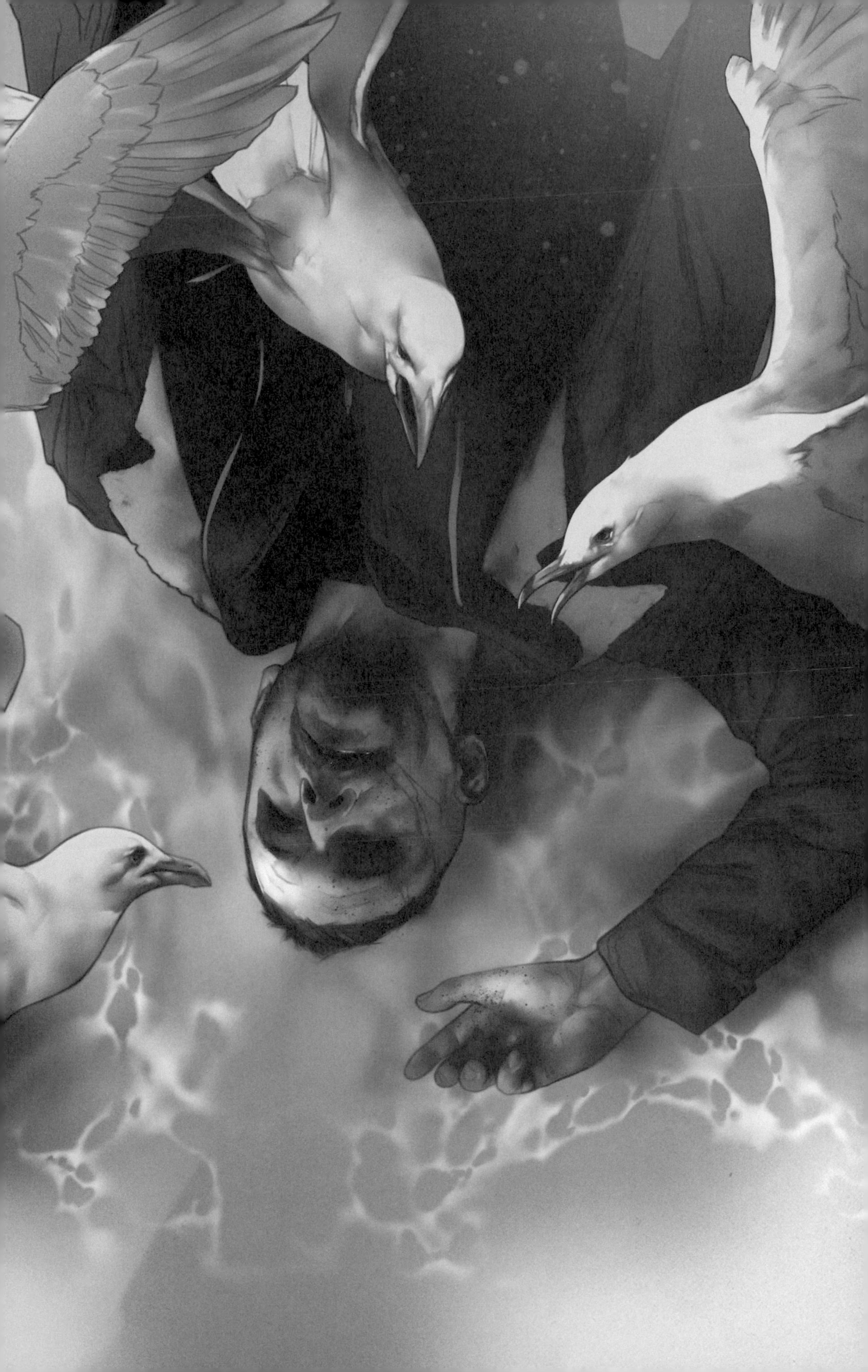

CHAPTER FIVE: WAR

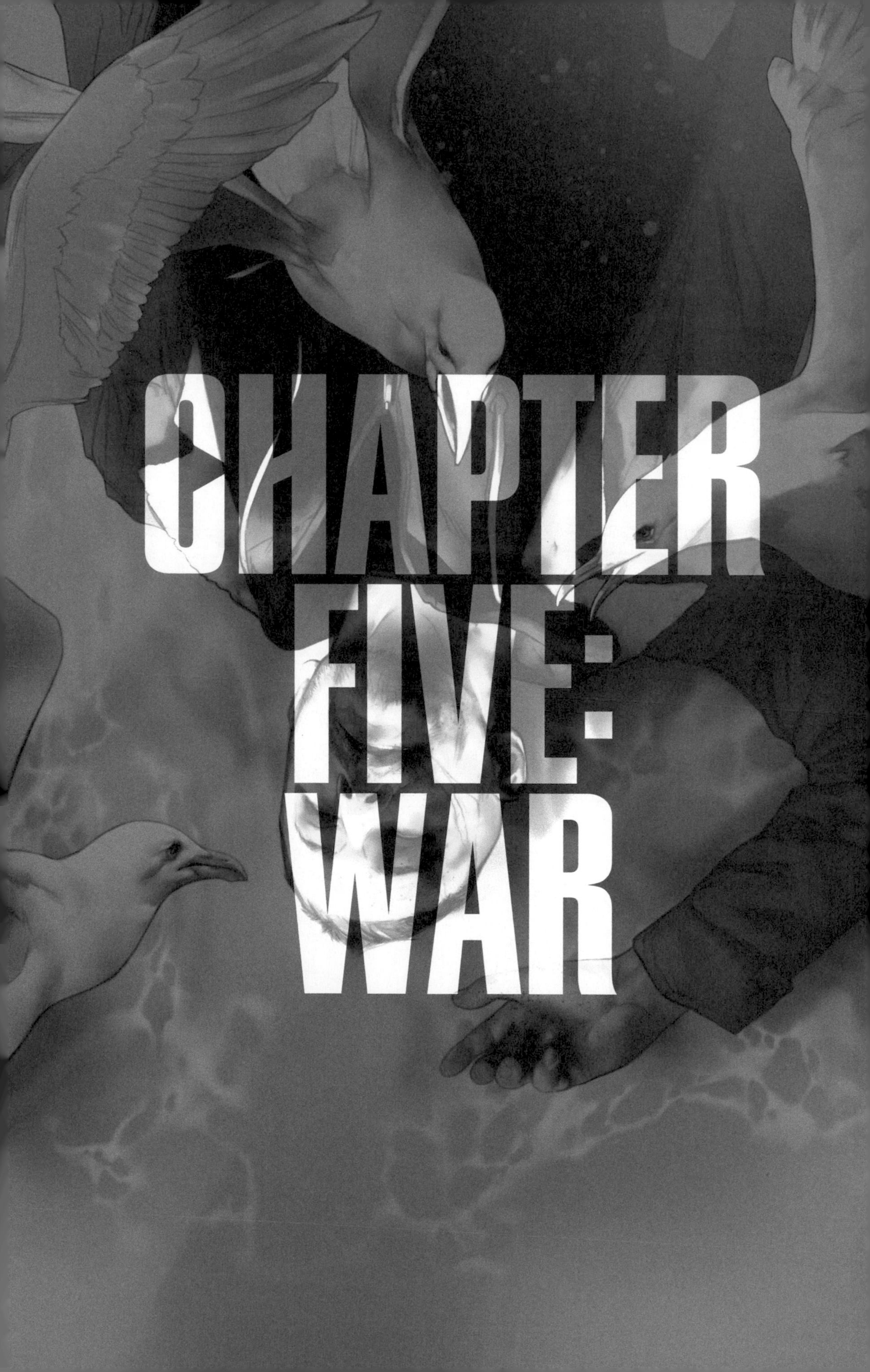

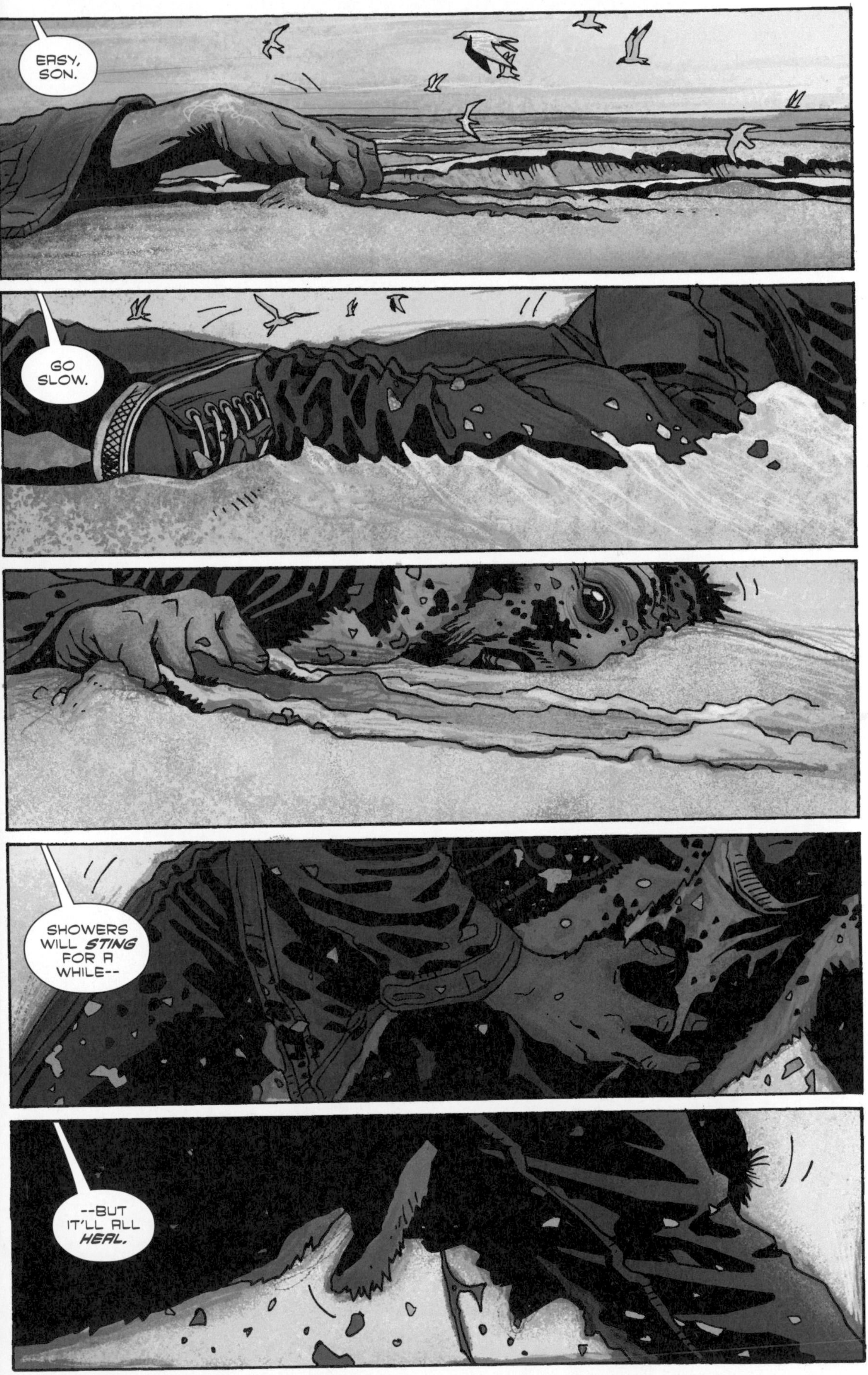
EASY, SON.
GO SLOW.
SHOWERS WILL STING FOR A WHILE--
--BUT IT'LL ALL HEAL.

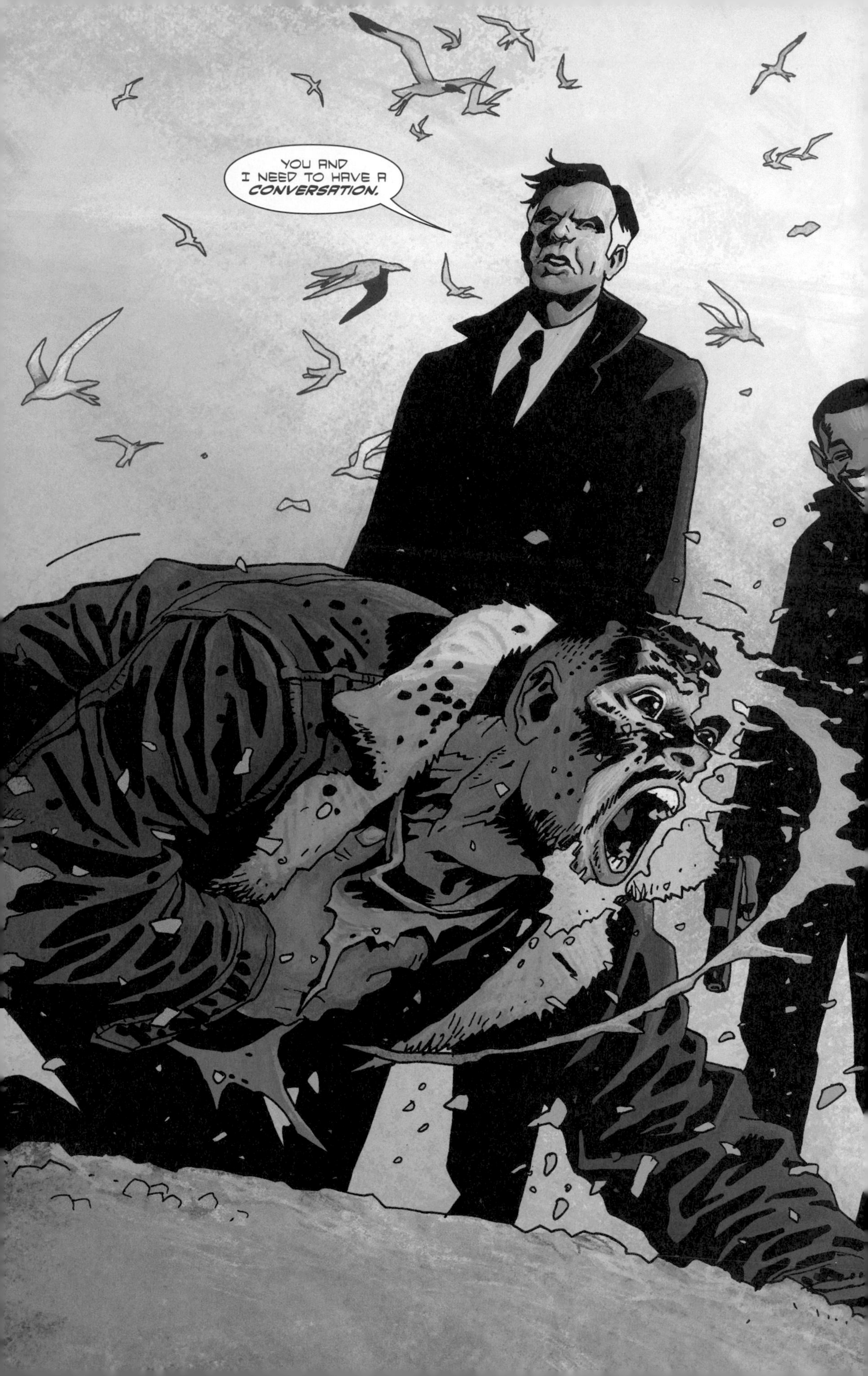
YOU AND I NEED TO HAVE A CONVERSATION.

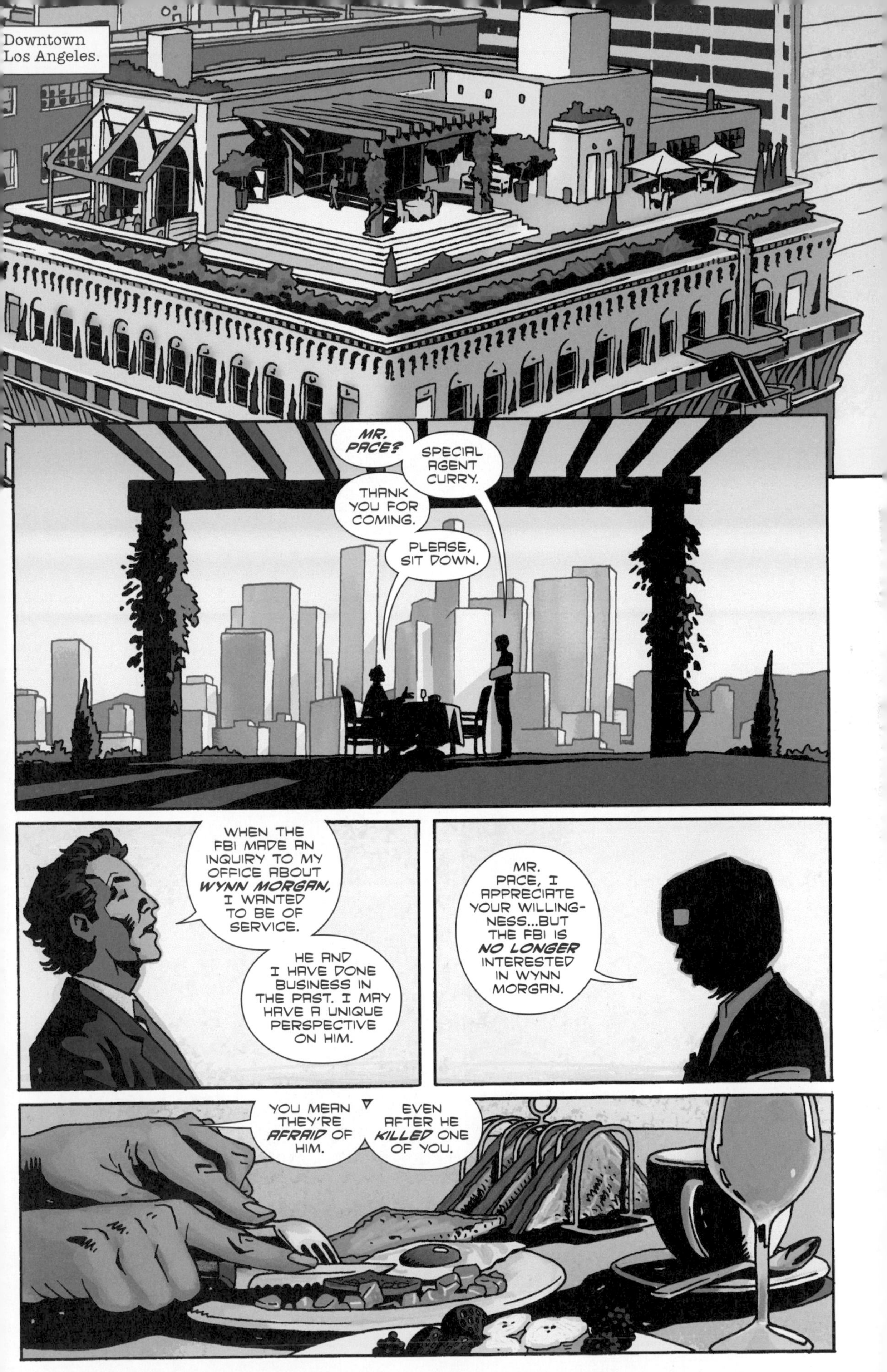
Downtown Los Angeles.
MR. PACE?
SPECIAL AGENT CURRY.
THANK YOU FOR COMING.
PLEASE, SIT DOWN.
WHEN THE FBI MADE AN INQUIRY TO MY OFFICE ABOUT WYNN MORGAN, I WANTED TO BE OF SERVICE.
HE AND I HAVE DONE BUSINESS IN THE PAST. I MAY HAVE A UNIQUE PERSPECTIVE ON HIM.
MR. PACE, I APPRECIATE YOUR WILLINGNESS...BUT THE FBI IS NO LONGER INTERESTED IN WYNN MORGAN.
YOU MEAN THEY'RE AFRAID OF HIM.
EVEN AFTER HE KILLED ONE OF YOU.

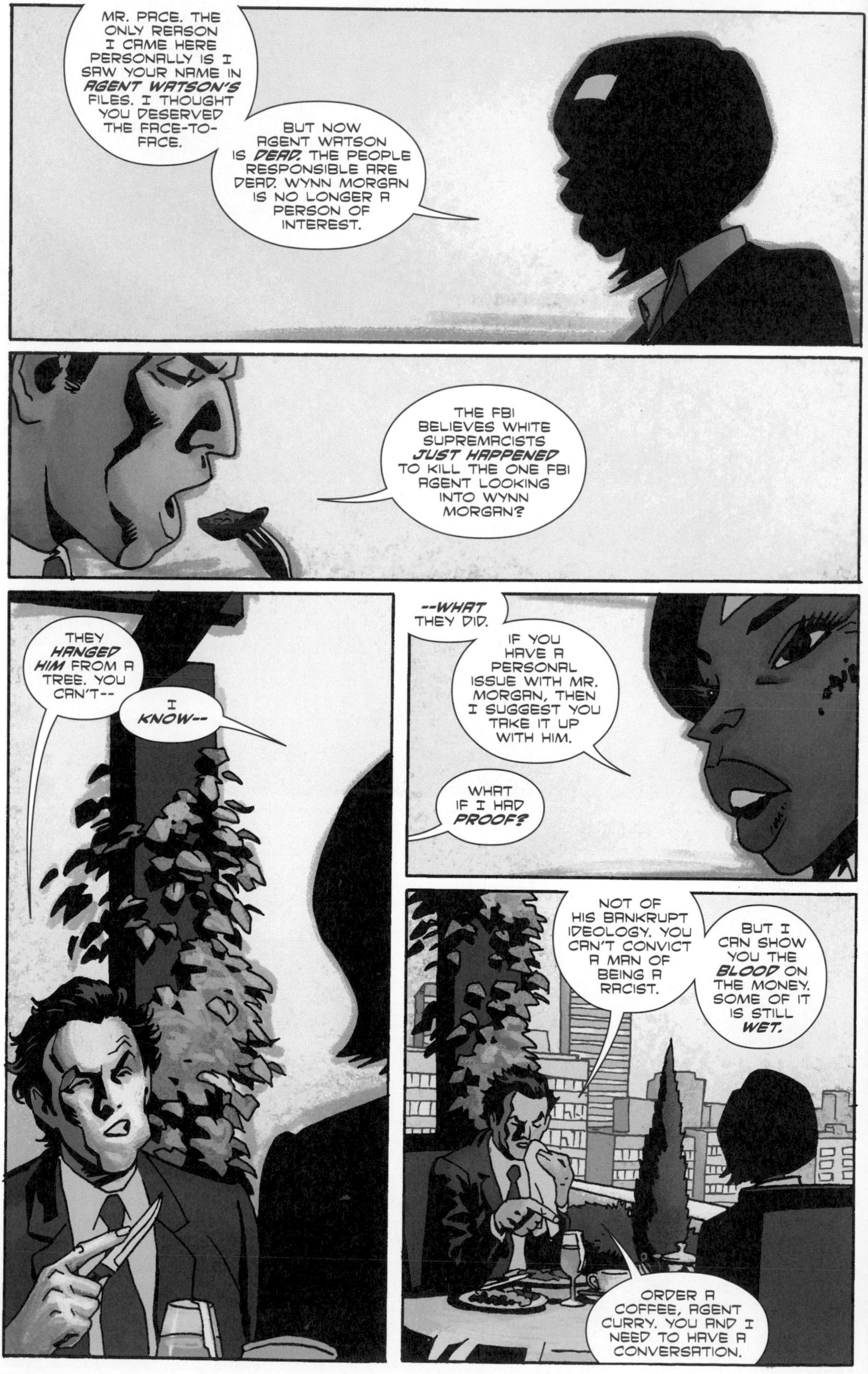
MR. PACE. THE ONLY REASON I CAME HERE PERSONALLY IS I SAW YOUR NAME IN AGENT WATSON'S FILES. I THOUGHT YOU DESERVED THE FACE-TO-FACE.
BUT NOW AGENT WATSON IS DEAD, THE PEOPLE RESPONSIBLE ARE DEAD. WYNN MORGAN IS NO LONGER A PERSON OF INTEREST.
THE FBI BELIEVES WHITE SUPREMACISTS JUST HAPPENED TO KILL THE ONE FBI AGENT LOOKING INTO WYNN MORGAN?
THEY HANGED HIM FROM A TREE. YOU CAN'T--
I KNOW--
--WHAT THEY DID.
IF YOU HAVE A PERSONAL ISSUE WITH MR. MORGAN, THEN I SUGGEST YOU TAKE IT UP WITH HIM.
WHAT IF I HAD PROOF?
NOT OF HIS BANKRUPT IDEOLOGY. YOU CAN'T CONVICT A MAN OF BEING A RACIST.
BUT I CAN SHOW YOU THE BLOOD ON THE MONEY. SOME OF IT IS STILL WET.
ORDER A COFFEE, AGENT CURRY. YOU AND I NEED TO HAVE A CONVERSATION.

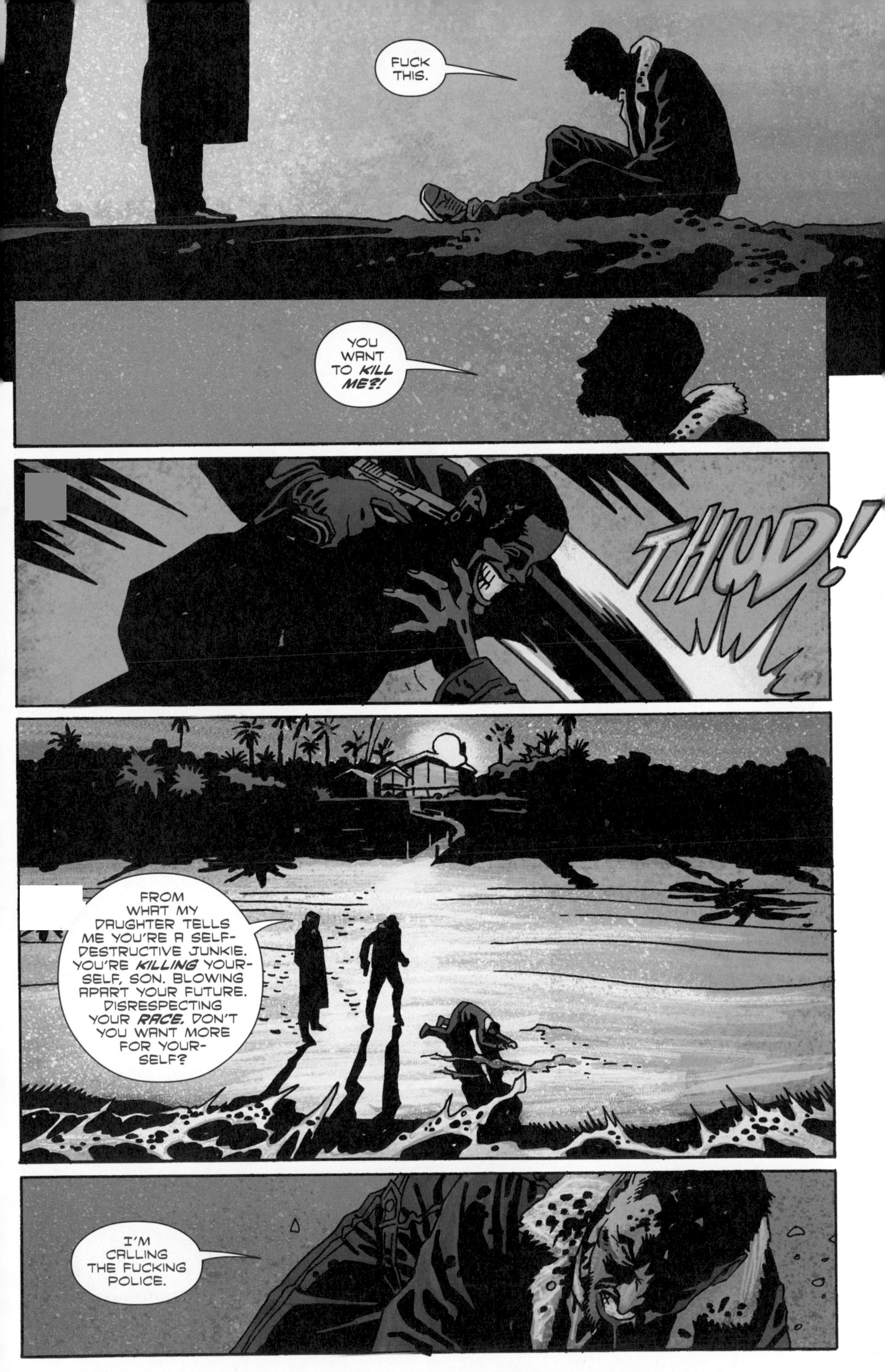
FUCK THIS.
YOU WANT TO KILL ME?!
THUD!
FROM WHAT MY DAUGHTER TELLS ME YOU'RE A SELF-DESTRUCTIVE JUNKIE. YOU'RE KILLING YOURSELF, SON. BLOWING APART YOUR FUTURE. DISRESPECTING YOUR RACE. DON'T YOU WANT MORE FOR YOURSELF?
I'M CALLING THE FUCKING POLICE.

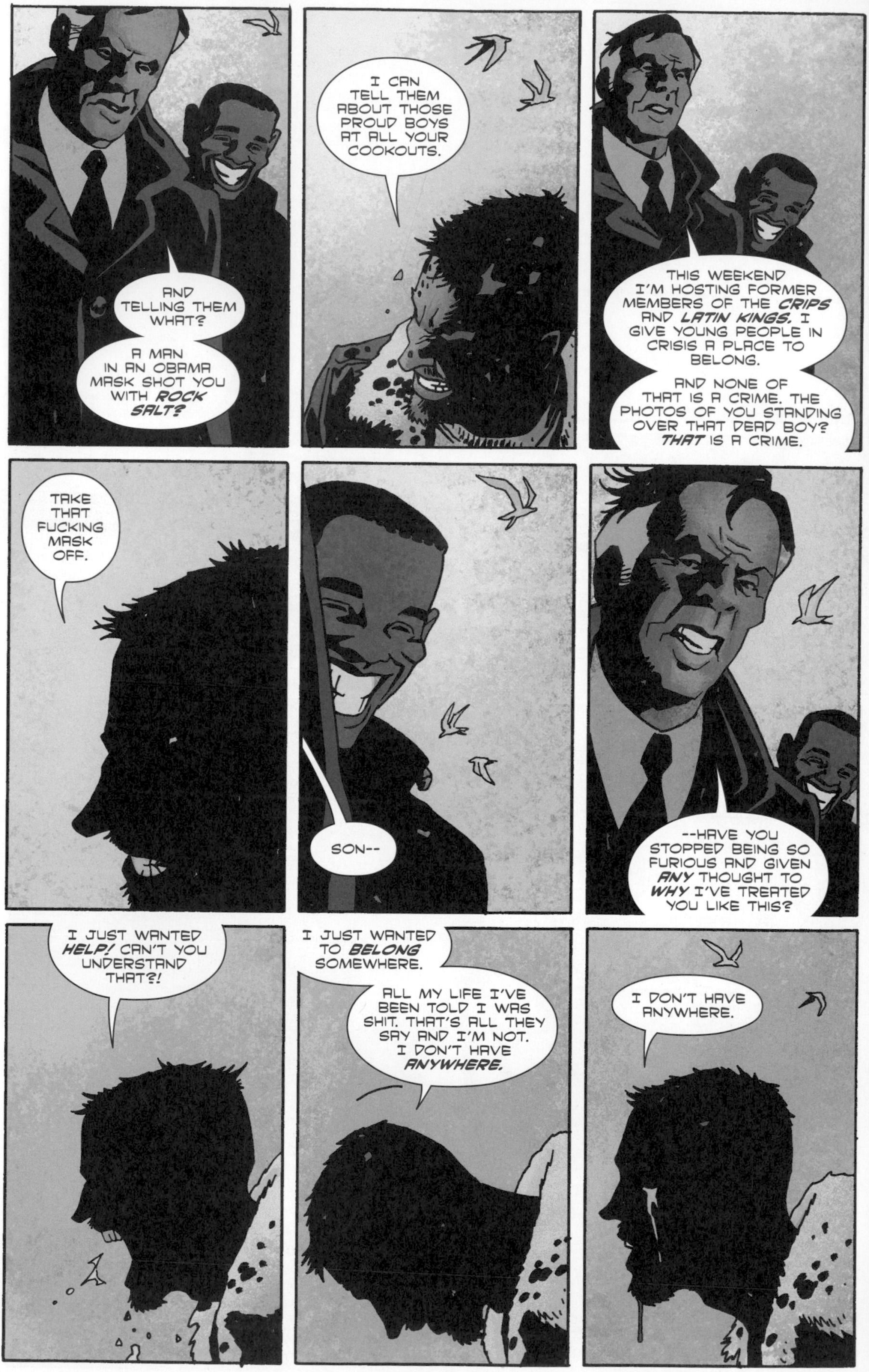
AND TELLING THEM WHAT?
A MAN IN AN OBAMA MASK SHOT YOU WITH ROCK SALT?
I CAN TELL THEM ABOUT THOSE PROUD BOYS AT ALL YOUR COOKOUTS.
THIS WEEKEND I'M HOSTING FORMER MEMBERS OF THE CRIPS AND LATIN KINGS. I GIVE YOUNG PEOPLE IN CRISIS A PLACE TO BELONG.
AND NONE OF THAT IS A CRIME. THE PHOTOS OF YOU STANDING OVER THAT DEAD BOY? THAT IS A CRIME.
TAKE THAT FUCKING MASK OFF.
SON--
--HAVE YOU STOPPED BEING SO FURIOUS AND GIVEN ANY THOUGHT TO WHY I'VE TREATED YOU LIKE THIS?
I JUST WANTED HELP! CAN'T YOU UNDERSTAND THAT?!
I JUST WANTED TO BELONG SOMEWHERE.
ALL MY LIFE I'VE BEEN TOLD I WAS SHIT. THAT'S ALL THEY SAY AND I'M NOT. I DON'T HAVE ANYWHERE.
I DON'T HAVE ANYWHERE.

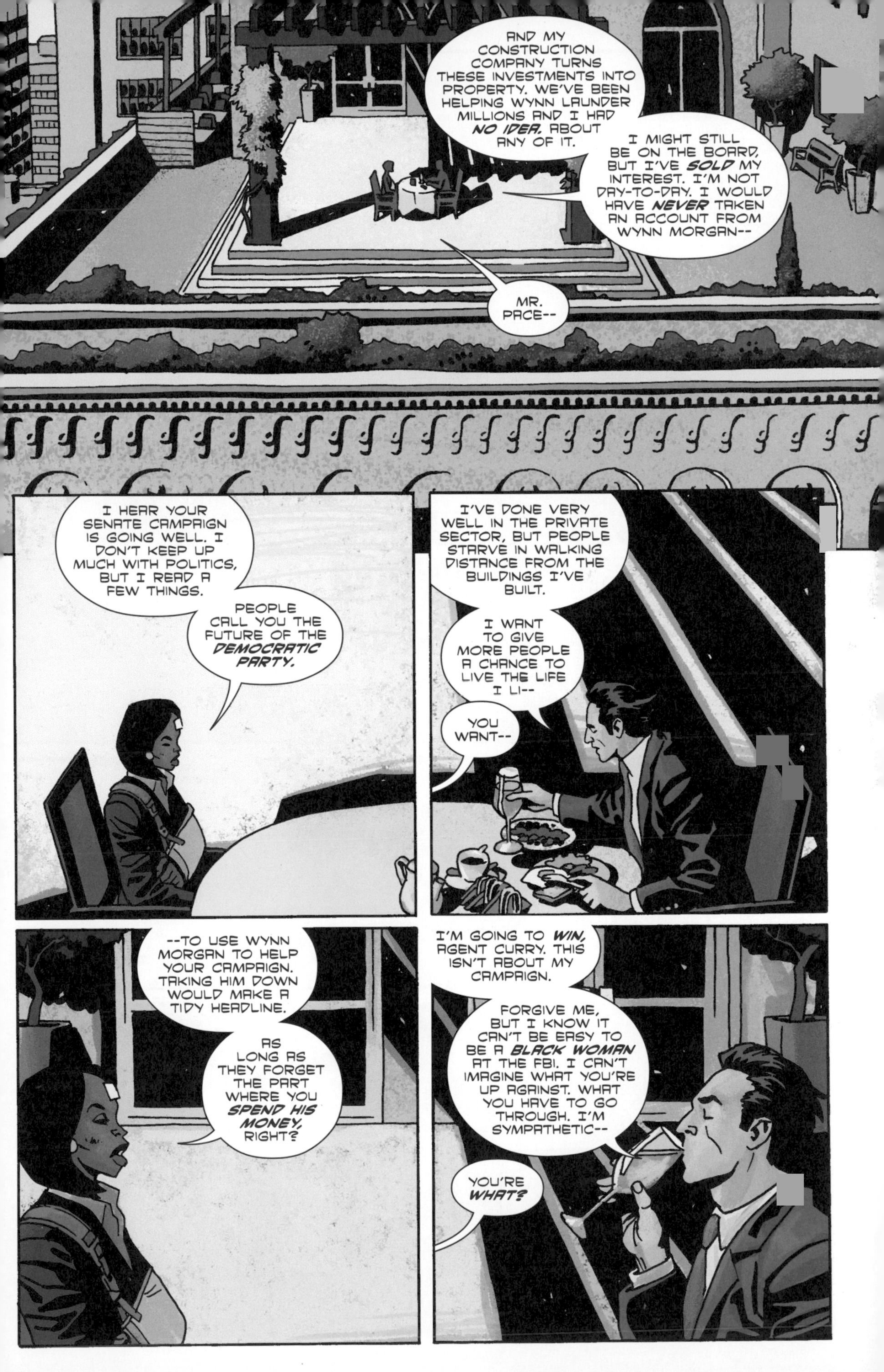
AND MY CONSTRUCTION COMPANY TURNS THESE INVESTMENTS INTO PROPERTY. WE'VE BEEN HELPING WYNN LAUNDER MILLIONS AND I HAD NO IDEA ABOUT ANY OF IT.
I MIGHT STILL BE ON THE BOARD, BUT I'VE SOLD MY INTEREST. I'M NOT DAY-TO-DAY. I WOULD HAVE NEVER TAKEN AN ACCOUNT FROM WYNN MORGAN--
MR. PACE--
I HEAR YOUR SENATE CAMPAIGN IS GOING WELL. I DON'T KEEP UP MUCH WITH POLITICS, BUT I READ A FEW THINGS.
PEOPLE CALL YOU THE FUTURE OF THE DEMOCRATIC PARTY.
I'VE DONE VERY WELL IN THE PRIVATE SECTOR, BUT PEOPLE STARVE IN WALKING DISTANCE FROM THE BUILDINGS I'VE BUILT.
I WANT TO GIVE MORE PEOPLE A CHANCE TO LIVE THE LIFE I LI--
YOU WANT--
--TO USE WYNN MORGAN TO HELP YOUR CAMPAIGN. TAKING HIM DOWN WOULD MAKE A TIDY HEADLINE.
AS LONG AS THEY FORGET THE PART WHERE YOU SPEND HIS MONEY, RIGHT?
I'M GOING TO WIN, AGENT CURRY. THIS ISN'T ABOUT MY CAMPAIGN.
FORGIVE ME, BUT I KNOW IT CAN'T BE EASY TO BE A BLACK WOMAN AT THE FBI. I CAN'T IMAGINE WHAT YOU'RE UP AGAINST. WHAT YOU HAVE TO GO THROUGH. I'M SYMPATHETIC--
YOU'RE WHAT?

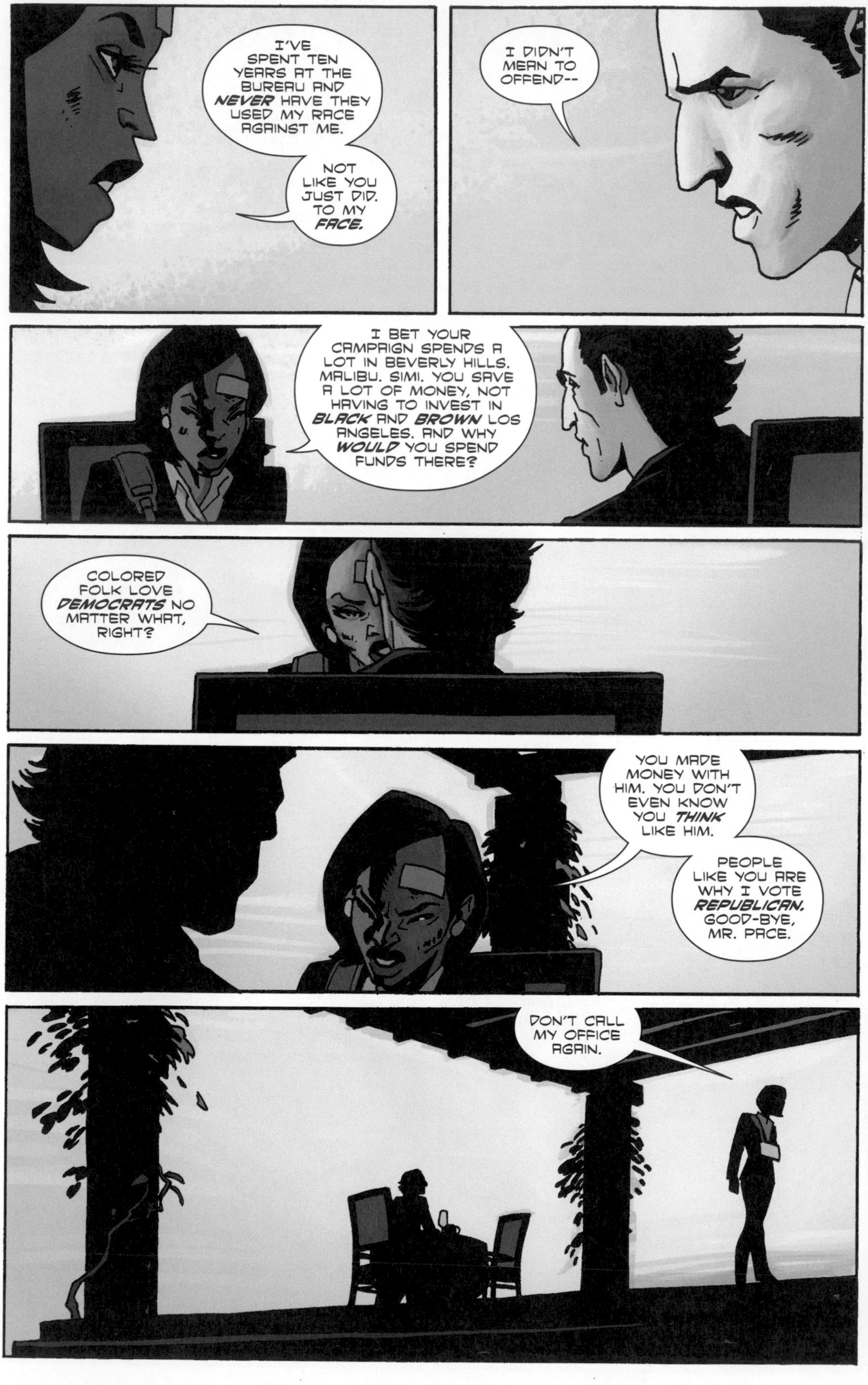
I'VE SPENT TEN YEARS AT THE BUREAU AND NEVER HAVE THEY USED MY RACE AGAINST ME.
NOT LIKE YOU JUST DID. TO MY FACE.
I DIDN'T MEAN TO OFFEND--
I BET YOUR CAMPAIGN SPENDS A LOT IN BEVERLY HILLS. MALIBU. SIMI. YOU SAVE A LOT OF MONEY, NOT HAVING TO INVEST IN BLACK AND BROWN LOS ANGELES. AND WHY WOULD YOU SPEND FUNDS THERE?
COLORED FOLK LOVE DEMOCRATS NO MATTER WHAT, RIGHT?
YOU MADE MONEY WITH HIM. YOU DON'T EVEN KNOW YOU THINK LIKE HIM.
PEOPLE LIKE YOU ARE WHY I VOTE REPUBLICAN. GOOD-BYE, MR. PACE.
DON'T CALL MY OFFICE AGAIN.

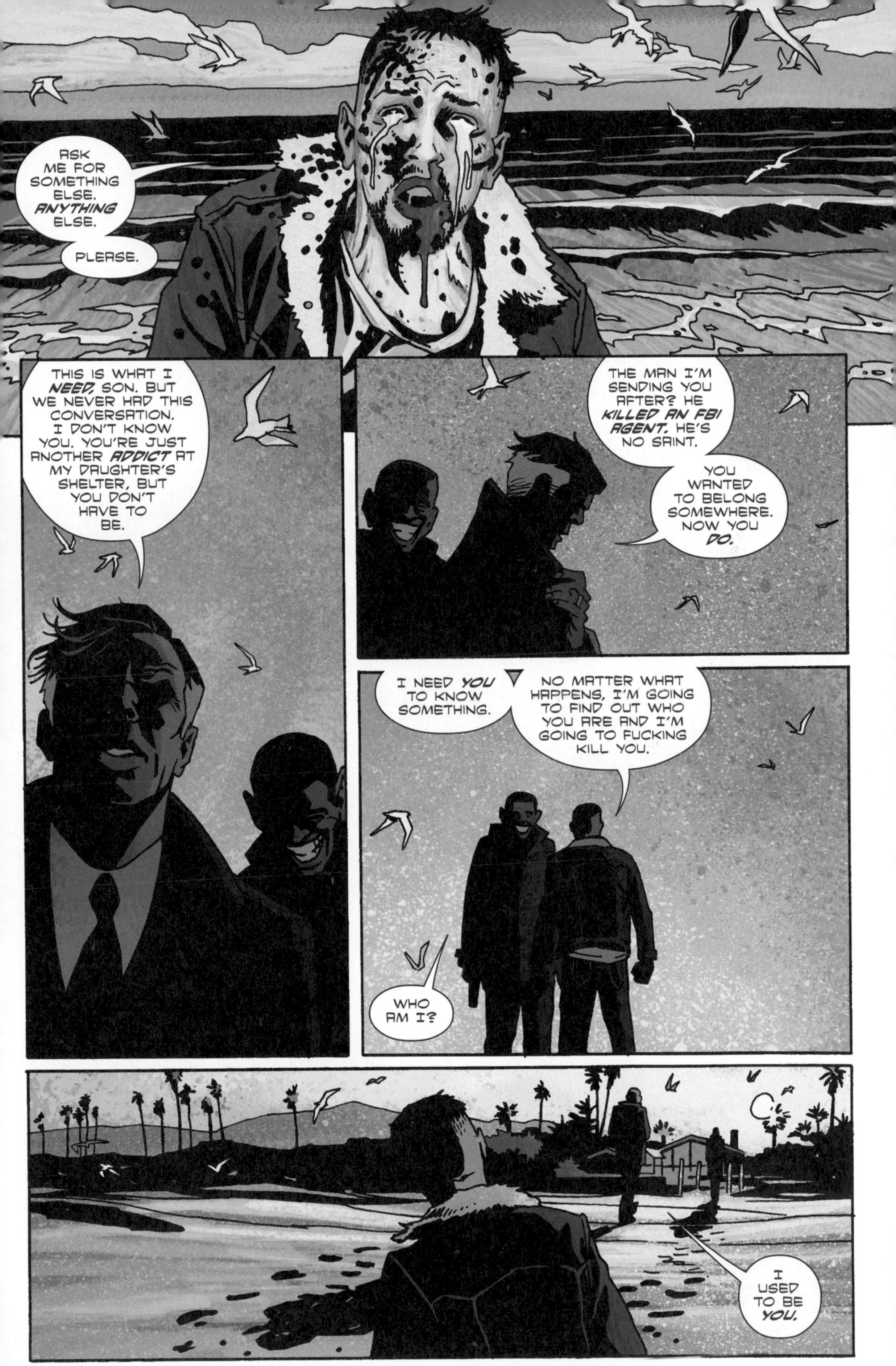
ASK ME FOR SOMETHING ELSE. ANYTHING ELSE.
PLEASE.
THIS IS WHAT I NEED, SON. BUT WE NEVER HAD THIS CONVERSATION. I DON'T KNOW YOU. YOU'RE JUST ANOTHER ADDICT AT MY DAUGHTER'S SHELTER, BUT YOU DON'T HAVE TO BE.
THE MAN I'M SENDING YOU AFTER? HE KILLED AN FBI AGENT. HE'S NO SAINT.
YOU WANTED TO BELONG SOMEWHERE. NOW YOU DO.
I NEED YOU TO KNOW SOMETHING.
NO MATTER WHAT HAPPENS, I'M GOING TO FIND OUT WHO YOU ARE AND I'M GOING TO FUCKING KILL YOU.
WHO AM I?
I USED TO BE YOU.

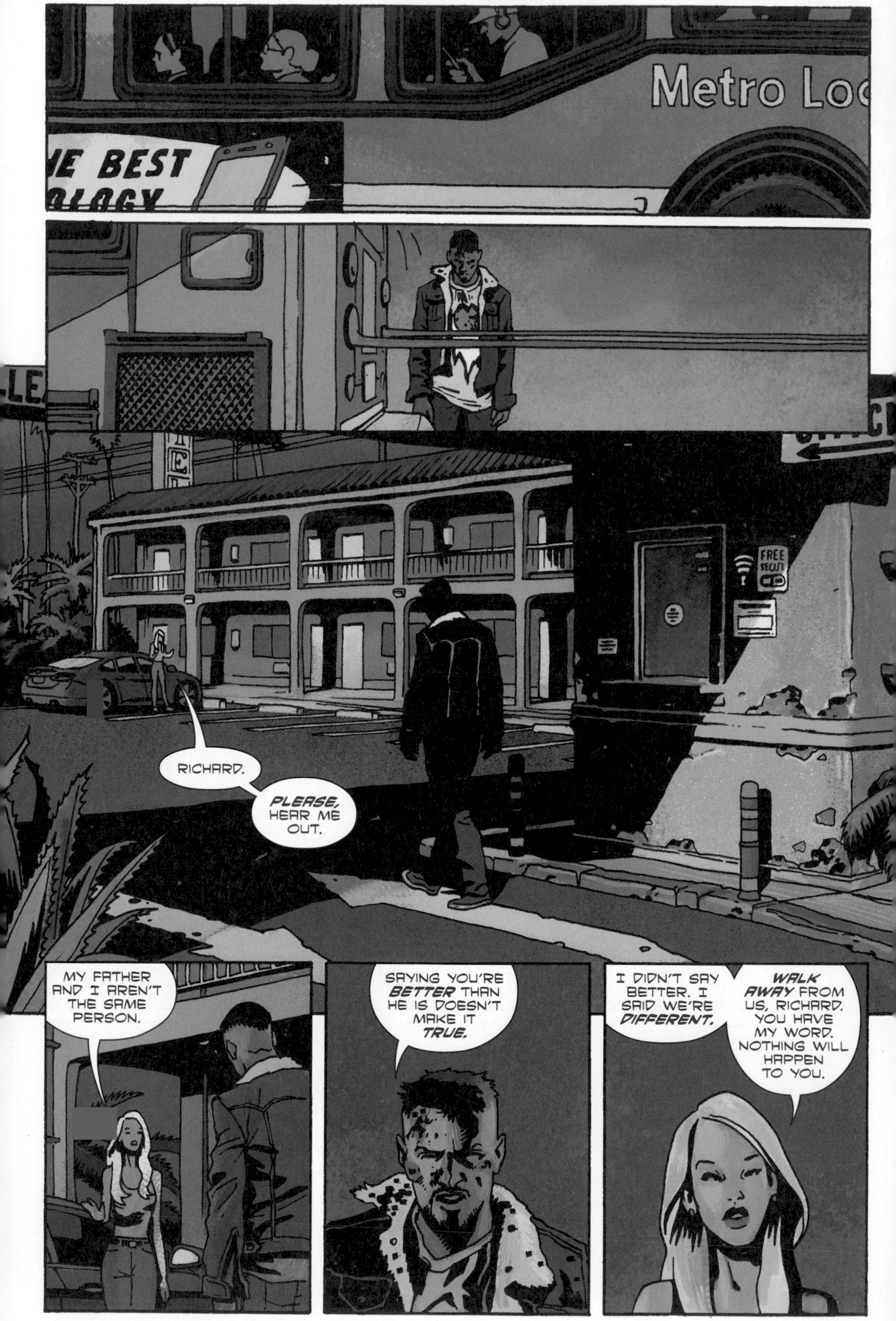
Metro Lo
HE BEST
RICHARD.
PLEASE, HEAR ME OUT.
MY FATHER AND I AREN'T THE SAME PERSON.
SAYING YOU'RE BETTER THAN HE IS DOESN'T MAKE IT TRUE.
I DIDN'T SAY BETTER. I SAID WE'RE DIFFERENT.
WALK AWAY FROM US, RICHARD. YOU HAVE MY WORD. NOTHING WILL HAPPEN TO YOU.

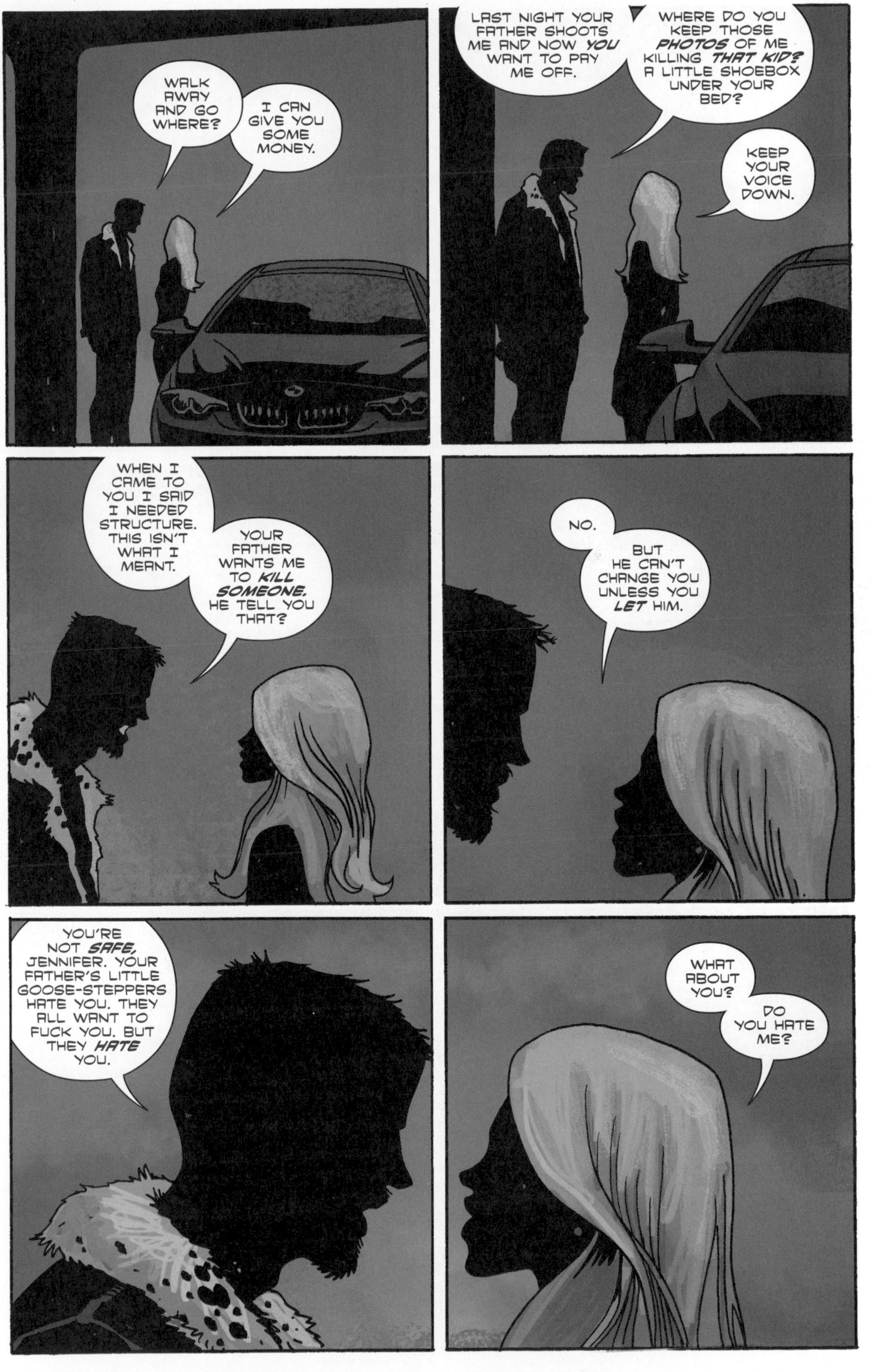
WALK AWAY AND GO WHERE?
I CAN GIVE YOU SOME MONEY.
LAST NIGHT YOUR FATHER SHOOTS ME AND NOW YOU WANT TO PAY ME OFF.
WHERE DO YOU KEEP THOSE PHOTOS OF ME KILLING THAT KID? A LITTLE SHOEBOX UNDER YOUR BED?
KEEP YOUR VOICE DOWN.
WHEN I CAME TO YOU I SAID I NEEDED STRUCTURE. THIS ISN'T WHAT I MEANT.
YOUR FATHER WANTS ME TO KILL SOMEONE. HE TELL YOU THAT?
NO.
BUT HE CAN'T CHANGE YOU UNLESS YOU LET HIM.
YOU'RE NOT SAFE, JENNIFER. YOUR FATHER'S LITTLE GOOSE-STEPPERS HATE YOU. THEY ALL WANT TO FUCK YOU. BUT THEY HATE YOU.
WHAT ABOUT YOU?
DO YOU HATE ME?

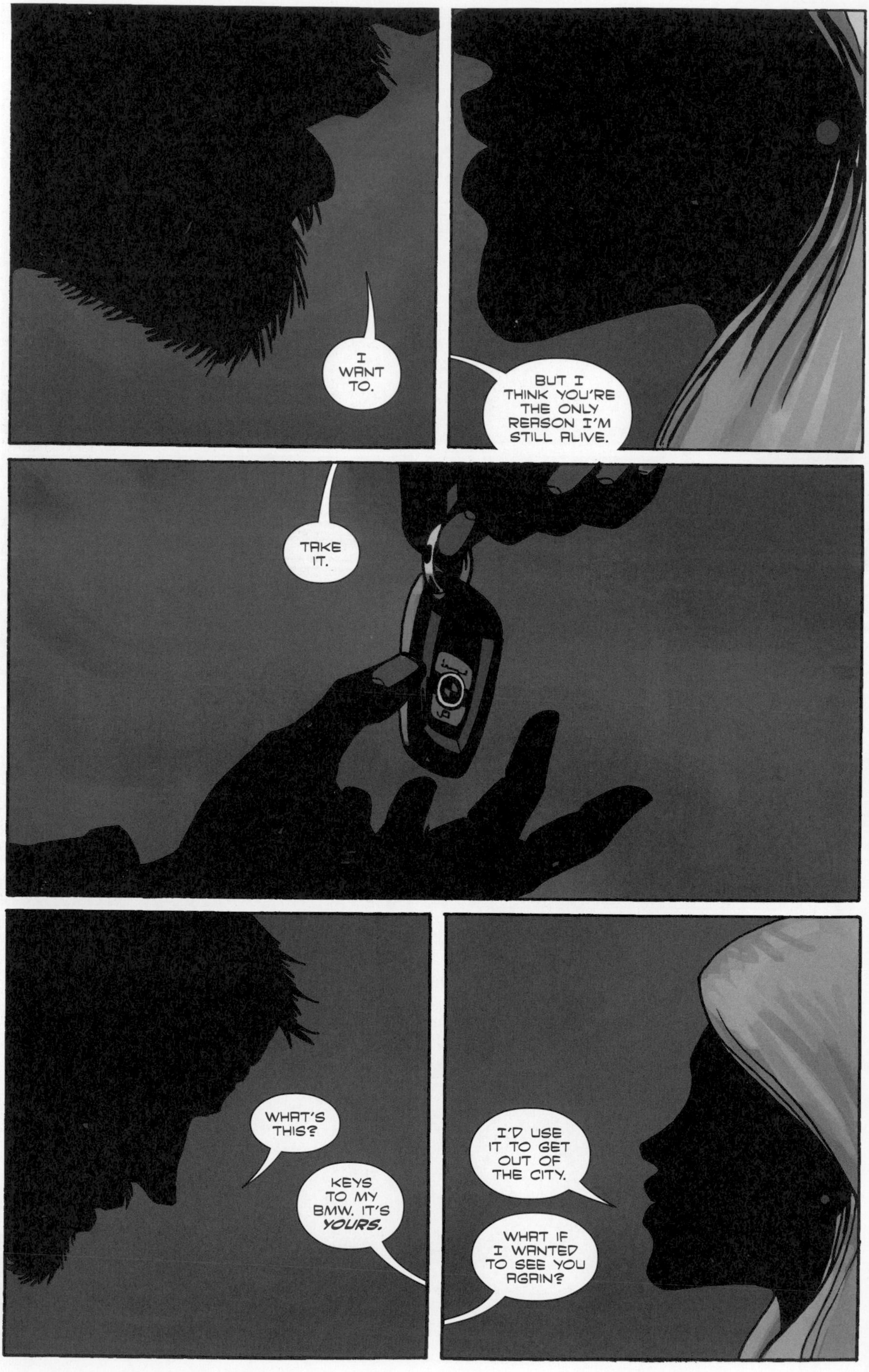
I WANT TO.
BUT I THINK YOU'RE THE ONLY REASON I'M STILL ALIVE.
TAKE IT.
WHAT'S THIS?
KEYS TO MY BMW. IT'S *YOURS.*
I'D USE IT TO GET OUT OF THE CITY.
WHAT IF I WANTED TO SEE YOU AGAIN?

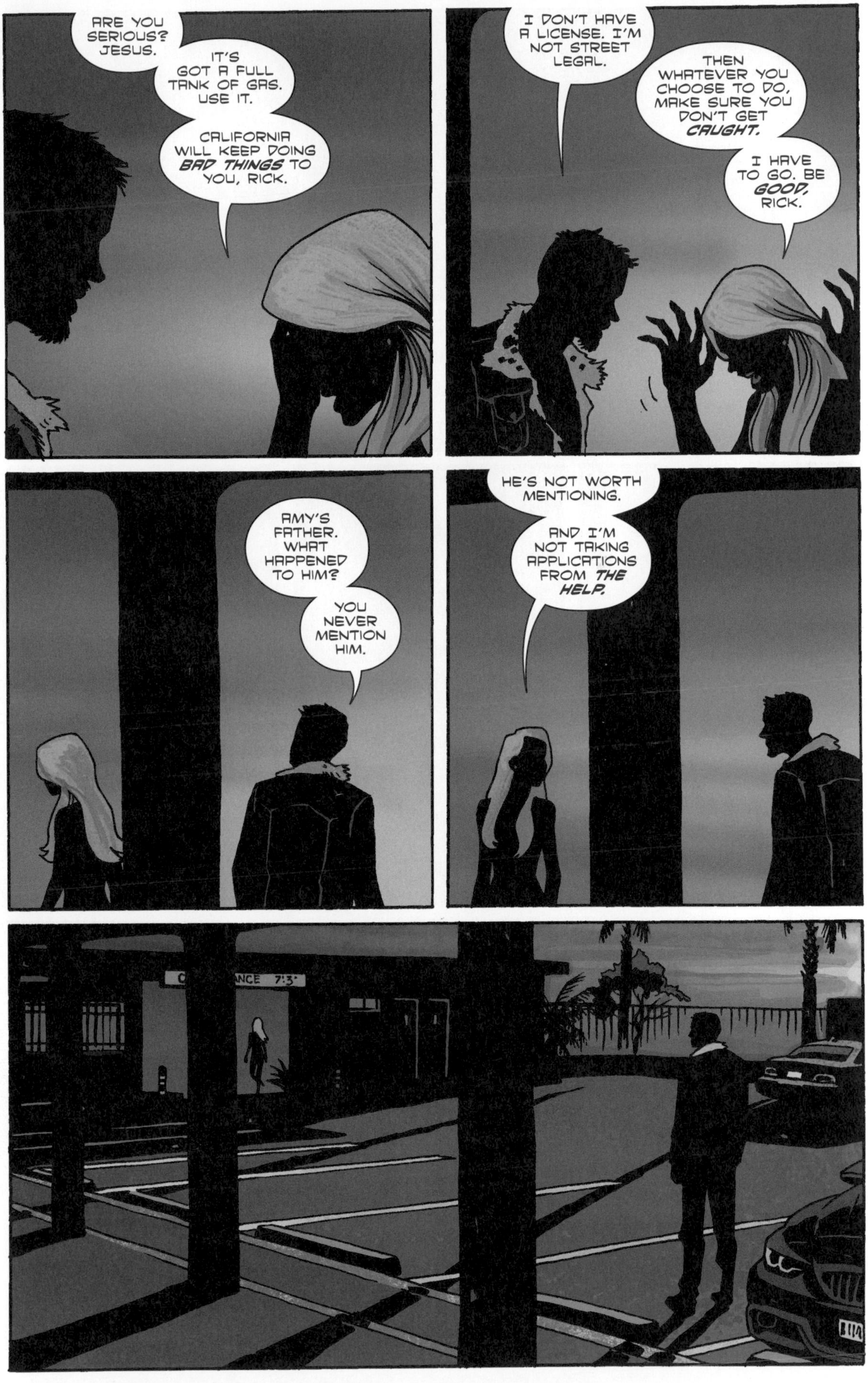
ARE YOU SERIOUS? JESUS.
IT'S GOT A FULL TANK OF GAS. USE IT.
CALIFORNIA WILL KEEP DOING *BAD THINGS* TO YOU, RICK.
I DON'T HAVE A LICENSE. I'M NOT STREET LEGAL.
THEN WHATEVER YOU CHOOSE TO DO, MAKE SURE YOU DON'T GET *CAUGHT.*
I HAVE TO GO. BE *GOOD,* RICK.
AMY'S FATHER. WHAT HAPPENED TO HIM?
YOU NEVER MENTION HIM.
HE'S NOT WORTH MENTIONING.
AND I'M NOT TAKING APPLICATIONS FROM *THE HELP.*

FIND IT *INSIDE*, RICK.

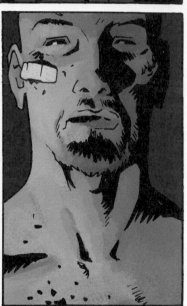

YOU JUST HAVE TO FIND IT.

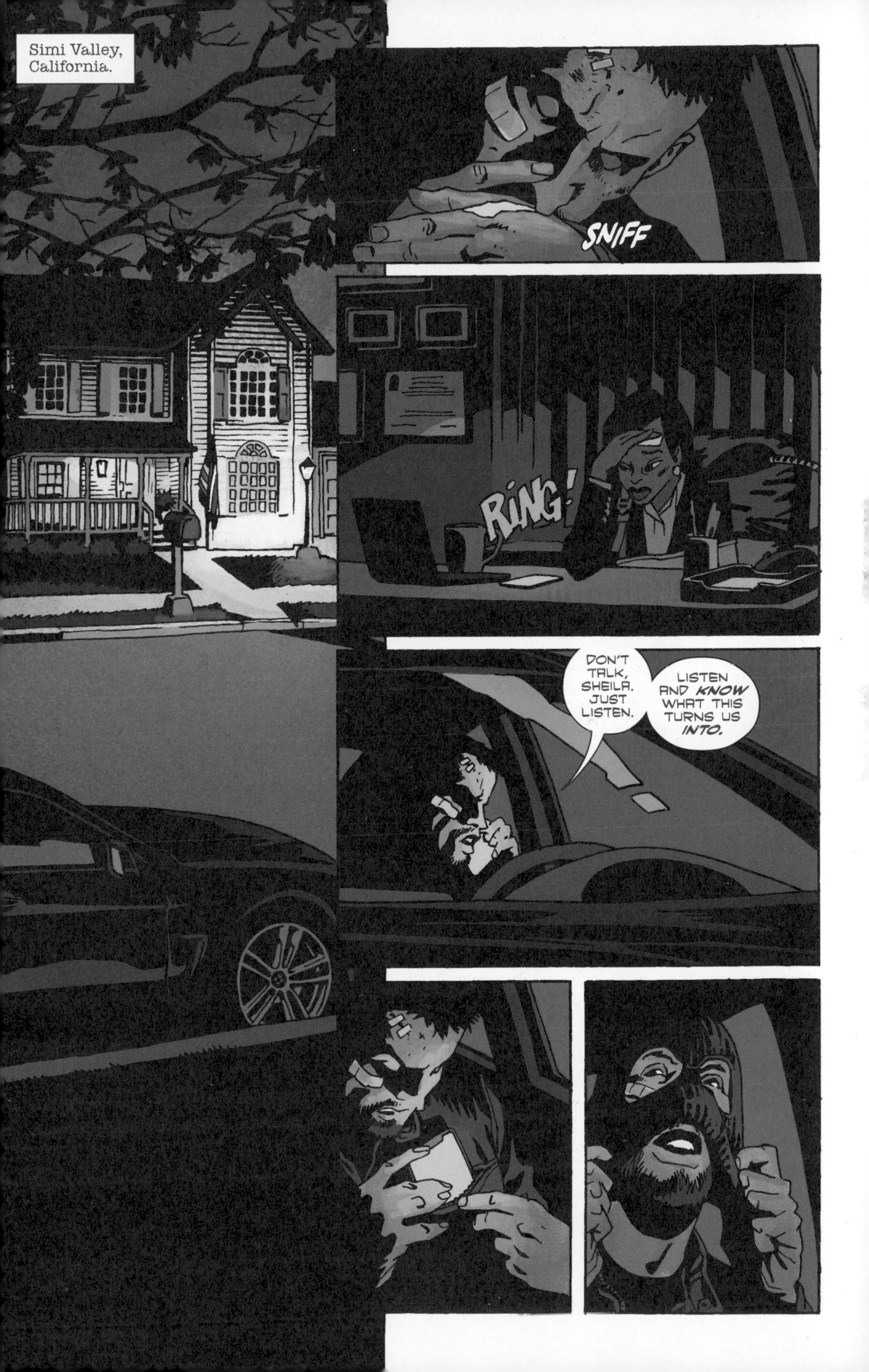
Simi Valley, California.
SNIFF
RING!
DON'T TALK, SHEILA. JUST LISTEN.
LISTEN AND KNOW WHAT THIS TURNS US INTO.

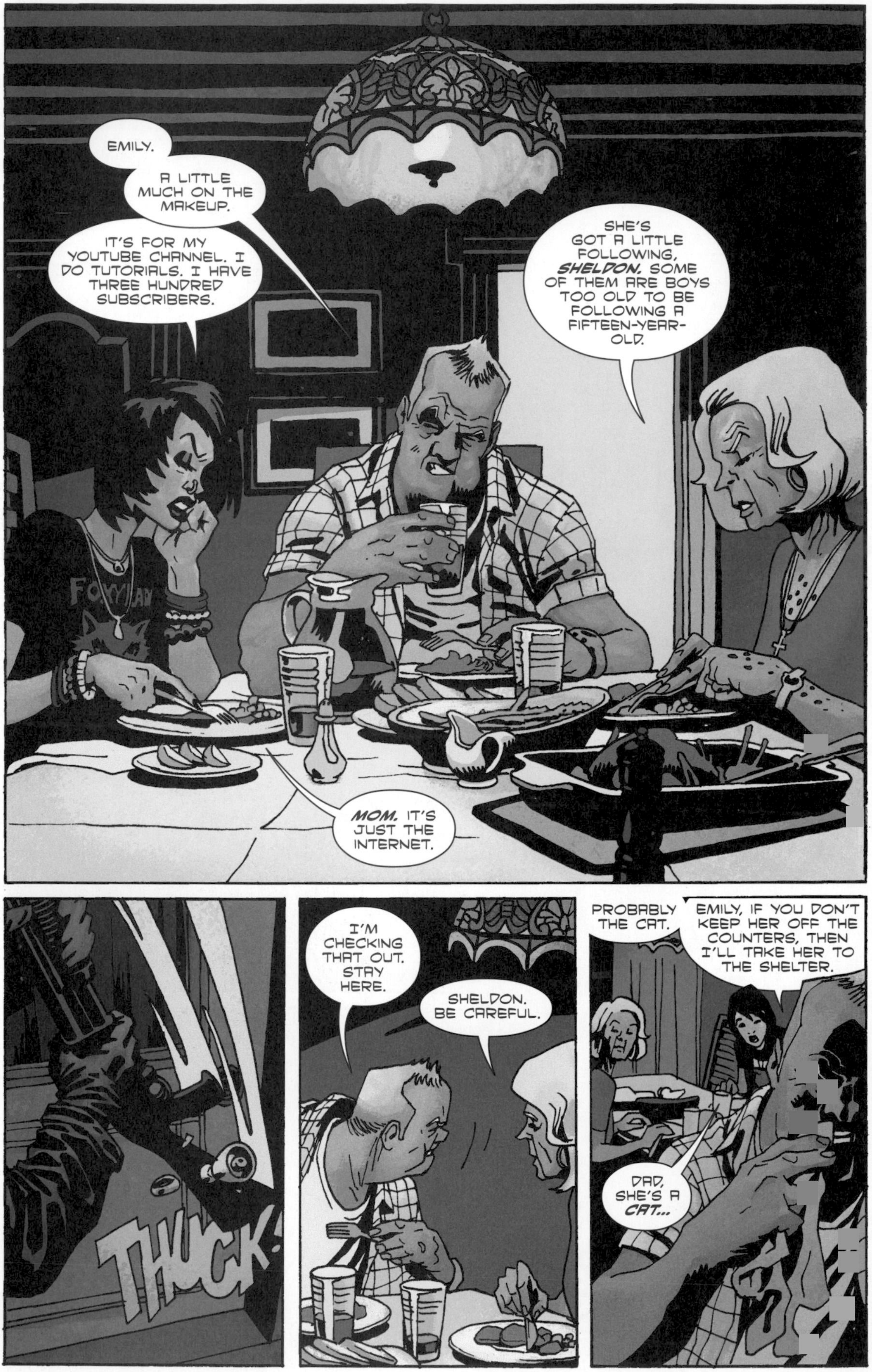
EMILY.
A LITTLE MUCH ON THE MAKEUP.
IT'S FOR MY YOUTUBE CHANNEL. I DO TUTORIALS. I HAVE THREE HUNDRED SUBSCRIBERS.
SHE'S GOT A LITTLE FOLLOWING, SHELDON. SOME OF THEM ARE BOYS TOO OLD TO BE FOLLOWING A FIFTEEN-YEAR-OLD.
MOM. IT'S JUST THE INTERNET.
THUCK!
I'M CHECKING THAT OUT. STAY HERE.
SHELDON. BE CAREFUL.
PROBABLY THE CAT.
EMILY, IF YOU DON'T KEEP HER OFF THE COUNTERS, THEN I'LL TAKE HER TO THE SHELTER.
DAD, SHE'S A CAT...

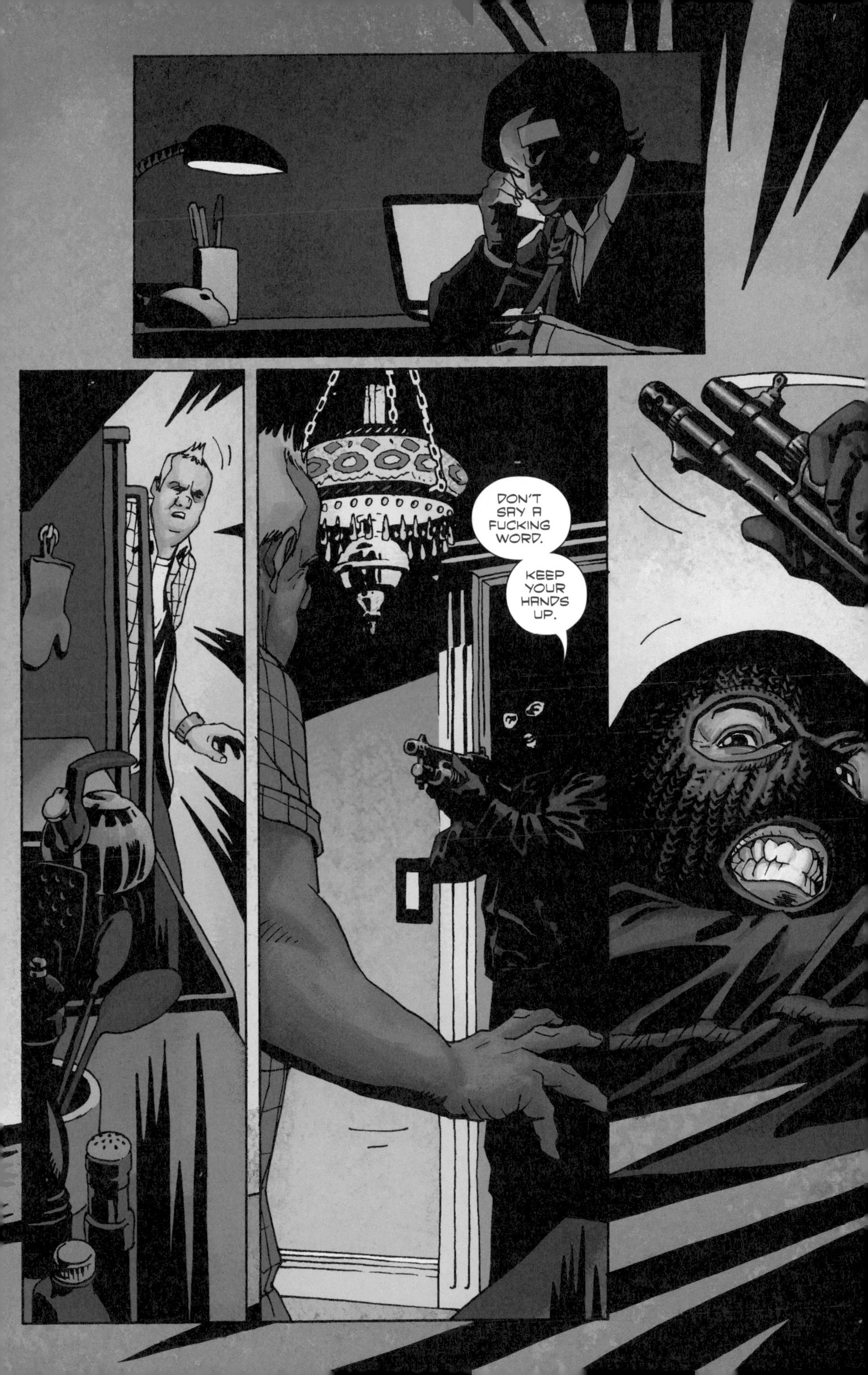
DON'T SAY A FUCKING WORD.
KEEP YOUR HANDS UP.

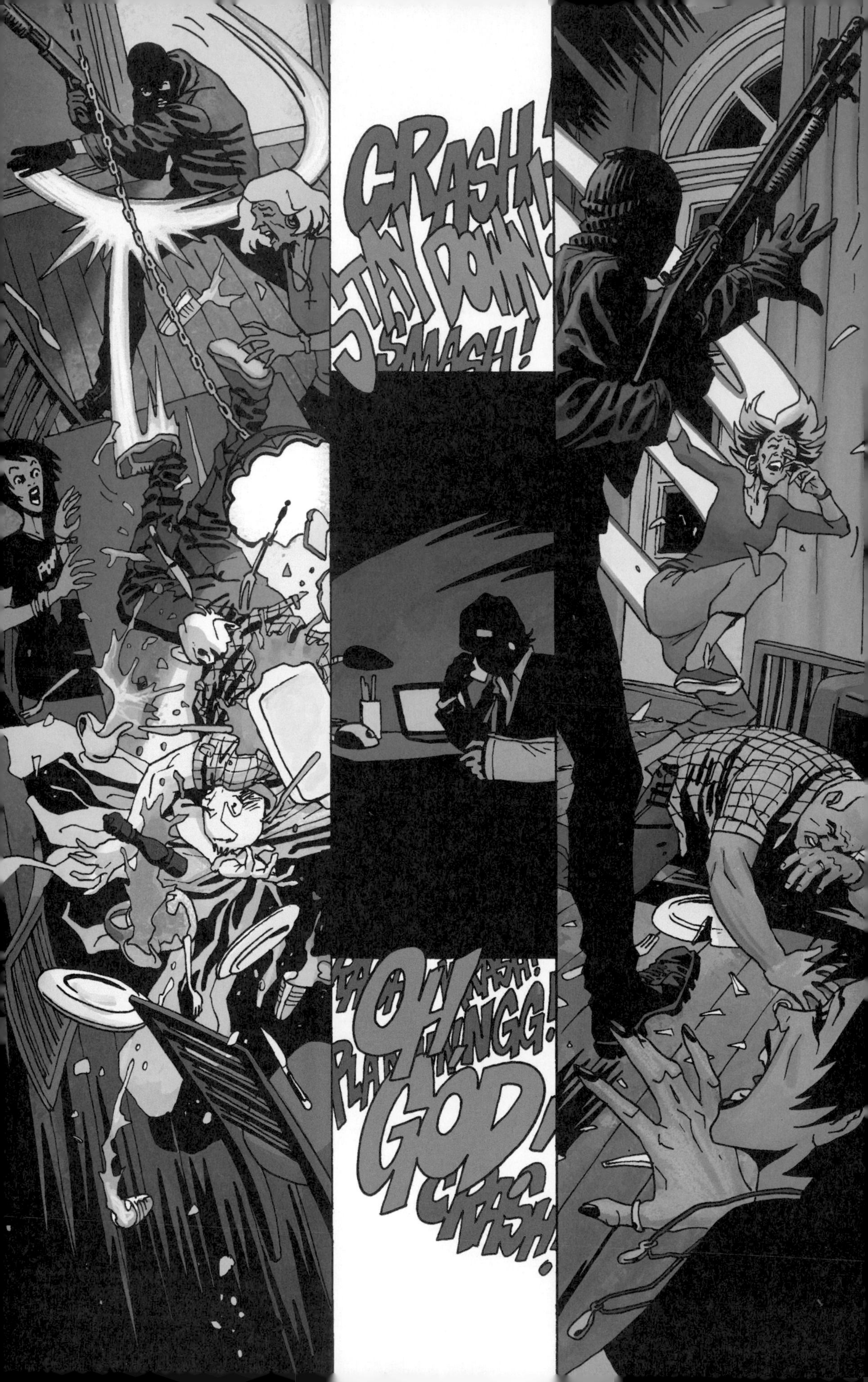
CRASH!
STAY DOWN!
SMASH!
OH GOD!

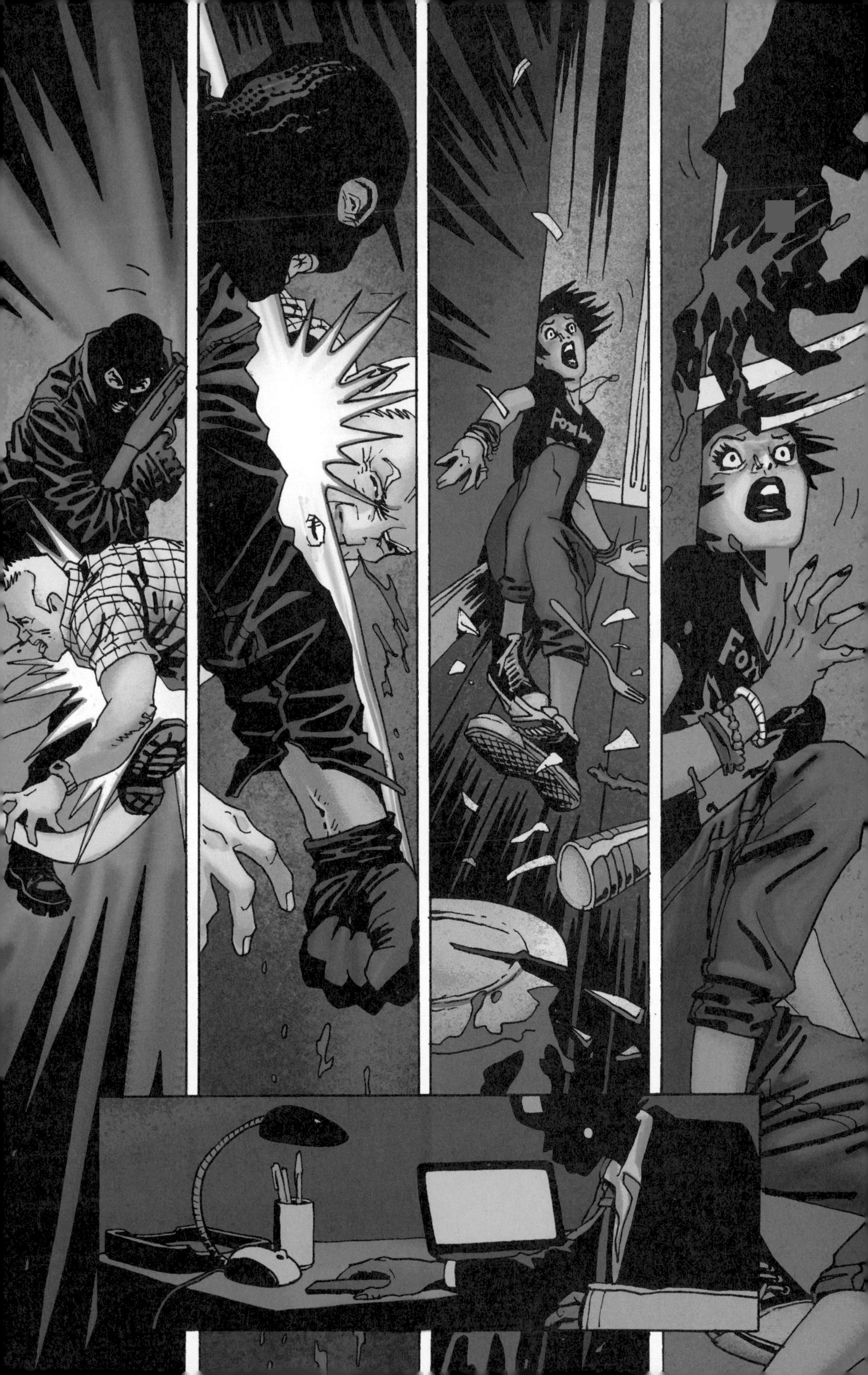

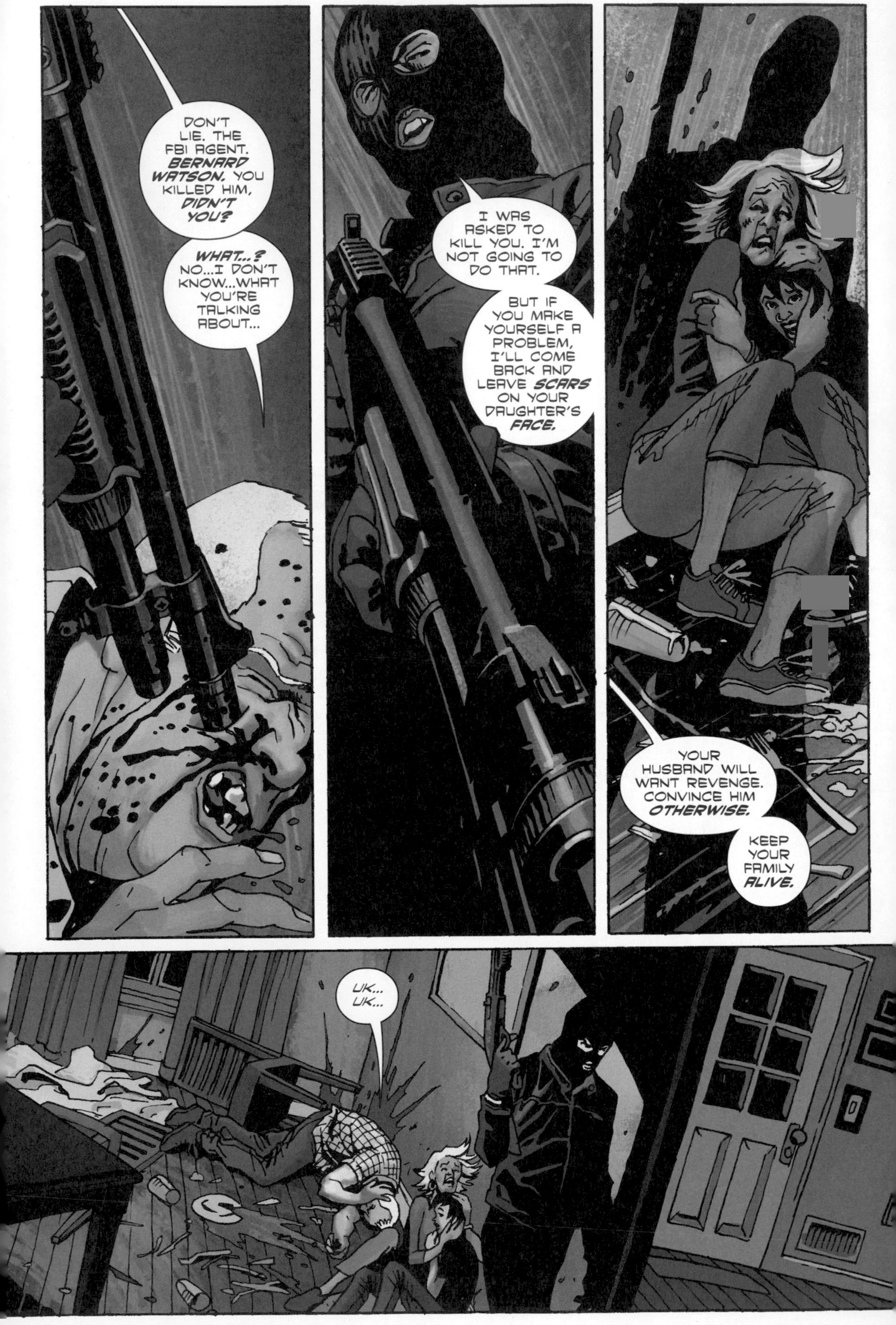
DON'T LIE. THE FBI AGENT. BERNARD WATSON. YOU KILLED HIM, DIDN'T YOU?
WHAT...? NO...I DON'T KNOW...WHAT YOU'RE TALKING ABOUT...
I WAS ASKED TO KILL YOU. I'M NOT GOING TO DO THAT.
BUT IF YOU MAKE YOURSELF A PROBLEM, I'LL COME BACK AND LEAVE SCARS ON YOUR DAUGHTER'S FACE.
YOUR HUSBAND WILL WANT REVENGE. CONVINCE HIM OTHERWISE.
KEEP YOUR FAMILY ALIVE.
UK... UK...

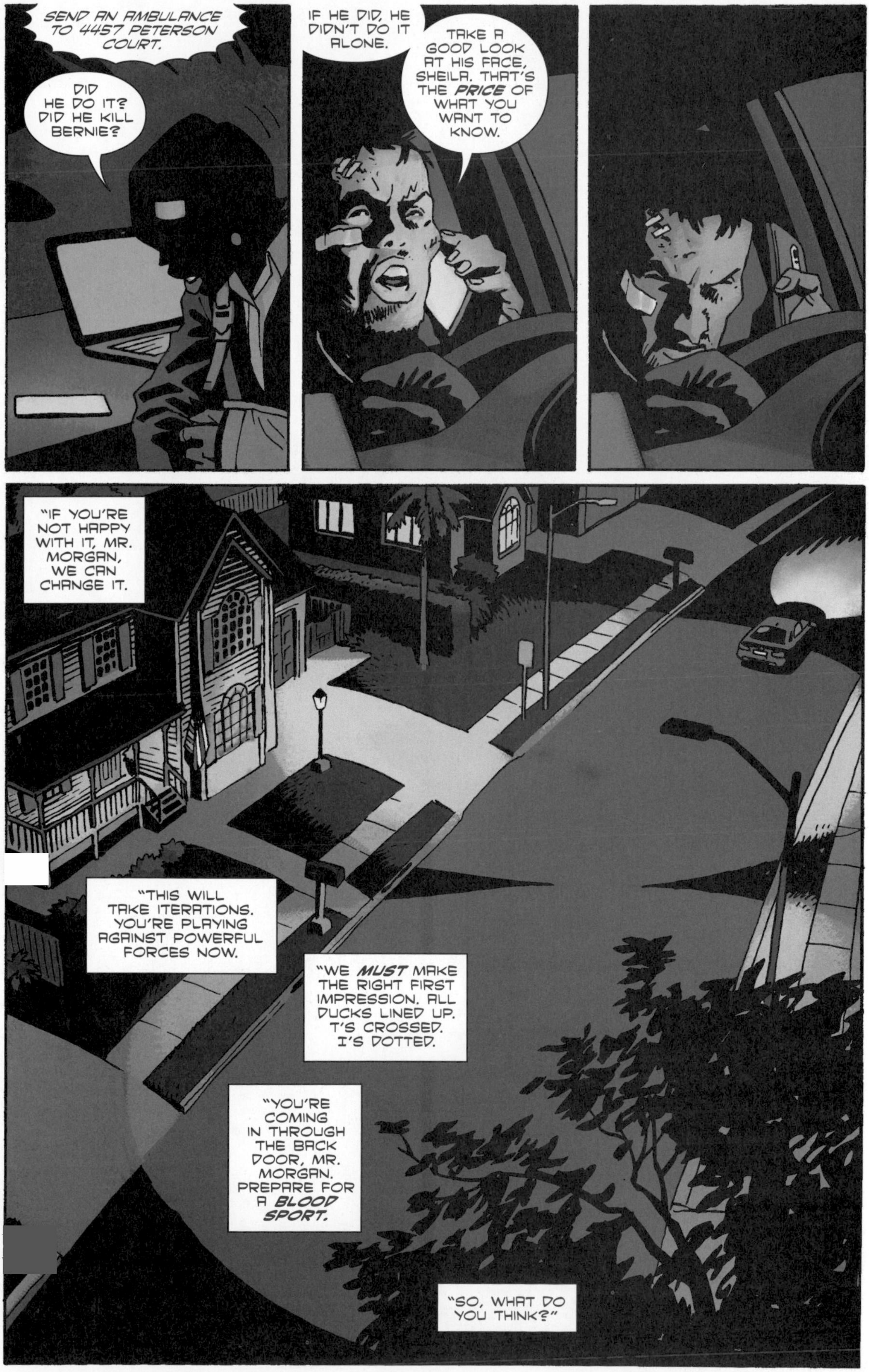
SEND AN AMBULANCE TO 4457 PETERSON COURT.
DID HE DO IT? DID HE KILL BERNIE?
IF HE DID, HE DIDN'T DO IT ALONE.
TAKE A GOOD LOOK AT HIS FACE, SHEILA. THAT'S THE PRICE OF WHAT YOU WANT TO KNOW.
"IF YOU'RE NOT HAPPY WITH IT, MR. MORGAN, WE CAN CHANGE IT.
"THIS WILL TAKE ITERATIONS. YOU'RE PLAYING AGAINST POWERFUL FORCES NOW.
"WE MUST MAKE THE RIGHT FIRST IMPRESSION. ALL DUCKS LINED UP. T'S CROSSED. I'S DOTTED.
"YOU'RE COMING IN THROUGH THE BACK DOOR, MR. MORGAN. PREPARE FOR A BLOOD SPORT.
"SO, WHAT DO YOU THINK?"

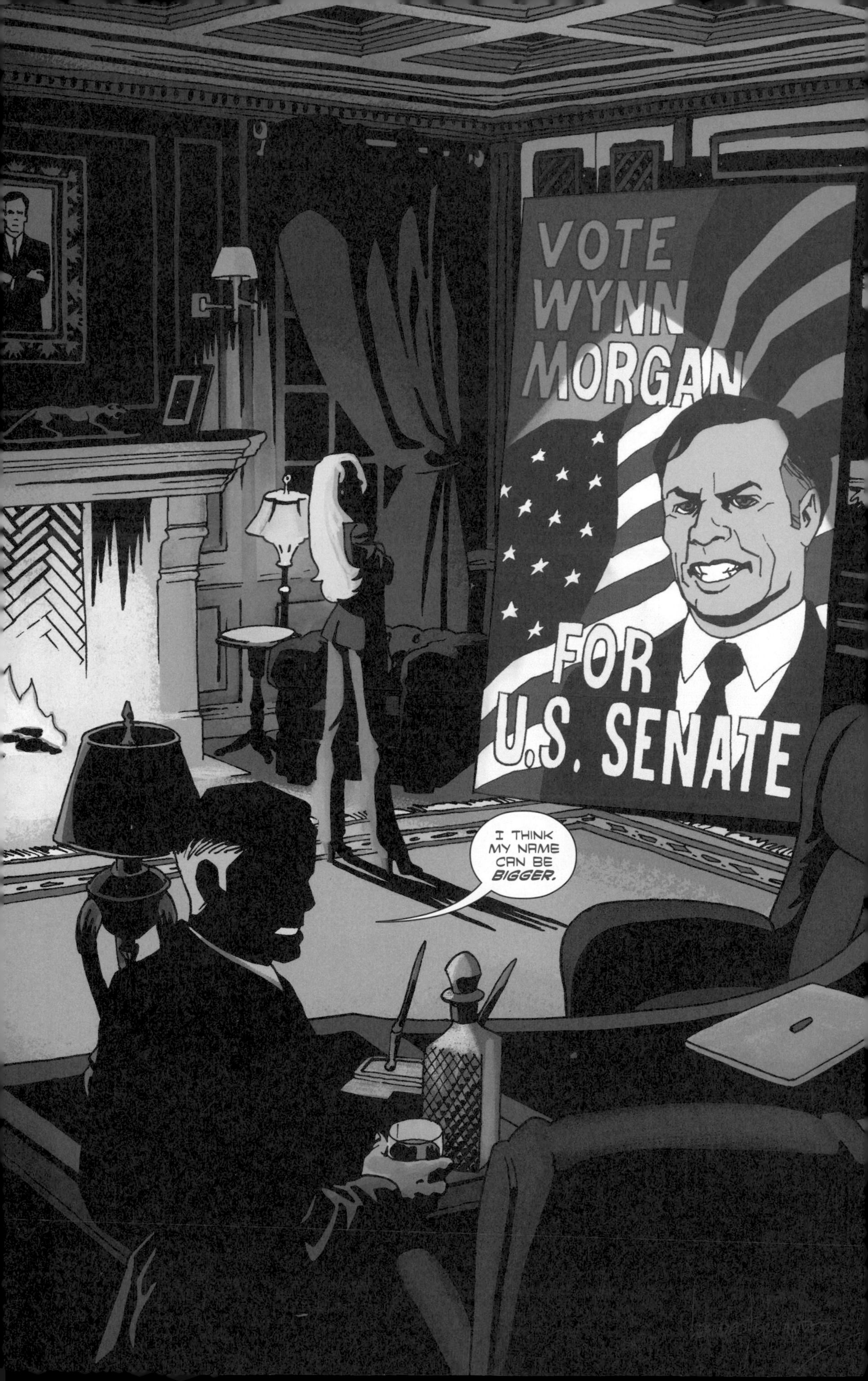
VOTE WYNN MORGAN FOR U.S. SENATE
I THINK MY NAME CAN BE *BIGGER.*

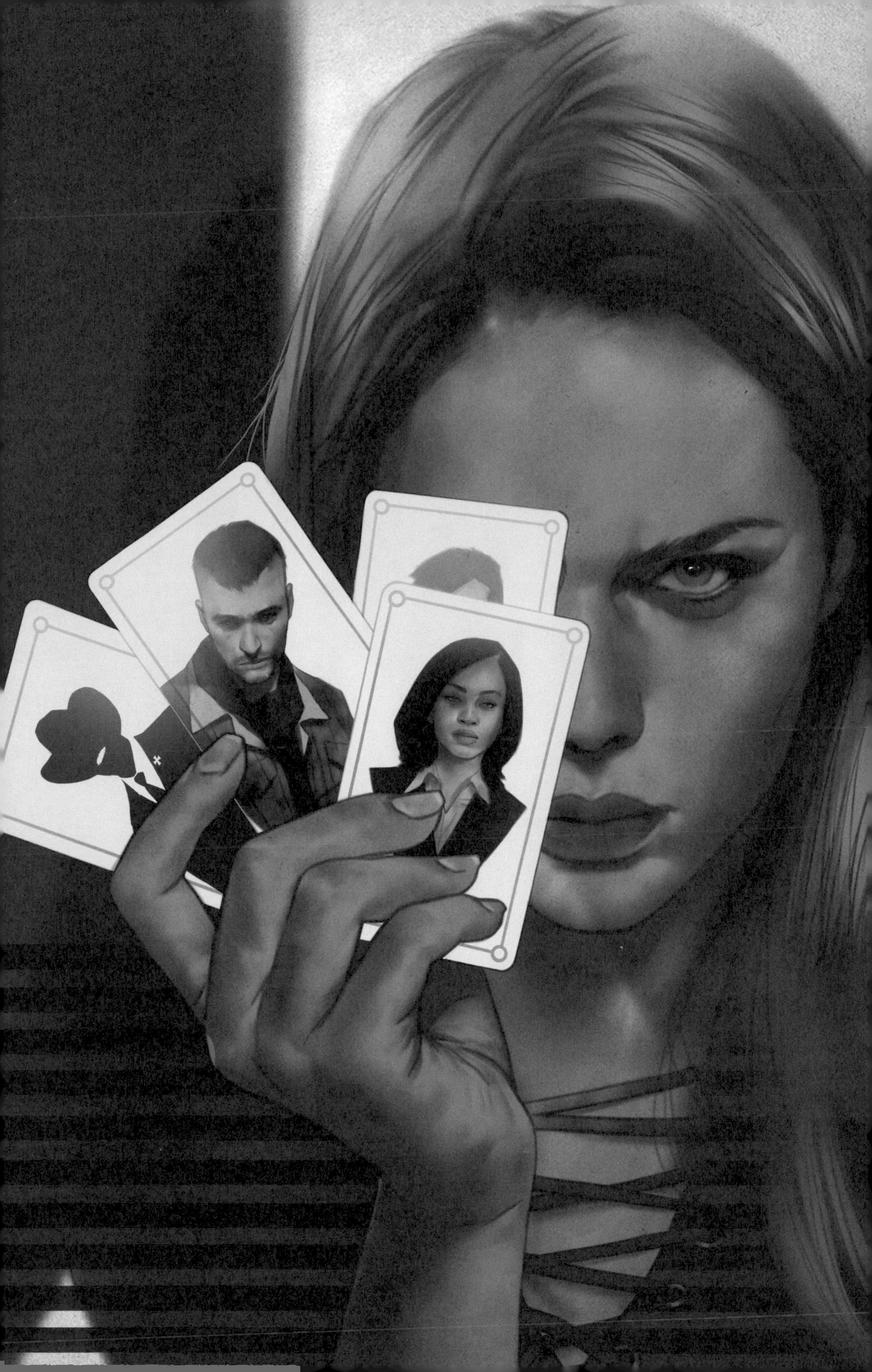

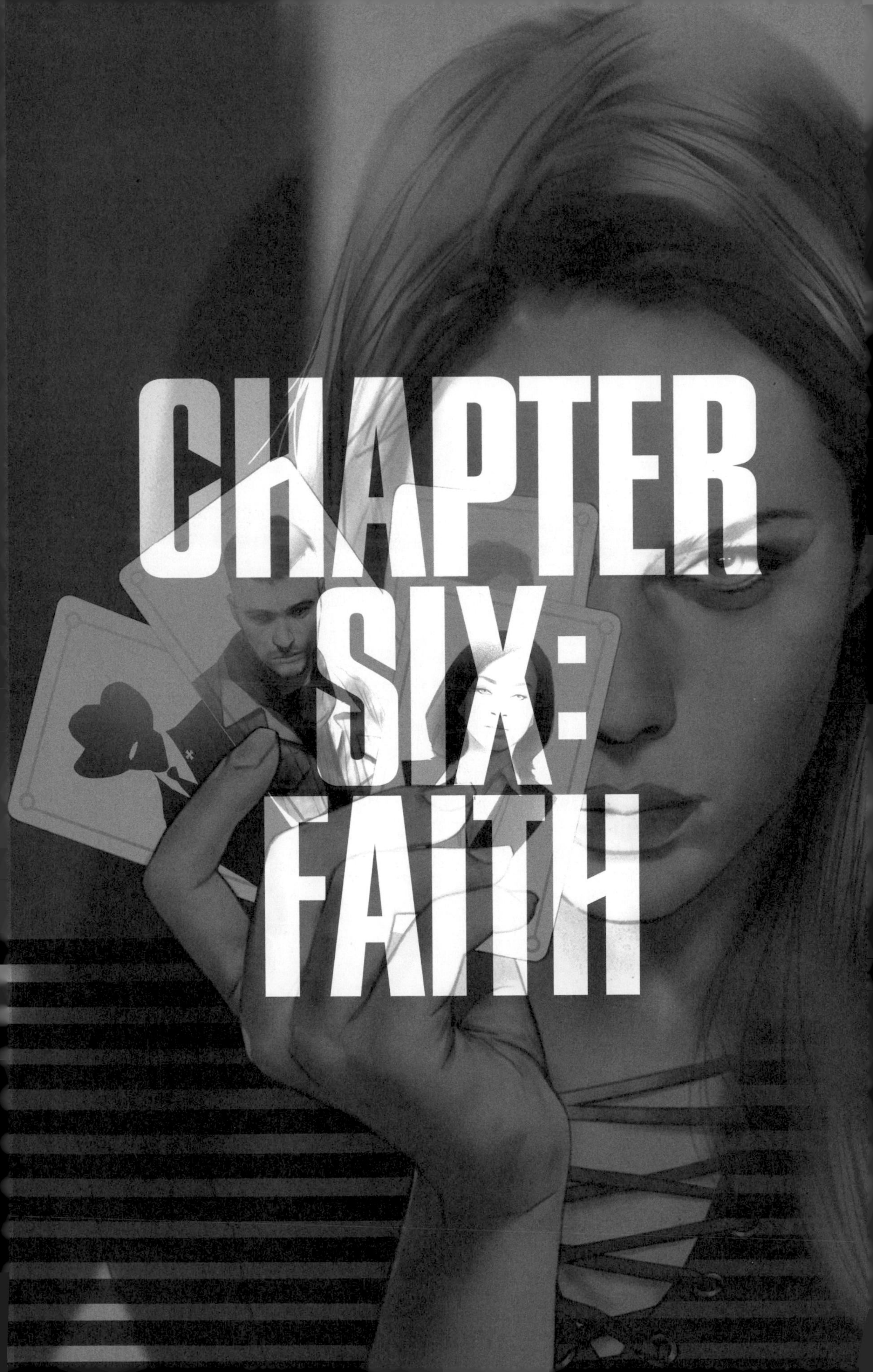
CHAPTER
SIX:
FAITH

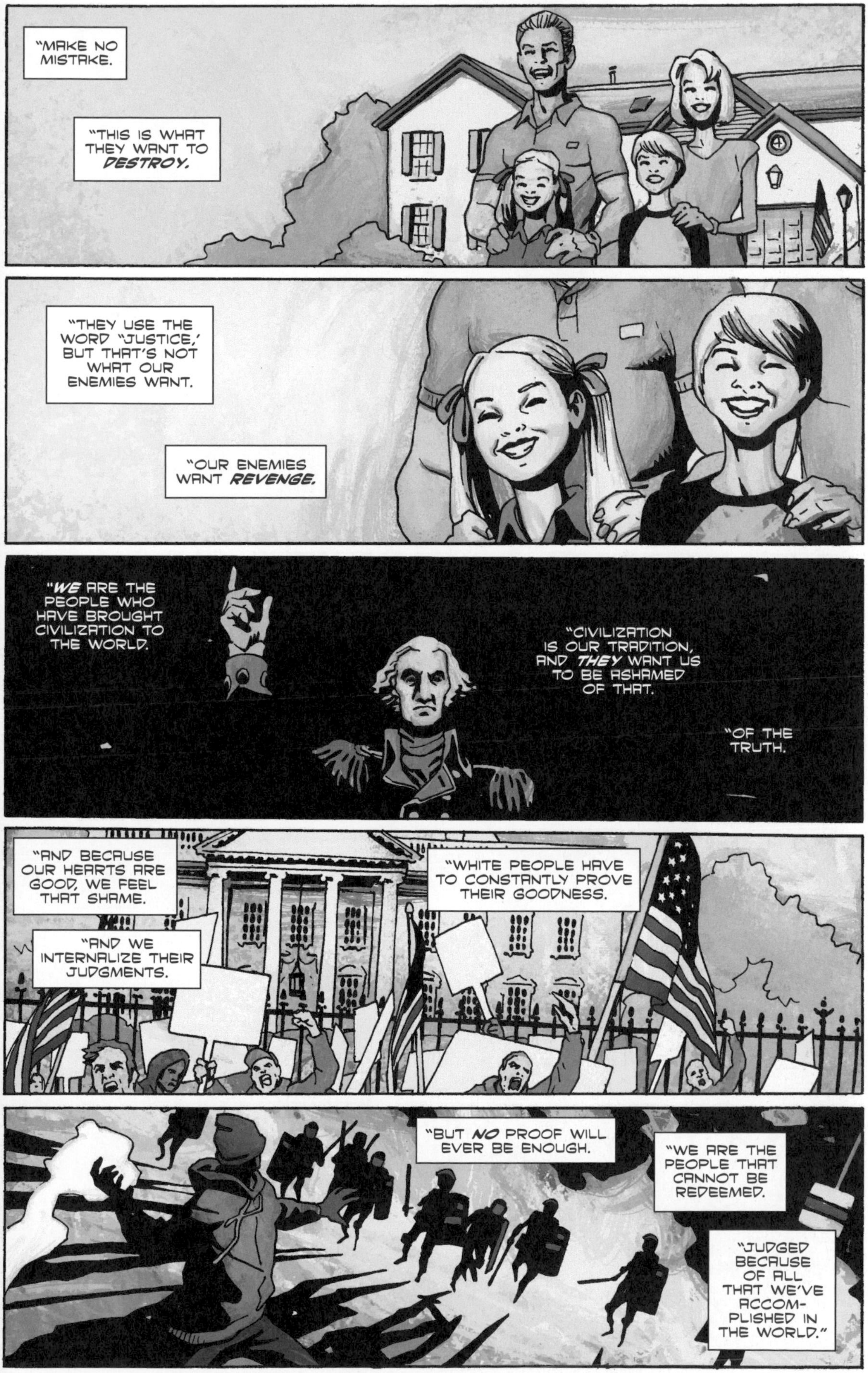
"MAKE NO MISTAKE.
"THIS IS WHAT THEY WANT TO *DESTROY.*
"THEY USE THE WORD 'JUSTICE,' BUT THAT'S NOT WHAT OUR ENEMIES WANT.
"OUR ENEMIES WANT *REVENGE.*
"*WE* ARE THE PEOPLE WHO HAVE BROUGHT CIVILIZATION TO THE WORLD.
"CIVILIZATION IS OUR TRADITION, AND *THEY* WANT US TO BE ASHAMED OF THAT.
"OF THE TRUTH.
"AND BECAUSE OUR HEARTS ARE GOOD, WE FEEL THAT SHAME.
"AND WE INTERNALIZE THEIR JUDGMENTS.
"WHITE PEOPLE HAVE TO CONSTANTLY PROVE THEIR GOODNESS.
"BUT *NO* PROOF WILL EVER BE ENOUGH.
"WE ARE THE PEOPLE THAT CANNOT BE REDEEMED.
"JUDGED BECAUSE OF ALL THAT WE'VE ACCOM-PLISHED IN THE WORLD."

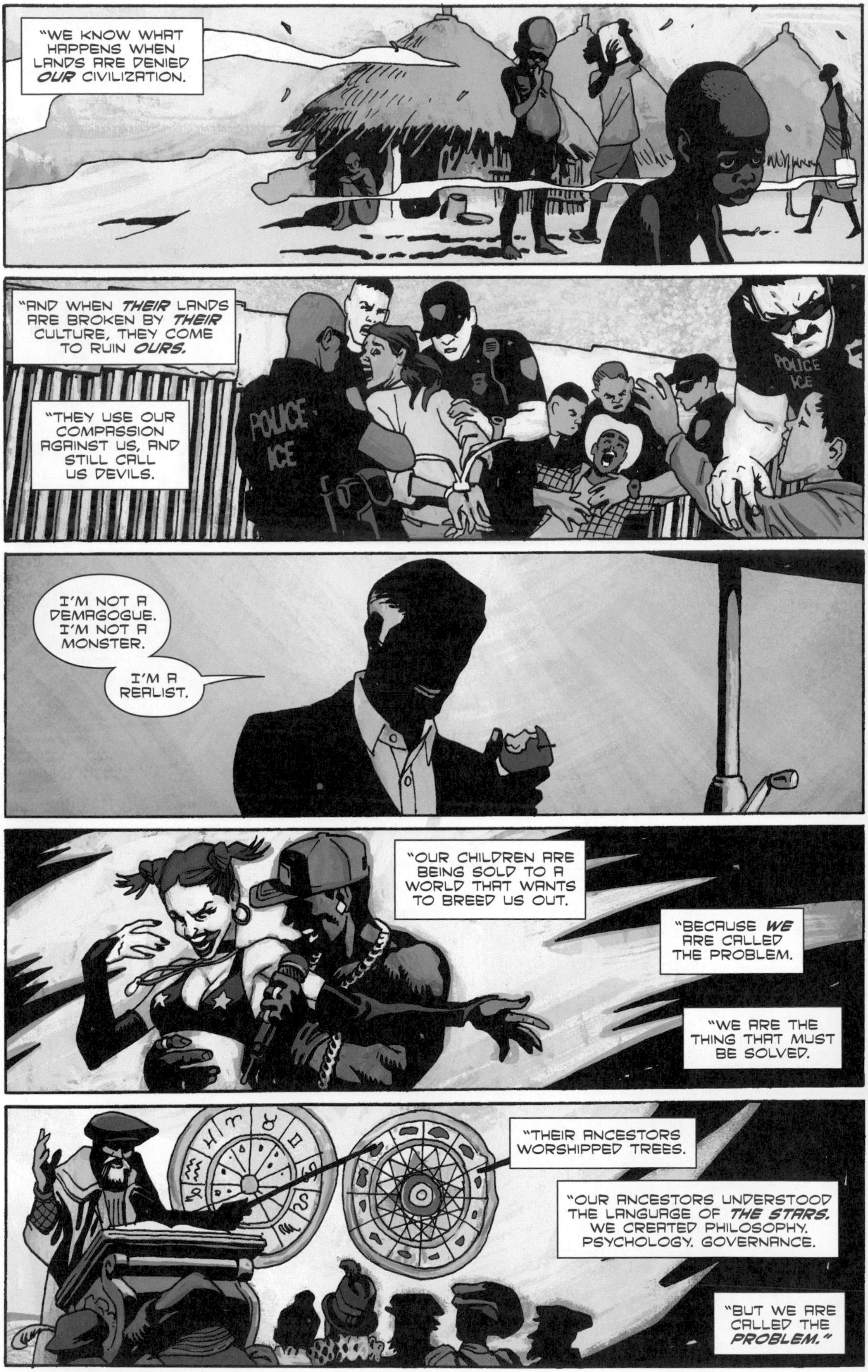
"WE KNOW WHAT HAPPENS WHEN LANDS ARE DENIED OUR CIVILIZATION.
"AND WHEN THEIR LANDS ARE BROKEN BY THEIR CULTURE, THEY COME TO RUIN OURS.
"THEY USE OUR COMPASSION AGAINST US, AND STILL CALL US DEVILS.
POLICE ICE
POLICE ICE
I'M NOT A DEMAGOGUE. I'M NOT A MONSTER.
I'M A REALIST.
"OUR CHILDREN ARE BEING SOLD TO A WORLD THAT WANTS TO BREED US OUT.
"BECAUSE WE ARE CALLED THE PROBLEM.
"WE ARE THE THING THAT MUST BE SOLVED.
"THEIR ANCESTORS WORSHIPPED TREES.
"OUR ANCESTORS UNDERSTOOD THE LANGUAGE OF THE STARS. WE CREATED PHILOSOPHY. PSYCHOLOGY. GOVERNANCE.
"BUT WE ARE CALLED THE PROBLEM."

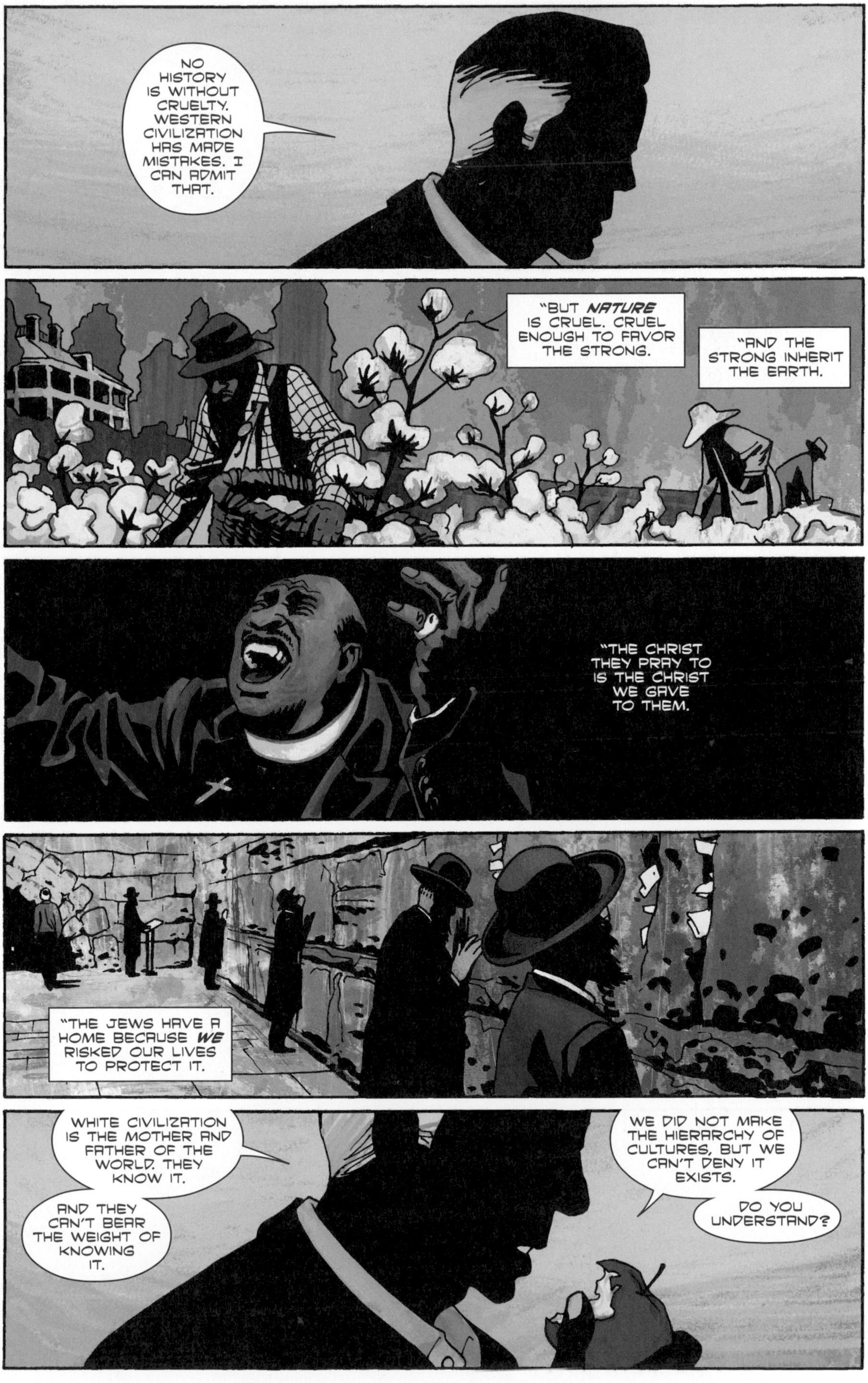
NO HISTORY IS WITHOUT CRUELTY. WESTERN CIVILIZATION HAS MADE MISTAKES. I CAN ADMIT THAT.
"BUT NATURE IS CRUEL. CRUEL ENOUGH TO FAVOR THE STRONG.
"AND THE STRONG INHERIT THE EARTH.
"THE CHRIST THEY PRAY TO IS THE CHRIST WE GAVE TO THEM.
"THE JEWS HAVE A HOME BECAUSE WE RISKED OUR LIVES TO PROTECT IT.
WHITE CIVILIZATION IS THE MOTHER AND FATHER OF THE WORLD. THEY KNOW IT.
AND THEY CAN'T BEAR THE WEIGHT OF KNOWING IT.
WE DID NOT MAKE THE HIERARCHY OF CULTURES, BUT WE CAN'T DENY IT EXISTS.
DO YOU UNDERSTAND?

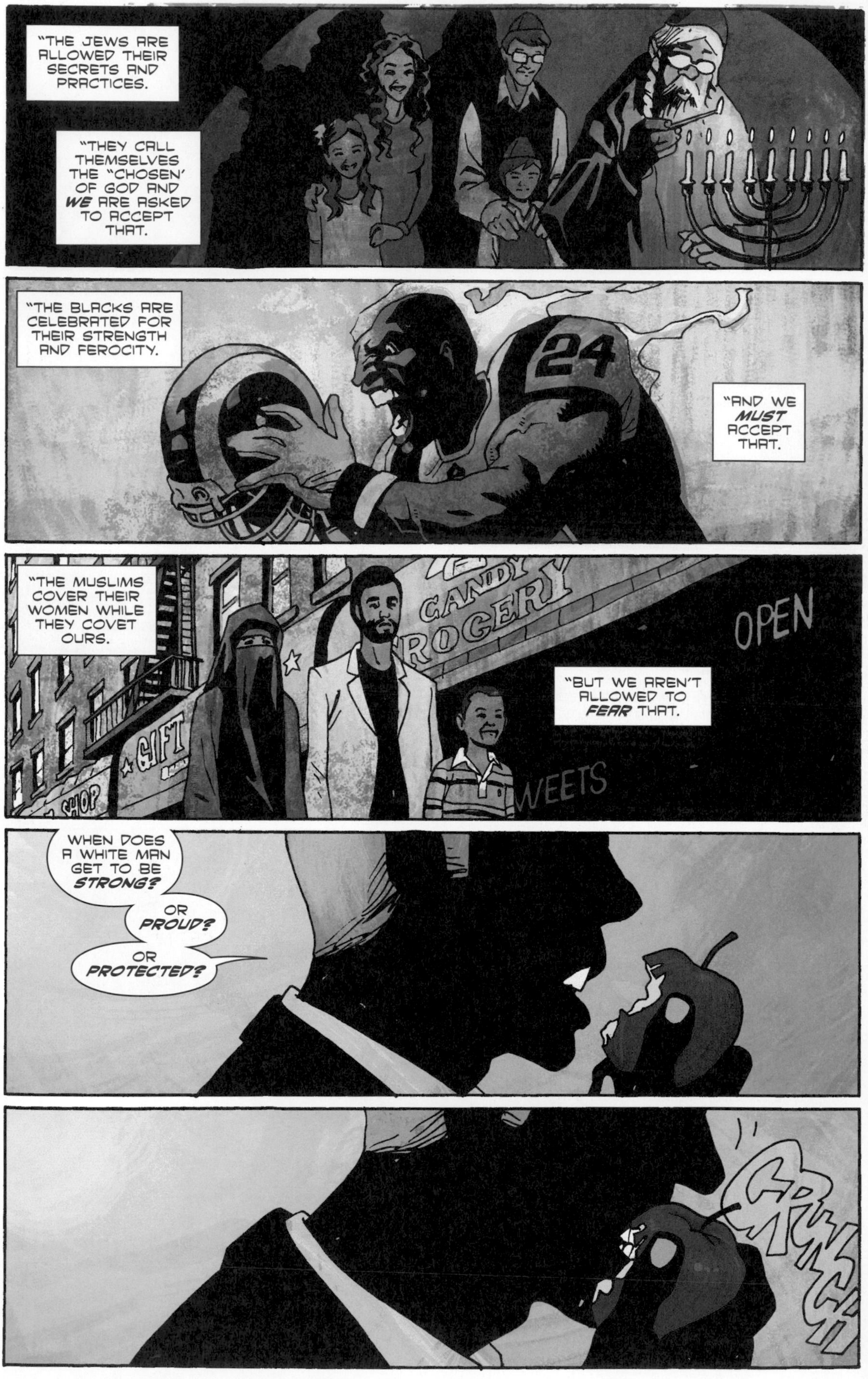
"THE JEWS ARE ALLOWED THEIR SECRETS AND PRACTICES.
"THEY CALL THEMSELVES THE "CHOSEN' OF GOD AND *WE* ARE ASKED TO ACCEPT THAT.
"THE BLACKS ARE CELEBRATED FOR THEIR STRENGTH AND FEROCITY.
24
"AND WE *MUST* ACCEPT THAT.
"THE MUSLIMS COVER THEIR WOMEN WHILE THEY COVET OURS.
CANDY
OPEN
"BUT WE AREN'T ALLOWED TO *FEAR* THAT.
WHEN DOES A WHITE MAN GET TO BE *STRONG?*
OR *PROUD?*
OR *PROTECTED?*
CRUNCH

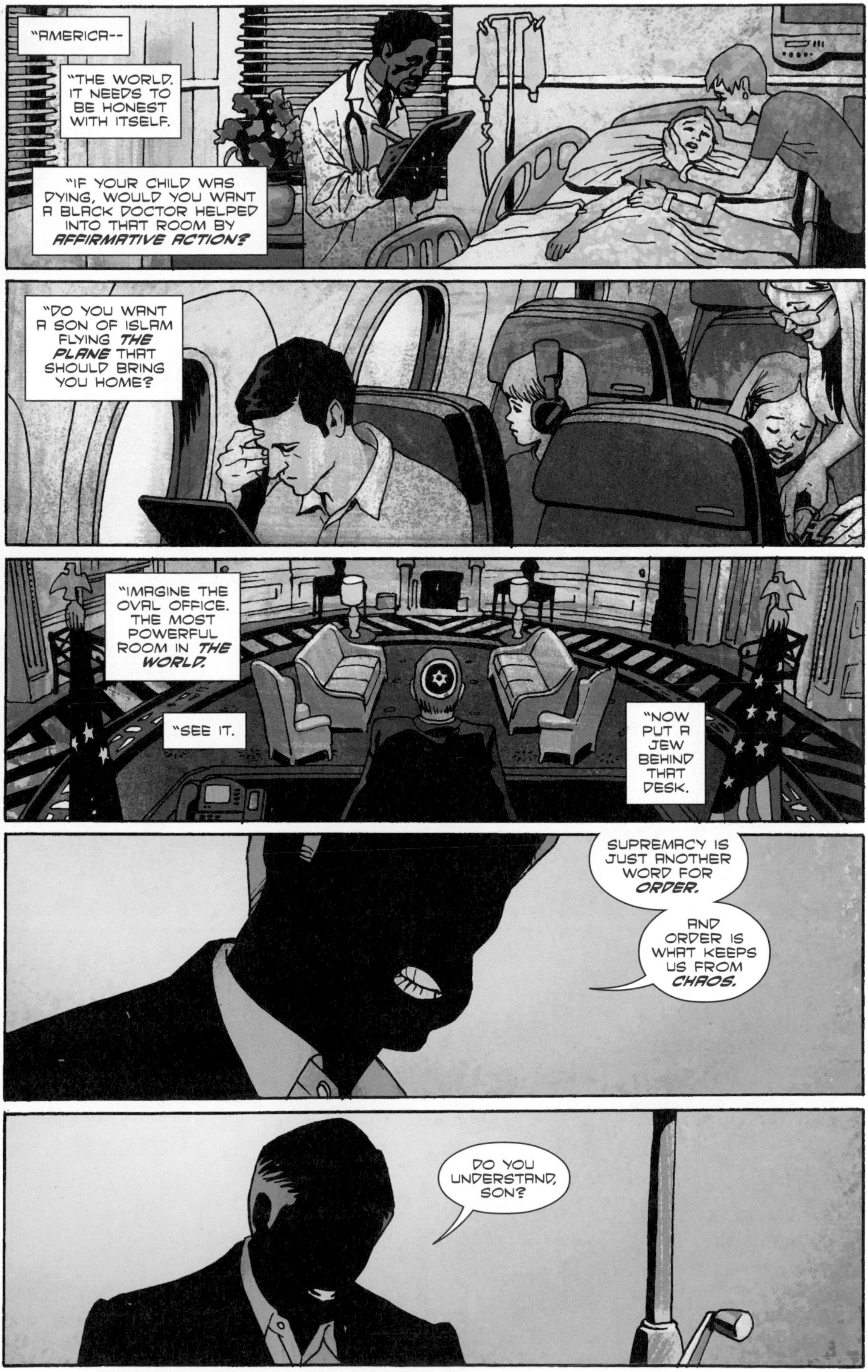
"AMERICA--
"THE WORLD. IT NEEDS TO BE HONEST WITH ITSELF.
"IF YOUR CHILD WAS DYING, WOULD YOU WANT A BLACK DOCTOR HELPED INTO THAT ROOM BY *AFFIRMATIVE ACTION?*
"DO YOU WANT A SON OF ISLAM FLYING *THE PLANE* THAT SHOULD BRING YOU HOME?
"IMAGINE THE OVAL OFFICE. THE MOST POWERFUL ROOM IN *THE WORLD.*
"SEE IT.
"NOW PUT A JEW BEHIND THAT DESK.
SUPREMACY IS JUST ANOTHER WORD FOR *ORDER.*
AND ORDER IS WHAT KEEPS US FROM *CHAOS.*
DO YOU UNDERSTAND, SON?

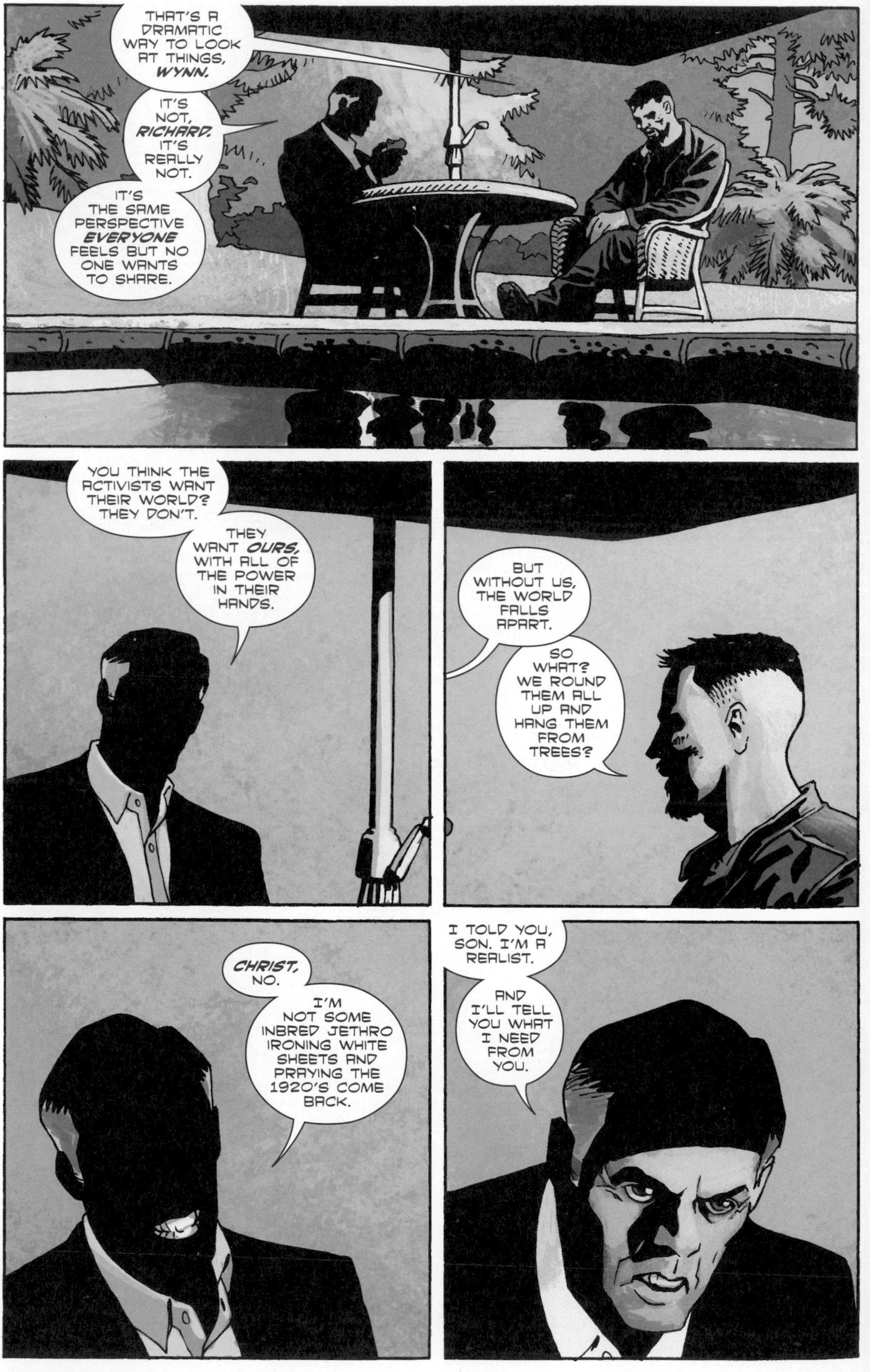
THAT'S A DRAMATIC WAY TO LOOK AT THINGS, WYNN.
IT'S NOT, RICHARD. IT'S REALLY NOT.
IT'S THE SAME PERSPECTIVE EVERYONE FEELS BUT NO ONE WANTS TO SHARE.
YOU THINK THE ACTIVISTS WANT THEIR WORLD? THEY DON'T.
THEY WANT OURS, WITH ALL OF THE POWER IN THEIR HANDS.
BUT WITHOUT US, THE WORLD FALLS APART.
SO WHAT? WE ROUND THEM ALL UP AND HANG THEM FROM TREES?
CHRIST, NO.
I'M NOT SOME INBRED JETHRO IRONING WHITE SHEETS AND PRAYING THE 1920'S COME BACK.
I TOLD YOU, SON. I'M A REALIST.
AND I'LL TELL YOU WHAT I NEED FROM YOU.

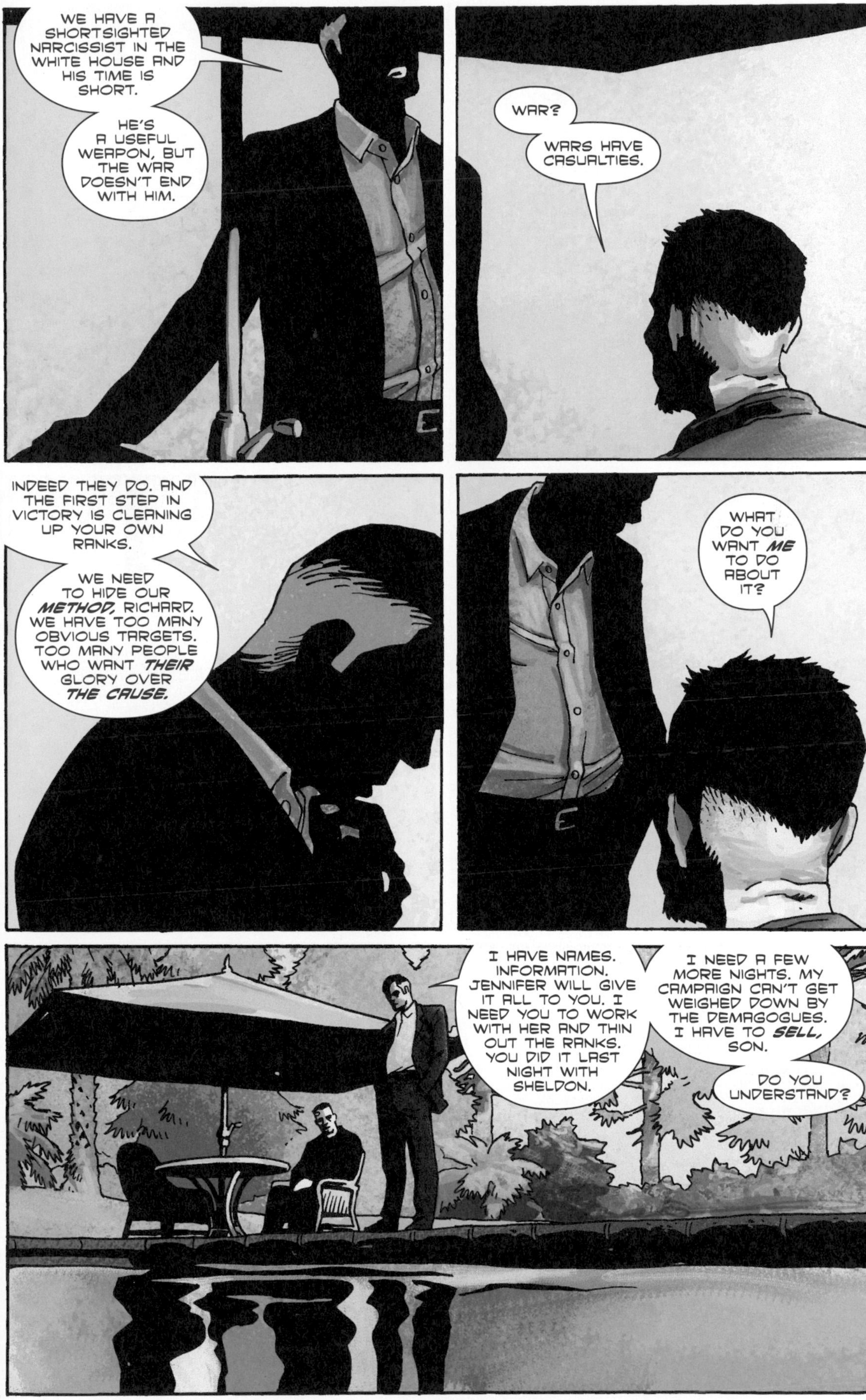
WE HAVE A SHORTSIGHTED NARCISSIST IN THE WHITE HOUSE AND HIS TIME IS SHORT.
HE'S A USEFUL WEAPON, BUT THE WAR DOESN'T END WITH HIM.
WAR?
WARS HAVE CASUALTIES.
INDEED THEY DO. AND THE FIRST STEP IN VICTORY IS CLEANING UP YOUR OWN RANKS.
WE NEED TO HIDE OUR *METHOD,* RICHARD. WE HAVE TOO MANY OBVIOUS TARGETS. TOO MANY PEOPLE WHO WANT *THEIR* GLORY OVER *THE CAUSE.*
WHAT DO YOU WANT *ME* TO DO ABOUT IT?
I HAVE NAMES. INFORMATION. JENNIFER WILL GIVE IT ALL TO YOU. I NEED YOU TO WORK WITH HER AND THIN OUT THE RANKS. YOU DID IT LAST NIGHT WITH SHELDON.
I NEED A FEW MORE NIGHTS. MY CAMPAIGN CAN'T GET WEIGHED DOWN BY THE DEMAGOGUES. I HAVE TO *SELL,* SON.
DO YOU UNDERSTAND?

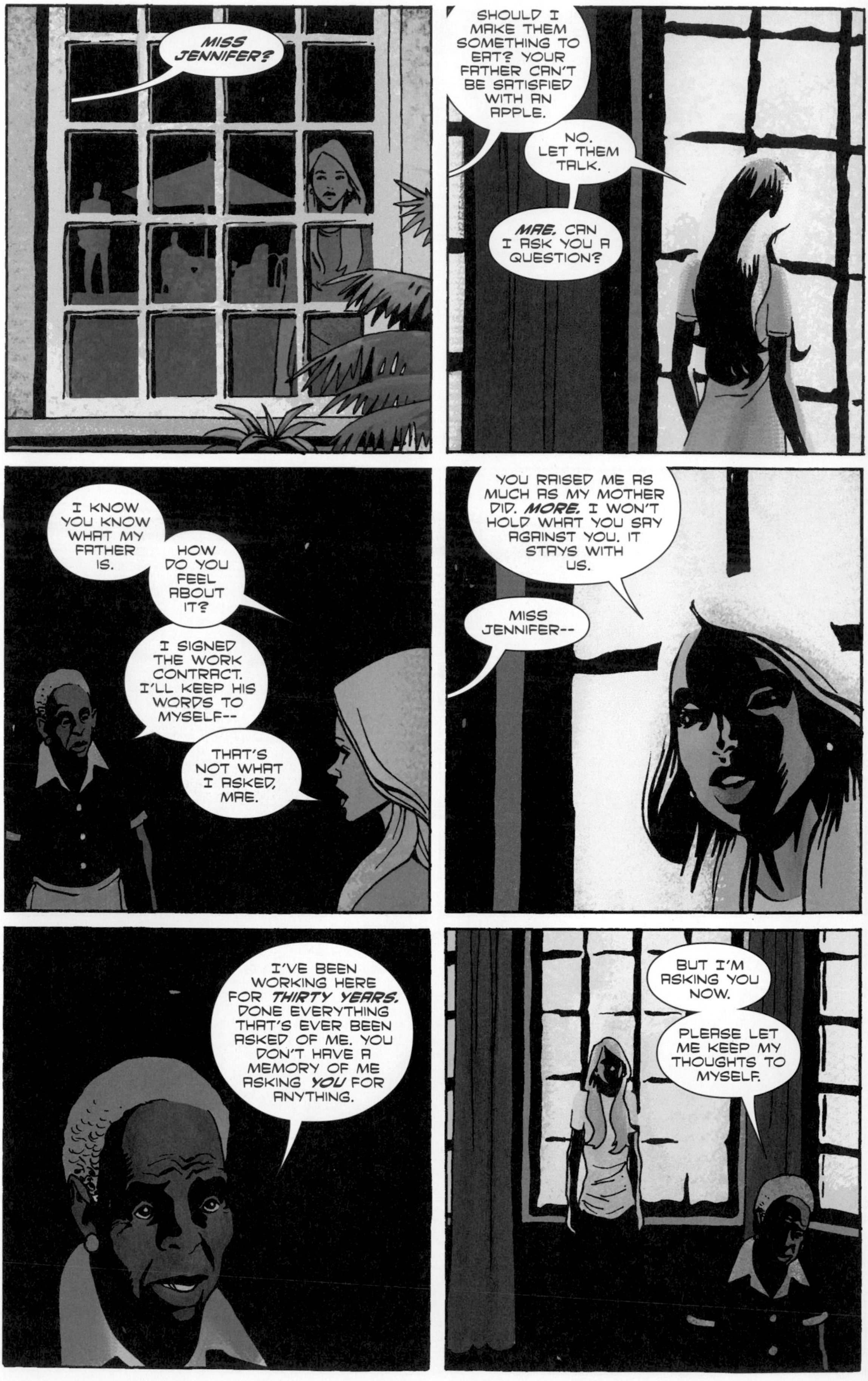
MISS JENNIFER?
SHOULD I MAKE THEM SOMETHING TO EAT? YOUR FATHER CAN'T BE SATISFIED WITH AN APPLE.
NO. LET THEM TALK.
MAE, CAN I ASK YOU A QUESTION?
I KNOW YOU KNOW WHAT MY FATHER IS.
HOW DO YOU FEEL ABOUT IT?
I SIGNED THE WORK CONTRACT. I'LL KEEP HIS WORDS TO MYSELF--
THAT'S NOT WHAT I ASKED, MAE.
YOU RAISED ME AS MUCH AS MY MOTHER DID. MORE. I WON'T HOLD WHAT YOU SAY AGAINST YOU. IT STAYS WITH US.
MISS JENNIFER--
I'VE BEEN WORKING HERE FOR THIRTY YEARS. DONE EVERYTHING THAT'S EVER BEEN ASKED OF ME. YOU DON'T HAVE A MEMORY OF ME ASKING YOU FOR ANYTHING.
BUT I'M ASKING YOU NOW.
PLEASE LET ME KEEP MY THOUGHTS TO MYSELF.

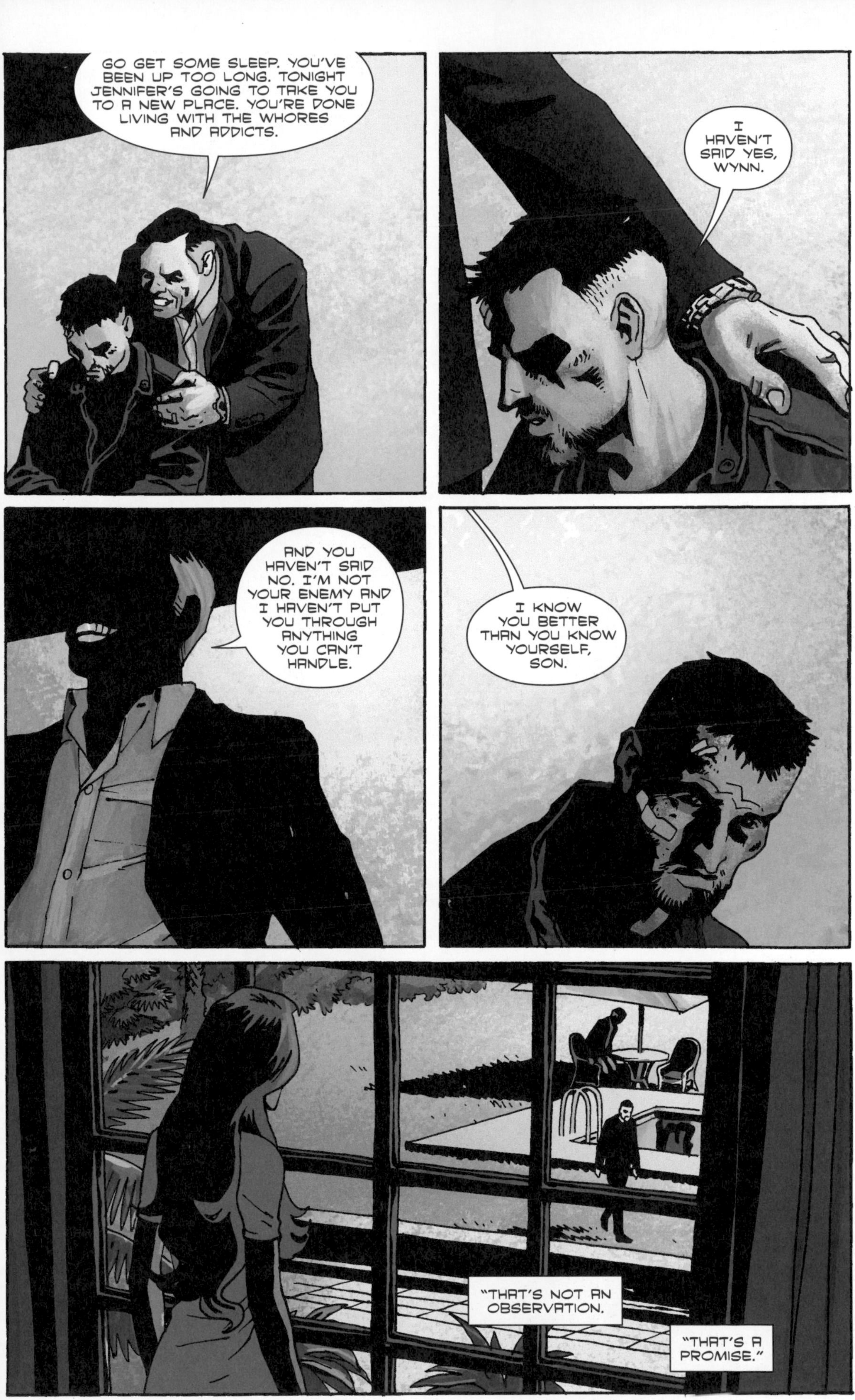
GO GET SOME SLEEP. YOU'VE BEEN UP TOO LONG. TONIGHT JENNIFER'S GOING TO TAKE YOU TO A NEW PLACE. YOU'RE DONE LIVING WITH THE WHORES AND ADDICTS.
I HAVEN'T SAID YES, WYNN.
AND YOU HAVEN'T SAID NO. I'M NOT YOUR ENEMY AND I HAVEN'T PUT YOU THROUGH ANYTHING YOU CAN'T HANDLE.
I KNOW YOU BETTER THAN YOU KNOW YOURSELF, SON.
"THAT'S NOT AN OBSERVATION.
"THAT'S A PROMISE."

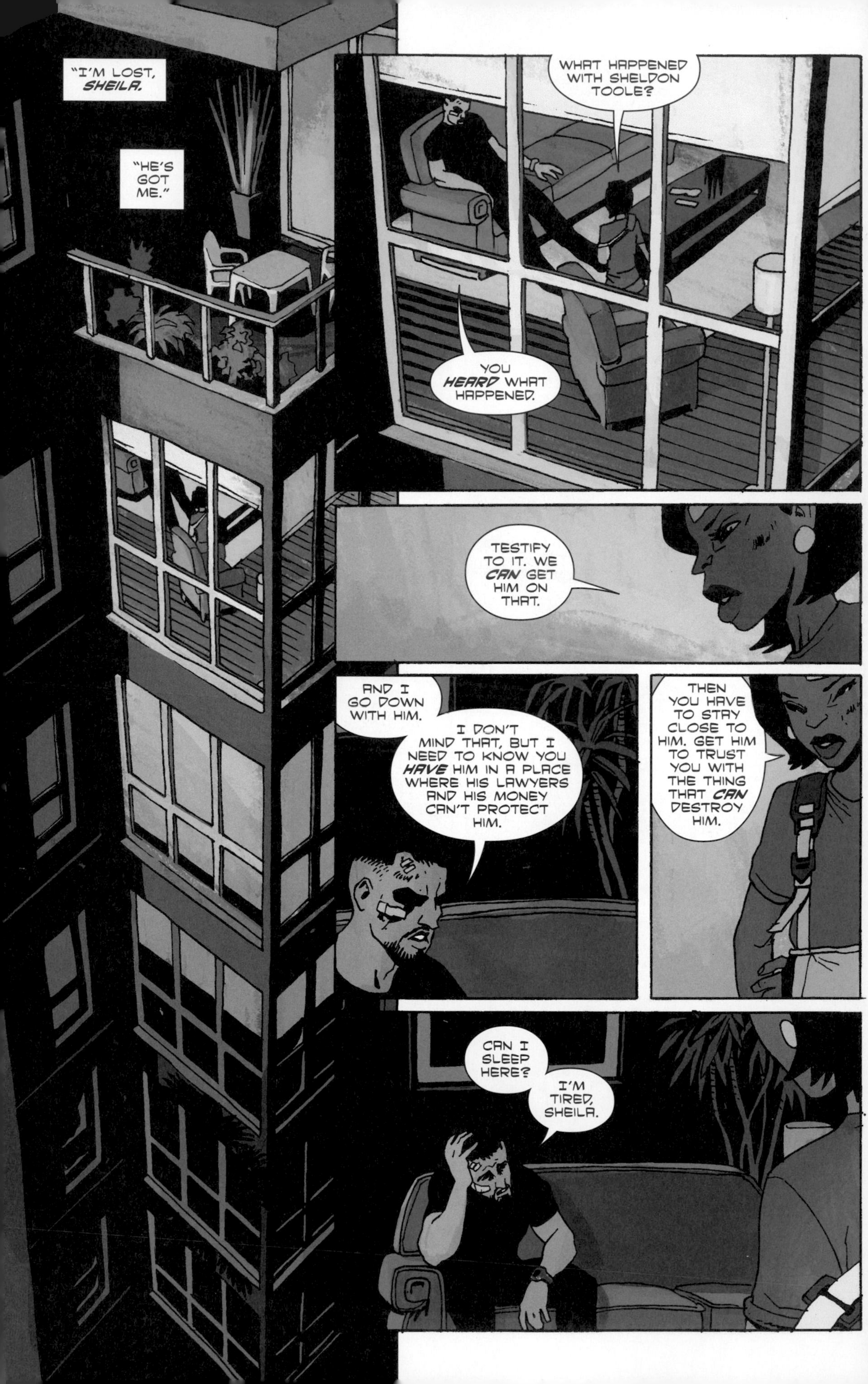
"I'M LOST, SHEILA.
"HE'S GOT ME."
WHAT HAPPENED WITH SHELDON TOOLE?
YOU HEARD WHAT HAPPENED.
TESTIFY TO IT. WE CAN GET HIM ON THAT.
AND I GO DOWN WITH HIM.
I DON'T MIND THAT, BUT I NEED TO KNOW YOU HAVE HIM IN A PLACE WHERE HIS LAWYERS AND HIS MONEY CAN'T PROTECT HIM.
THEN YOU HAVE TO STAY CLOSE TO HIM. GET HIM TO TRUST YOU WITH THE THING THAT CAN DESTROY HIM.
CAN I SLEEP HERE?
I'M TIRED, SHEILA.

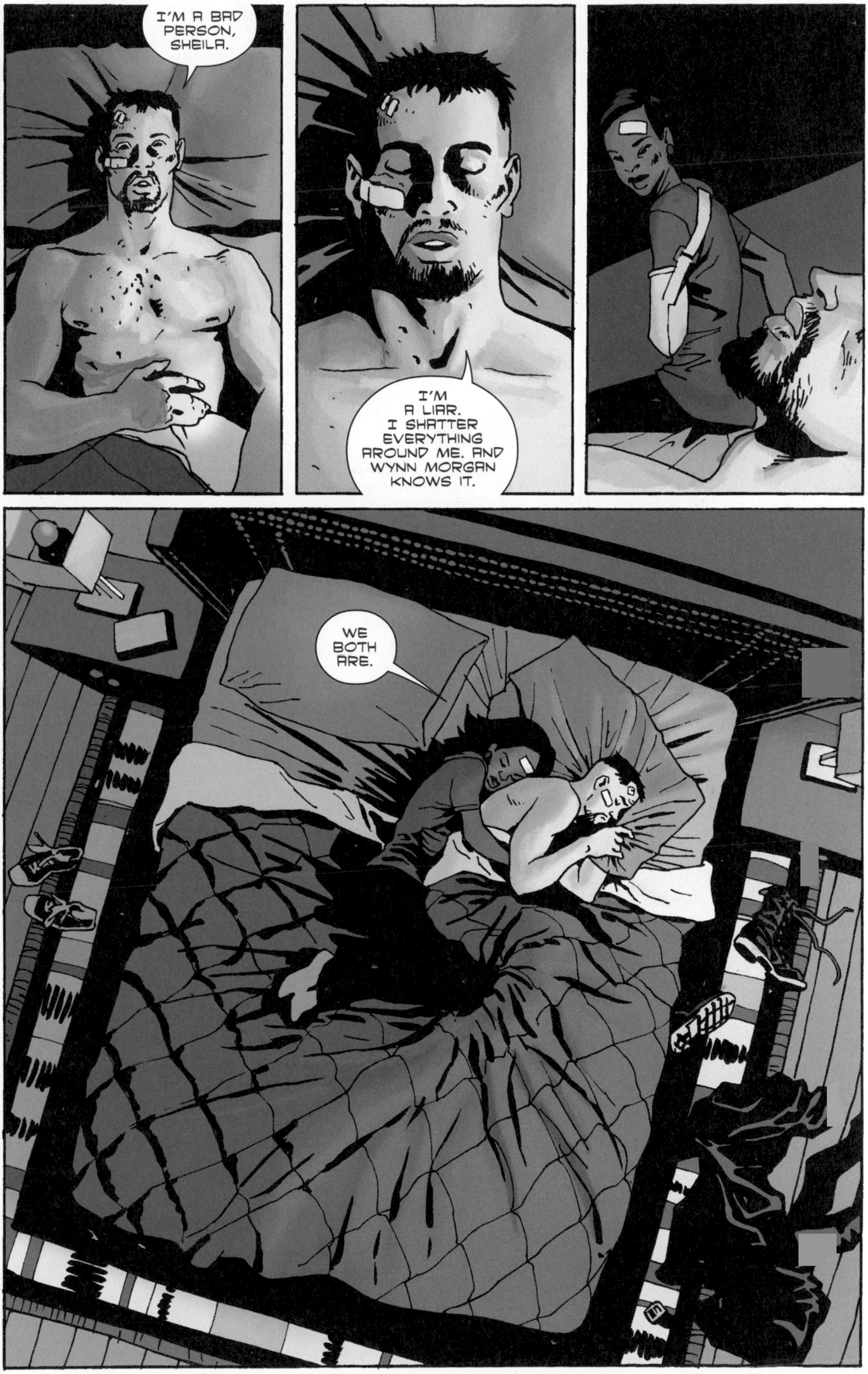
I'M A BAD PERSON, SHEILA.
I'M A LIAR. I SHATTER EVERYTHING AROUND ME. AND WYNN MORGAN KNOWS IT.
WE BOTH ARE.

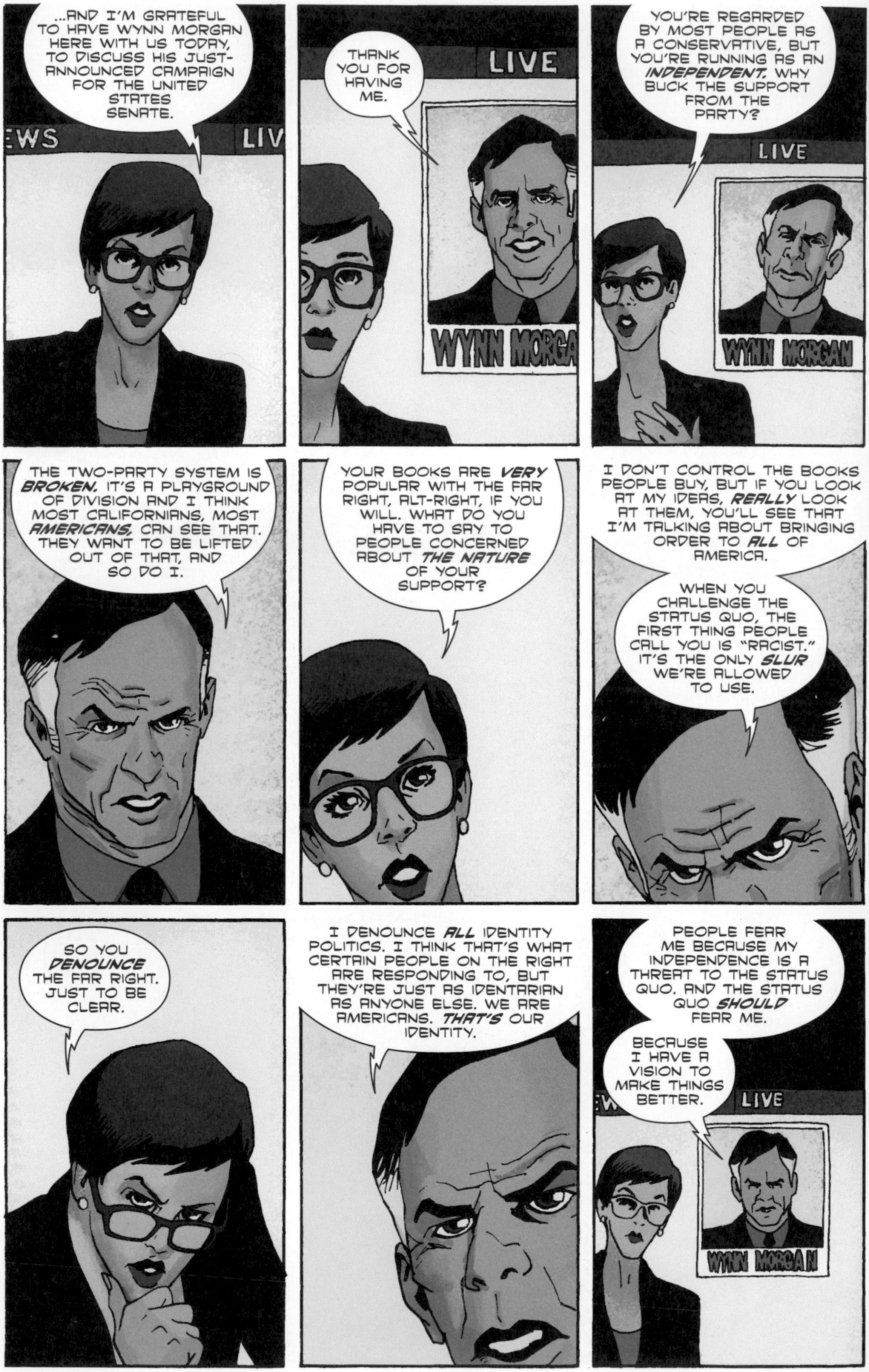
...AND I'M GRATEFUL TO HAVE WYNN MORGAN HERE WITH US TODAY, TO DISCUSS HIS JUST-ANNOUNCED CAMPAIGN FOR THE UNITED STATES SENATE.
EWS
LIV
THANK YOU FOR HAVING ME.
LIVE
WYNN MORGA
YOU'RE REGARDED BY MOST PEOPLE AS A CONSERVATIVE, BUT YOU'RE RUNNING AS AN *INDEPENDENT.* WHY BUCK THE SUPPORT FROM THE PARTY?
LIVE
WYNN MORGAN
THE TWO-PARTY SYSTEM IS *BROKEN.* IT'S A PLAYGROUND OF DIVISION AND I THINK MOST CALIFORNIANS, MOST *AMERICANS,* CAN SEE THAT. THEY WANT TO BE LIFTED OUT OF THAT, AND SO DO I.
YOUR BOOKS ARE *VERY* POPULAR WITH THE FAR RIGHT, ALT-RIGHT, IF YOU WILL. WHAT DO YOU HAVE TO SAY TO PEOPLE CONCERNED ABOUT *THE NATURE* OF YOUR SUPPORT?
I DON'T CONTROL THE BOOKS PEOPLE BUY, BUT IF YOU LOOK AT MY IDEAS, *REALLY* LOOK AT THEM, YOU'LL SEE THAT I'M TALKING ABOUT BRINGING ORDER TO *ALL* OF AMERICA.
WHEN YOU CHALLENGE THE STATUS QUO, THE FIRST THING PEOPLE CALL YOU IS "RACIST." IT'S THE ONLY *SLUR* WE'RE ALLOWED TO USE.
SO YOU *DENOUNCE* THE FAR RIGHT. JUST TO BE CLEAR.
I DENOUNCE *ALL* IDENTITY POLITICS. I THINK THAT'S WHAT CERTAIN PEOPLE ON THE RIGHT ARE RESPONDING TO, BUT THEY'RE JUST AS IDENTARIAN AS ANYONE ELSE. WE ARE AMERICANS. *THAT'S* OUR IDENTITY.
PEOPLE FEAR ME BECAUSE MY INDEPENDENCE IS A THREAT TO THE STATUS QUO. AND THE STATUS QUO *SHOULD* FEAR ME.
BECAUSE I HAVE A VISION TO MAKE THINGS BETTER.
EWS
LIVE
WYNN MORGAN

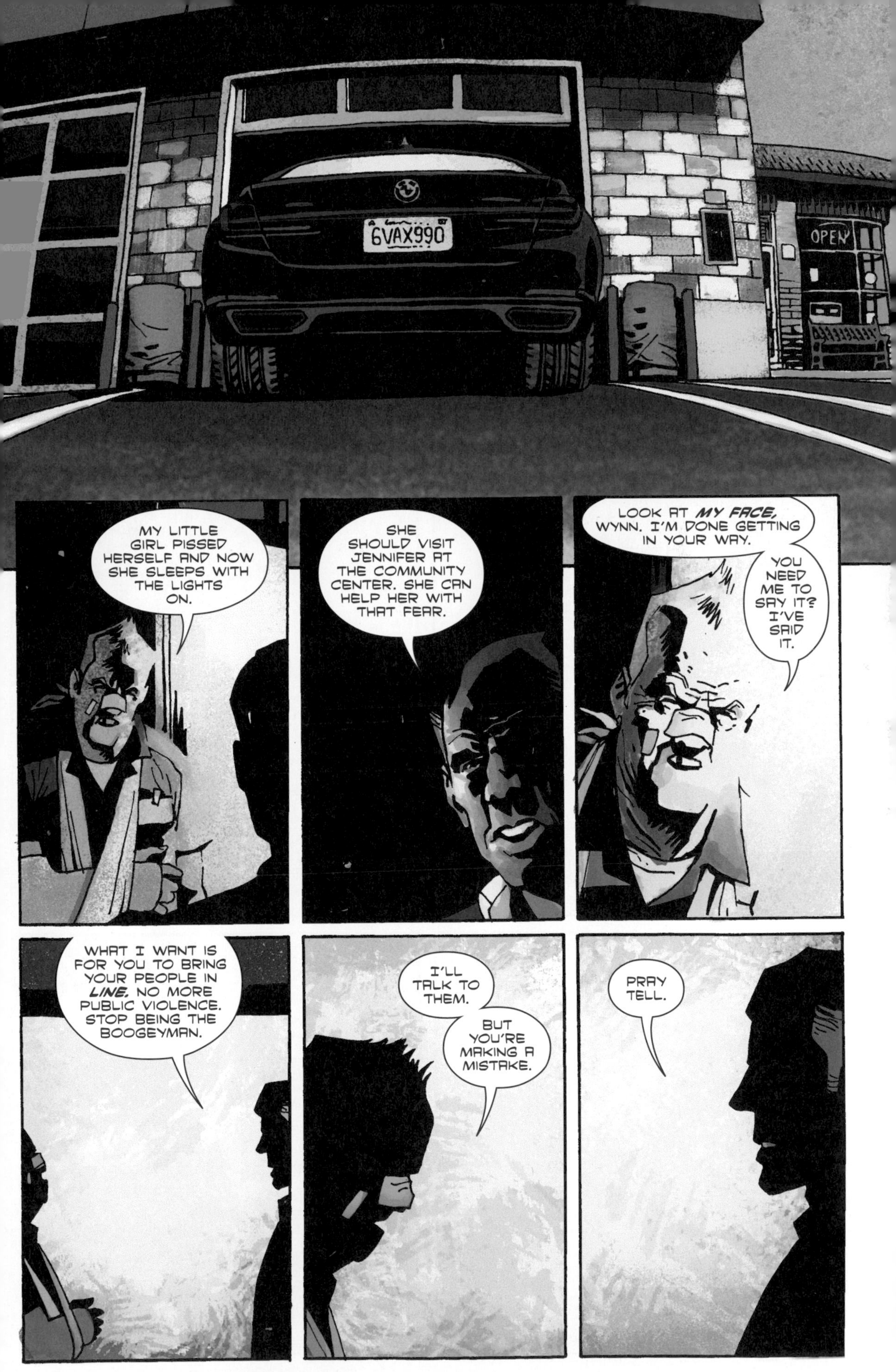
6VAX990
OPEN
MY LITTLE GIRL PISSED HERSELF AND NOW SHE SLEEPS WITH THE LIGHTS ON.
SHE SHOULD VISIT JENNIFER AT THE COMMUNITY CENTER. SHE CAN HELP HER WITH THAT FEAR.
LOOK AT *MY FACE,* WYNN. I'M DONE GETTING IN YOUR WAY.
YOU NEED ME TO SAY IT? I'VE SAID IT.
WHAT I WANT IS FOR YOU TO BRING YOUR PEOPLE IN *LINE.* NO MORE PUBLIC VIOLENCE. STOP BEING THE BOOGEYMAN.
I'LL TALK TO THEM.
BUT YOU'RE MAKING A MISTAKE.
PRAY TELL.

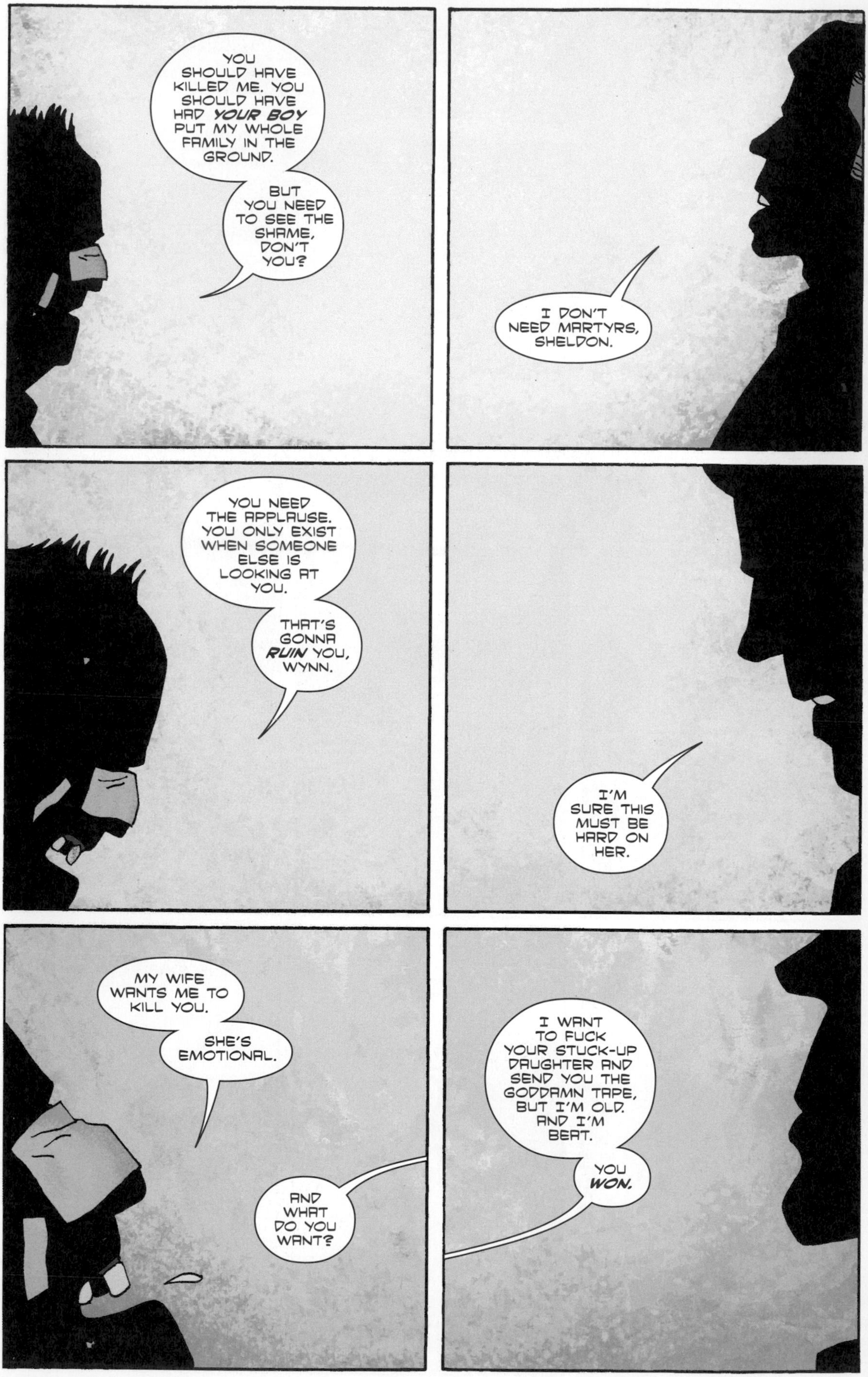
YOU SHOULD HAVE KILLED ME. YOU SHOULD HAVE HAD YOUR BOY PUT MY WHOLE FAMILY IN THE GROUND.
BUT YOU NEED TO SEE THE SHAME, DON'T YOU?
I DON'T NEED MARTYRS, SHELDON.
YOU NEED THE APPLAUSE. YOU ONLY EXIST WHEN SOMEONE ELSE IS LOOKING AT YOU.
THAT'S GONNA RUIN YOU, WYNN.
I'M SURE THIS MUST BE HARD ON HER.
MY WIFE WANTS ME TO KILL YOU.
SHE'S EMOTIONAL.
AND WHAT DO YOU WANT?
I WANT TO FUCK YOUR STUCK-UP DAUGHTER AND SEND YOU THE GODDAMN TAPE, BUT I'M OLD. AND I'M BEAT.
YOU WON.

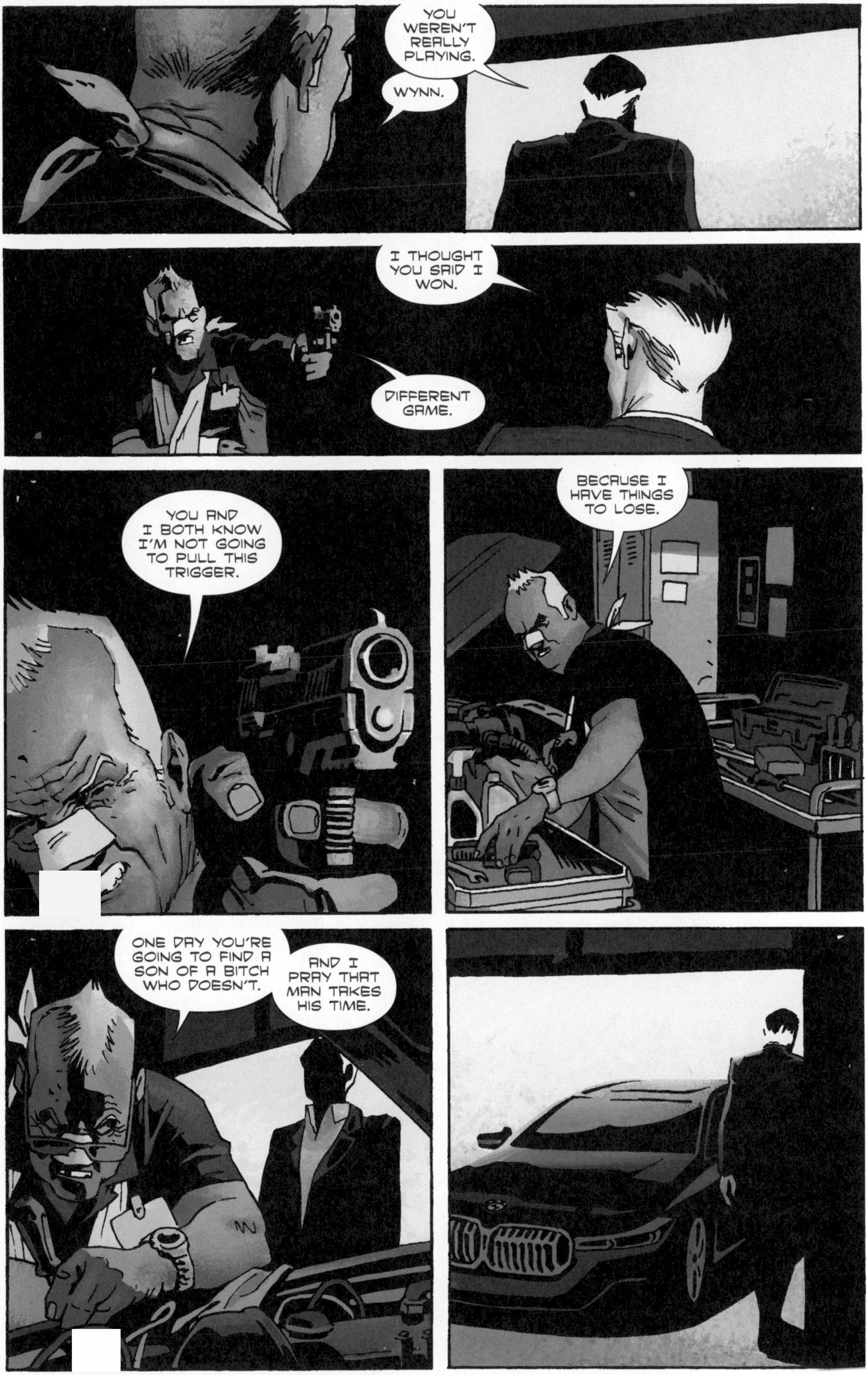
YOU WEREN'T REALLY PLAYING.
WYNN.
I THOUGHT YOU SAID I WON.
DIFFERENT GAME.
YOU AND I BOTH KNOW I'M NOT GOING TO PULL THIS TRIGGER.
BECAUSE I HAVE THINGS TO LOSE.
ONE DAY YOU'RE GOING TO FIND A SON OF A BITCH WHO DOESN'T.
AND I PRAY THAT MAN TAKES HIS TIME.

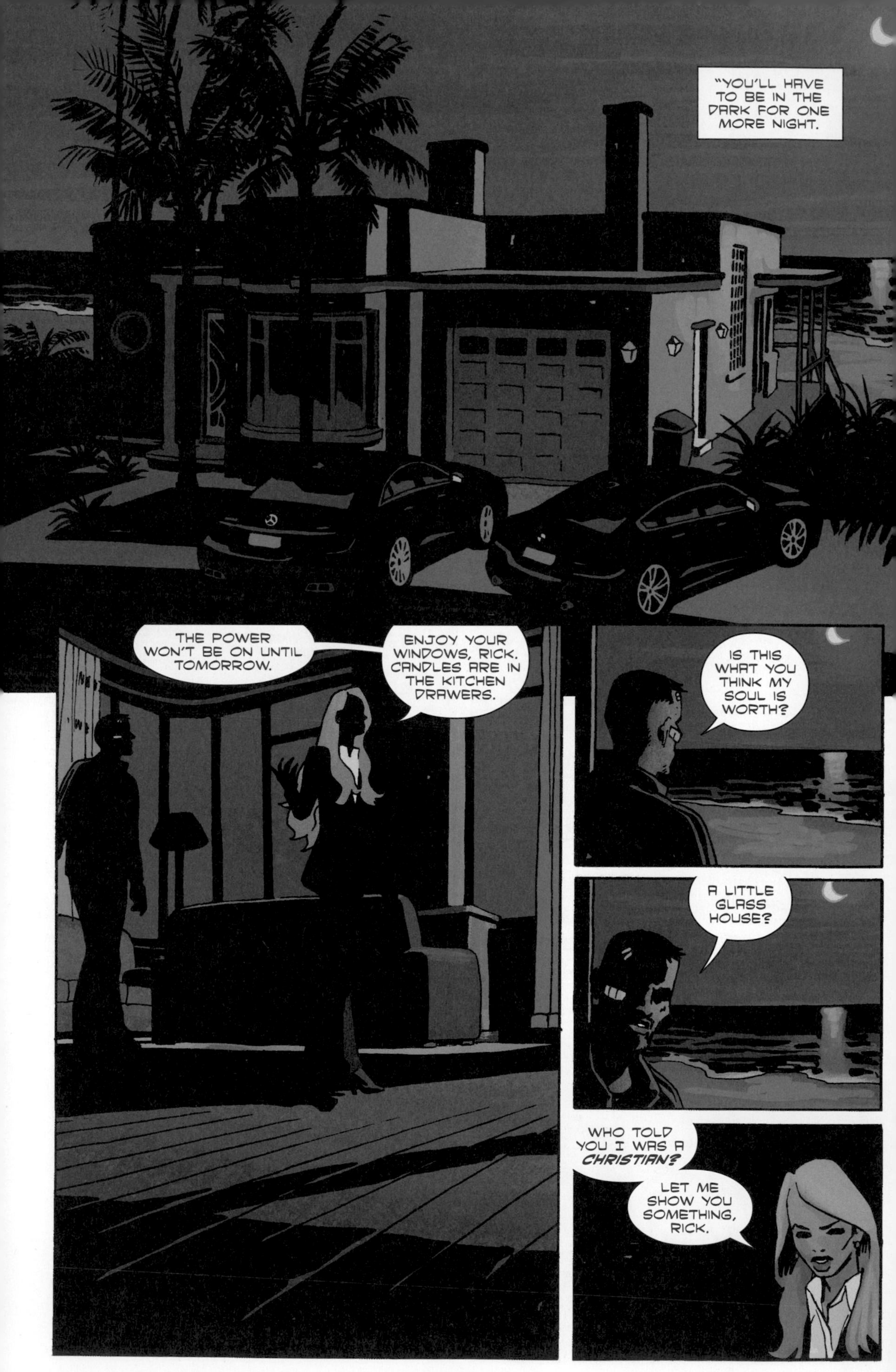
"YOU'LL HAVE TO BE IN THE DARK FOR ONE MORE NIGHT.
THE POWER WON'T BE ON UNTIL TOMORROW.
ENJOY YOUR WINDOWS, RICK. CANDLES ARE IN THE KITCHEN DRAWERS.
IS THIS WHAT YOU THINK MY SOUL IS WORTH?
A LITTLE GLASS HOUSE?
WHO TOLD YOU I WAS A CHRISTIAN?
LET ME SHOW YOU SOMETHING, RICK.

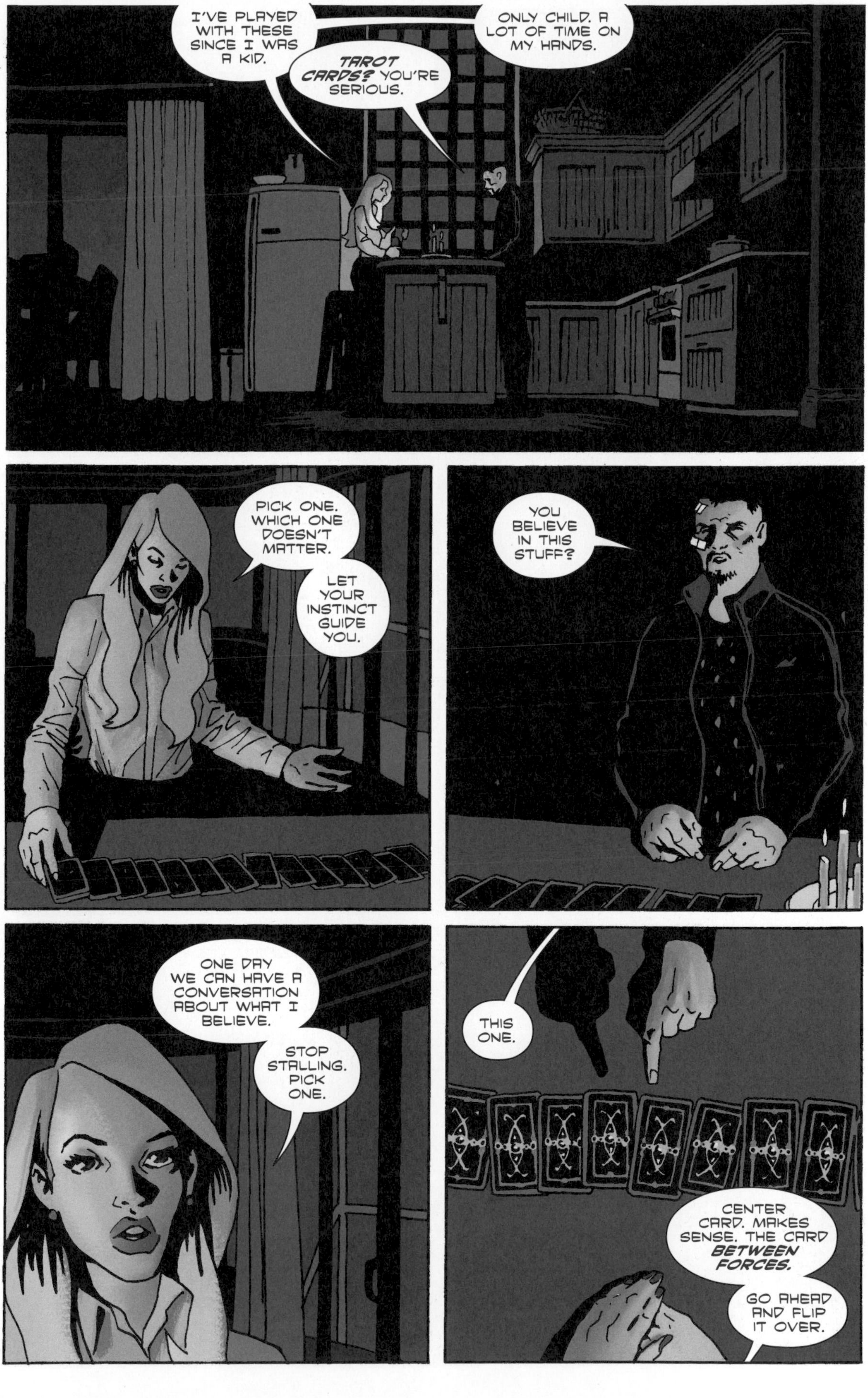
I'VE PLAYED WITH THESE SINCE I WAS A KID.
TAROT CARDS? YOU'RE SERIOUS.
ONLY CHILD. A LOT OF TIME ON MY HANDS.
PICK ONE. WHICH ONE DOESN'T MATTER.
LET YOUR INSTINCT GUIDE YOU.
YOU BELIEVE IN THIS STUFF?
ONE DAY WE CAN HAVE A CONVERSATION ABOUT WHAT I BELIEVE.
STOP STALLING. PICK ONE.
THIS ONE.
CENTER CARD. MAKES SENSE. THE CARD BETWEEN FORCES.
GO AHEAD AND FLIP IT OVER.

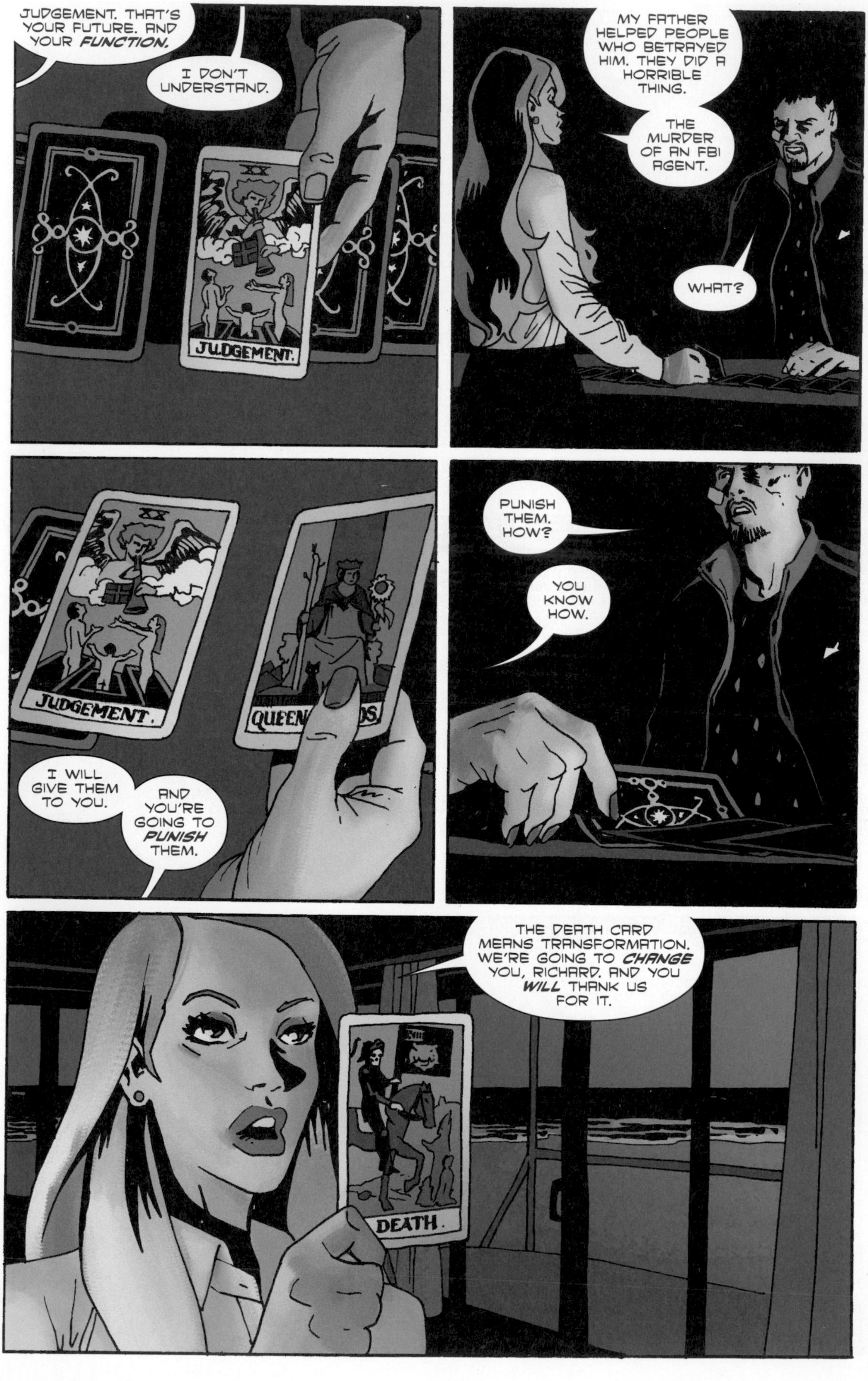

JUDGEMENT. THAT'S YOUR FUTURE. AND YOUR *FUNCTION.*
I DON'T UNDERSTAND.
JUDGEMENT.
MY FATHER HELPED PEOPLE WHO BETRAYED HIM. THEY DID A HORRIBLE THING.
THE MURDER OF AN FBI AGENT.
WHAT?
JUDGEMENT.
I WILL GIVE THEM TO YOU.
AND YOU'RE GOING TO *PUNISH* THEM.
PUNISH THEM. HOW?
YOU KNOW HOW.
THE DEATH CARD MEANS TRANSFORMATION. WE'RE GOING TO *CHANGE* YOU, RICHARD. AND YOU *WILL* THANK US FOR IT.
DEATH.

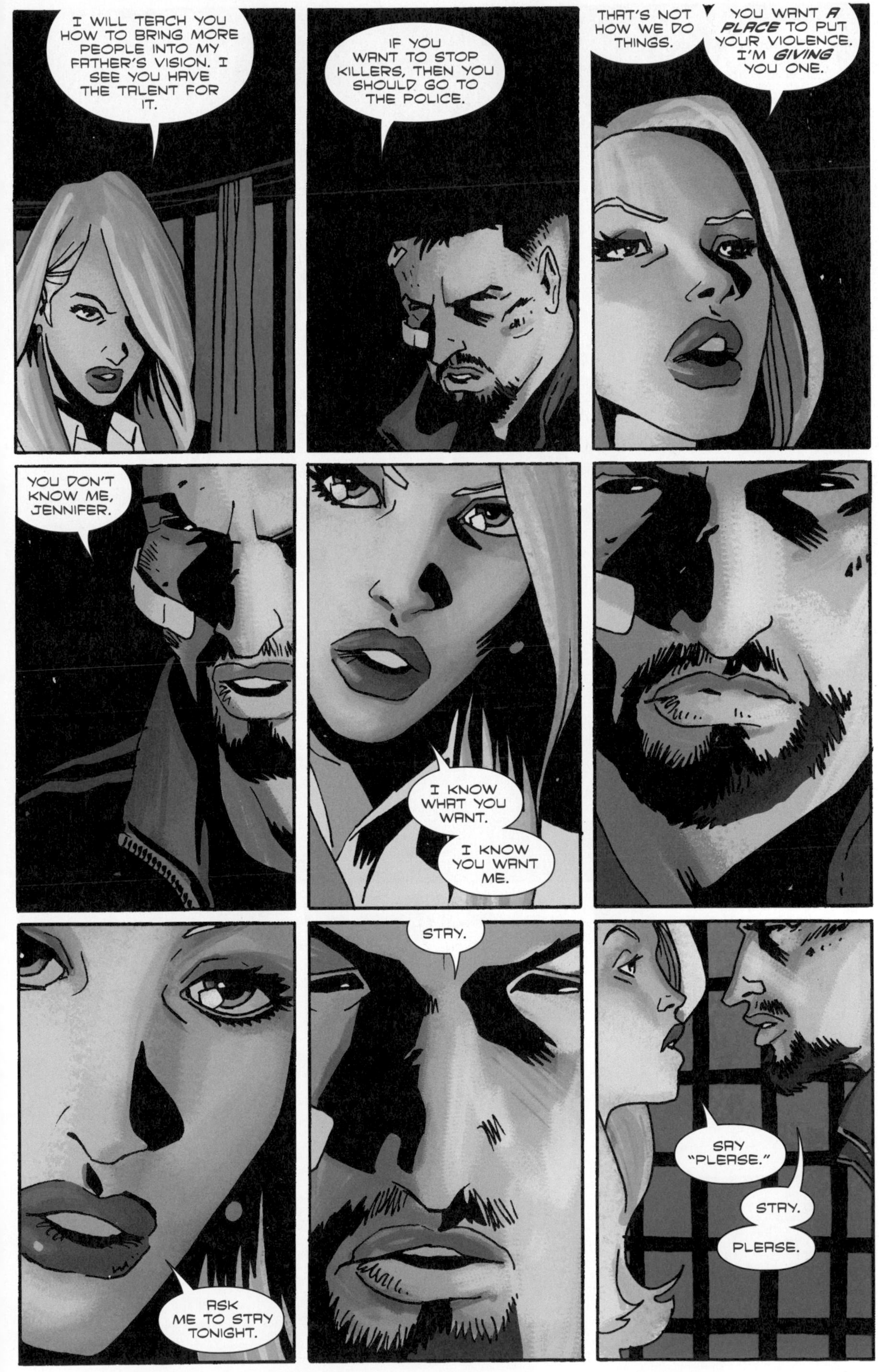
I WILL TEACH YOU HOW TO BRING MORE PEOPLE INTO MY FATHER'S VISION. I SEE YOU HAVE THE TALENT FOR IT.
IF YOU WANT TO STOP KILLERS, THEN YOU SHOULD GO TO THE POLICE.
THAT'S NOT HOW WE DO THINGS.
YOU WANT *A PLACE* TO PUT YOUR VIOLENCE. I'M *GIVING* YOU ONE.
YOU DON'T KNOW ME, JENNIFER.
I KNOW WHAT YOU WANT.
I KNOW YOU WANT ME.
ASK ME TO STAY TONIGHT.
STAY.
SAY "PLEASE."
STAY.
PLEASE.

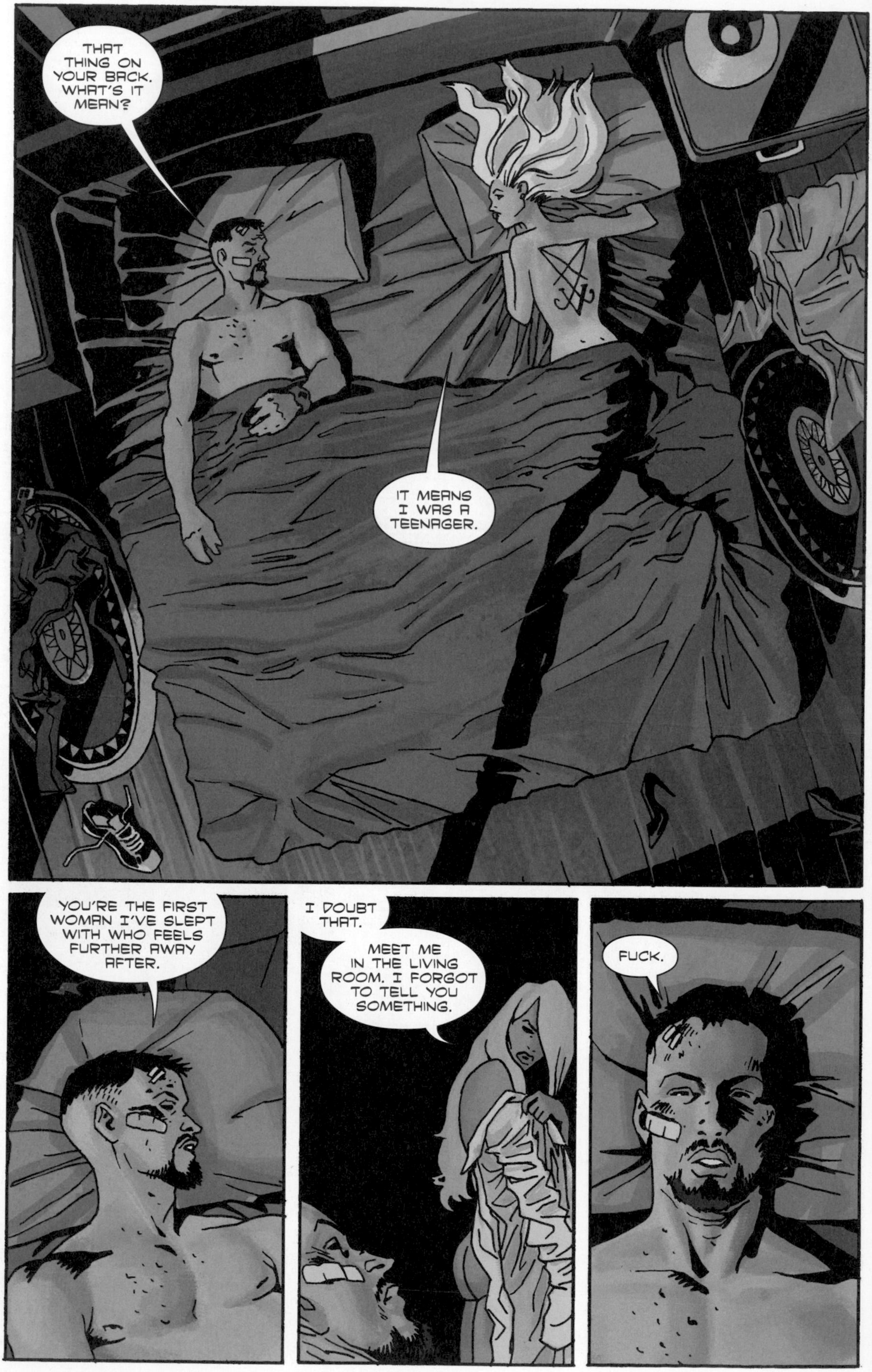
THAT THING ON YOUR BACK. WHAT'S IT MEAN?
IT MEANS I WAS A TEENAGER.
YOU'RE THE FIRST WOMAN I'VE SLEPT WITH WHO FEELS FURTHER AWAY AFTER.
I DOUBT THAT.
MEET ME IN THE LIVING ROOM. I FORGOT TO TELL YOU SOMETHING.
FUCK.

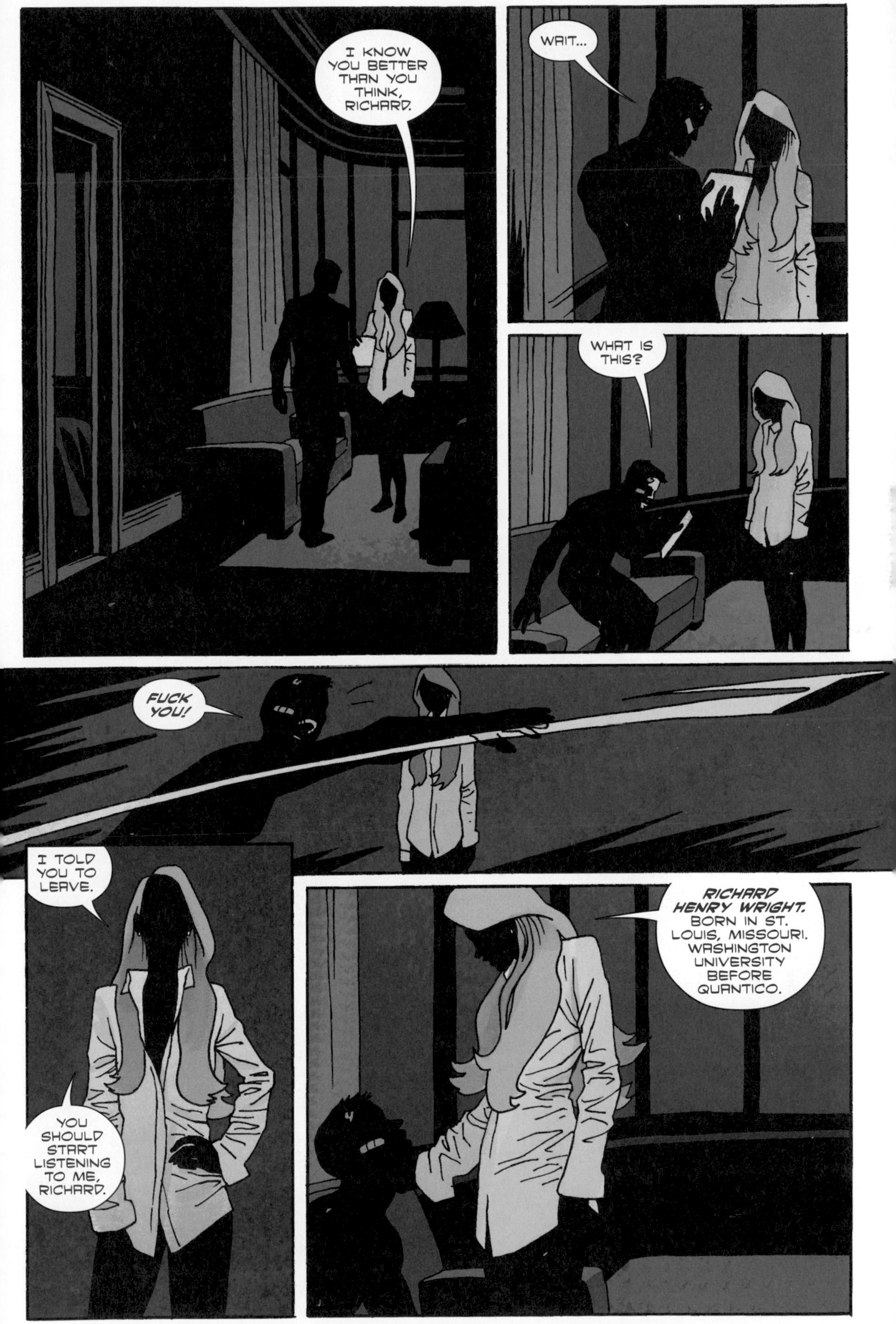
I KNOW YOU BETTER THAN YOU THINK, RICHARD.
WAIT...
WHAT IS THIS?
FUCK YOU!
I TOLD YOU TO LEAVE.
YOU SHOULD START LISTENING TO ME, RICHARD.
RICHARD HENRY WRIGHT. BORN IN ST. LOUIS, MISSOURI. WASHINGTON UNIVERSITY BEFORE QUANTICO.

I'M NOT ANGRY. WE'RE NOT GOING TO CRUCIFY YOU FOR IT.

SECRETS ARE HARD TO KEEP, RICHARD. THEY *EAT AWAY* AT YOU.

I BET IT FEELS GOOD TO KNOW YOU CAN FINALLY BE HONEST WITH *SOMEONE.*

YOU HAD TO KNOW WE'D FIND OUT. PART OF YOU MUST HAVE WANTED US TO.

HOW?

YOU THINK SOMEONE LIKE MY FATHER DOESN'T HAVE FRIENDS IN *THE FBI?*

FRIENDS WHO KNOW ABOUT THE BLACK BITCH WHO'S TRYING TO RUIN HIS LIFE. AND YOURS?

NOT BLACK. NOT WHITE. YOU'RE A STRUGGLING THING CAUGHT BETWEEN FORCES. YOU REALLY SHOULDN'T EXIST.

"NO MATTER WHAT HAPPENS NEXT.

"REMEMBER--

"--I ASKED YOU TO LEAVE."

LEANDRO FERNANDEZ

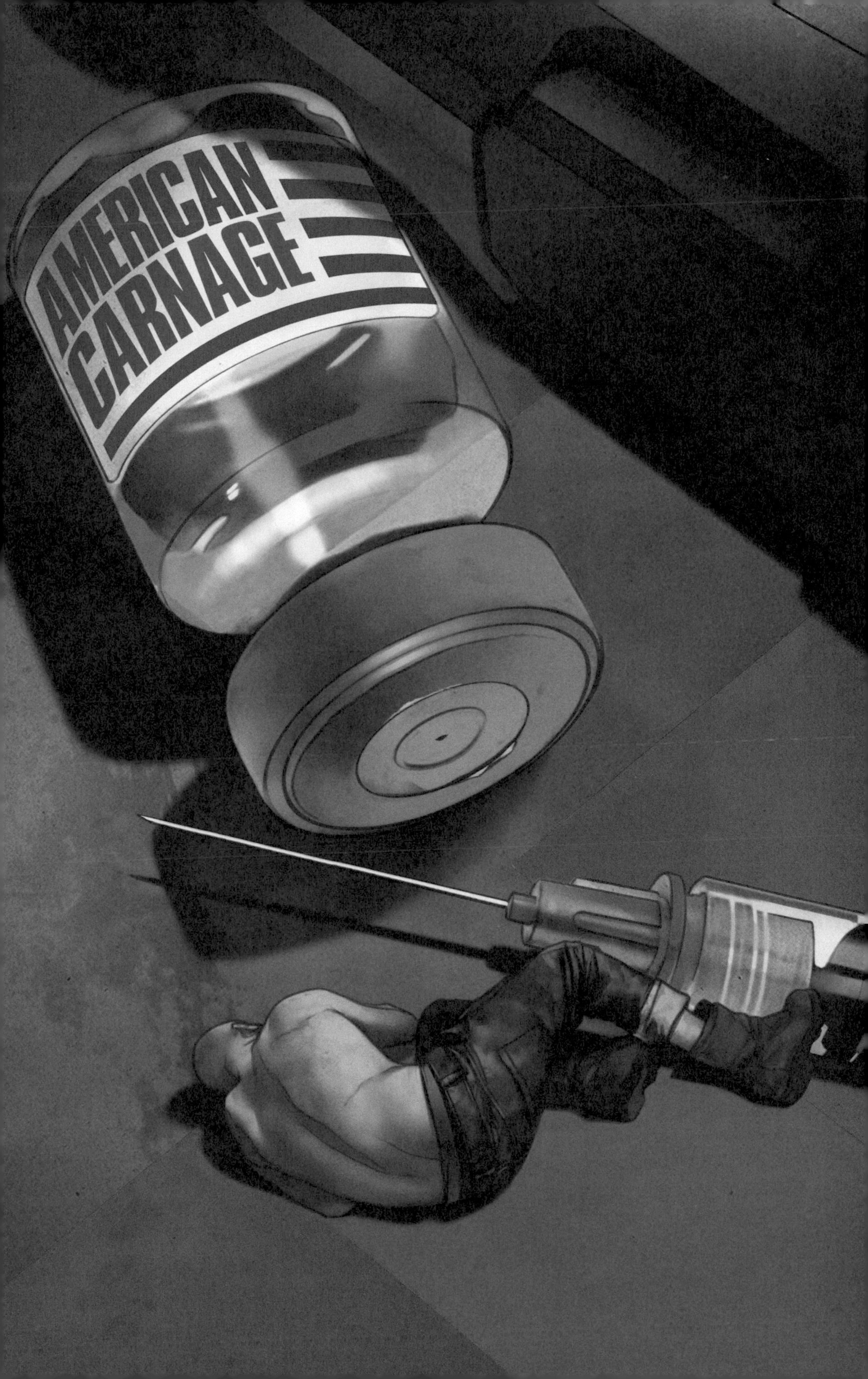
AMERICAN
CARNAGE

CHAPTER SEVEN: JUDGMENT

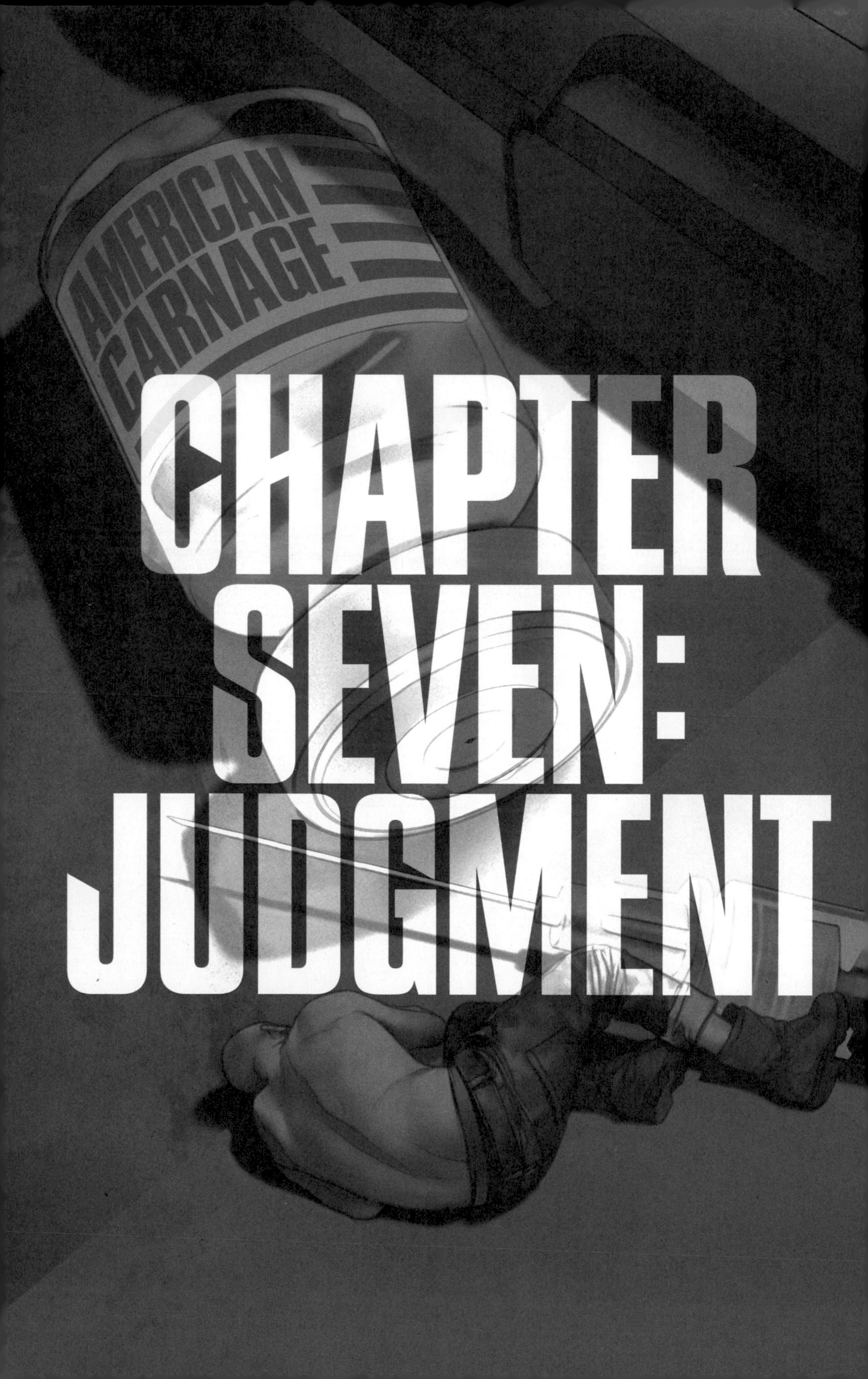
AMERICAN CARNAGE

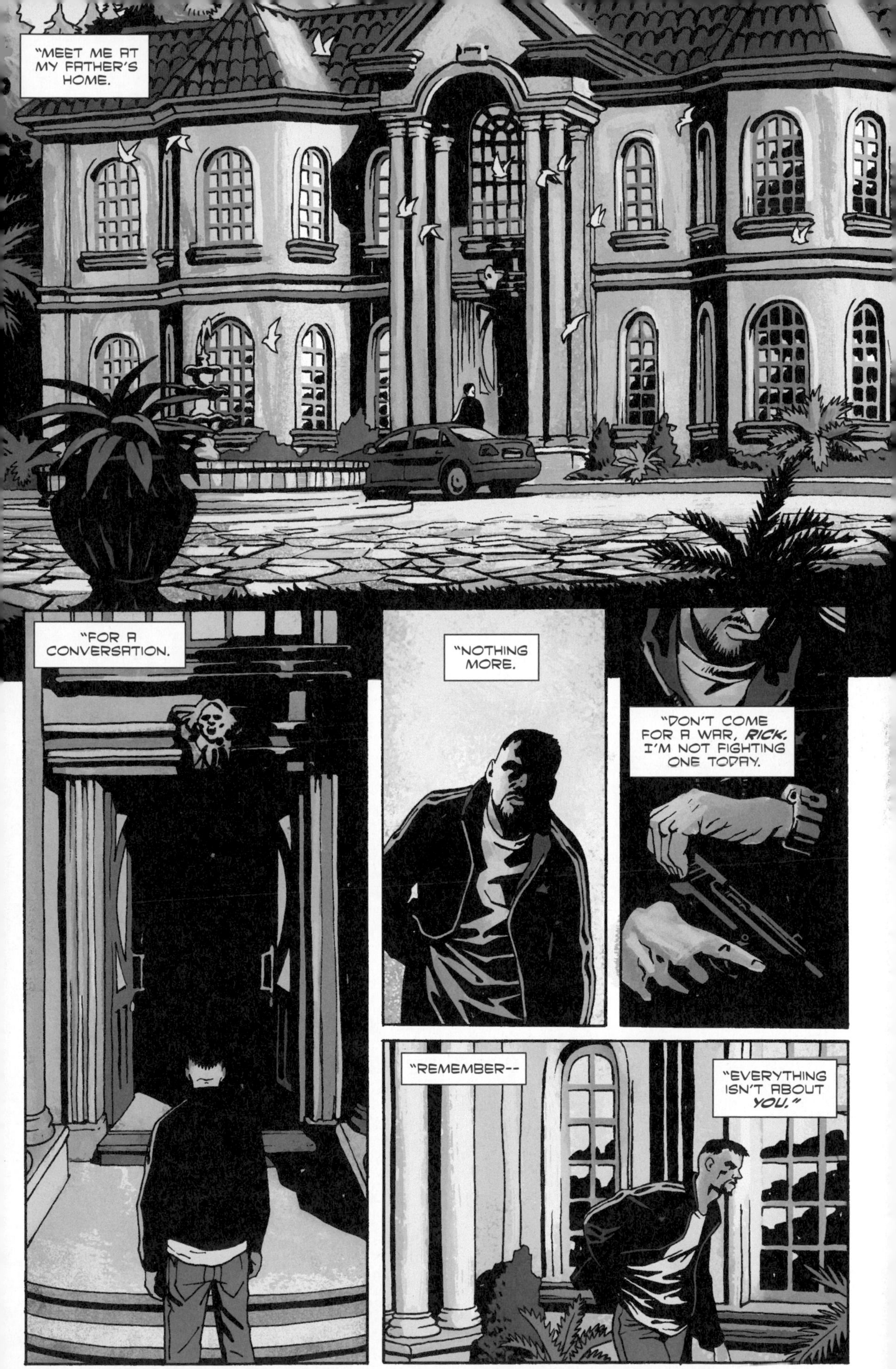
"MEET ME AT MY FATHER'S HOME.
"FOR A CONVERSATION.
"NOTHING MORE.
"DON'T COME FOR A WAR, *RICK.* I'M NOT FIGHTING ONE TODAY.
"REMEMBER--
"EVERYTHING ISN'T ABOUT *YOU.*"

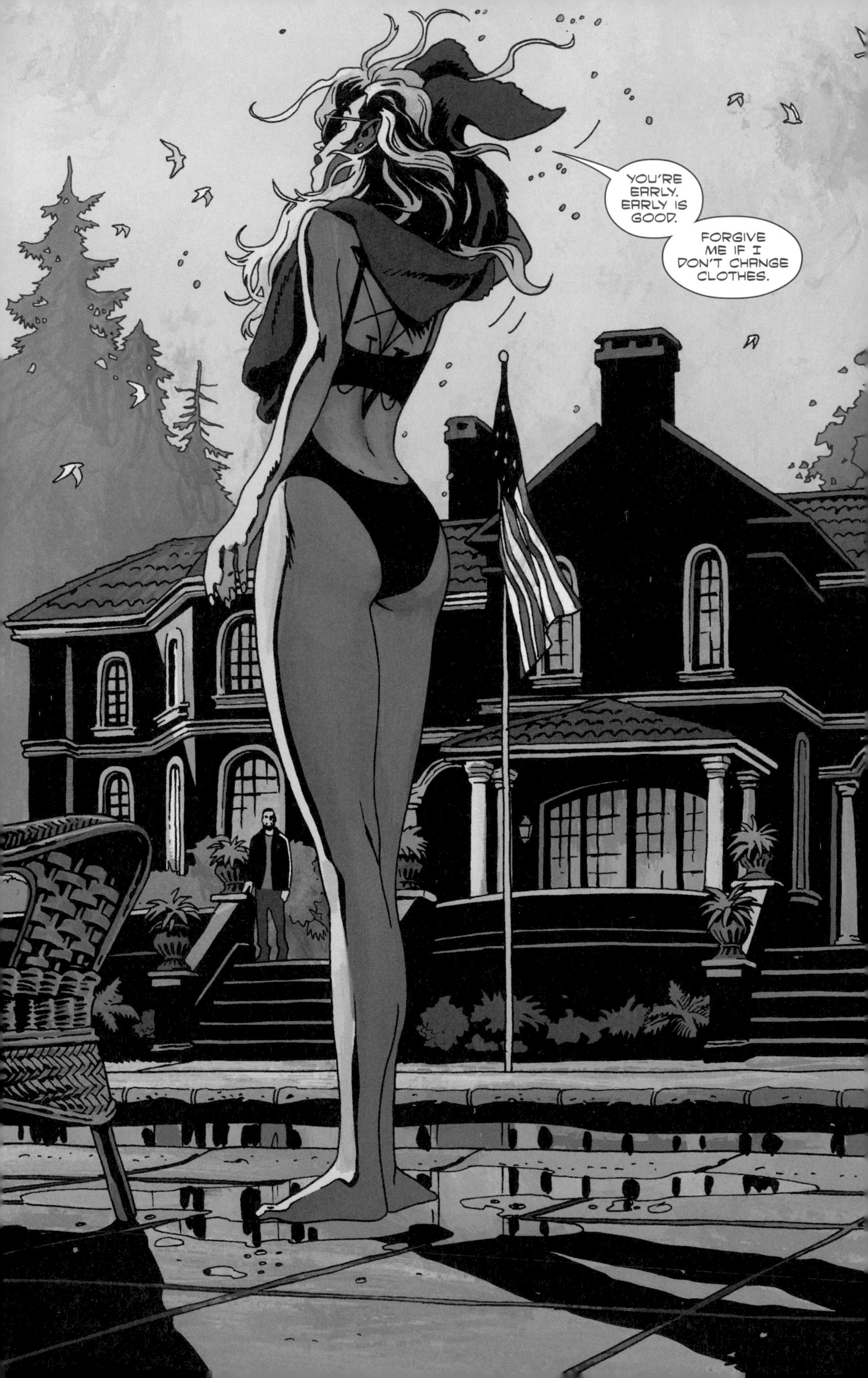
YOU'RE EARLY. EARLY IS GOOD.
FORGIVE ME IF I DON'T CHANGE CLOTHES.

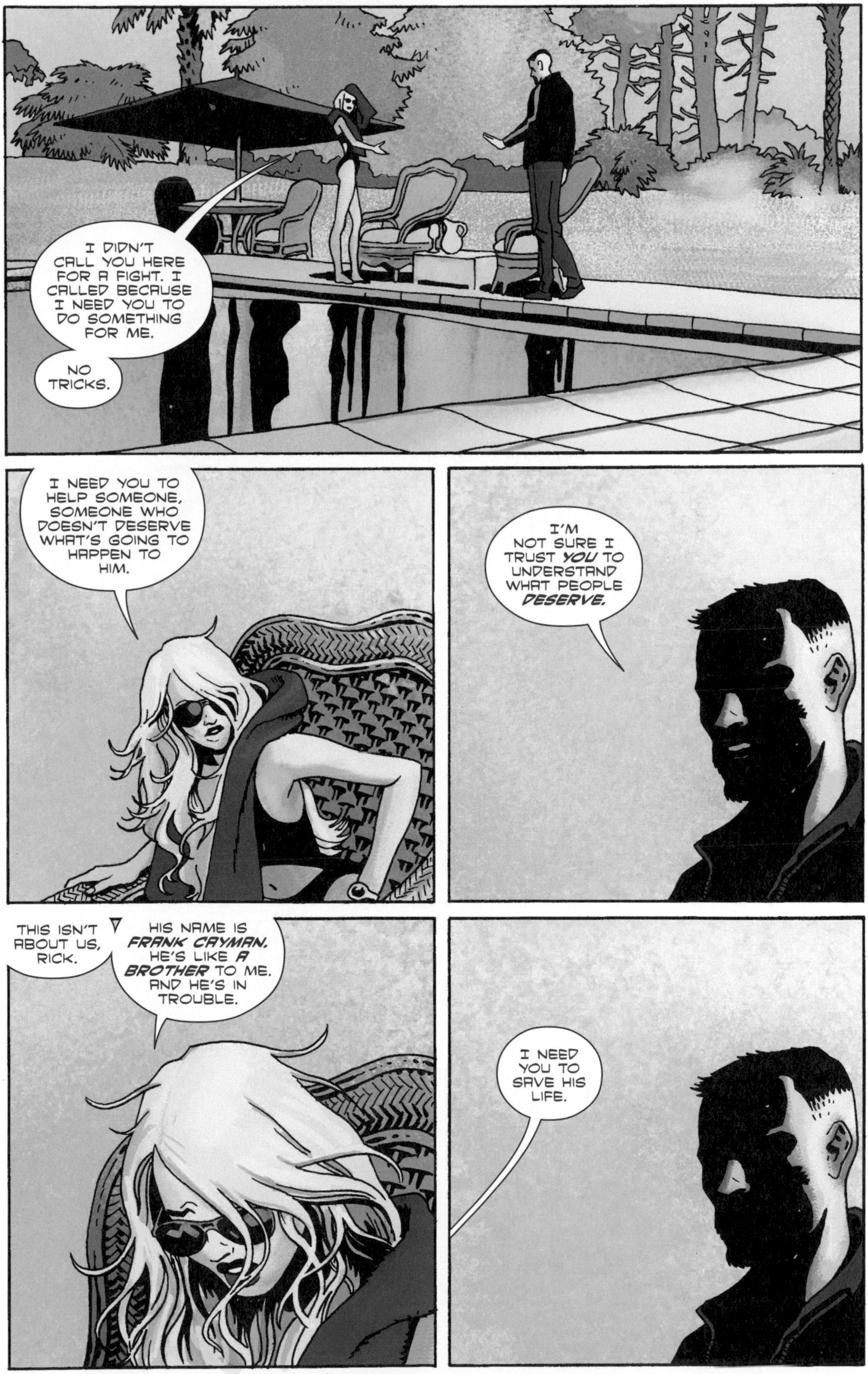
I DIDN'T CALL YOU HERE FOR A FIGHT. I CALLED BECAUSE I NEED YOU TO DO SOMETHING FOR ME.
NO TRICKS.
I NEED YOU TO HELP SOMEONE, SOMEONE WHO DOESN'T DESERVE WHAT'S GOING TO HAPPEN TO HIM.
I'M NOT SURE I TRUST *YOU* TO UNDERSTAND WHAT PEOPLE *DESERVE.*
THIS ISN'T ABOUT US, RICK.
HIS NAME IS *FRANK CAYMAN.* HE'S LIKE *A BROTHER* TO ME. AND HE'S IN TROUBLE.
I NEED YOU TO SAVE HIS LIFE.

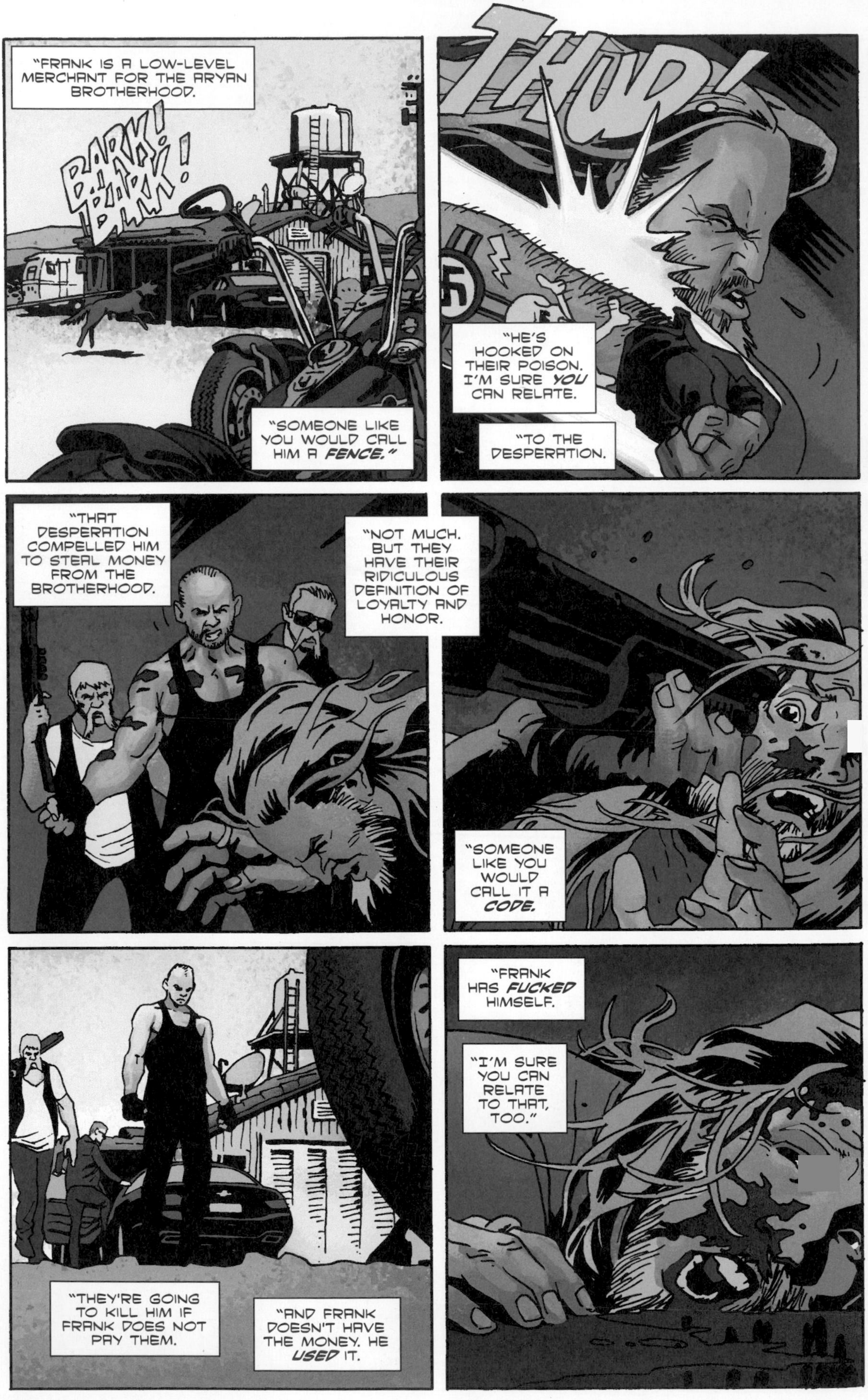
"FRANK IS A LOW-LEVEL MERCHANT FOR THE ARYAN BROTHERHOOD.
BARK! BARK!
"SOMEONE LIKE YOU WOULD CALL HIM A *FENCE.*"
THUD!
"HE'S HOOKED ON THEIR POISON. I'M SURE *YOU* CAN RELATE.
"TO THE DESPERATION.
"THAT DESPERATION COMPELLED HIM TO STEAL MONEY FROM THE BROTHERHOOD.
"NOT MUCH. BUT THEY HAVE THEIR RIDICULOUS DEFINITION OF LOYALTY AND HONOR.
"SOMEONE LIKE YOU WOULD CALL IT A *CODE.*
"THEY'RE GOING TO KILL HIM IF FRANK DOES NOT PAY THEM.
"AND FRANK DOESN'T HAVE THE MONEY. HE *USED* IT.
"FRANK HAS *FUCKED* HIMSELF.
"I'M SURE YOU CAN RELATE TO THAT, TOO."

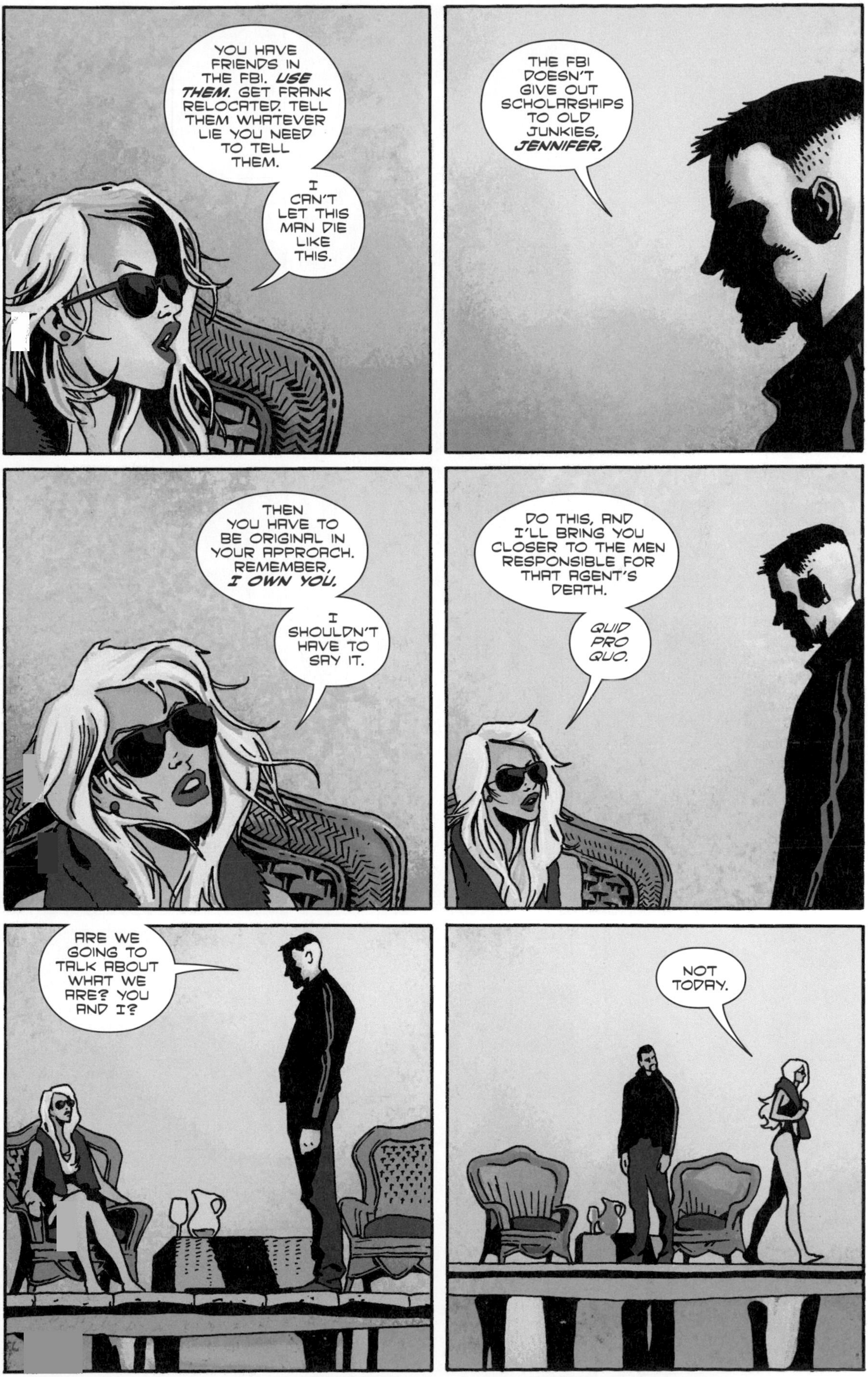
YOU HAVE FRIENDS IN THE FBI. *USE THEM.* GET FRANK RELOCATED. TELL THEM WHATEVER LIE YOU NEED TO TELL THEM.
I CAN'T LET THIS MAN DIE LIKE THIS.
THE FBI DOESN'T GIVE OUT SCHOLARSHIPS TO OLD JUNKIES, *JENNIFER.*
THEN YOU HAVE TO BE ORIGINAL IN YOUR APPROACH. REMEMBER, *I OWN YOU.*
I SHOULDN'T HAVE TO SAY IT.
DO THIS, AND I'LL BRING YOU CLOSER TO THE MEN RESPONSIBLE FOR THAT AGENT'S DEATH.
QUID PRO QUO.
ARE WE GOING TO TALK ABOUT WHAT WE ARE? YOU AND I?
NOT TODAY.

STEADY, *SHEILA.*

STEADY...

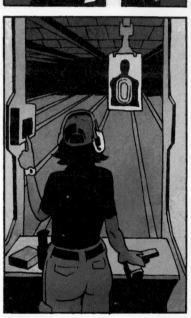

BLAM!

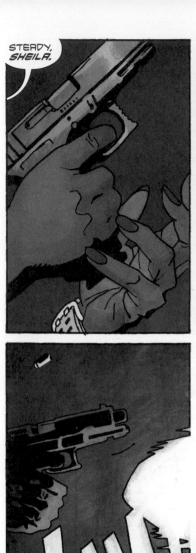

BLAM!

BLAM! BLAM! BLAM

"YOU WANT ME TO SAVE *THIS* BASTARD?"

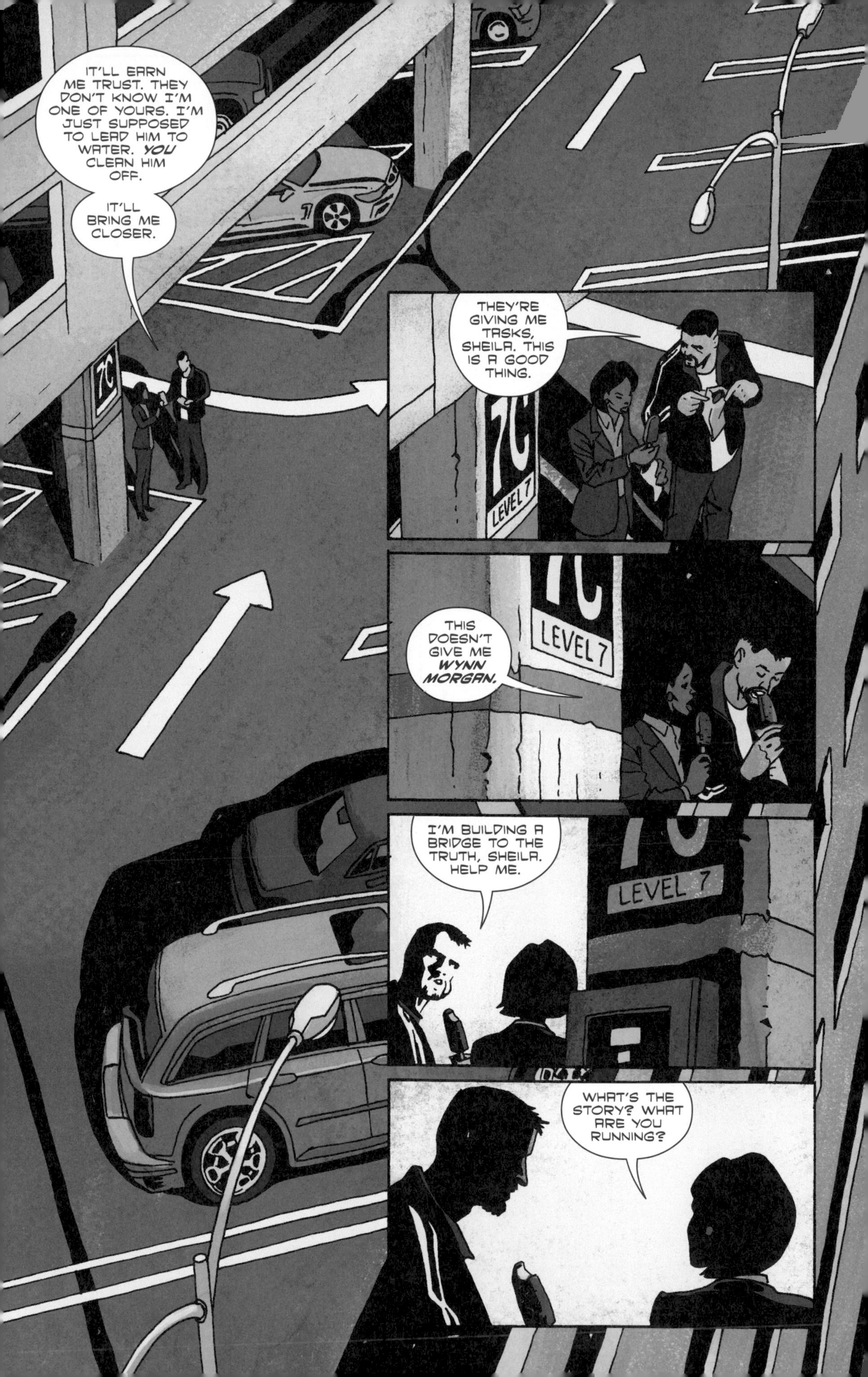
IT'LL EARN ME TRUST. THEY DON'T KNOW I'M ONE OF YOURS. I'M JUST SUPPOSED TO LEAD HIM TO WATER. YOU CLEAN HIM OFF.
IT'LL BRING ME CLOSER.
7C
THEY'RE GIVING ME TASKS, SHEILA. THIS IS A GOOD THING.
7C LEVEL 7
THIS DOESN'T GIVE ME WYNN MORGAN.
LEVEL 7
I'M BUILDING A BRIDGE TO THE TRUTH, SHEILA. HELP ME.
LEVEL 7
WHAT'S THE STORY? WHAT ARE YOU RUNNING?

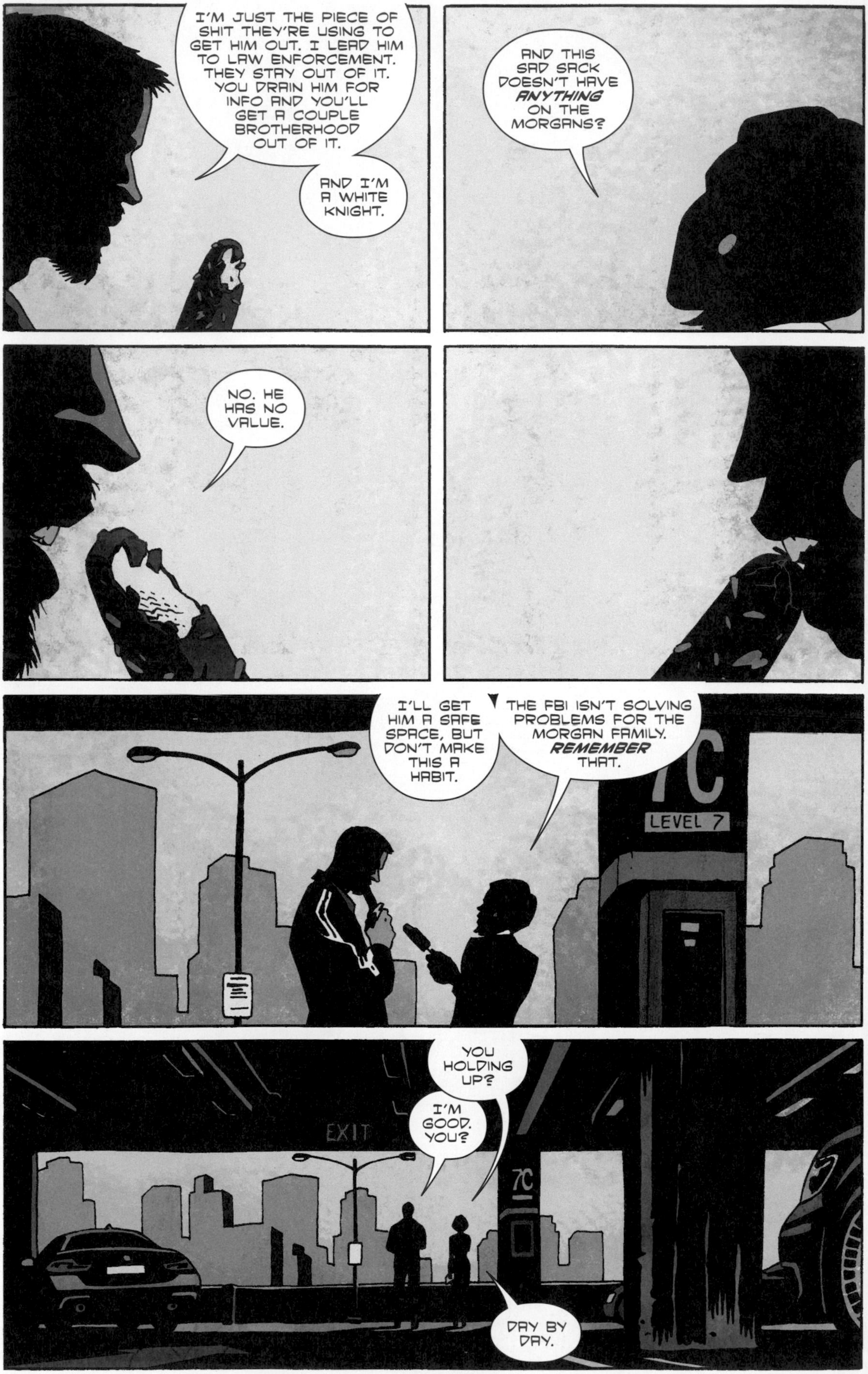

I'M JUST THE PIECE OF SHIT THEY'RE USING TO GET HIM OUT. I LEAD HIM TO LAW ENFORCEMENT. THEY STAY OUT OF IT. YOU DRAIN HIM FOR INFO AND YOU'LL GET A COUPLE BROTHERHOOD OUT OF IT.
AND I'M A WHITE KNIGHT.
AND THIS SAD SACK DOESN'T HAVE *ANYTHING* ON THE MORGANS?
NO. HE HAS NO VALUE.
I'LL GET HIM A SAFE SPACE, BUT DON'T MAKE THIS A HABIT.
THE FBI ISN'T SOLVING PROBLEMS FOR THE MORGAN FAMILY. *REMEMBER* THAT.
7C
LEVEL 7
YOU HOLDING UP?
I'M GOOD. YOU?
EXIT
7C
DAY BY DAY.

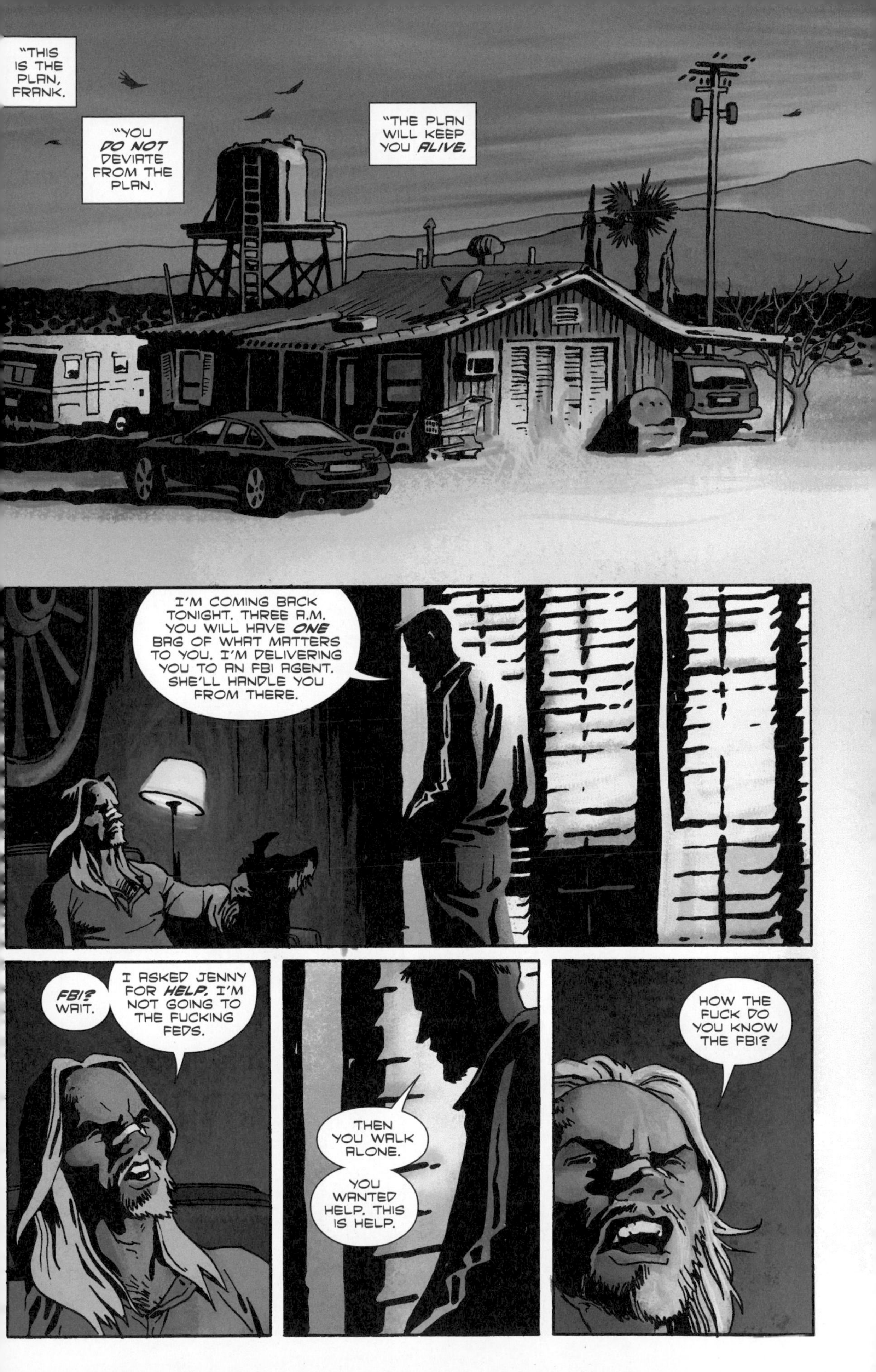
"THIS IS THE PLAN, FRANK.
"YOU DO NOT DEVIATE FROM THE PLAN.
"THE PLAN WILL KEEP YOU ALIVE.
I'M COMING BACK TONIGHT. THREE A.M. YOU WILL HAVE ONE BAG OF WHAT MATTERS TO YOU. I'M DELIVERING YOU TO AN FBI AGENT. SHE'LL HANDLE YOU FROM THERE.
FBI? WAIT.
I ASKED JENNY FOR HELP. I'M NOT GOING TO THE FUCKING FEDS.
THEN YOU WALK ALONE.
YOU WANTED HELP. THIS IS HELP.
HOW THE FUCK DO YOU KNOW THE FBI?

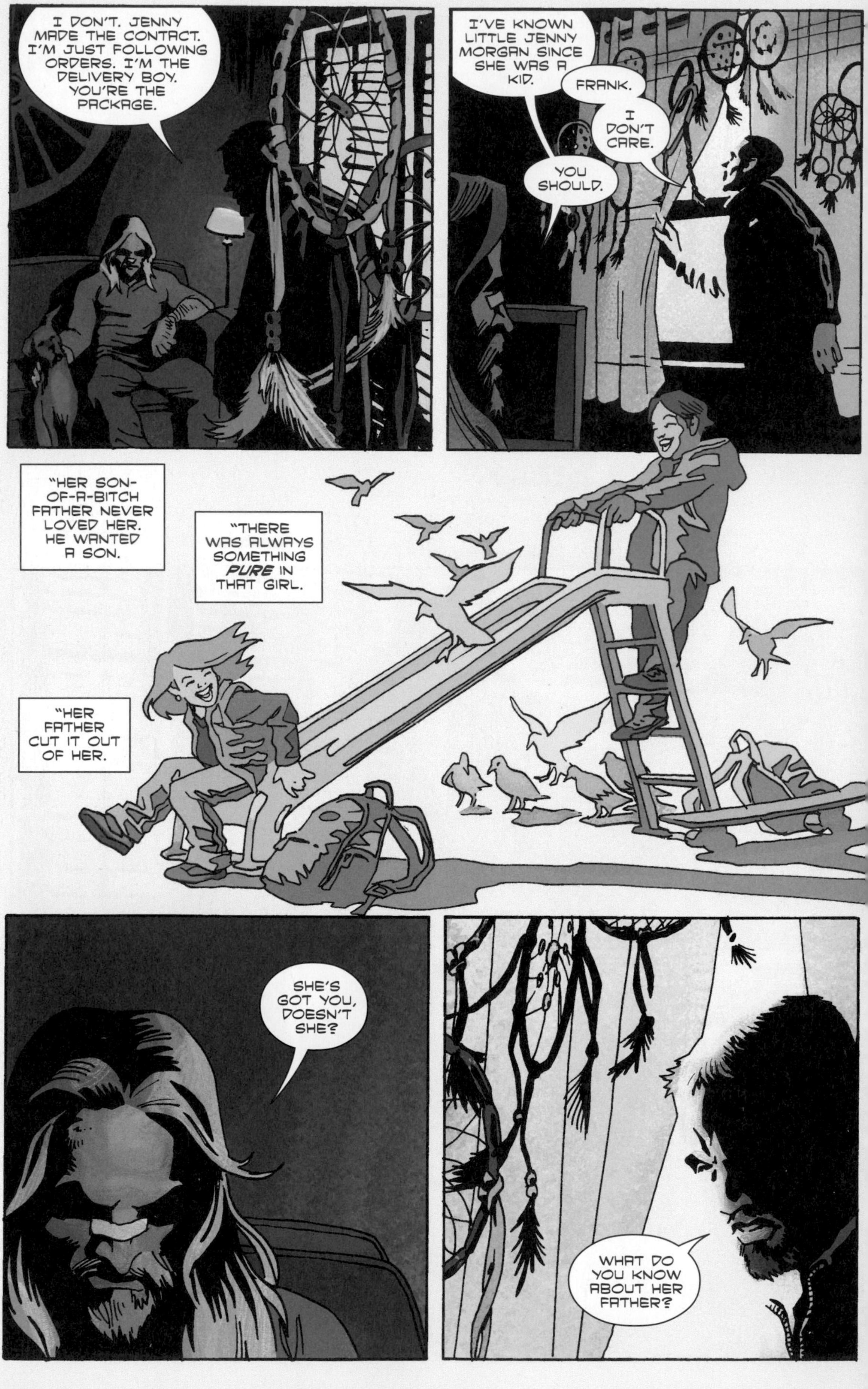
I DON'T. JENNY MADE THE CONTACT. I'M JUST FOLLOWING ORDERS. I'M THE DELIVERY BOY. YOU'RE THE PACKAGE.
I'VE KNOWN LITTLE JENNY MORGAN SINCE SHE WAS A KID.
FRANK.
I DON'T CARE.
YOU SHOULD.
"HER SON-OF-A-BITCH FATHER NEVER LOVED HER. HE WANTED A SON.
"THERE WAS ALWAYS SOMETHING *PURE* IN THAT GIRL.
"HER FATHER CUT IT OUT OF HER.
SHE'S GOT YOU, DOESN'T SHE?
WHAT DO YOU KNOW ABOUT HER FATHER?

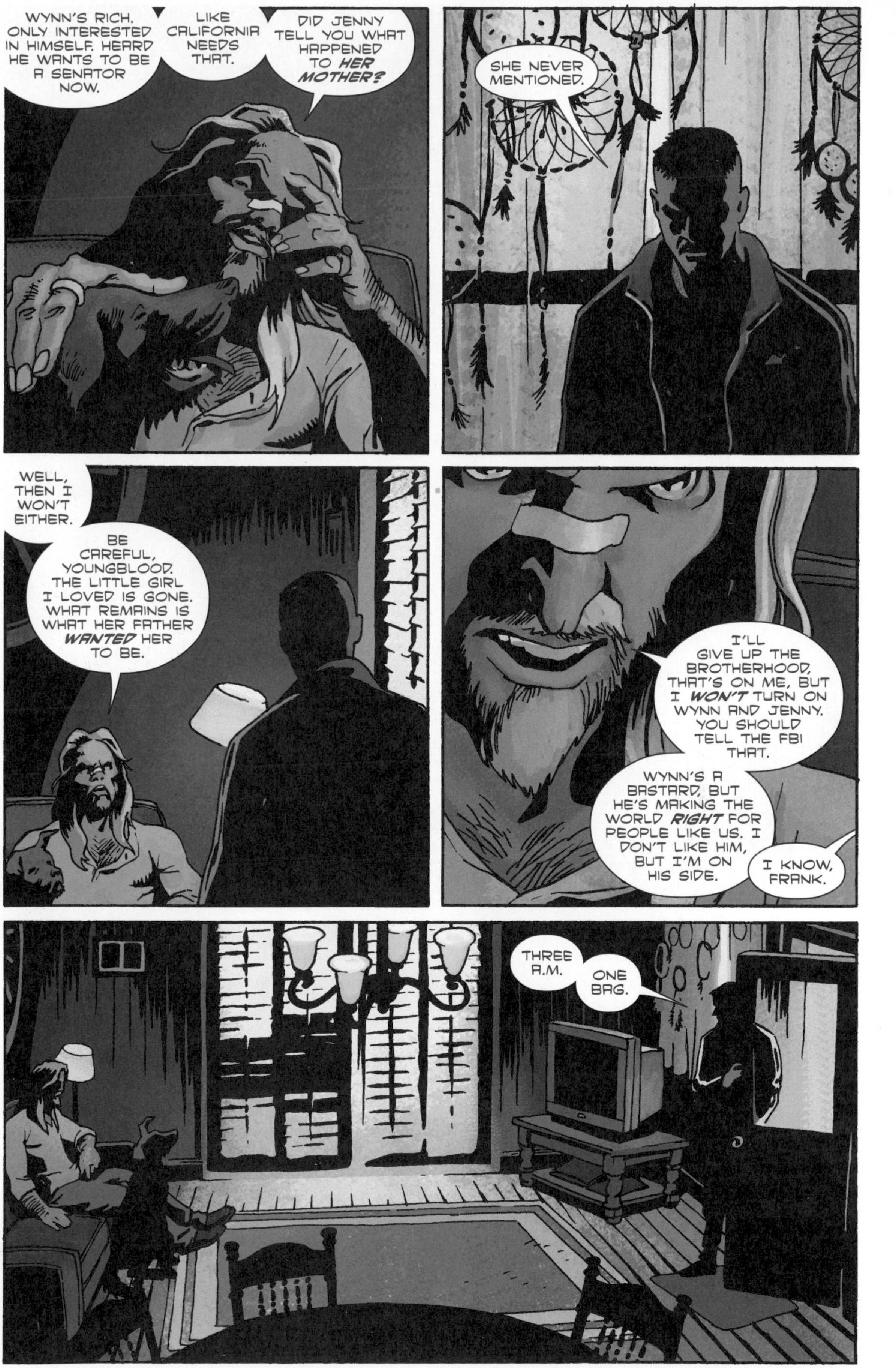
WYNN'S RICH. ONLY INTERESTED IN HIMSELF. HEARD HE WANTS TO BE A SENATOR NOW.
LIKE CALIFORNIA NEEDS THAT.
DID JENNY TELL YOU WHAT HAPPENED TO HER MOTHER?
SHE NEVER MENTIONED.
WELL, THEN I WON'T EITHER.
BE CAREFUL, YOUNGBLOOD. THE LITTLE GIRL I LOVED IS GONE. WHAT REMAINS IS WHAT HER FATHER WANTED HER TO BE.
I'LL GIVE UP THE BROTHERHOOD, THAT'S ON ME, BUT I WON'T TURN ON WYNN AND JENNY. YOU SHOULD TELL THE FBI THAT.
WYNN'S A BASTARD, BUT HE'S MAKING THE WORLD RIGHT FOR PEOPLE LIKE US. I DON'T LIKE HIM, BUT I'M ON HIS SIDE.
I KNOW, FRANK.
THREE A.M.
ONE BAG.

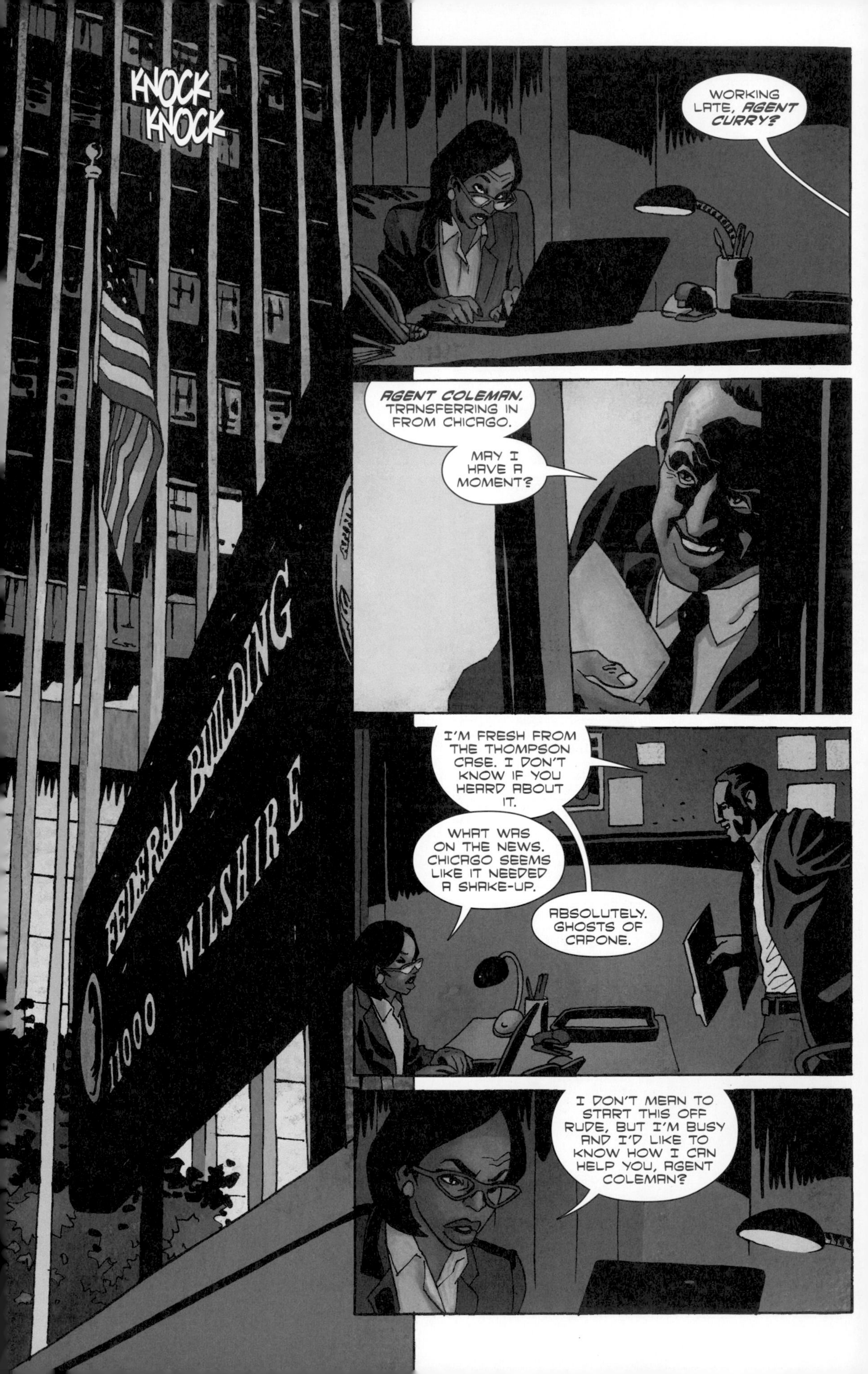
KNOCK KNOCK
FEDERAL BUILDING
11000 WILSHIRE
WORKING LATE, AGENT CURRY?
AGENT COLEMAN. TRANSFERRING IN FROM CHICAGO.
MAY I HAVE A MOMENT?
I'M FRESH FROM THE THOMPSON CASE. I DON'T KNOW IF YOU HEARD ABOUT IT.
WHAT WAS ON THE NEWS. CHICAGO SEEMS LIKE IT NEEDED A SHAKE-UP.
ABSOLUTELY. GHOSTS OF CAPONE.
I DON'T MEAN TO START THIS OFF RUDE, BUT I'M BUSY AND I'D LIKE TO KNOW HOW I CAN HELP YOU, AGENT COLEMAN?

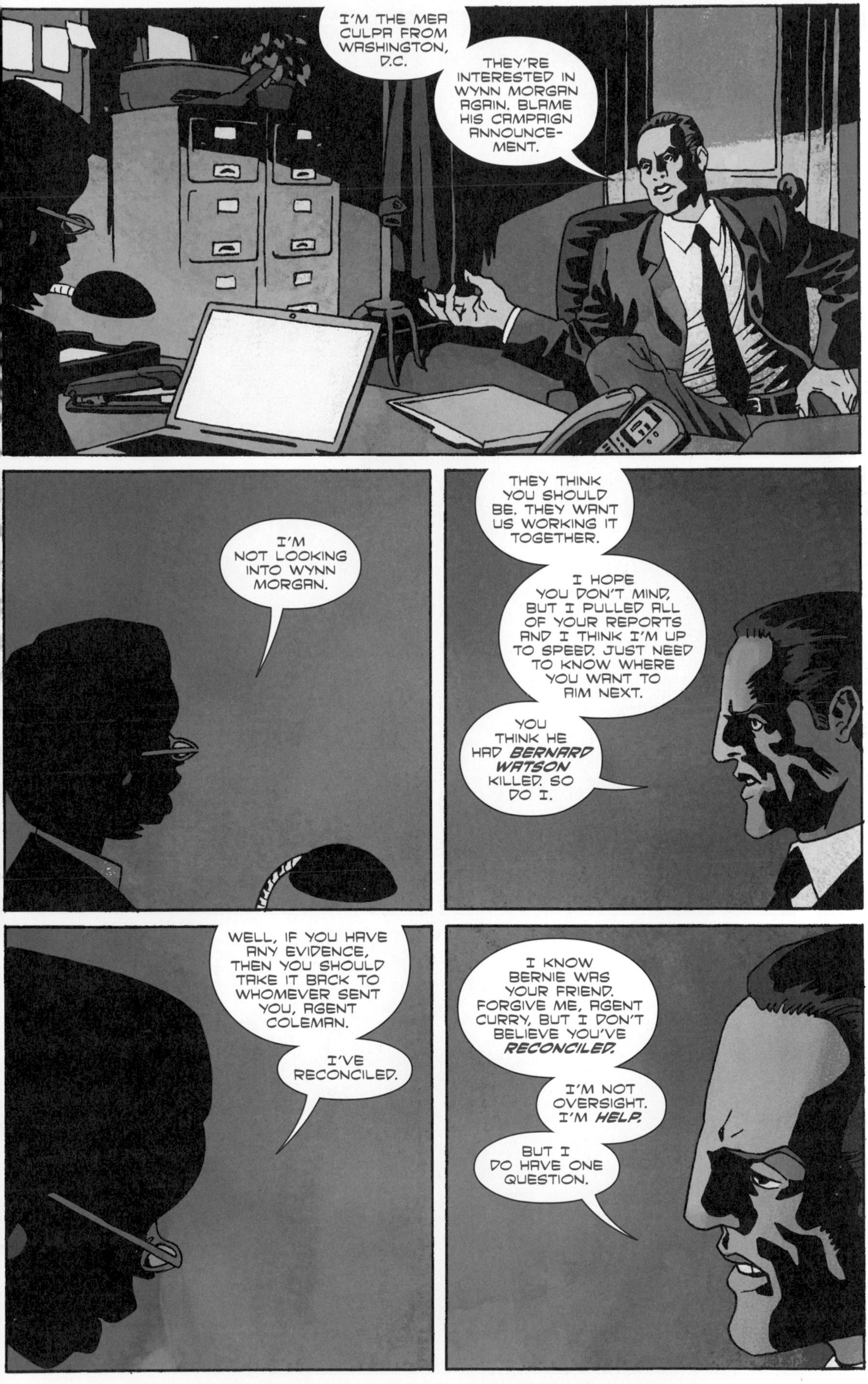
I'M THE MEA CULPA FROM WASHINGTON, D.C.
THEY'RE INTERESTED IN WYNN MORGAN AGAIN. BLAME HIS CAMPAIGN ANNOUNCEMENT.
I'M NOT LOOKING INTO WYNN MORGAN.
THEY THINK YOU SHOULD BE. THEY WANT US WORKING IT TOGETHER.
I HOPE YOU DON'T MIND, BUT I PULLED ALL OF YOUR REPORTS AND I THINK I'M UP TO SPEED. JUST NEED TO KNOW WHERE YOU WANT TO AIM NEXT.
YOU THINK HE HAD BERNARD WATSON KILLED. SO DO I.
WELL, IF YOU HAVE ANY EVIDENCE, THEN YOU SHOULD TAKE IT BACK TO WHOMEVER SENT YOU, AGENT COLEMAN.
I'VE RECONCILED.
I KNOW BERNIE WAS YOUR FRIEND. FORGIVE ME, AGENT CURRY, BUT I DON'T BELIEVE YOU'VE RECONCILED.
I'M NOT OVERSIGHT. I'M HELP.
BUT I DO HAVE ONE QUESTION.

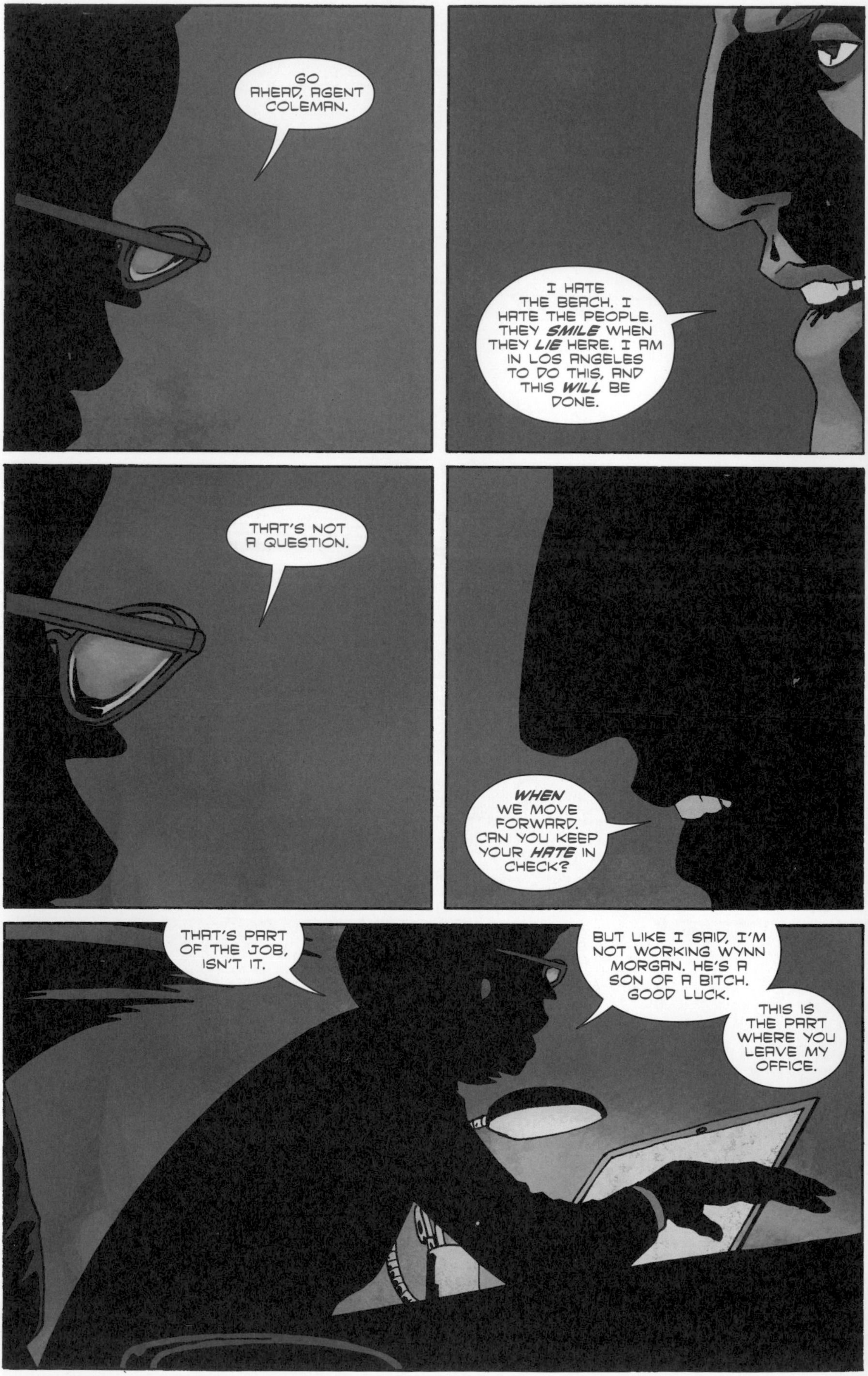
GO AHEAD, AGENT COLEMAN.
I HATE THE BEACH. I HATE THE PEOPLE. THEY SMILE WHEN THEY LIE HERE. I AM IN LOS ANGELES TO DO THIS, AND THIS WILL BE DONE.
THAT'S NOT A QUESTION.
WHEN WE MOVE FORWARD. CAN YOU KEEP YOUR HATE IN CHECK?
THAT'S PART OF THE JOB, ISN'T IT.
BUT LIKE I SAID, I'M NOT WORKING WYNN MORGAN. HE'S A SON OF A BITCH. GOOD LUCK.
THIS IS THE PART WHERE YOU LEAVE MY OFFICE.

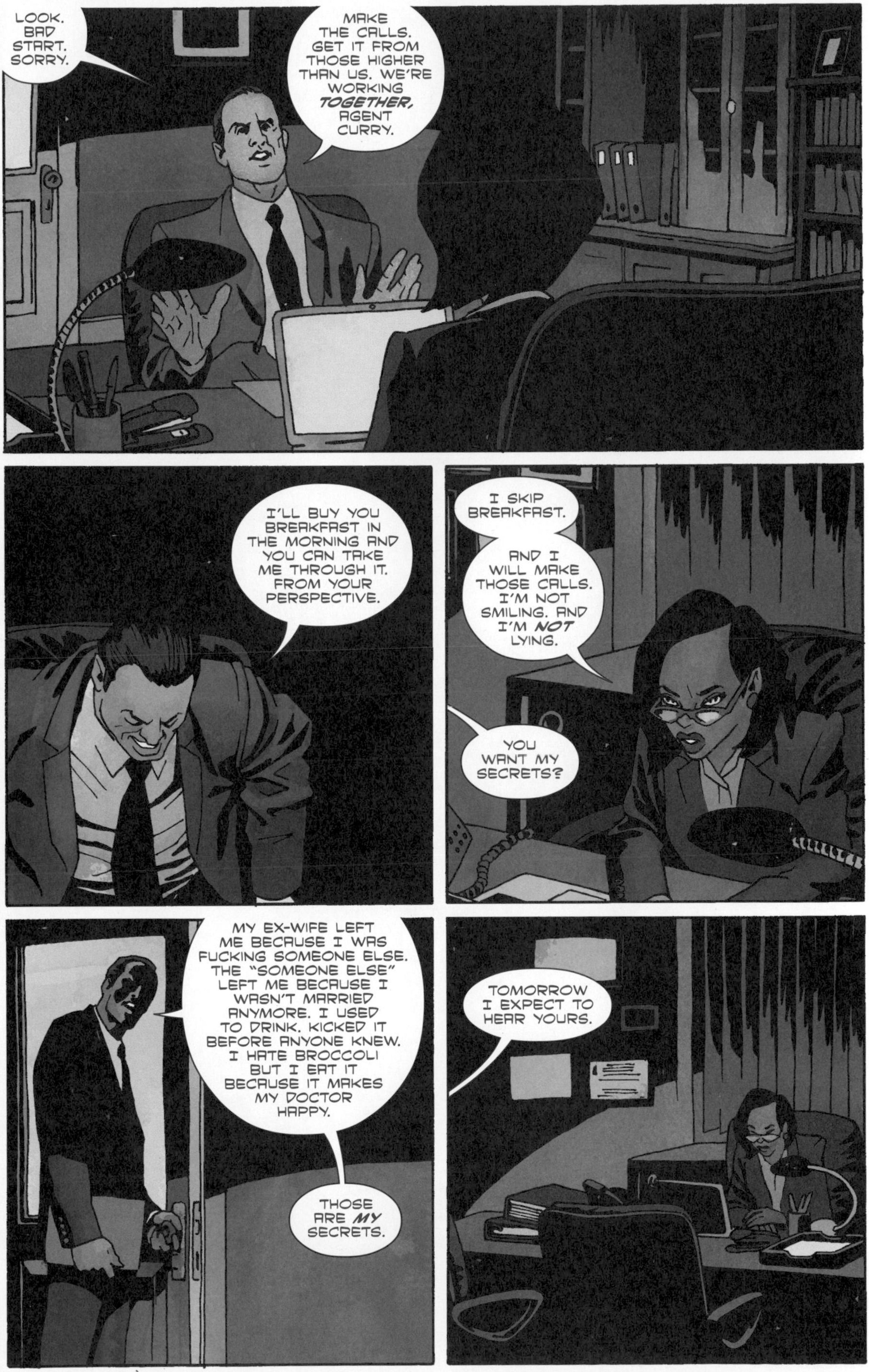
LOOK. BAD START. SORRY.
MAKE THE CALLS. GET IT FROM THOSE HIGHER THAN US. WE'RE WORKING *TOGETHER,* AGENT CURRY.
I'LL BUY YOU BREAKFAST IN THE MORNING AND YOU CAN TAKE ME THROUGH IT. FROM YOUR PERSPECTIVE.
I SKIP BREAKFAST.
AND I WILL MAKE THOSE CALLS. I'M NOT SMILING. AND I'M *NOT* LYING.
YOU WANT MY SECRETS?
MY EX-WIFE LEFT ME BECAUSE I WAS FUCKING SOMEONE ELSE. THE "SOMEONE ELSE" LEFT ME BECAUSE I WASN'T MARRIED ANYMORE. I USED TO DRINK. KICKED IT BEFORE ANYONE KNEW. I HATE BROCCOLI BUT I EAT IT BECAUSE IT MAKES MY DOCTOR HAPPY.
THOSE ARE *MY* SECRETS.
TOMORROW I EXPECT TO HEAR YOURS.

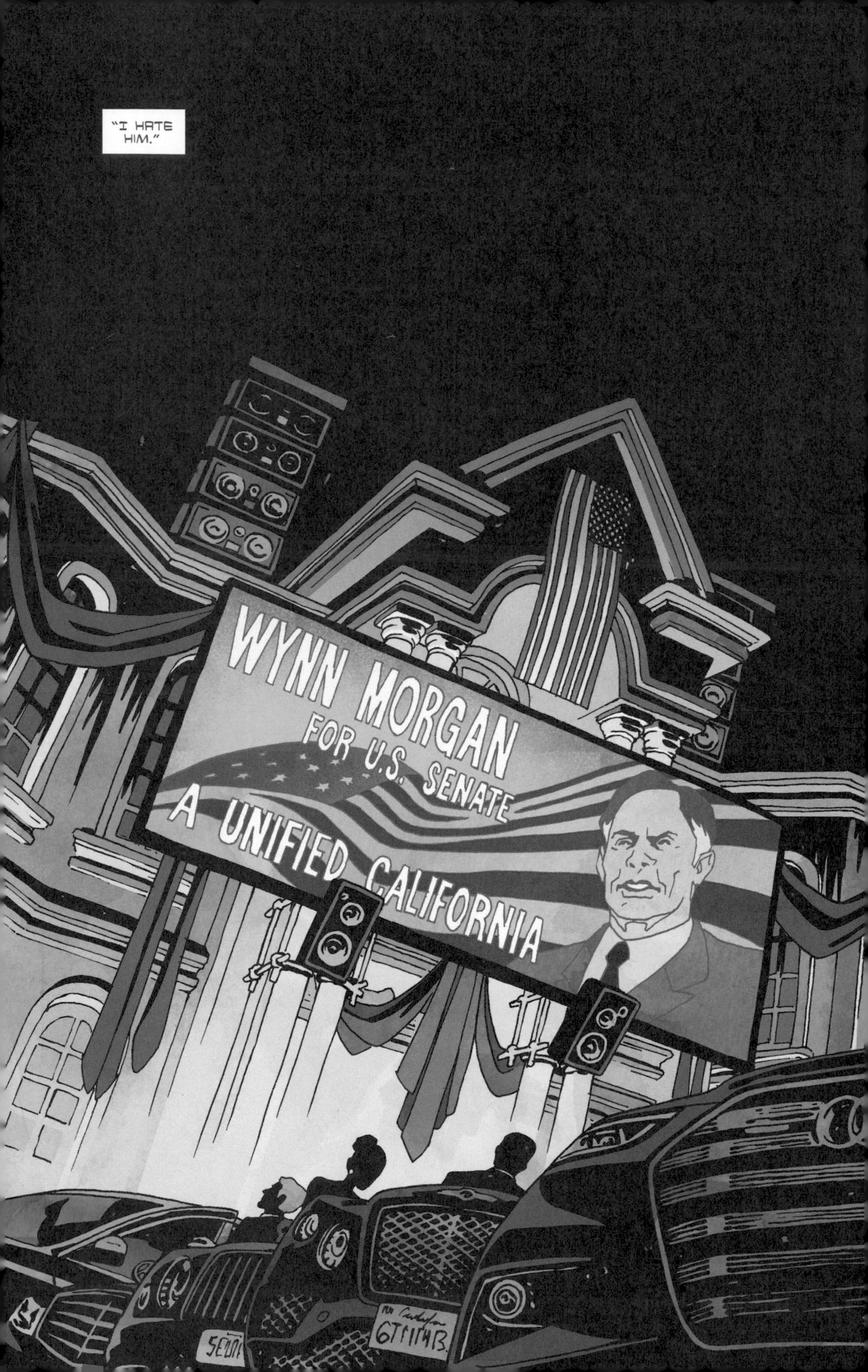
"I HATE HIM."
WYNN MORGAN
FOR U.S. SENATE
A UNIFIED CALIFORNIA

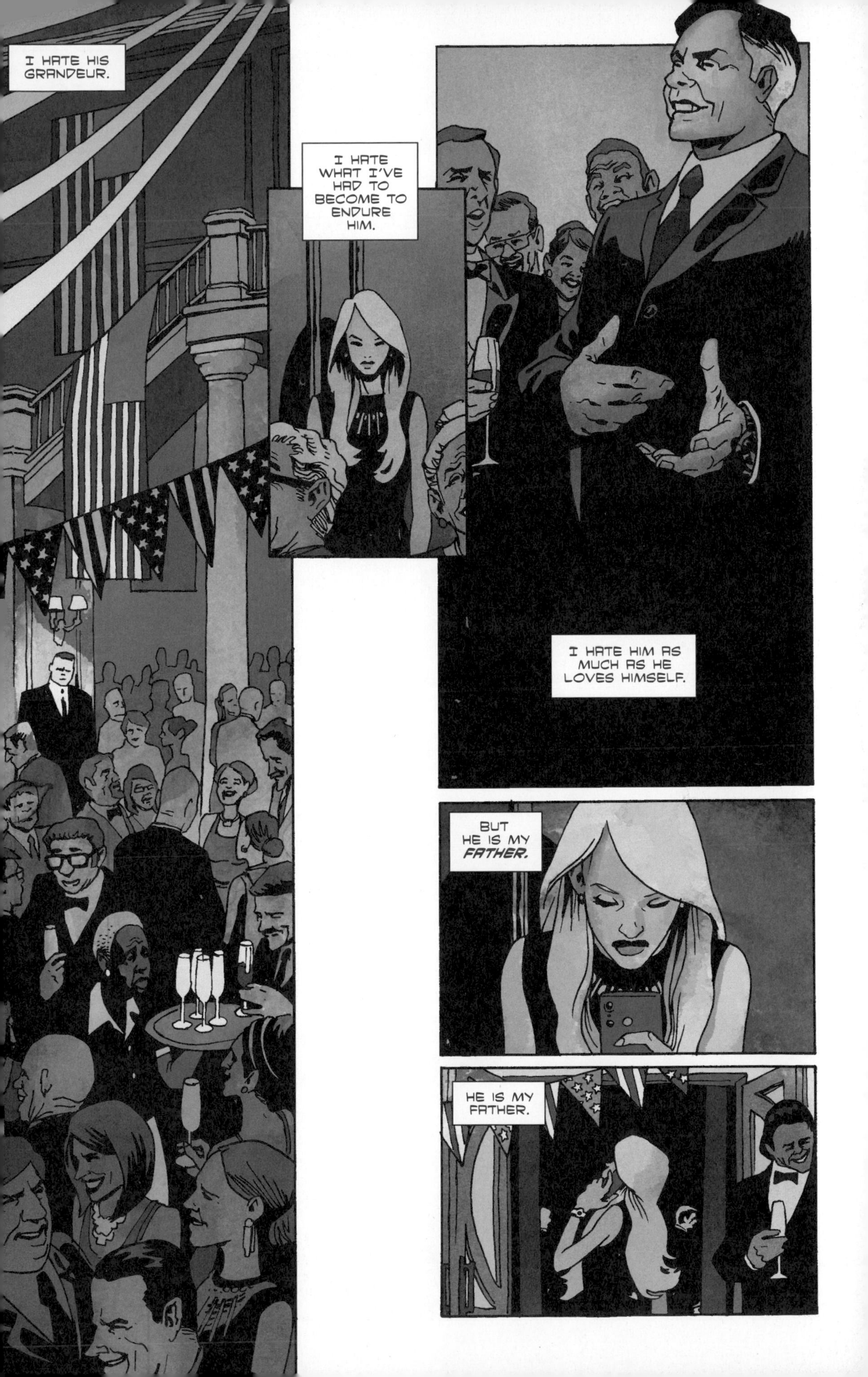
I HATE HIS GRANDEUR.
I HATE WHAT I'VE HAD TO BECOME TO ENDURE HIM.
I HATE HIM AS MUCH AS HE LOVES HIMSELF.
BUT HE IS MY *FATHER.*
HE IS MY FATHER.

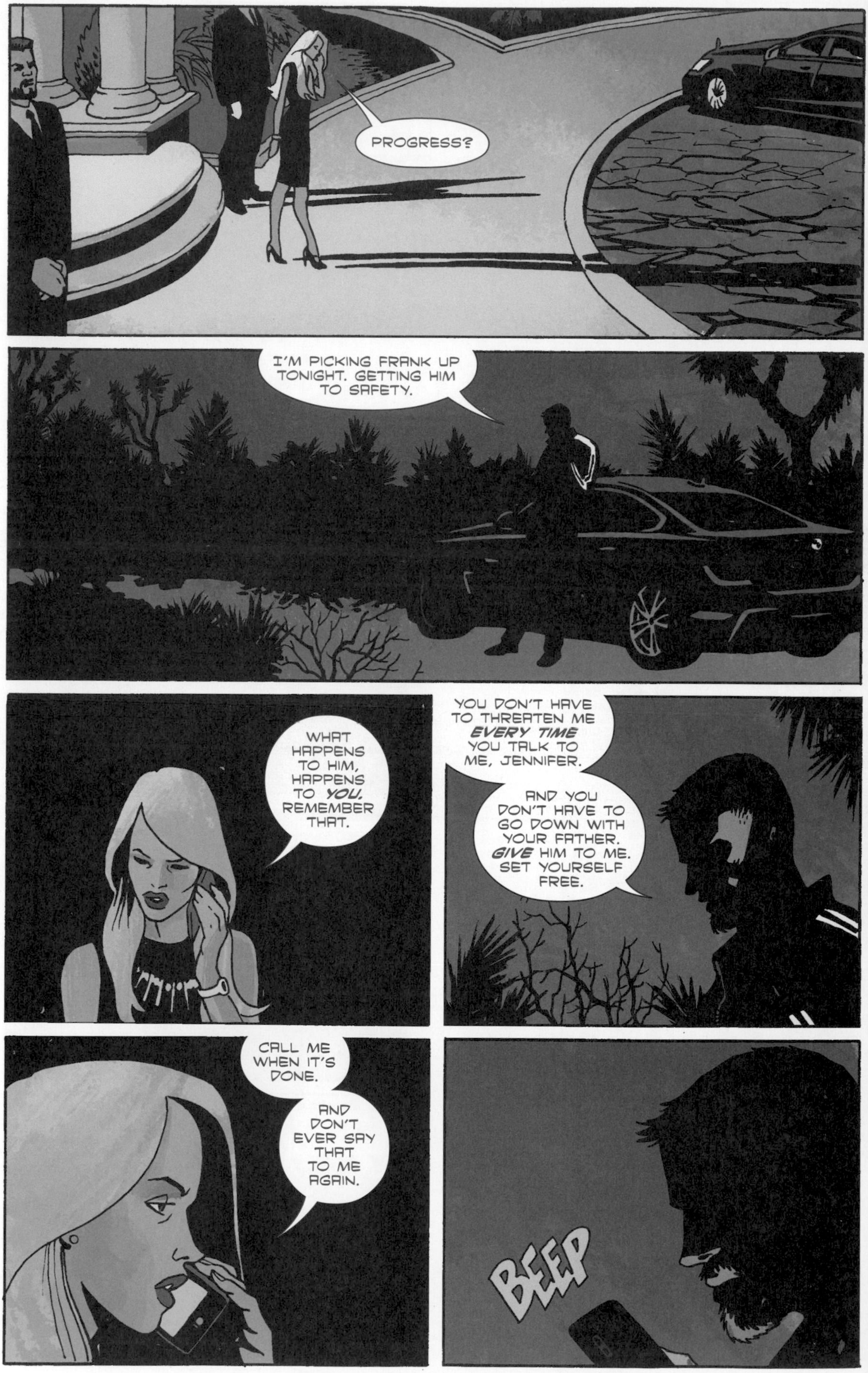
PROGRESS?
I'M PICKING FRANK UP TONIGHT. GETTING HIM TO SAFETY.
WHAT HAPPENS TO HIM, HAPPENS TO YOU. REMEMBER THAT.
YOU DON'T HAVE TO THREATEN ME EVERY TIME YOU TALK TO ME, JENNIFER.
AND YOU DON'T HAVE TO GO DOWN WITH YOUR FATHER. GIVE HIM TO ME. SET YOURSELF FREE.
CALL ME WHEN IT'S DONE.
AND DON'T EVER SAY THAT TO ME AGAIN.
BEEP

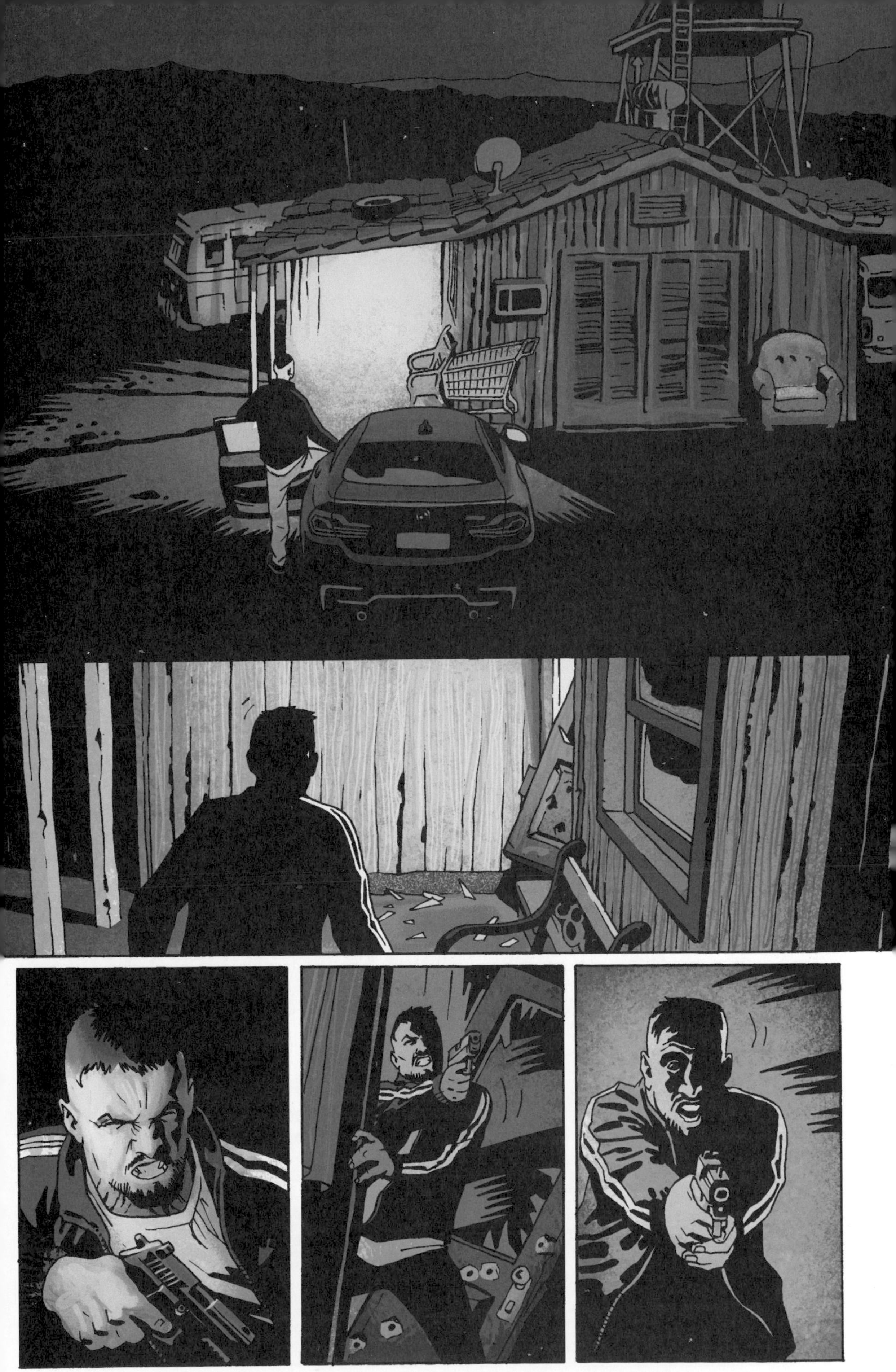

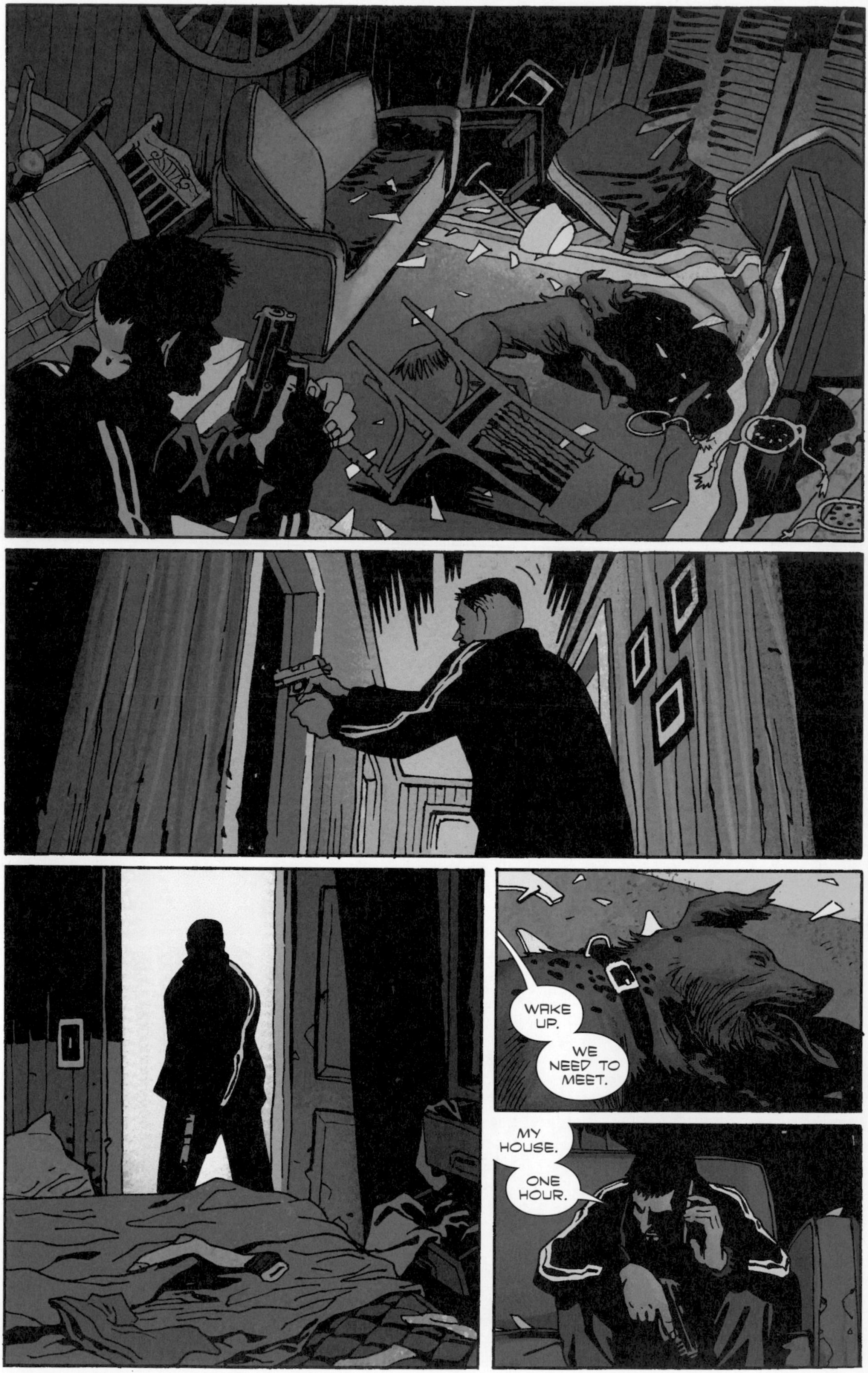
WAKE UP.
WE NEED TO MEET.
MY HOUSE.
ONE HOUR.

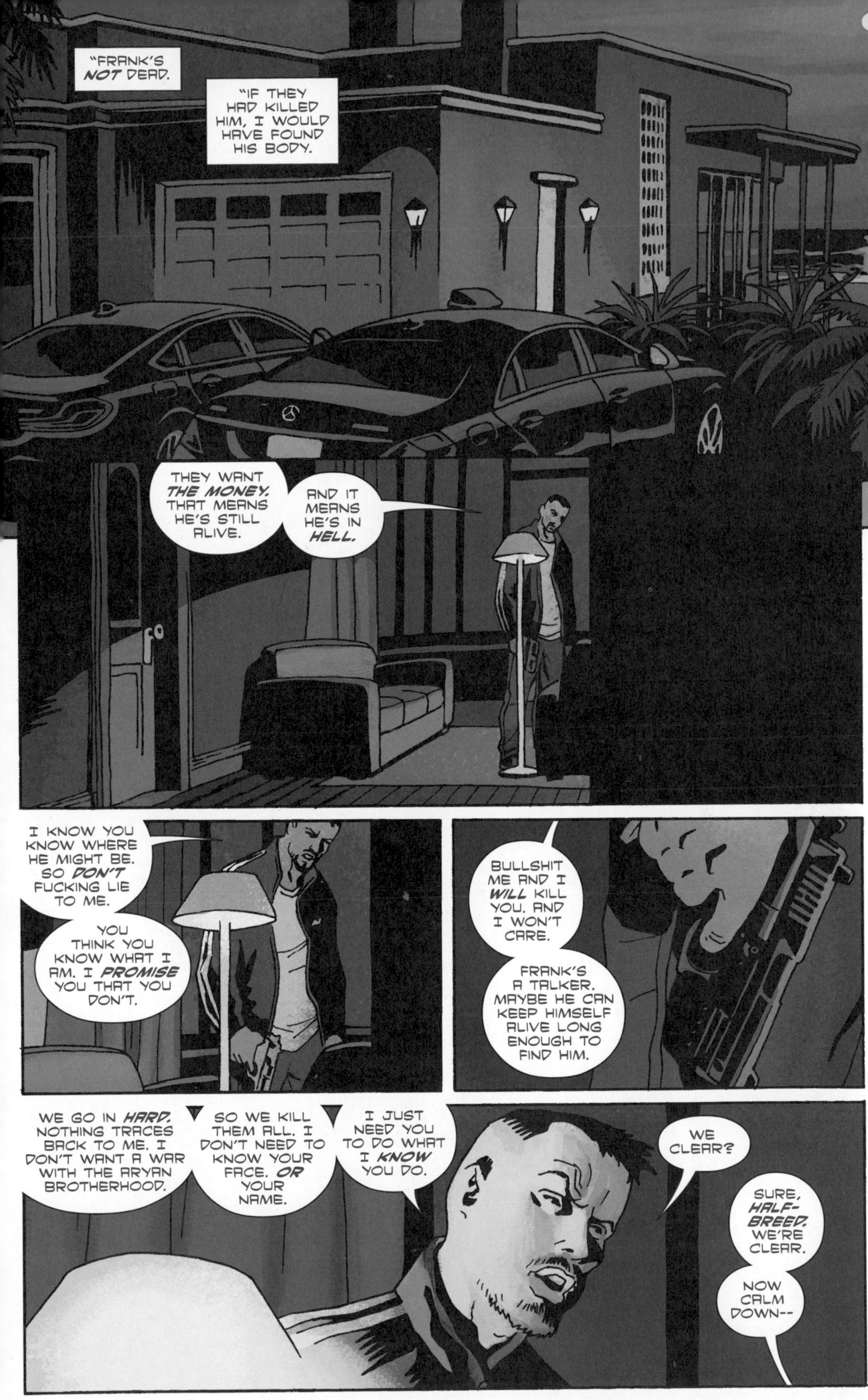
"FRANK'S NOT DEAD.
"IF THEY HAD KILLED HIM, I WOULD HAVE FOUND HIS BODY.
THEY WANT THE MONEY. THAT MEANS HE'S STILL ALIVE.
AND IT MEANS HE'S IN HELL.
I KNOW YOU KNOW WHERE HE MIGHT BE. SO DON'T FUCKING LIE TO ME.
YOU THINK YOU KNOW WHAT I AM. I PROMISE YOU THAT YOU DON'T.
BULLSHIT ME AND I WILL KILL YOU. AND I WON'T CARE.
FRANK'S A TALKER. MAYBE HE CAN KEEP HIMSELF ALIVE LONG ENOUGH TO FIND HIM.
WE GO IN HARD. NOTHING TRACES BACK TO ME. I DON'T WANT A WAR WITH THE ARYAN BROTHERHOOD.
SO WE KILL THEM ALL. I DON'T NEED TO KNOW YOUR FACE. OR YOUR NAME.
I JUST NEED YOU TO DO WHAT I KNOW YOU DO.
WE CLEAR?
SURE, HALF-BREED. WE'RE CLEAR.
NOW CALM DOWN--

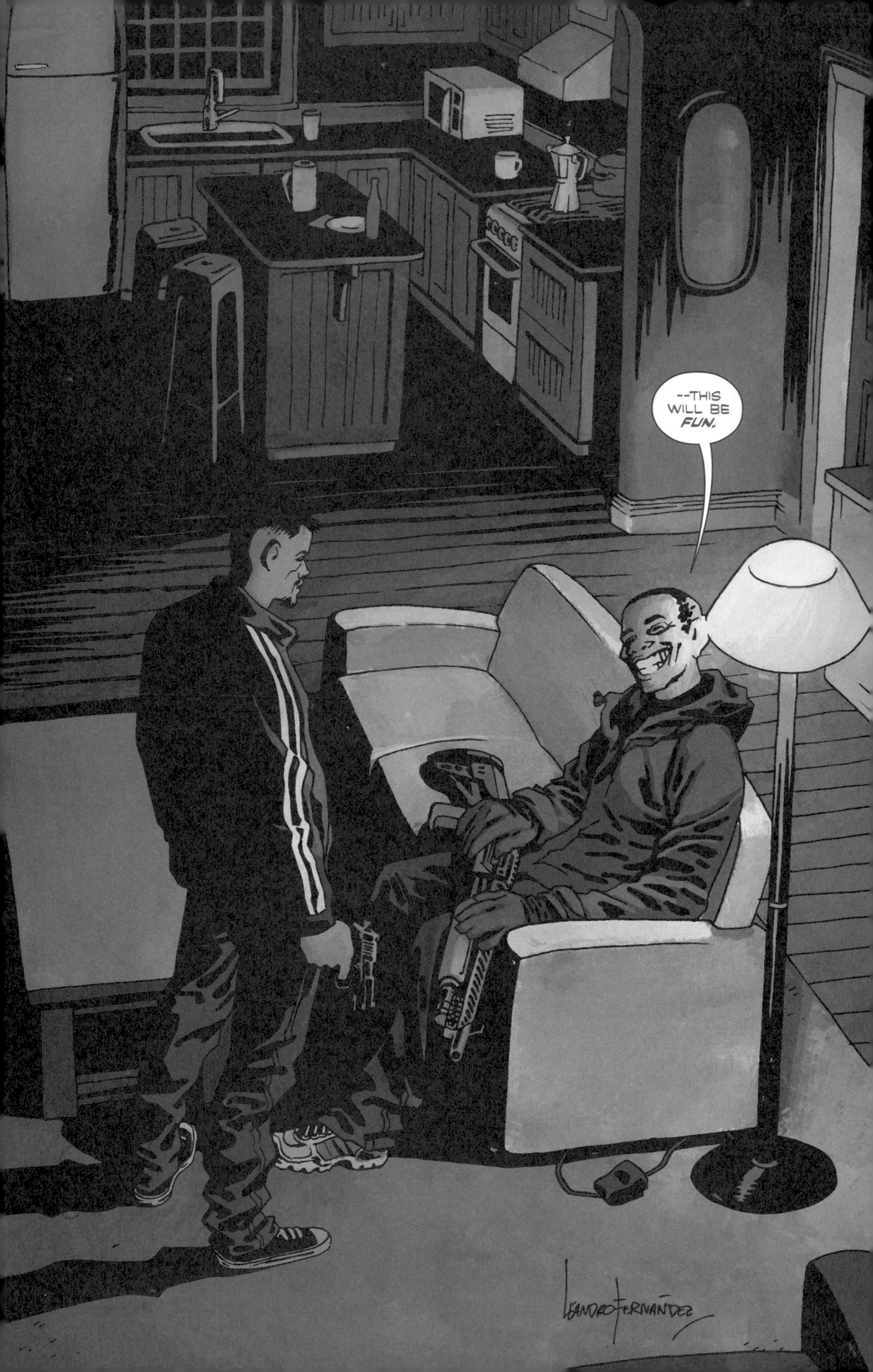
--THIS WILL BE FUN.

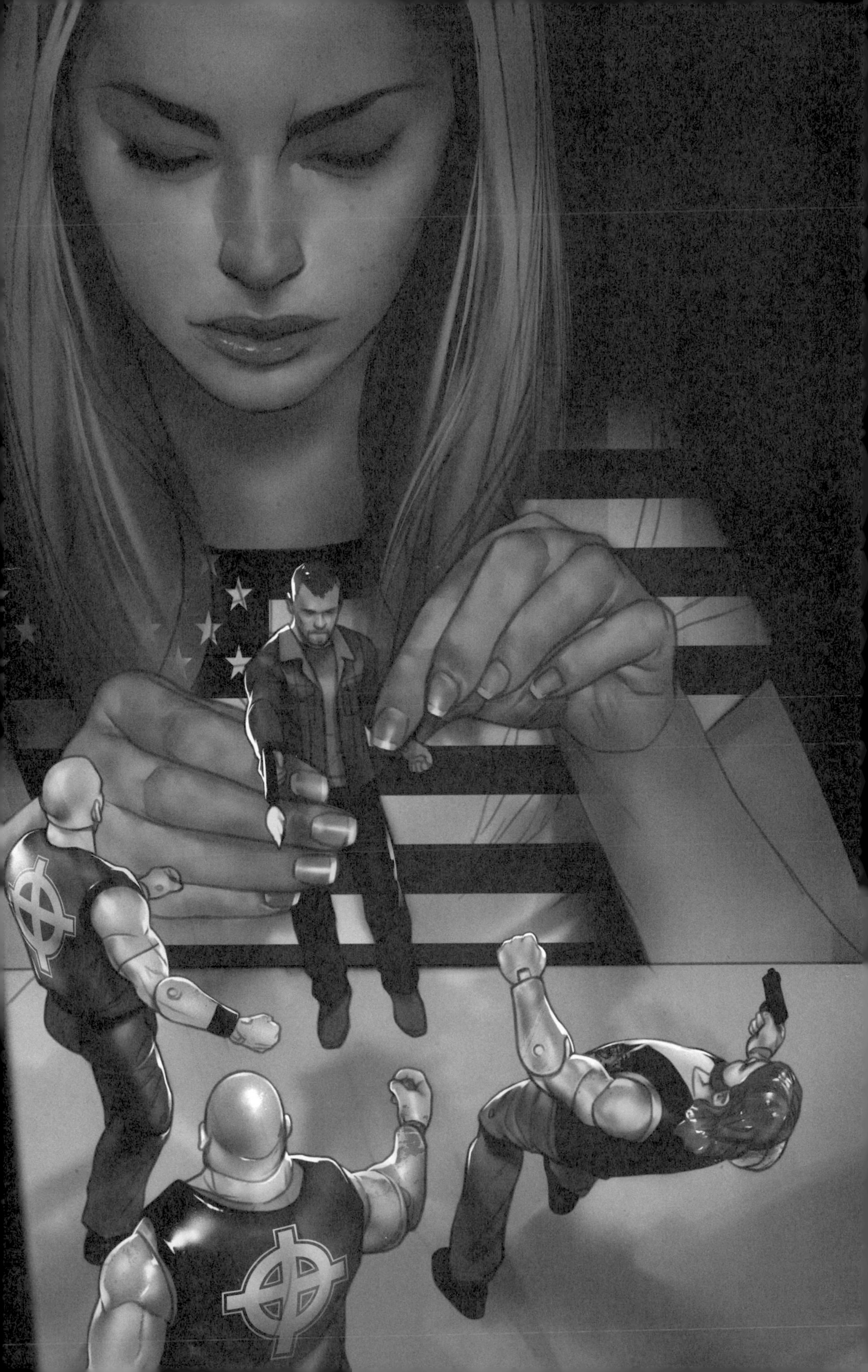

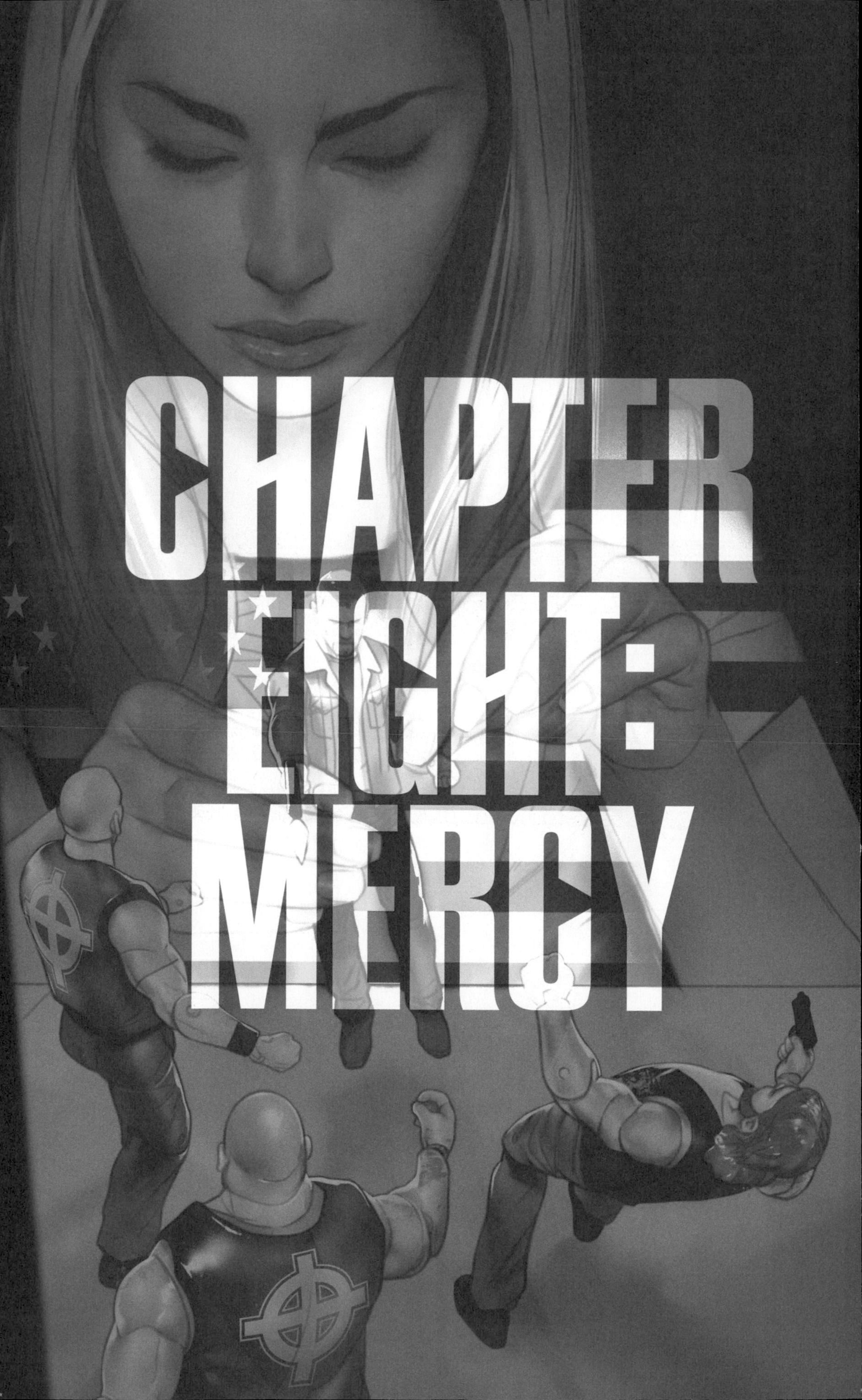
CHAPTER
EIGHT:
MERCY

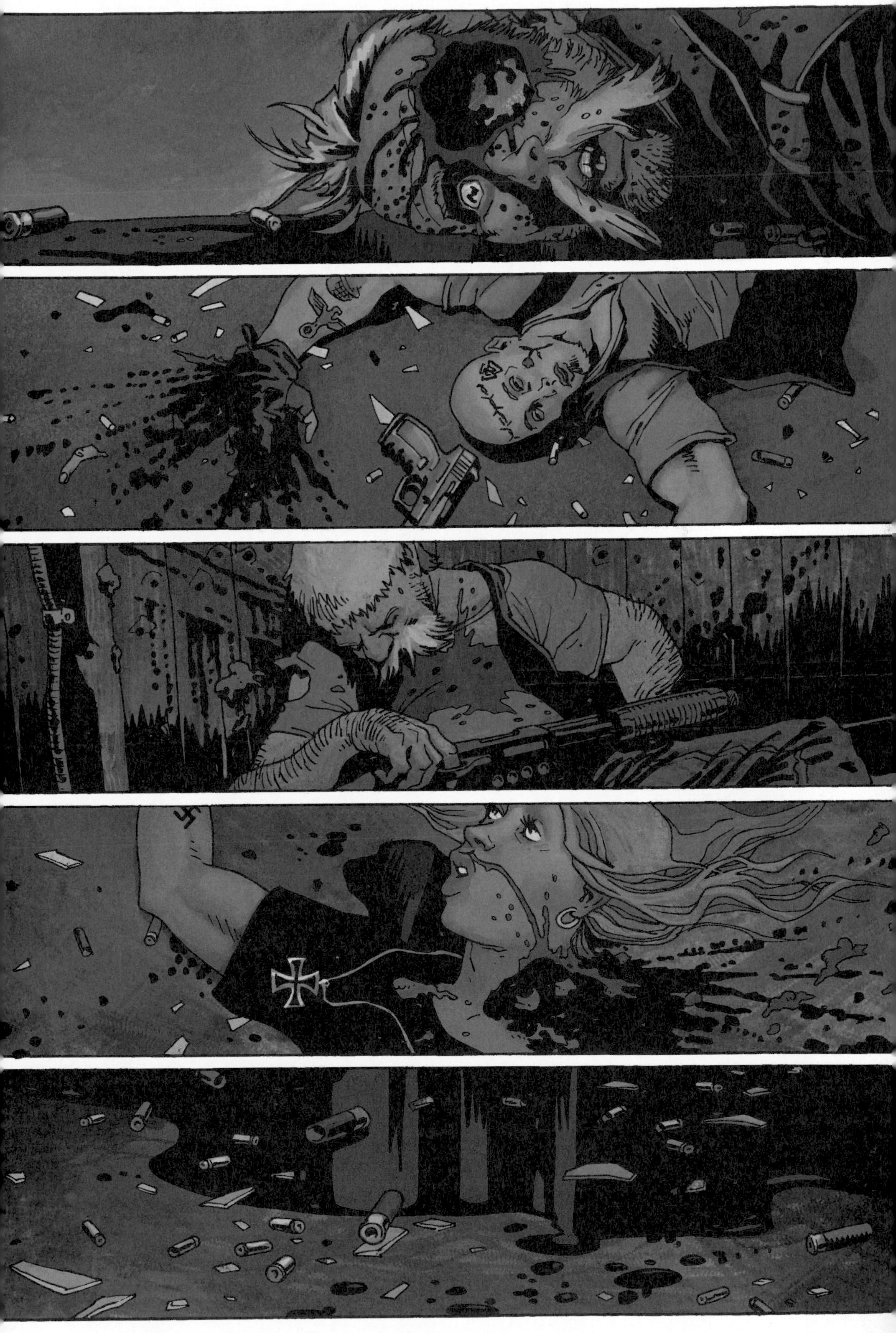

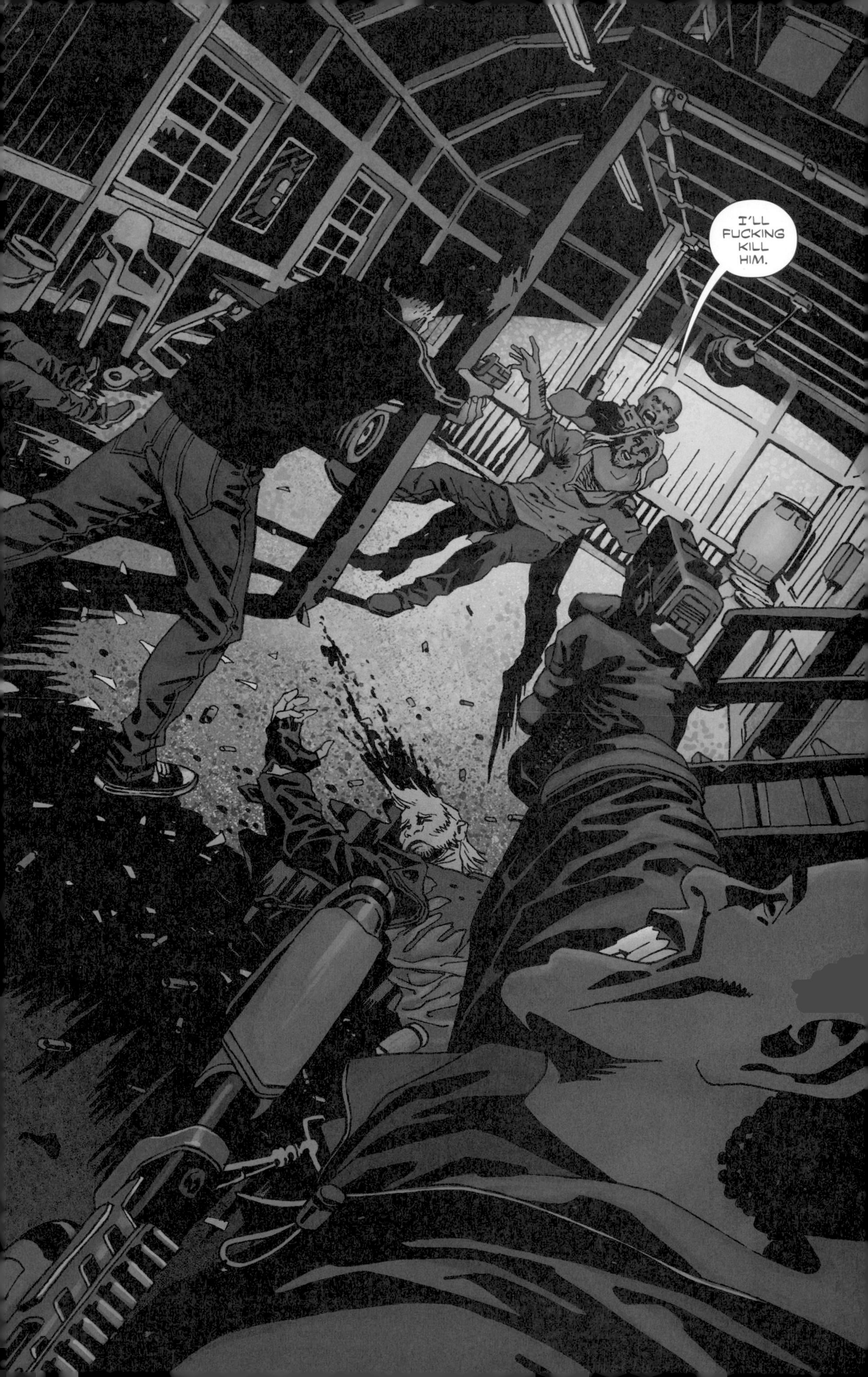
I'LL FUCKING KILL HIM.

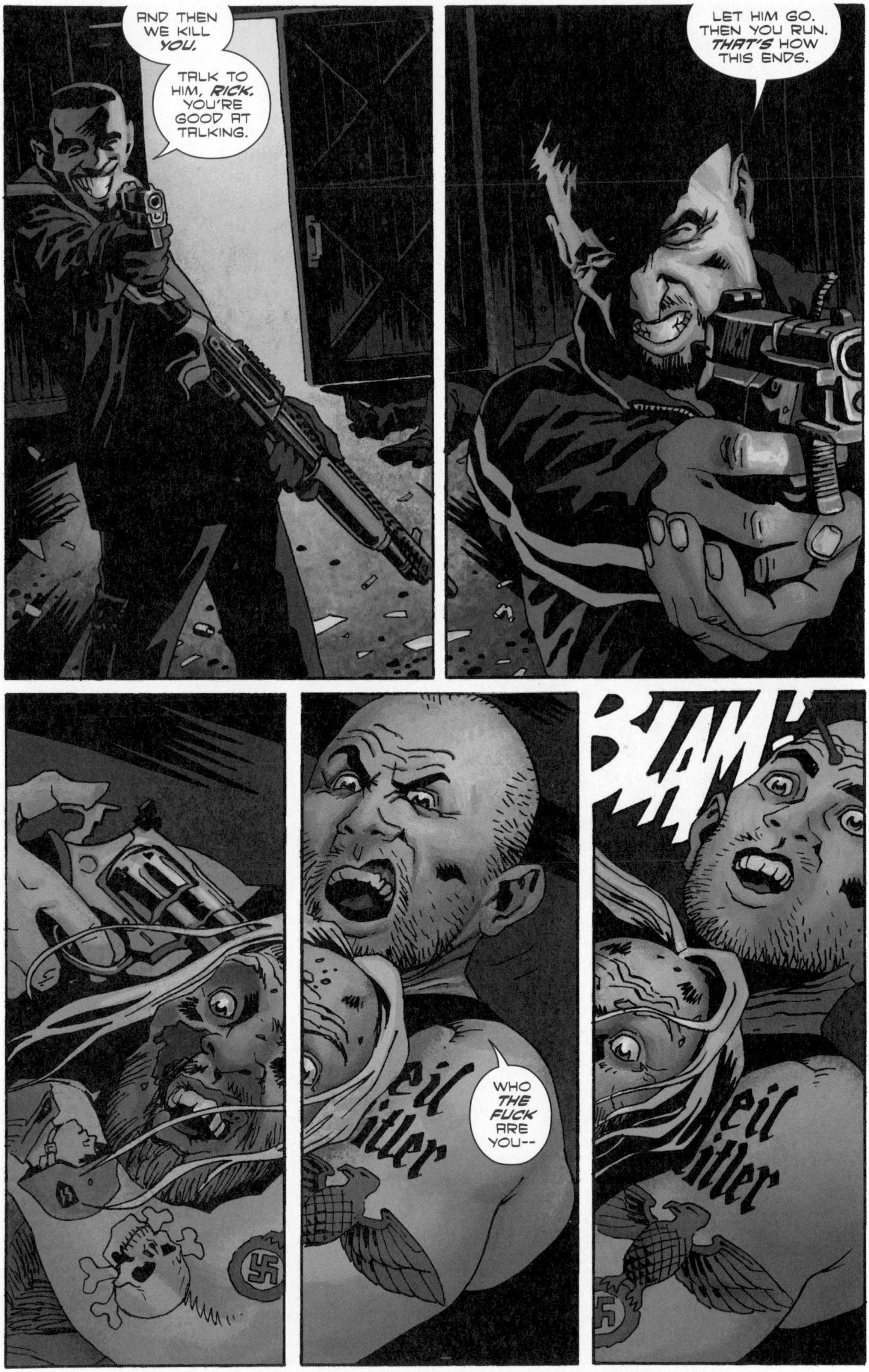
AND THEN WE KILL *YOU.*
TALK TO HIM, *RICK.* YOU'RE GOOD AT TALKING.
LET HIM GO. THEN YOU RUN. *THAT'S* HOW THIS ENDS.
WHO *THE FUCK* ARE YOU--
Heil Hitler
BLAM
Heil Hitler

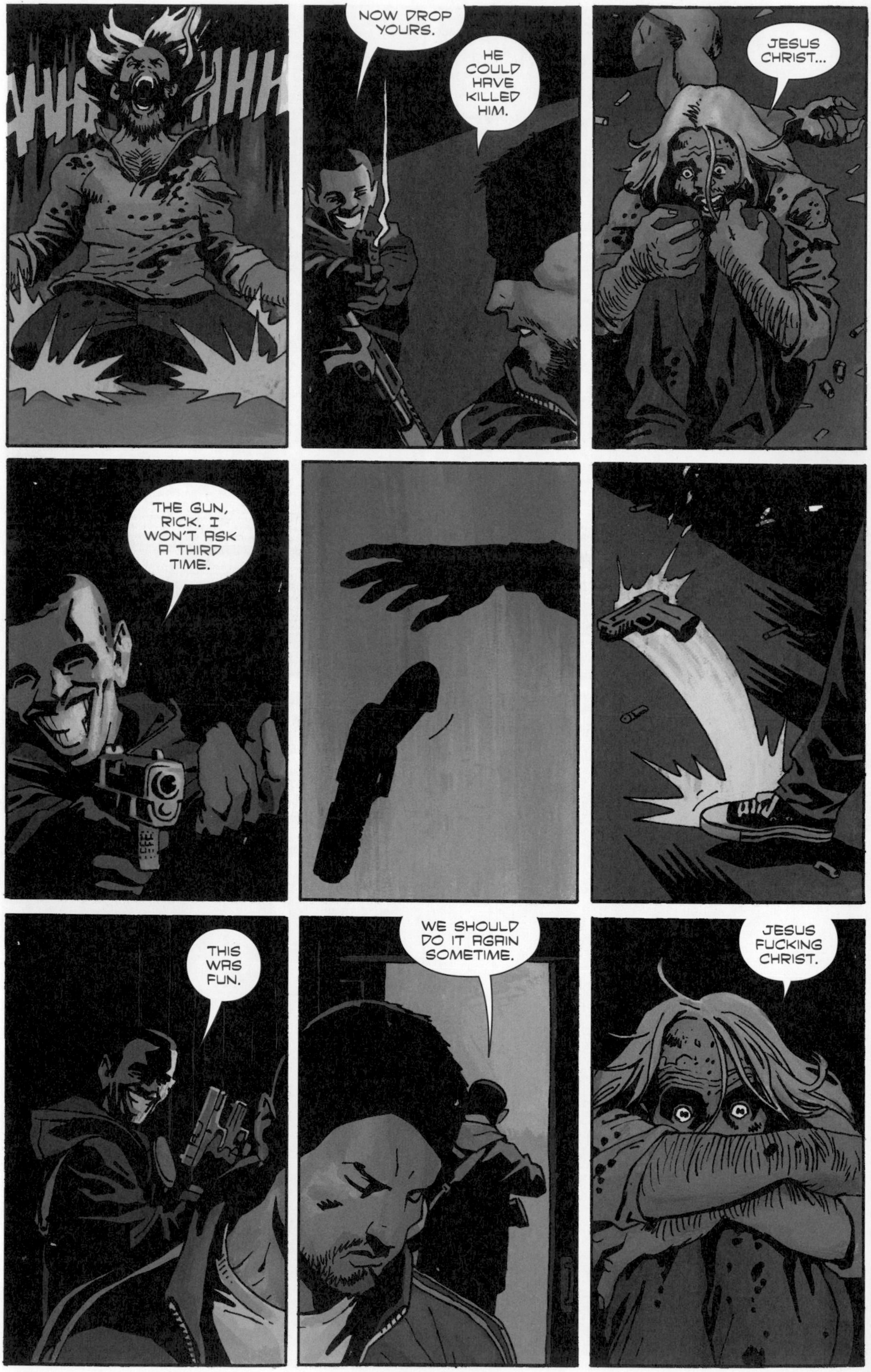
AHHHHHHH
NOW DROP YOURS.
HE COULD HAVE KILLED HIM.
JESUS CHRIST...
THE GUN, RICK. I WON'T ASK A THIRD TIME.
THIS WAS FUN.
WE SHOULD DO IT AGAIN SOMETIME.
JESUS FUCKING CHRIST.

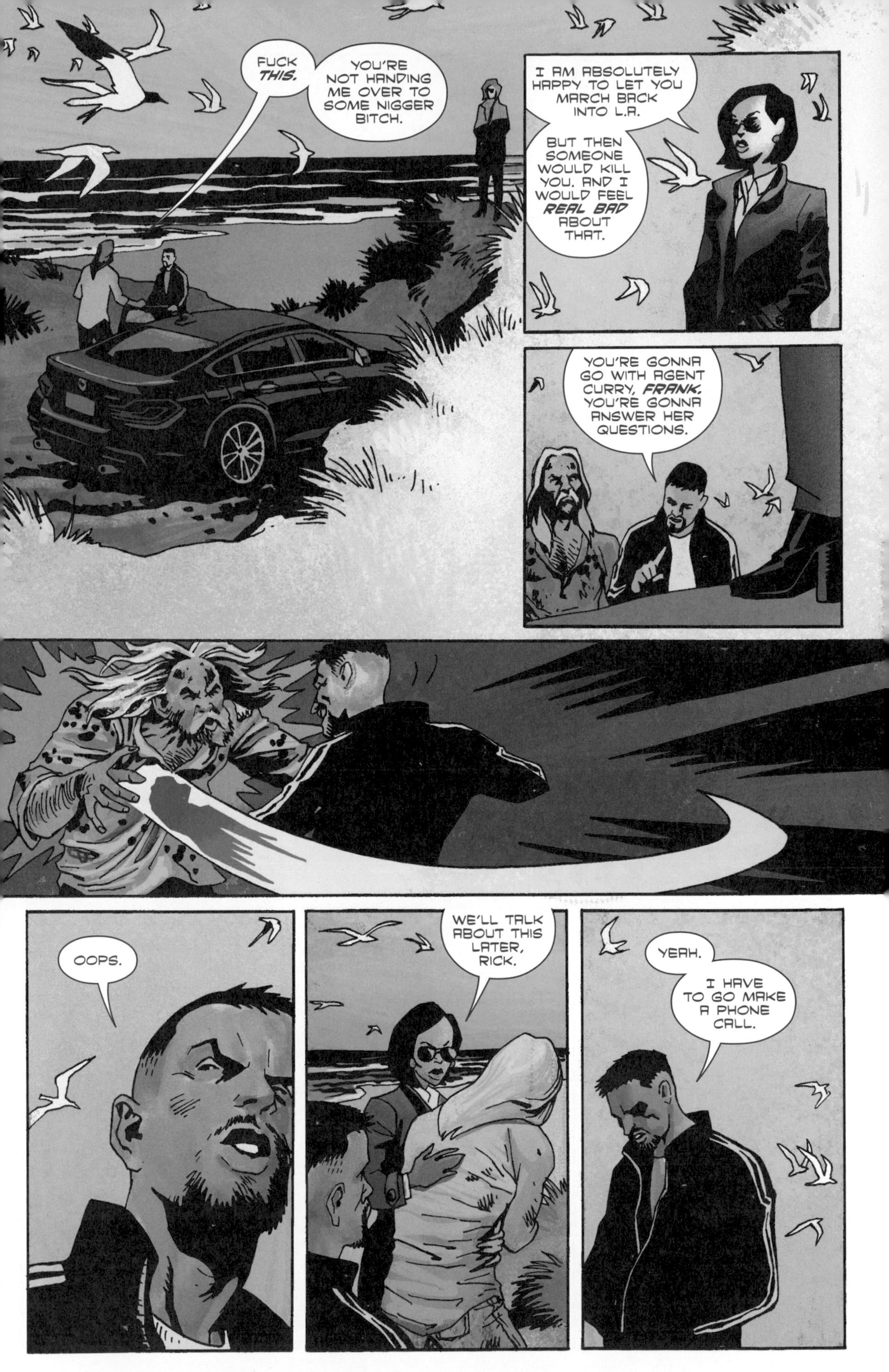
FUCK THIS.
YOU'RE NOT HANDING ME OVER TO SOME NIGGER BITCH.
I AM ABSOLUTELY HAPPY TO LET YOU MARCH BACK INTO L.A.
BUT THEN SOMEONE WOULD KILL YOU. AND I WOULD FEEL REAL BAD ABOUT THAT.
YOU'RE GONNA GO WITH AGENT CURRY, FRANK. YOU'RE GONNA ANSWER HER QUESTIONS.
OOPS.
WE'LL TALK ABOUT THIS LATER, RICK.
YEAH.
I HAVE TO GO MAKE A PHONE CALL.

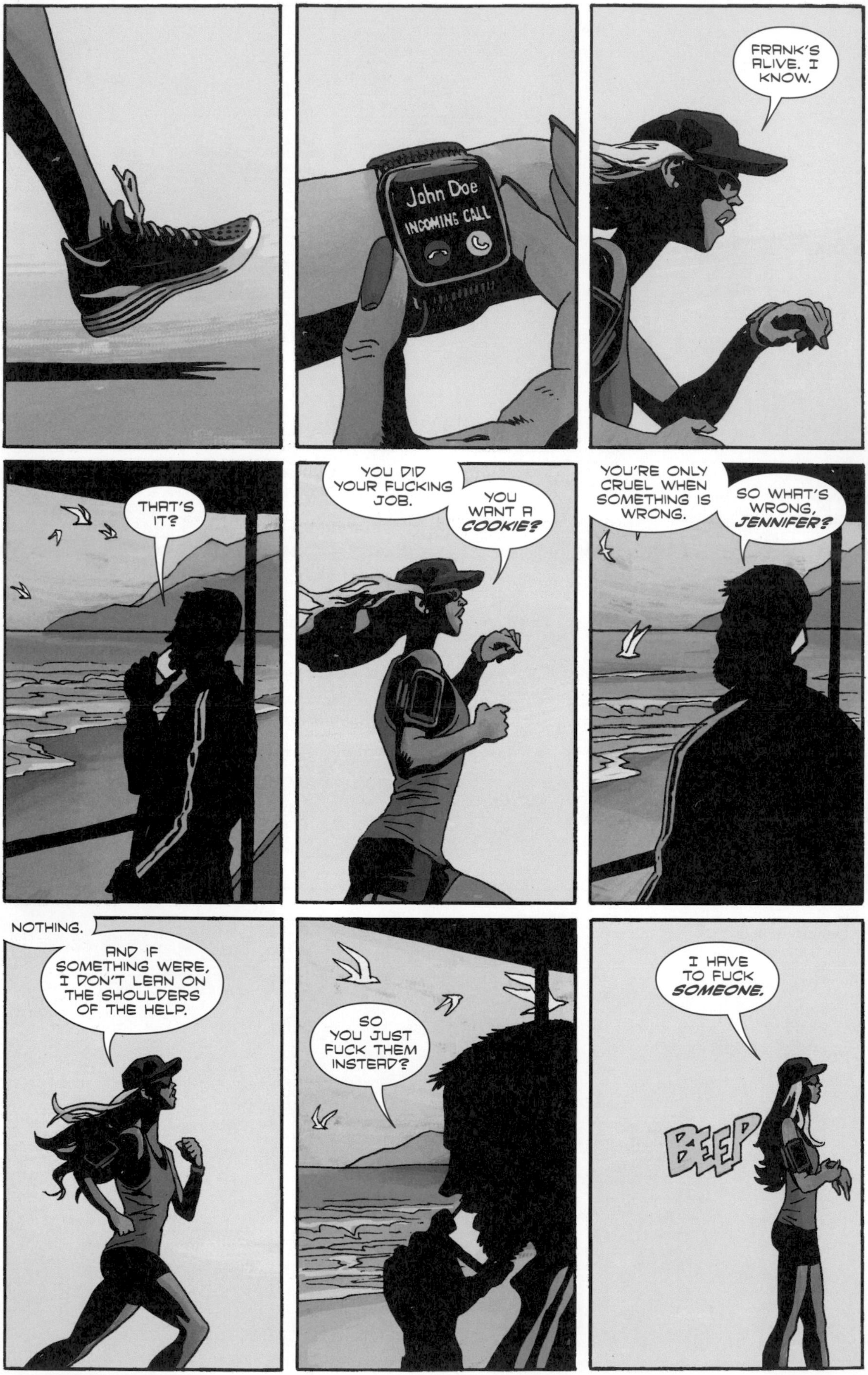
John Doe
INCOMING CALL
FRANK'S ALIVE. I KNOW.
THAT'S IT?
YOU DID YOUR FUCKING JOB.
YOU WANT A *COOKIE?*
YOU'RE ONLY CRUEL WHEN SOMETHING IS WRONG.
SO WHAT'S WRONG, *JENNIFER?*
NOTHING.
AND IF SOMETHING WERE, I DON'T LEAN ON THE SHOULDERS OF THE HELP.
SO YOU JUST FUCK THEM INSTEAD?
I HAVE TO FUCK *SOMEONE.*
BEEP

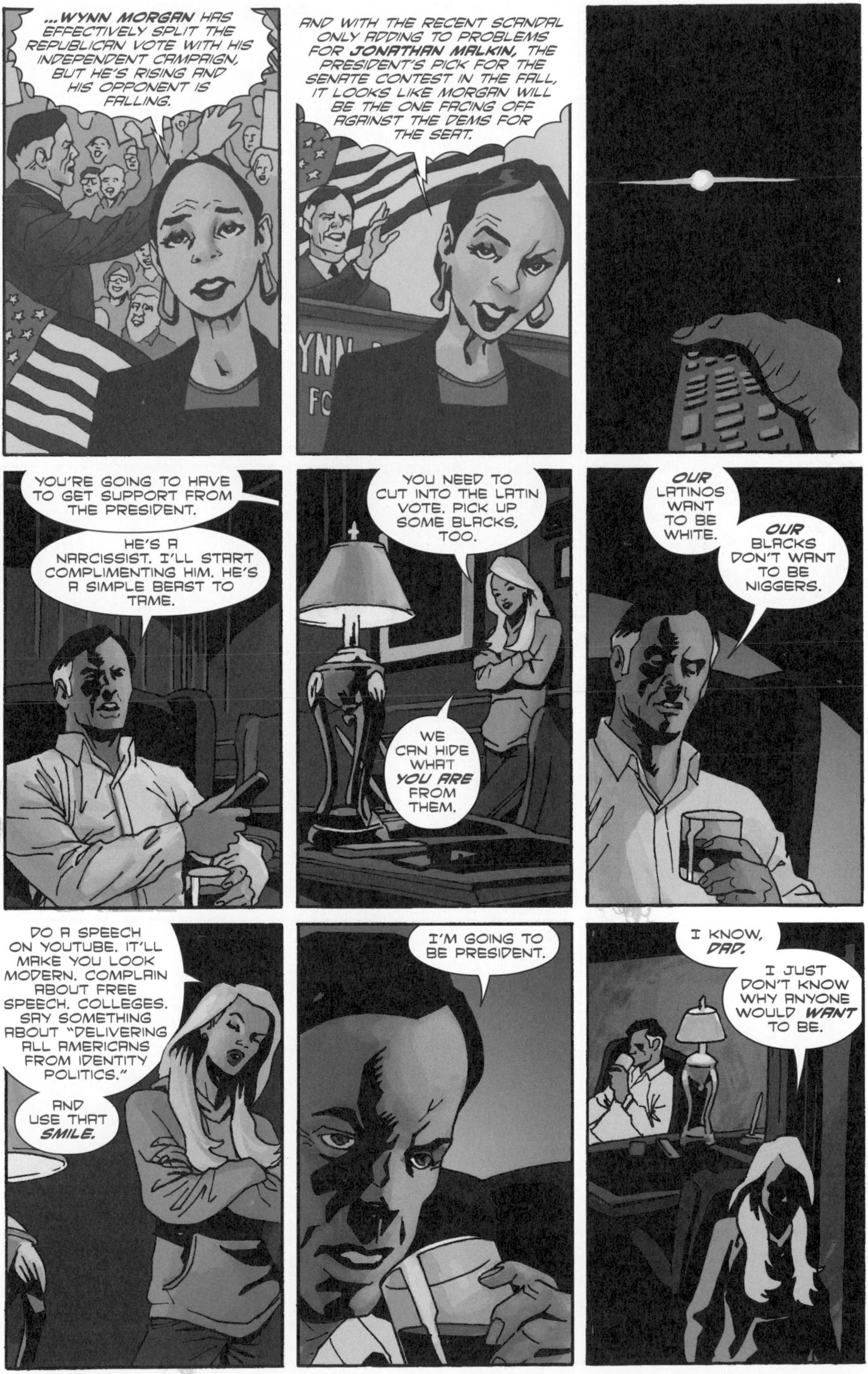
...WYNN MORGAN HAS EFFECTIVELY SPLIT THE REPUBLICAN VOTE WITH HIS INDEPENDENT CAMPAIGN, BUT HE'S RISING AND HIS OPPONENT IS FALLING.
AND WITH THE RECENT SCANDAL ONLY ADDING TO PROBLEMS FOR JONATHAN MALKIN, THE PRESIDENT'S PICK FOR THE SENATE CONTEST IN THE FALL, IT LOOKS LIKE MORGAN WILL BE THE ONE FACING OFF AGAINST THE DEMS FOR THE SEAT.
YOU'RE GOING TO HAVE TO GET SUPPORT FROM THE PRESIDENT.
HE'S A NARCISSIST. I'LL START COMPLIMENTING HIM. HE'S A SIMPLE BEAST TO TAME.
YOU NEED TO CUT INTO THE LATIN VOTE. PICK UP SOME BLACKS, TOO.
WE CAN HIDE WHAT YOU ARE FROM THEM.
OUR LATINOS WANT TO BE WHITE.
OUR BLACKS DON'T WANT TO BE NIGGERS.
DO A SPEECH ON YOUTUBE. IT'LL MAKE YOU LOOK MODERN. COMPLAIN ABOUT FREE SPEECH. COLLEGES. SAY SOMETHING ABOUT "DELIVERING ALL AMERICANS FROM IDENTITY POLITICS."
AND USE THAT SMILE.
I'M GOING TO BE PRESIDENT.
I KNOW, DAD.
I JUST DON'T KNOW WHY ANYONE WOULD WANT TO BE.

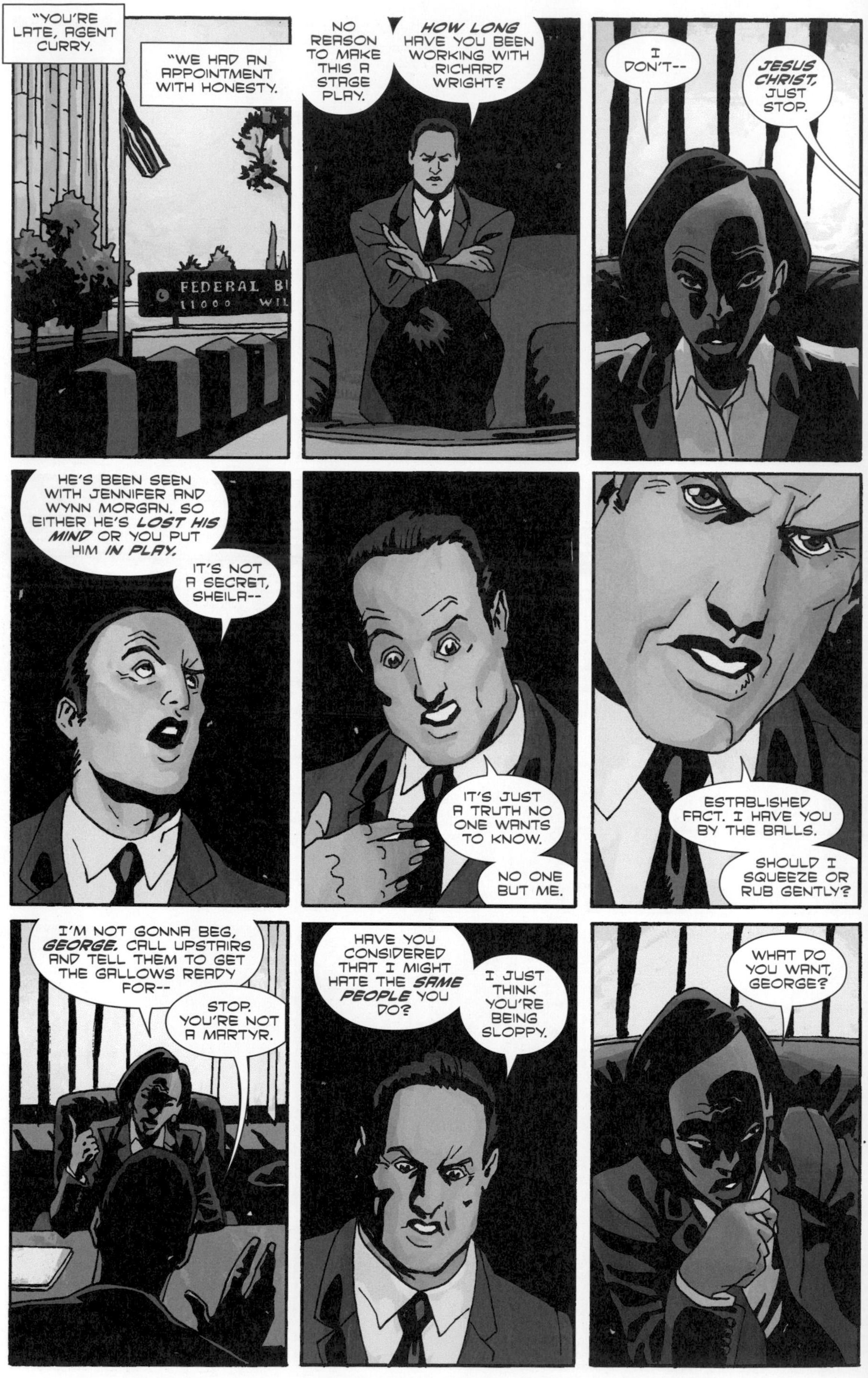
"YOU'RE LATE, AGENT CURRY.
"WE HAD AN APPOINTMENT WITH HONESTY.
FEDERAL B
11000 WIL
NO REASON TO MAKE THIS A STAGE PLAY.
HOW LONG HAVE YOU BEEN WORKING WITH RICHARD WRIGHT?
I DON'T--
JESUS CHRIST, JUST STOP.
HE'S BEEN SEEN WITH JENNIFER AND WYNN MORGAN. SO EITHER HE'S LOST HIS MIND OR YOU PUT HIM IN PLAY.
IT'S NOT A SECRET, SHEILA--
IT'S JUST A TRUTH NO ONE WANTS TO KNOW.
NO ONE BUT ME.
ESTABLISHED FACT. I HAVE YOU BY THE BALLS.
SHOULD I SQUEEZE OR RUB GENTLY?
I'M NOT GONNA BEG, GEORGE. CALL UPSTAIRS AND TELL THEM TO GET THE GALLOWS READY FOR--
STOP. YOU'RE NOT A MARTYR.
HAVE YOU CONSIDERED THAT I MIGHT HATE THE SAME PEOPLE YOU DO?
I JUST THINK YOU'RE BEING SLOPPY.
WHAT DO YOU WANT, GEORGE?

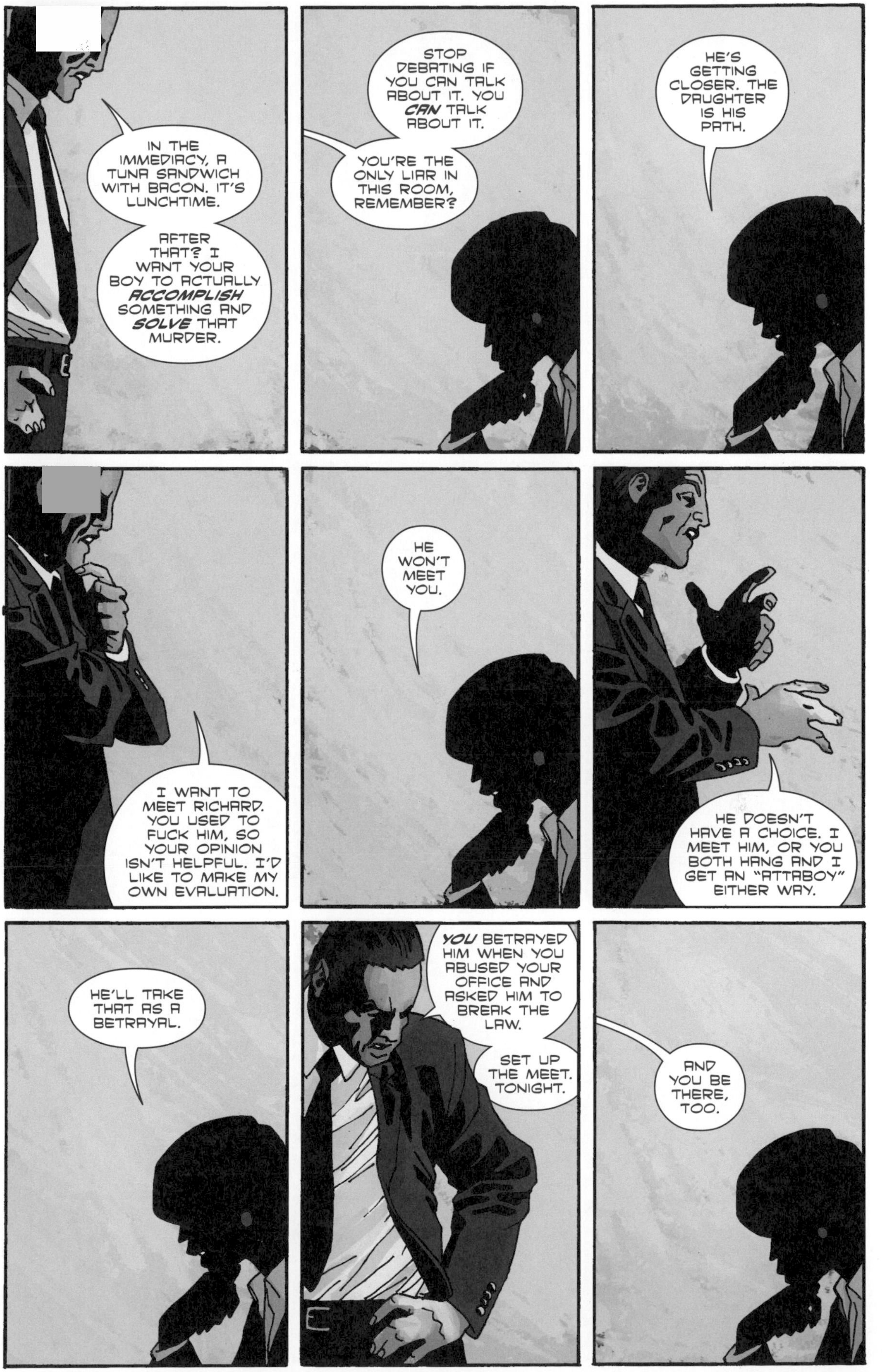

IN THE IMMEDIACY, A TUNA SANDWICH WITH BACON. IT'S LUNCHTIME.
AFTER THAT? I WANT YOUR BOY TO ACTUALLY ACCOMPLISH SOMETHING AND SOLVE THAT MURDER.
STOP DEBATING IF YOU CAN TALK ABOUT IT. YOU CAN TALK ABOUT IT.
YOU'RE THE ONLY LIAR IN THIS ROOM, REMEMBER?
HE'S GETTING CLOSER. THE DAUGHTER IS HIS PATH.
I WANT TO MEET RICHARD. YOU USED TO FUCK HIM, SO YOUR OPINION ISN'T HELPFUL. I'D LIKE TO MAKE MY OWN EVALUATION.
HE WON'T MEET YOU.
HE DOESN'T HAVE A CHOICE. I MEET HIM, OR YOU BOTH HANG AND I GET AN "ATTABOY" EITHER WAY.
HE'LL TAKE THAT AS A BETRAYAL.
YOU BETRAYED HIM WHEN YOU ABUSED YOUR OFFICE AND ASKED HIM TO BREAK THE LAW.
SET UP THE MEET. TONIGHT.
AND YOU BE THERE, TOO.

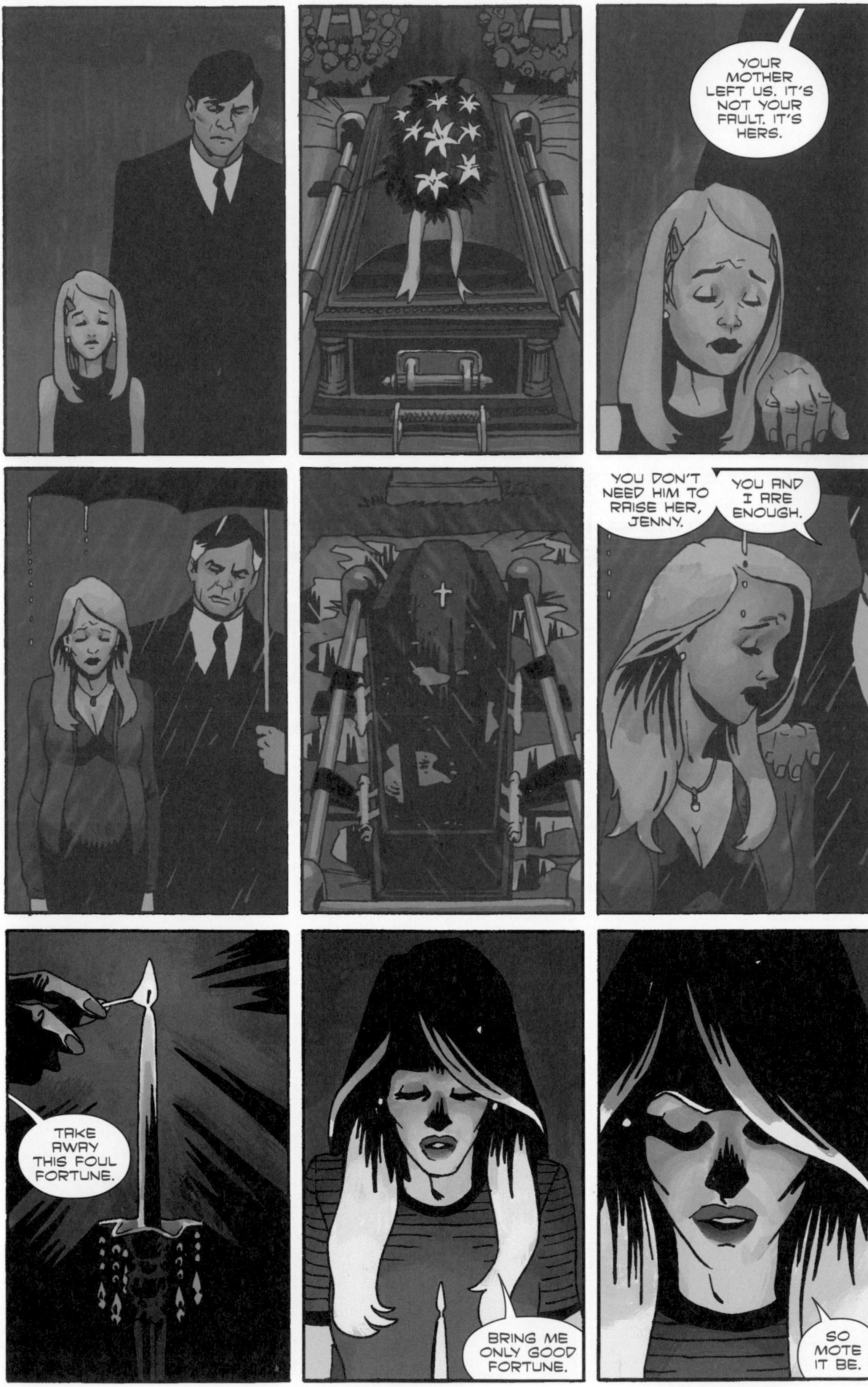

YOUR MOTHER LEFT US. IT'S NOT YOUR FAULT. IT'S HERS.
YOU DON'T NEED HIM TO RAISE HER, JENNY.
YOU AND I ARE ENOUGH.
TAKE AWAY THIS FOUL FORTUNE.
BRING ME ONLY GOOD FORTUNE.
SO MOTE IT BE.

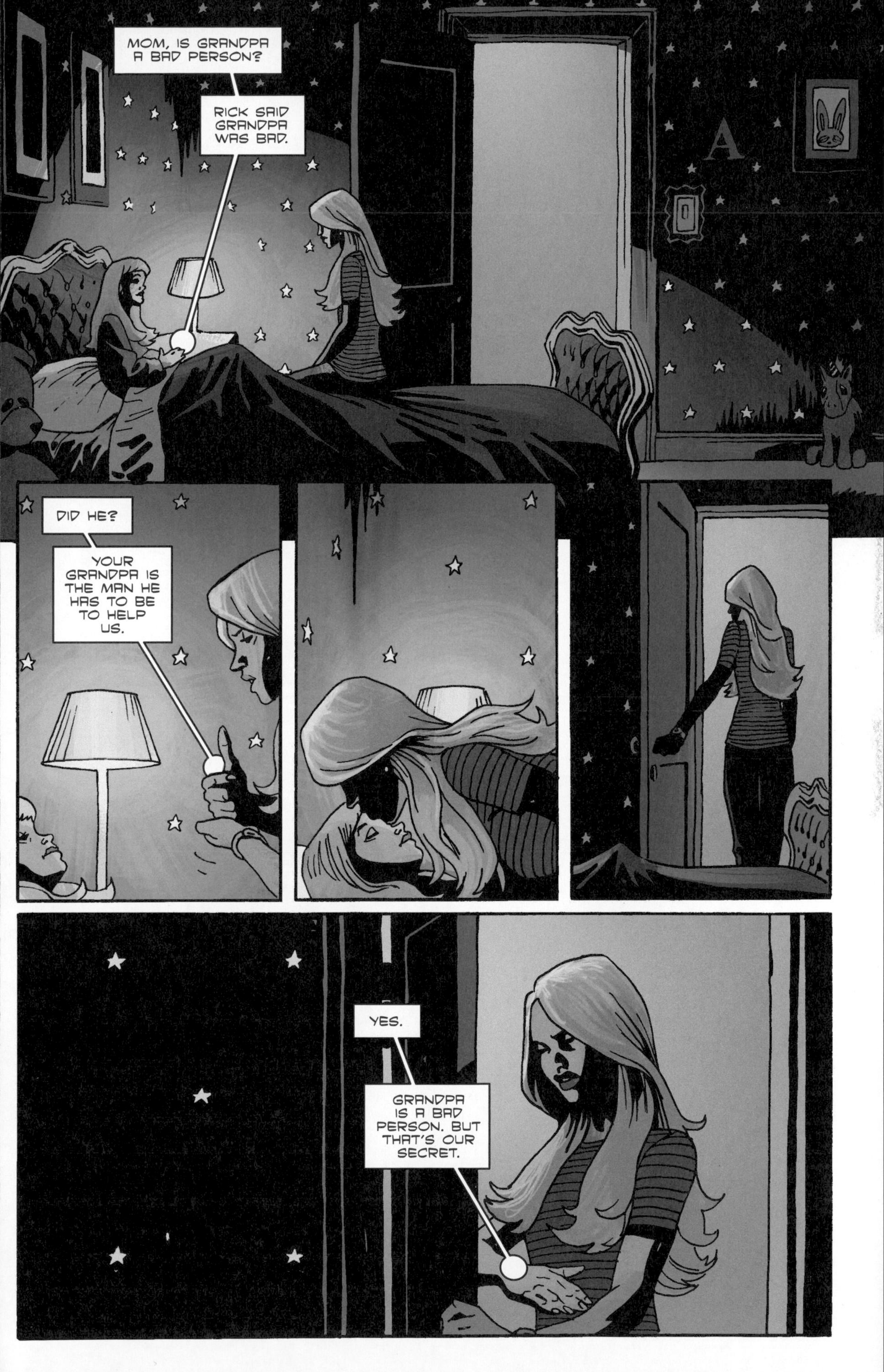
MOM, IS GRANDPA A BAD PERSON?
RICK SAID GRANDPA WAS BAD.
DID HE?
YOUR GRANDPA IS THE MAN HE HAS TO BE TO HELP US.
YES.
GRANDPA IS A BAD PERSON. BUT THAT'S OUR SECRET.

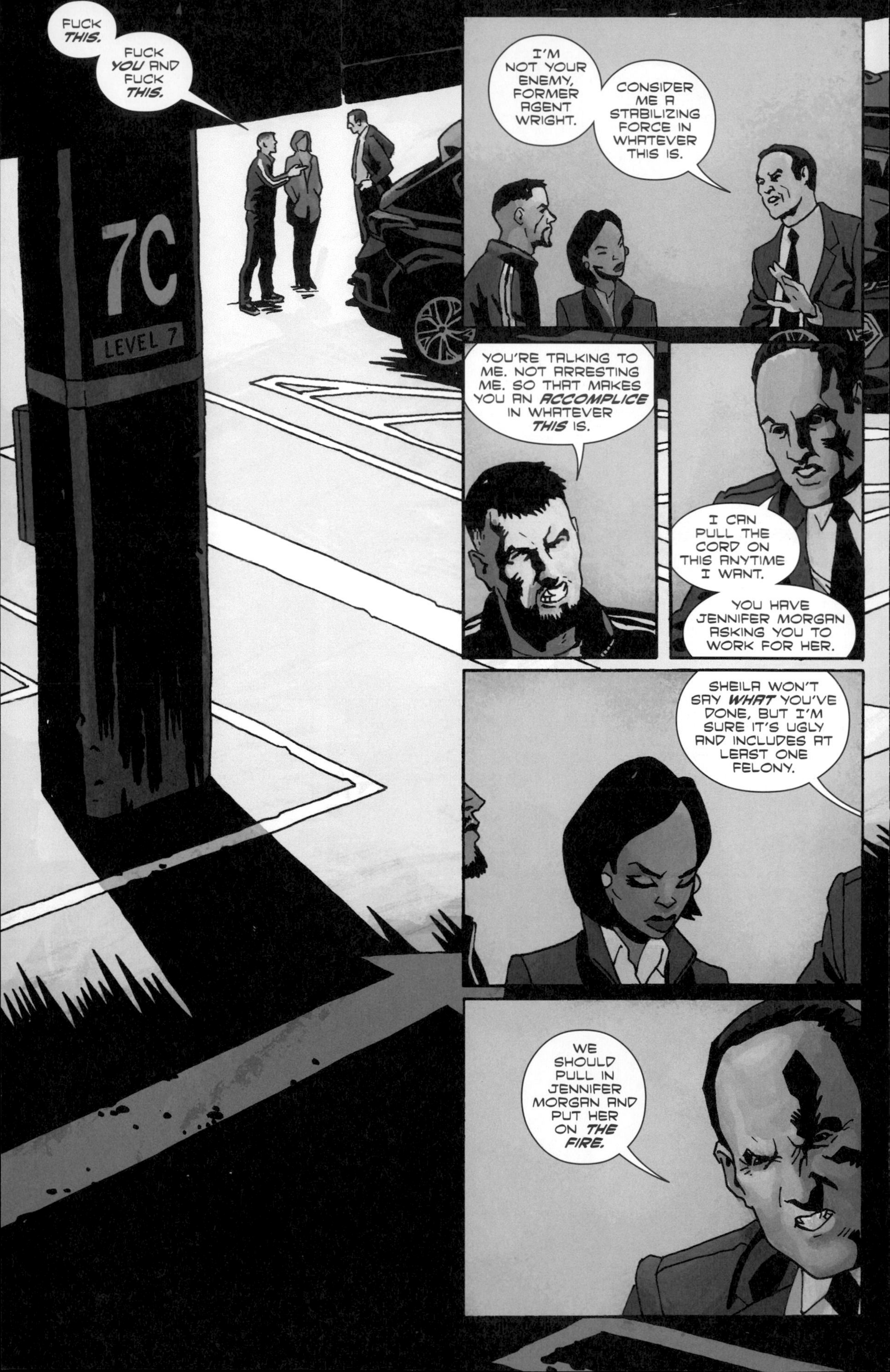
FUCK *THIS.*
FUCK *YOU* AND FUCK *THIS.*
7C
LEVEL 7
I'M NOT YOUR ENEMY, FORMER AGENT WRIGHT.
CONSIDER ME A STABILIZING FORCE IN WHATEVER THIS IS.
YOU'RE TALKING TO ME. NOT ARRESTING ME. SO THAT MAKES YOU AN *ACCOMPLICE* IN WHATEVER *THIS* IS.
I CAN PULL THE CORD ON THIS ANYTIME I WANT.
YOU HAVE JENNIFER MORGAN ASKING YOU TO WORK FOR HER.
SHEILA WON'T SAY *WHAT* YOU'VE DONE, BUT I'M SURE IT'S UGLY AND INCLUDES AT LEAST ONE FELONY.
WE SHOULD PULL IN JENNIFER MORGAN AND PUT HER ON *THE FIRE.*

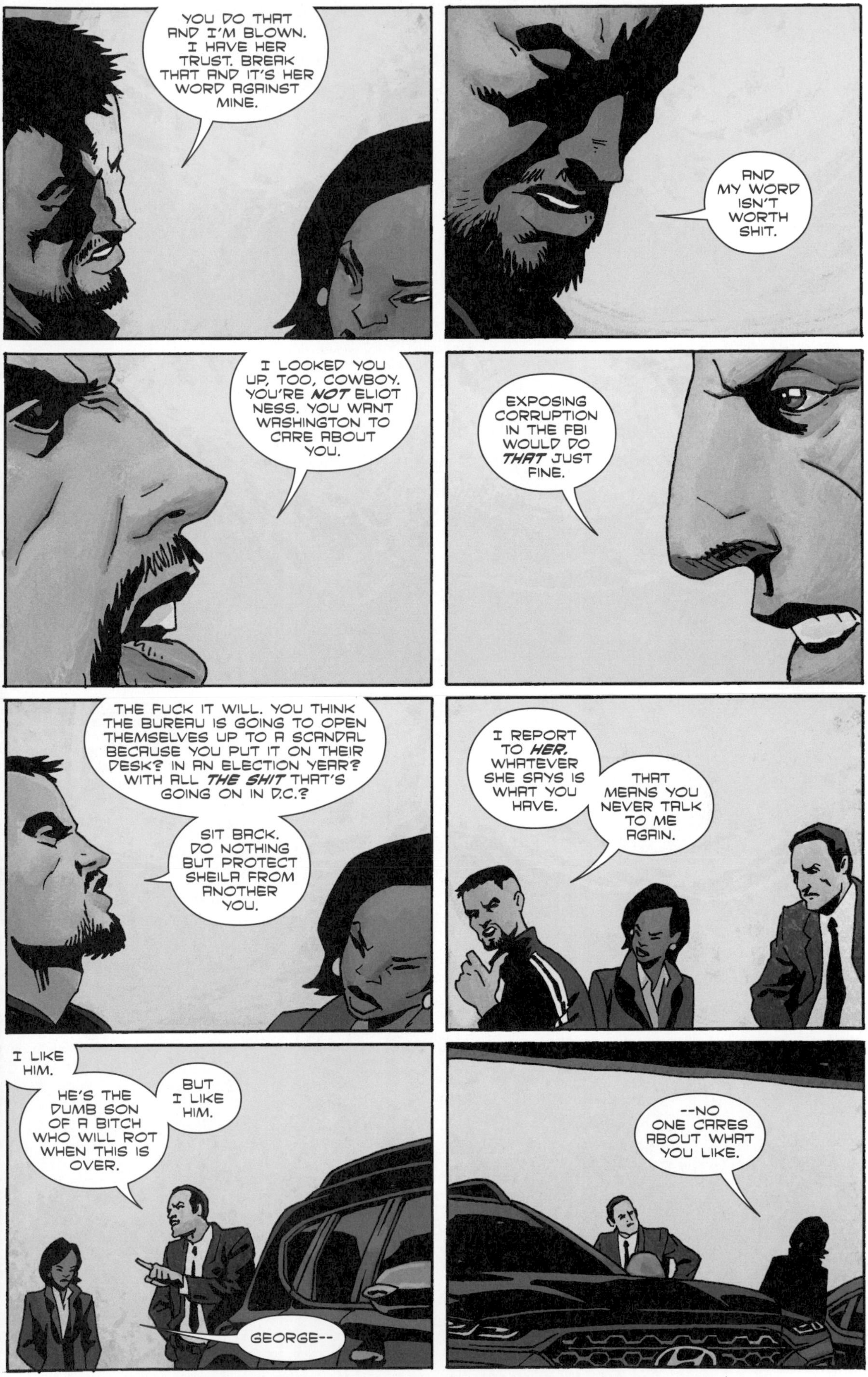
YOU DO THAT AND I'M BLOWN. I HAVE HER TRUST. BREAK THAT AND IT'S HER WORD AGAINST MINE.
AND MY WORD ISN'T WORTH SHIT.
I LOOKED YOU UP, TOO, COWBOY. YOU'RE *NOT* ELIOT NESS. YOU WANT WASHINGTON TO CARE ABOUT YOU.
EXPOSING CORRUPTION IN THE FBI WOULD DO *THAT* JUST FINE.
THE FUCK IT WILL. YOU THINK THE BUREAU IS GOING TO OPEN THEMSELVES UP TO A SCANDAL BECAUSE YOU PUT IT ON THEIR DESK? IN AN ELECTION YEAR? WITH ALL *THE SHIT* THAT'S GOING ON IN D.C.?
SIT BACK. DO NOTHING BUT PROTECT SHEILA FROM ANOTHER YOU.
I REPORT TO *HER.* WHATEVER SHE SAYS IS WHAT YOU HAVE.
THAT MEANS YOU NEVER TALK TO ME AGAIN.
I LIKE HIM.
HE'S THE DUMB SON OF A BITCH WHO WILL ROT WHEN THIS IS OVER.
BUT I LIKE HIM.
GEORGE--
--NO ONE CARES ABOUT WHAT YOU LIKE.

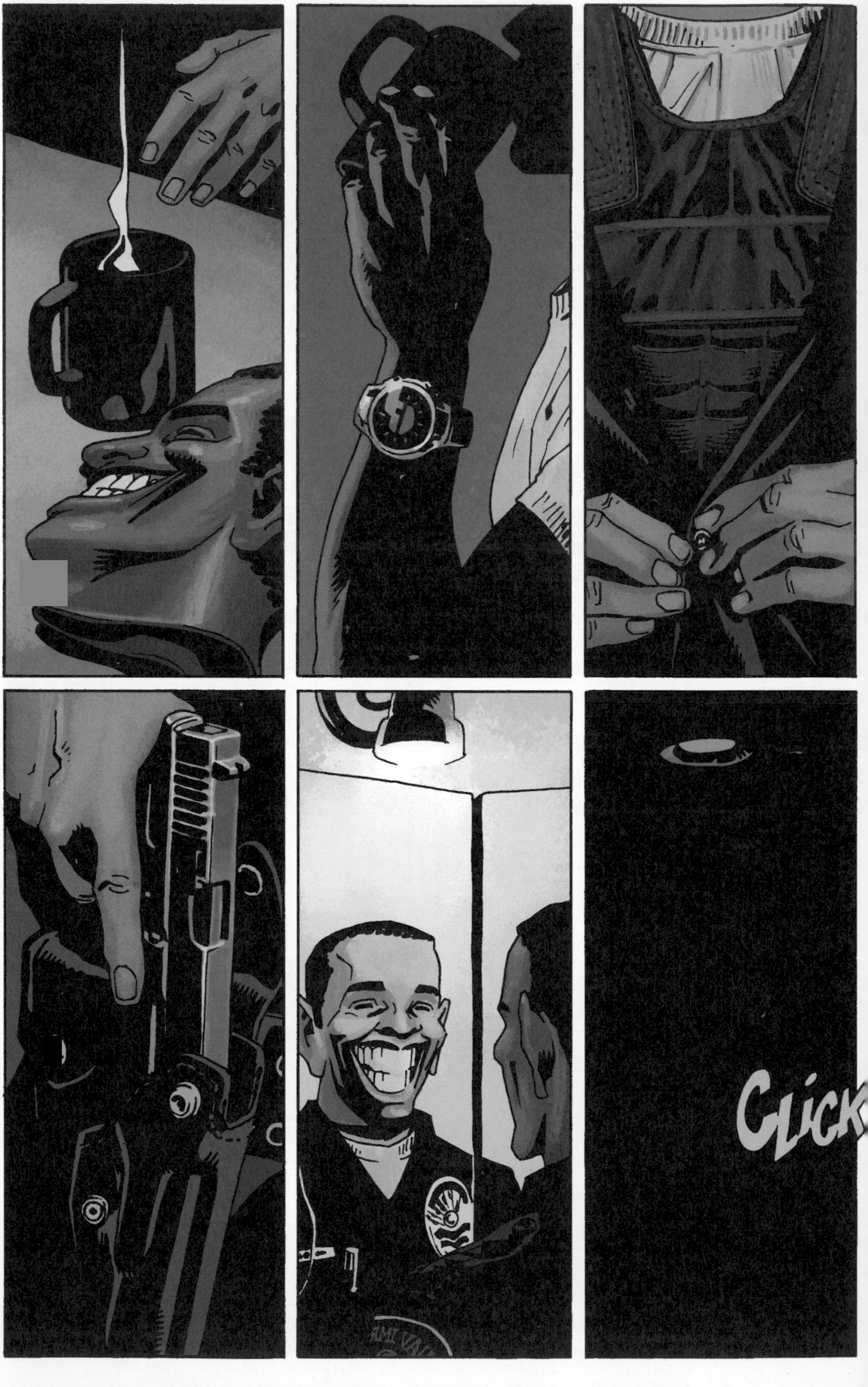
CLICK

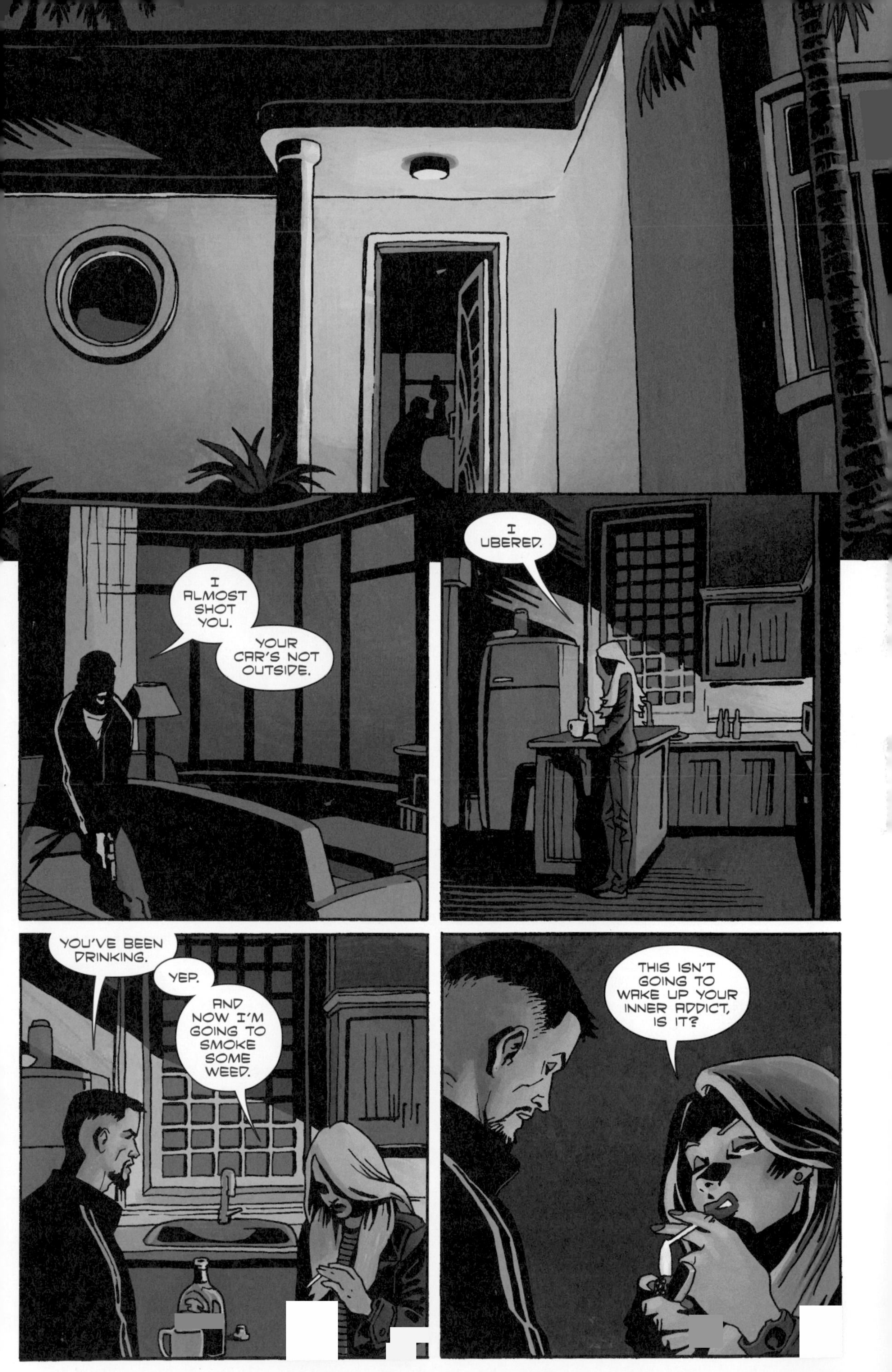
I ALMOST SHOT YOU.
YOUR CAR'S NOT OUTSIDE.
I UBERED.
YOU'VE BEEN DRINKING.
YEP.
AND NOW I'M GOING TO SMOKE SOME WEED.
THIS ISN'T GOING TO WAKE UP YOUR INNER ADDICT, IS IT?

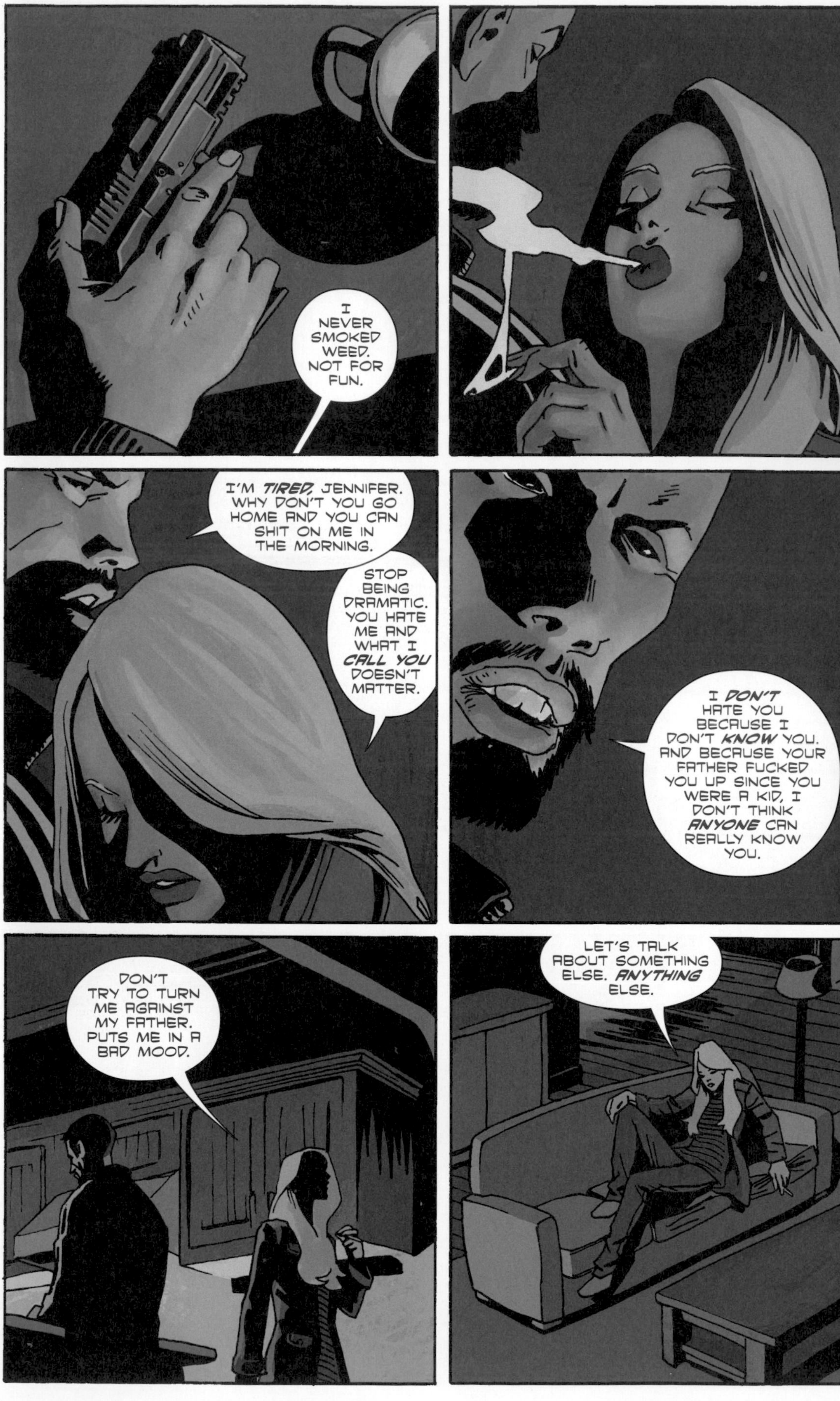
I NEVER SMOKED WEED. NOT FOR FUN.
I'M *TIRED,* JENNIFER. WHY DON'T YOU GO HOME AND YOU CAN SHIT ON ME IN THE MORNING.
STOP BEING DRAMATIC. YOU HATE ME AND WHAT I *CALL YOU* DOESN'T MATTER.
I *DON'T* HATE YOU BECAUSE I DON'T *KNOW* YOU. AND BECAUSE YOUR FATHER FUCKED YOU UP SINCE YOU WERE A KID, I DON'T THINK *ANYONE* CAN REALLY KNOW YOU.
DON'T TRY TO TURN ME AGAINST MY FATHER. PUTS ME IN A BAD MOOD.
LET'S TALK ABOUT SOMETHING ELSE. *ANYTHING* ELSE.

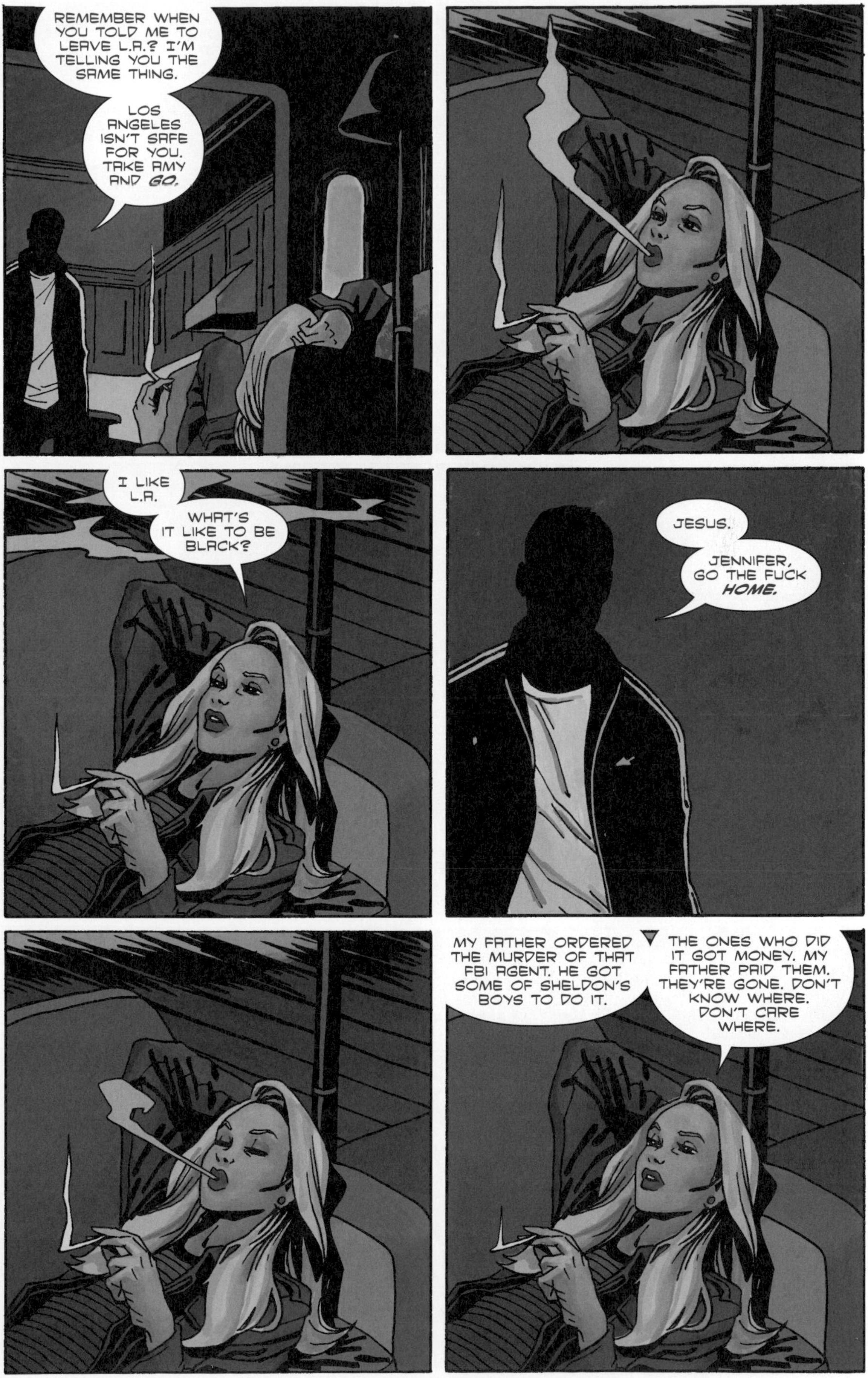
REMEMBER WHEN YOU TOLD ME TO LEAVE L.A.? I'M TELLING YOU THE SAME THING.
LOS ANGELES ISN'T SAFE FOR YOU. TAKE AMY AND *GO.*
I LIKE L.A.
WHAT'S IT LIKE TO BE BLACK?
JESUS.
JENNIFER, GO THE FUCK *HOME.*
MY FATHER ORDERED THE MURDER OF THAT FBI AGENT. HE GOT SOME OF SHELDON'S BOYS TO DO IT.
THE ONES WHO DID IT GOT MONEY. MY FATHER PAID THEM. THEY'RE GONE. DON'T KNOW WHERE. DON'T CARE WHERE.

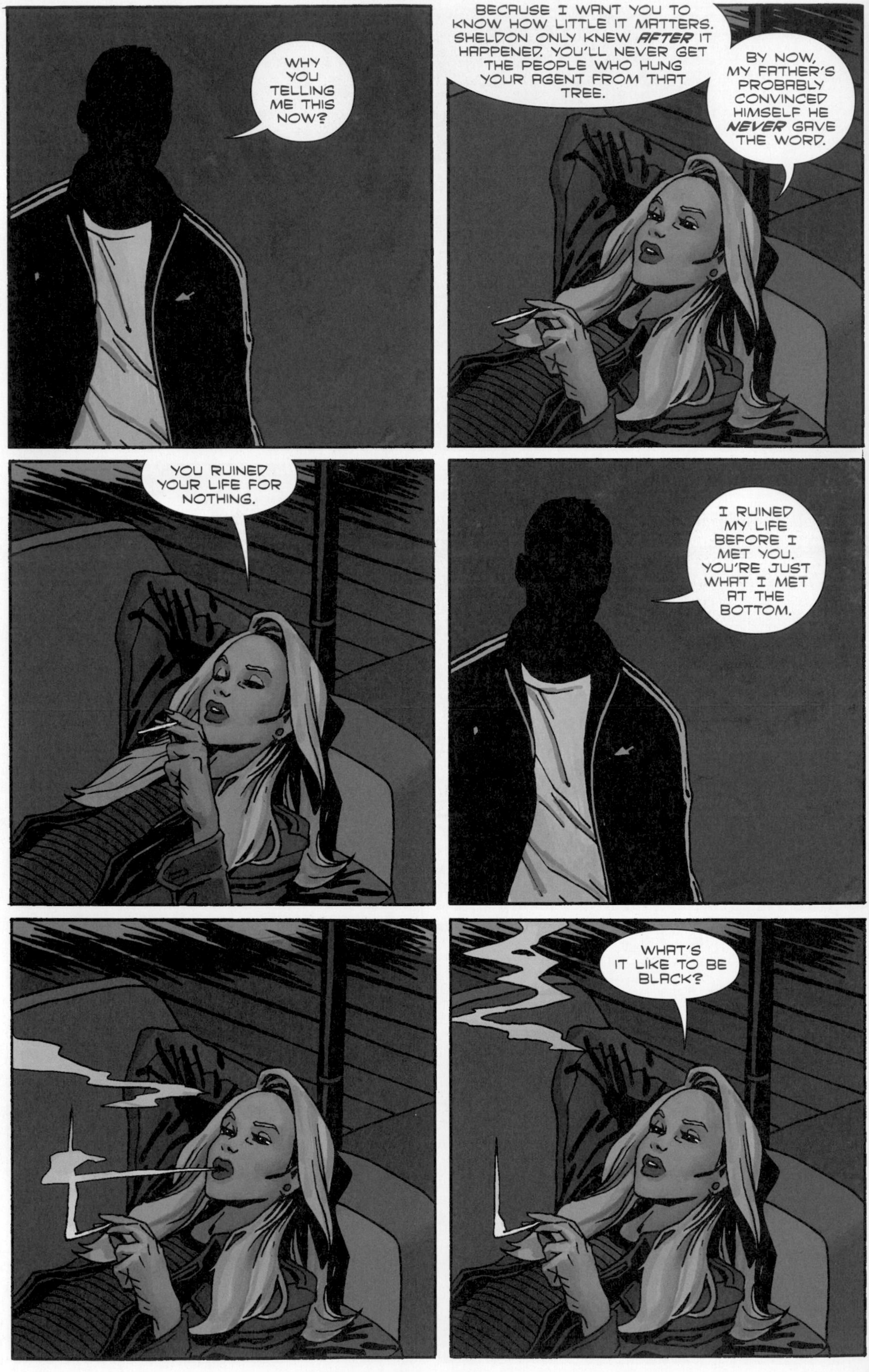
WHY YOU TELLING ME THIS NOW?
BECAUSE I WANT YOU TO KNOW HOW LITTLE IT MATTERS. SHELDON ONLY KNEW *AFTER* IT HAPPENED. YOU'LL NEVER GET THE PEOPLE WHO HUNG YOUR AGENT FROM THAT TREE.
BY NOW, MY FATHER'S PROBABLY CONVINCED HIMSELF HE *NEVER* GAVE THE WORD.
YOU RUINED YOUR LIFE FOR NOTHING.
I RUINED MY LIFE BEFORE I MET YOU. YOU'RE JUST WHAT I MET AT THE BOTTOM.
WHAT'S IT LIKE TO BE BLACK?

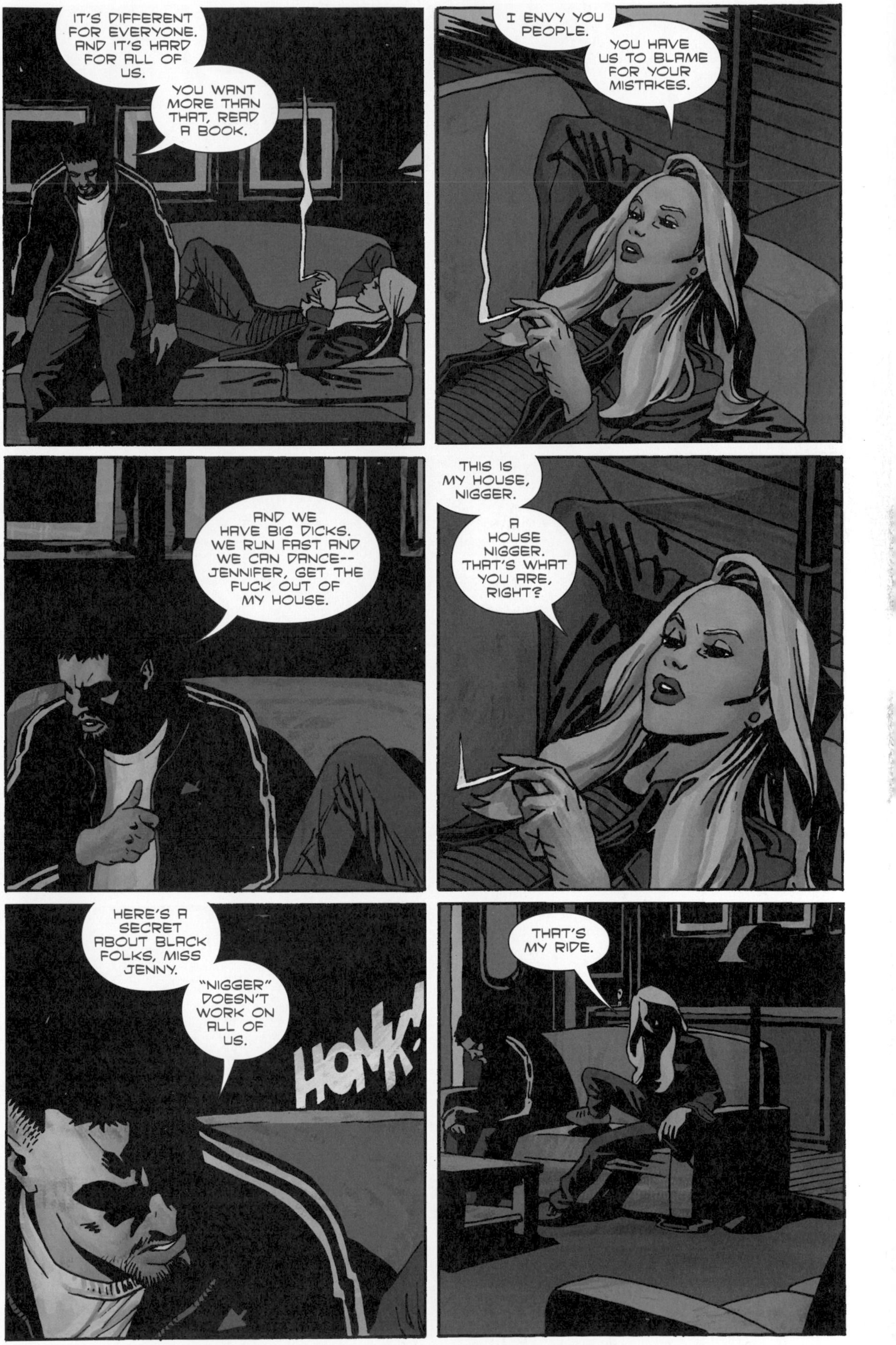
IT'S DIFFERENT FOR EVERYONE. AND IT'S HARD FOR ALL OF US.
YOU WANT MORE THAN THAT, READ A BOOK.
I ENVY YOU PEOPLE.
YOU HAVE US TO BLAME FOR YOUR MISTAKES.
AND WE HAVE BIG DICKS. WE RUN FAST AND WE CAN DANCE-- JENNIFER, GET THE FUCK OUT OF MY HOUSE.
THIS IS MY HOUSE, NIGGER.
A HOUSE NIGGER. THAT'S WHAT YOU ARE, RIGHT?
HERE'S A SECRET ABOUT BLACK FOLKS, MISS JENNY.
"NIGGER" DOESN'T WORK ON ALL OF US.
HONK!
THAT'S MY RIDE.

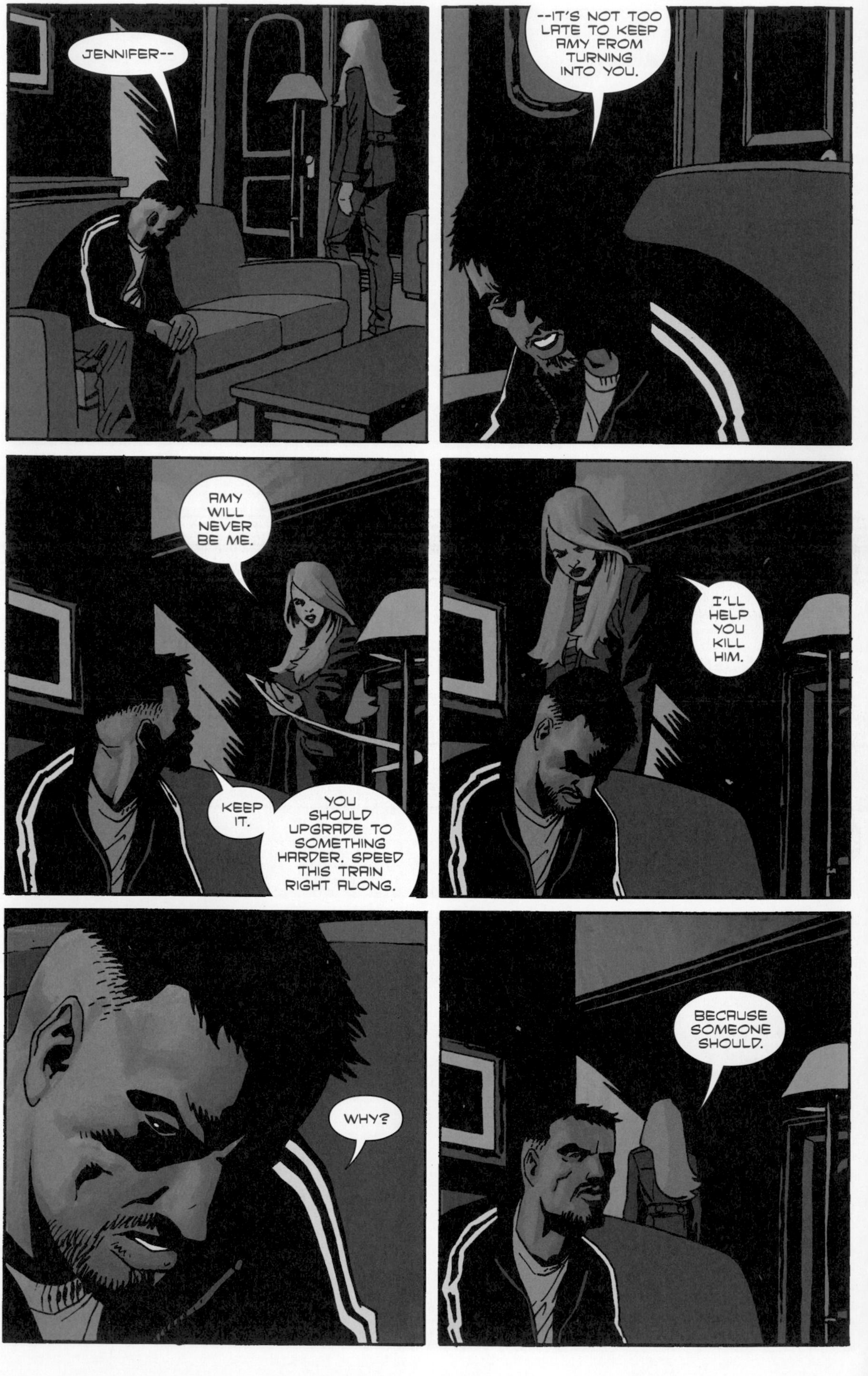
JENNIFER--
--IT'S NOT TOO LATE TO KEEP AMY FROM TURNING INTO YOU.
AMY WILL NEVER BE ME.
KEEP IT.
YOU SHOULD UPGRADE TO SOMETHING HARDER. SPEED THIS TRAIN RIGHT ALONG.
I'LL HELP YOU KILL HIM.
WHY?
BECAUSE SOMEONE SHOULD.

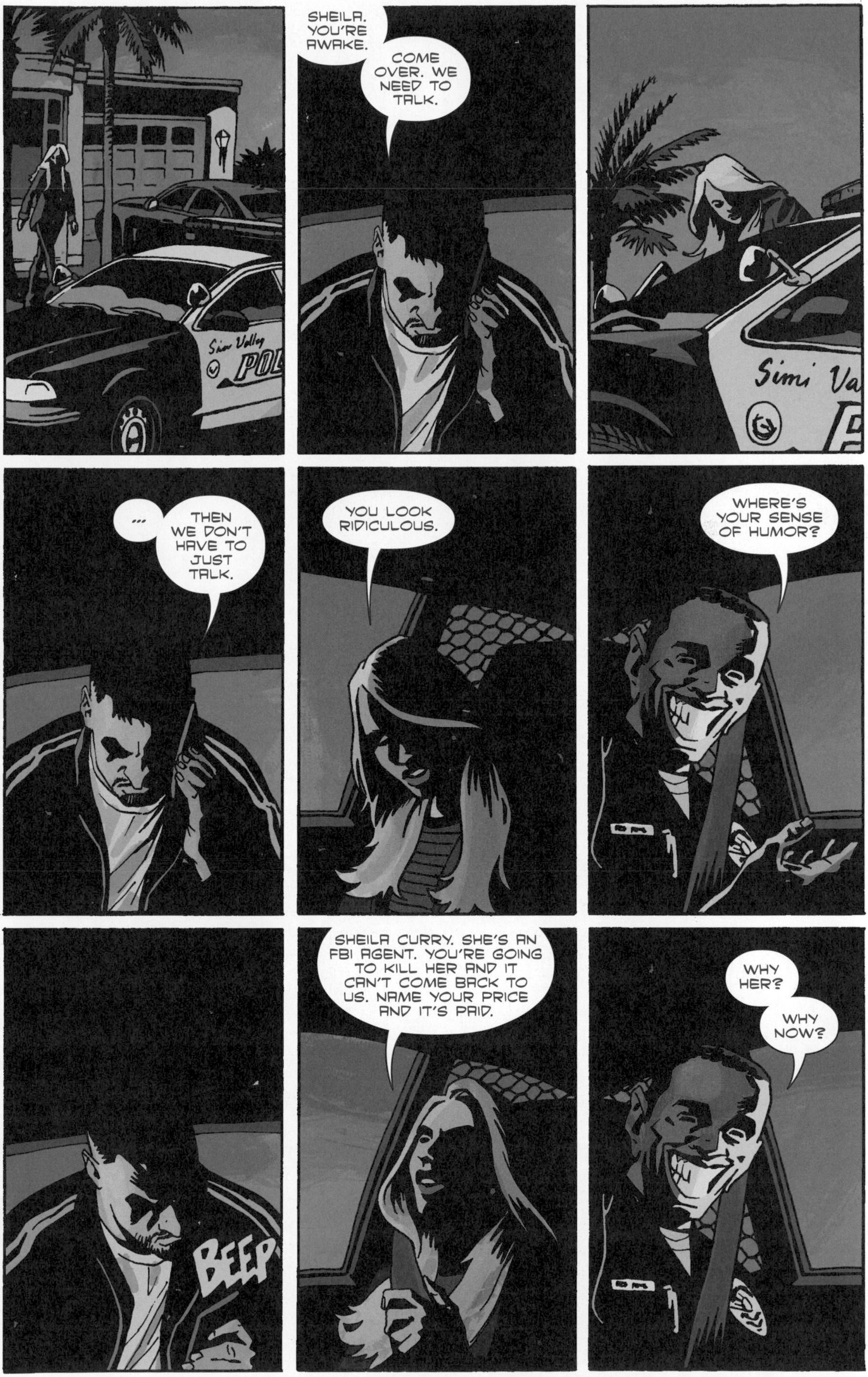

Simi Valley
POL
SHEILA. YOU'RE AWAKE.
COME OVER. WE NEED TO TALK.
Simi Va
...
THEN WE DON'T HAVE TO JUST TALK.
YOU LOOK RIDICULOUS.
WHERE'S YOUR SENSE OF HUMOR?
BEEP
SHEILA CURRY. SHE'S AN FBI AGENT. YOU'RE GOING TO KILL HER AND IT CAN'T COME BACK TO US. NAME YOUR PRICE AND IT'S PAID.
WHY HER?
WHY NOW?

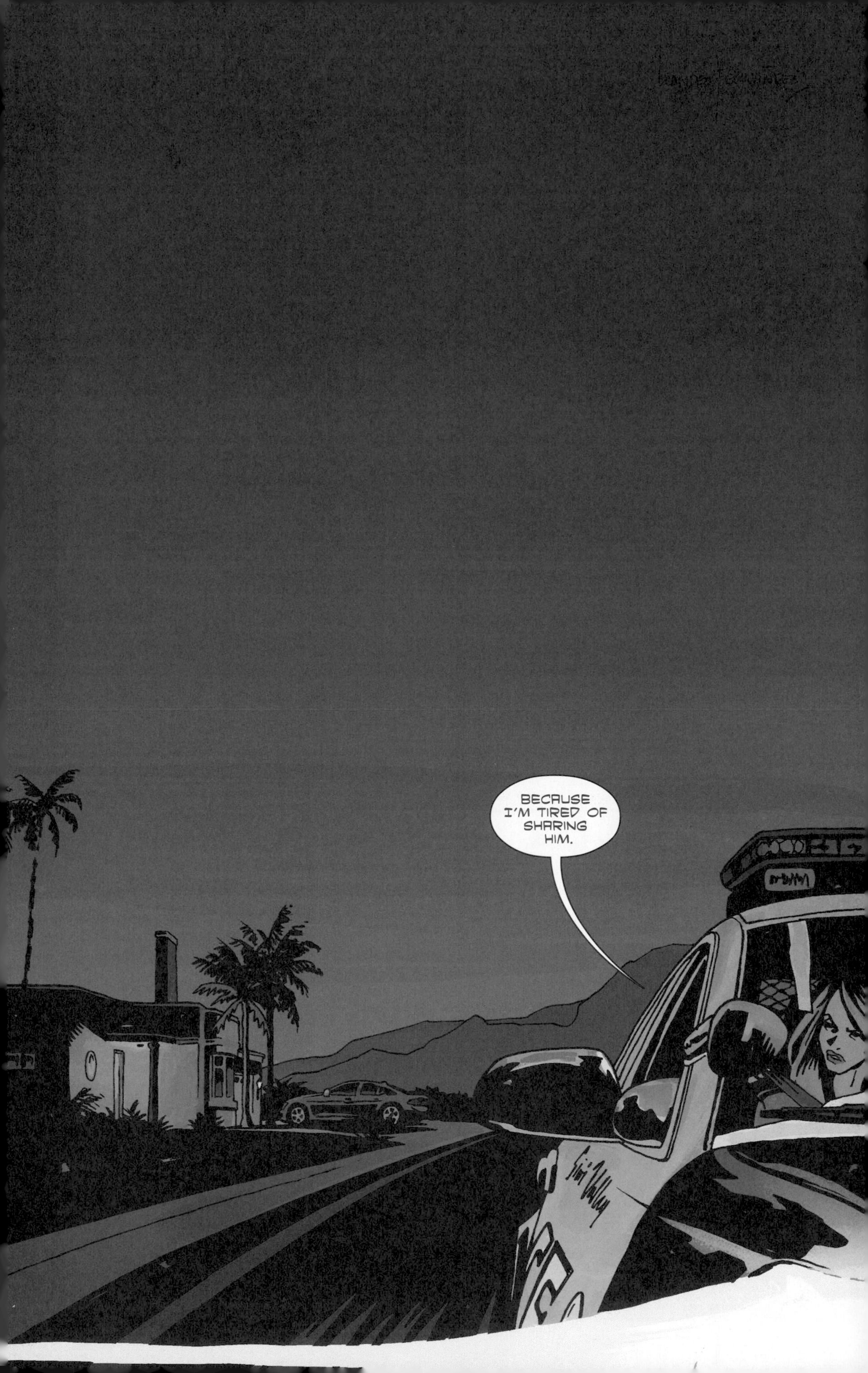
BECAUSE I'M TIRED OF SHARING HIM.

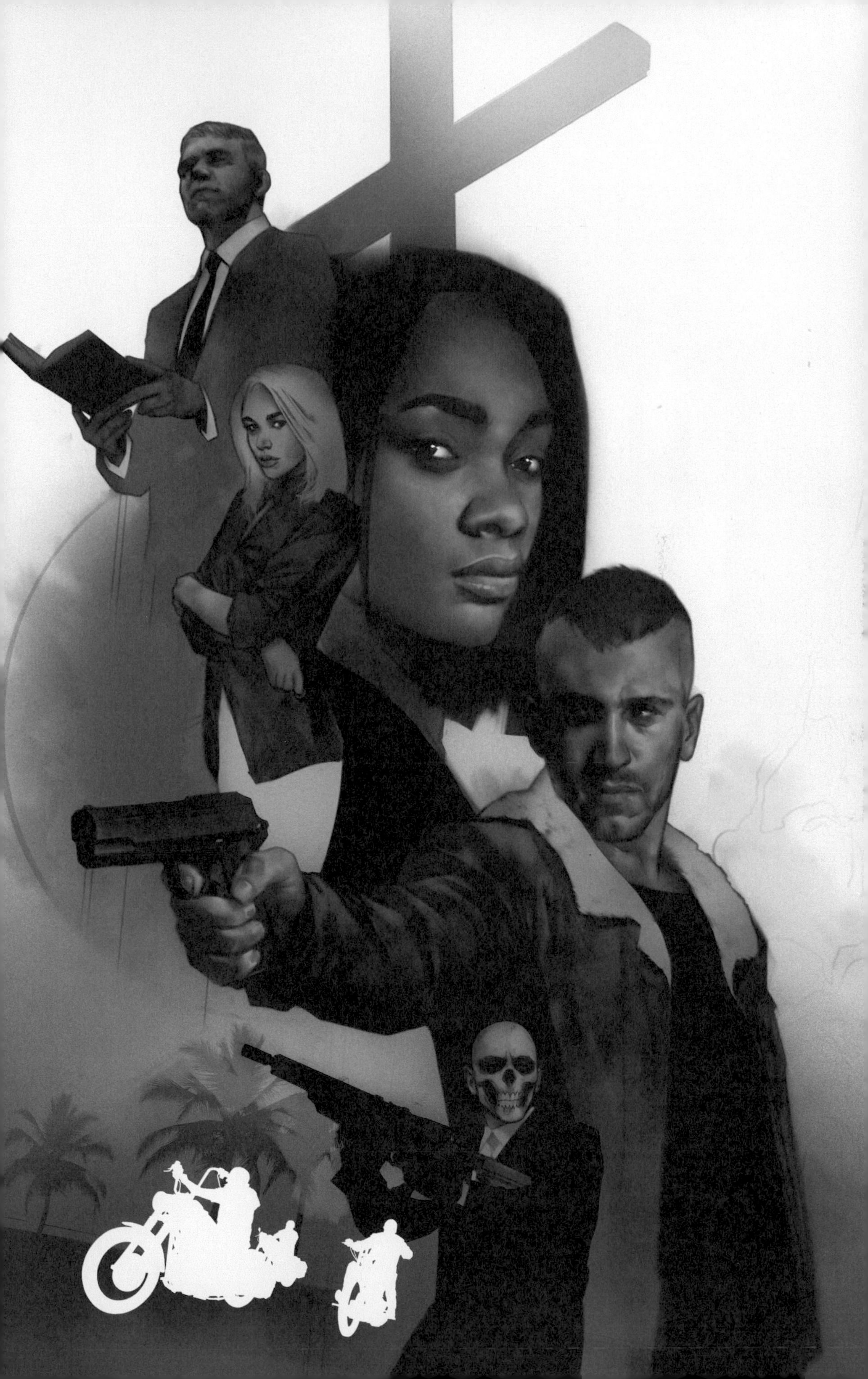

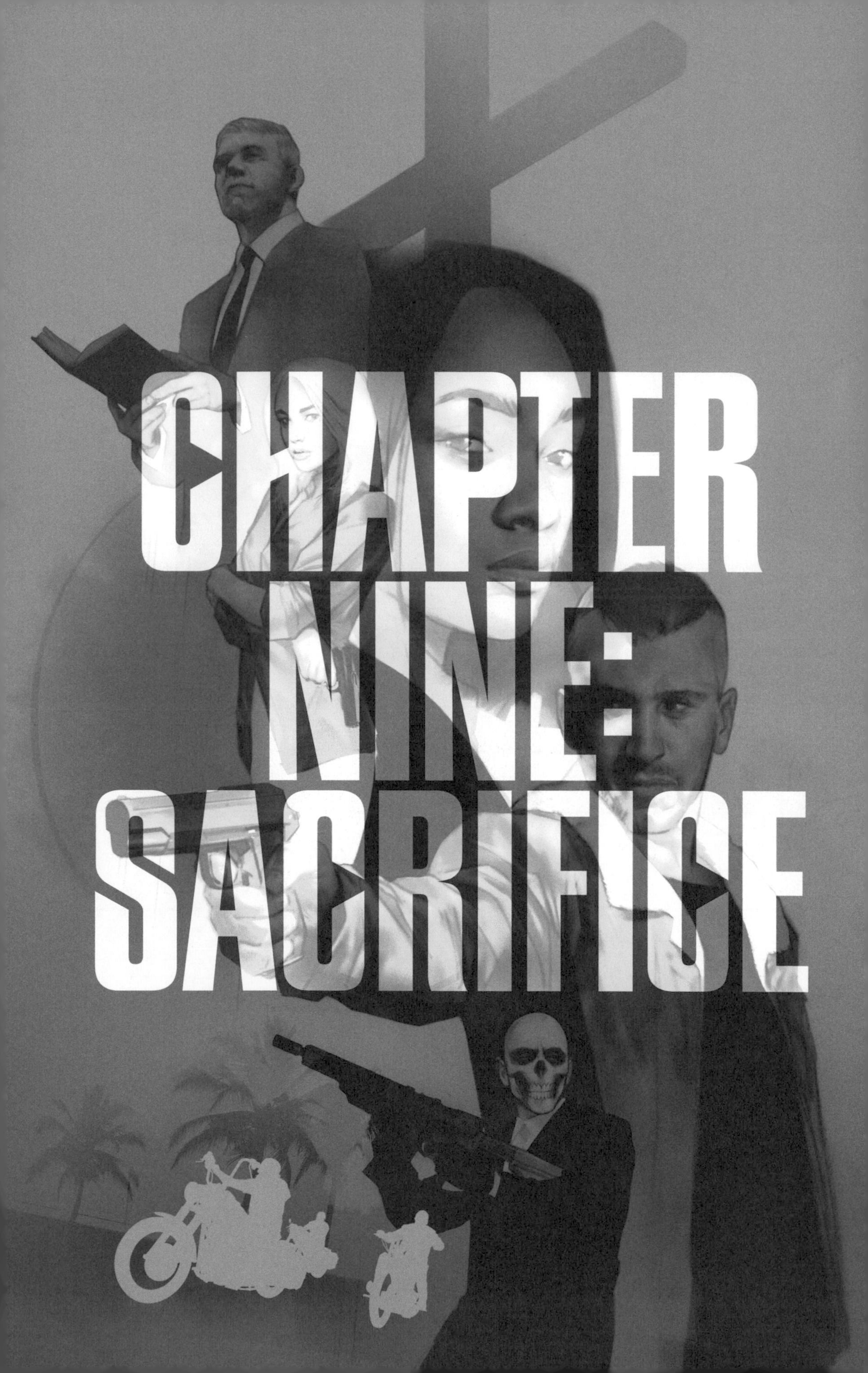
CHAPTER
NINE:
SACRIFICE

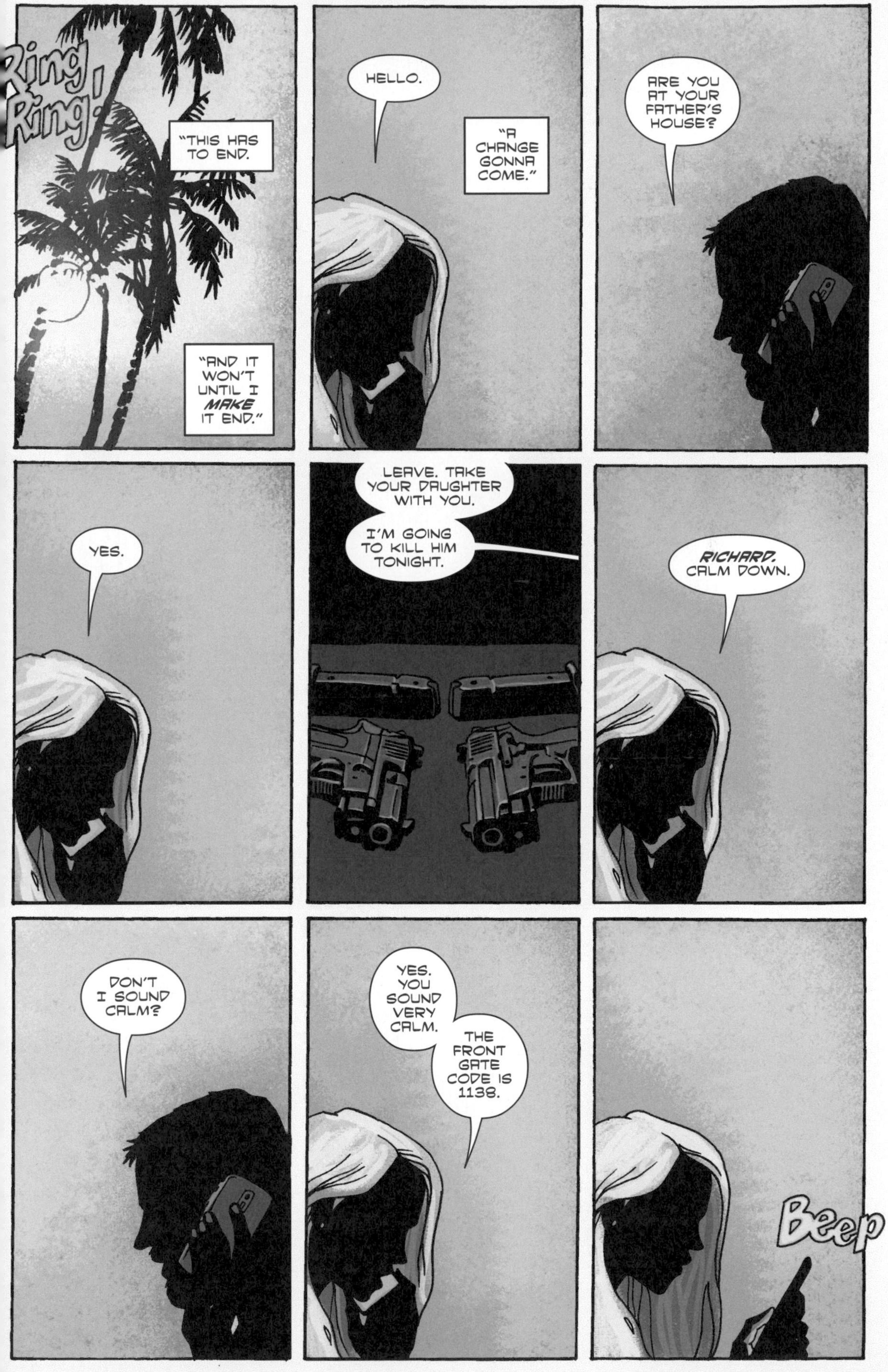
Ring, Ring!
"THIS HAS TO END.
"AND IT WON'T UNTIL I MAKE IT END."
HELLO.
"A CHANGE GONNA COME."
ARE YOU AT YOUR FATHER'S HOUSE?
YES.
LEAVE. TAKE YOUR DAUGHTER WITH YOU.
I'M GOING TO KILL HIM TONIGHT.
RICHARD. CALM DOWN.
DON'T I SOUND CALM?
YES. YOU SOUND VERY CALM.
THE FRONT GATE CODE IS 1138.
Beep

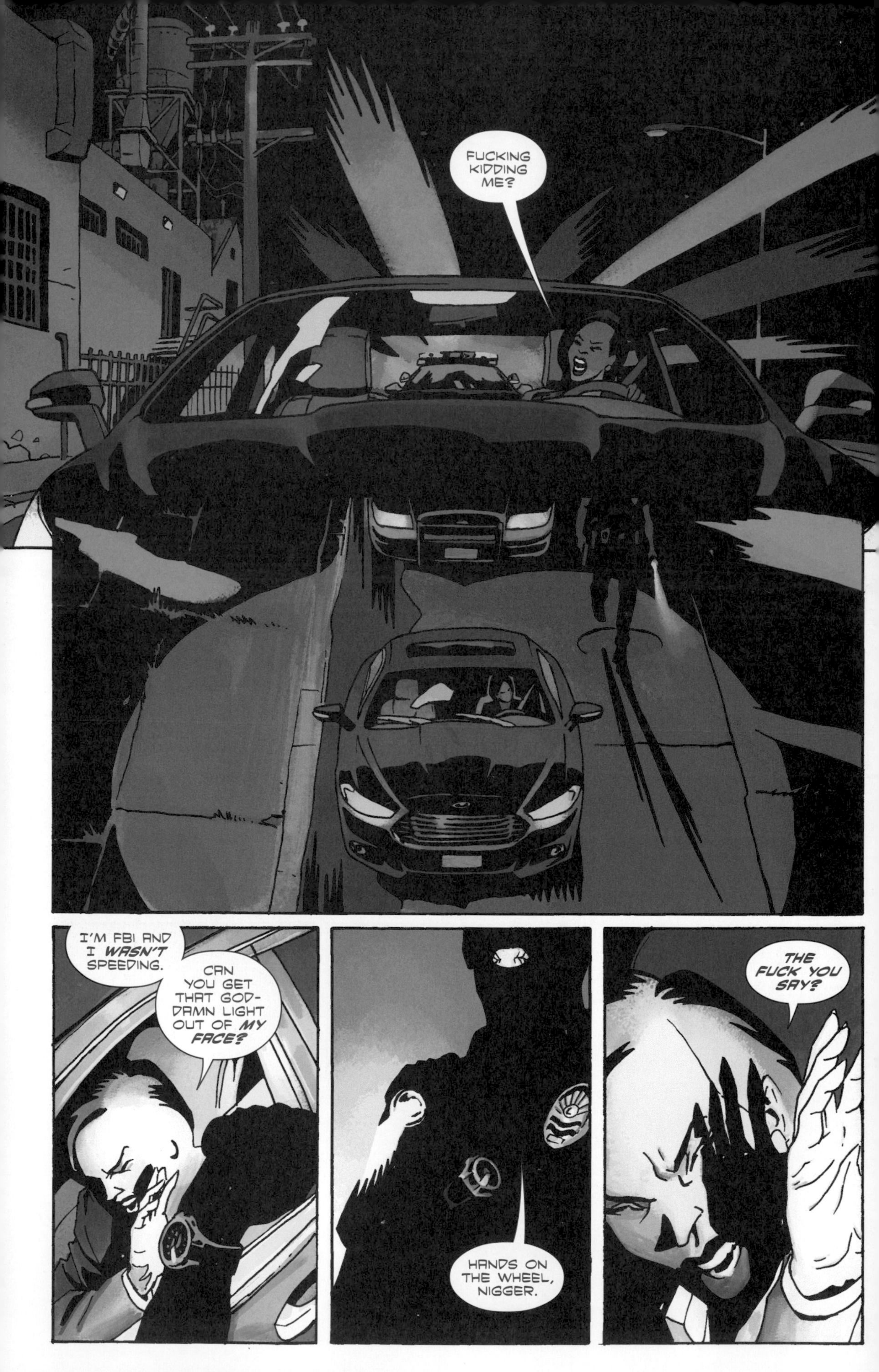
FUCKING KIDDING ME?
I'M FBI AND I *WASN'T* SPEEDING.
CAN YOU GET THAT GOD-DAMN LIGHT OUT OF *MY FACE?*
HANDS ON THE WHEEL, NIGGER.
THE FUCK YOU SAY?

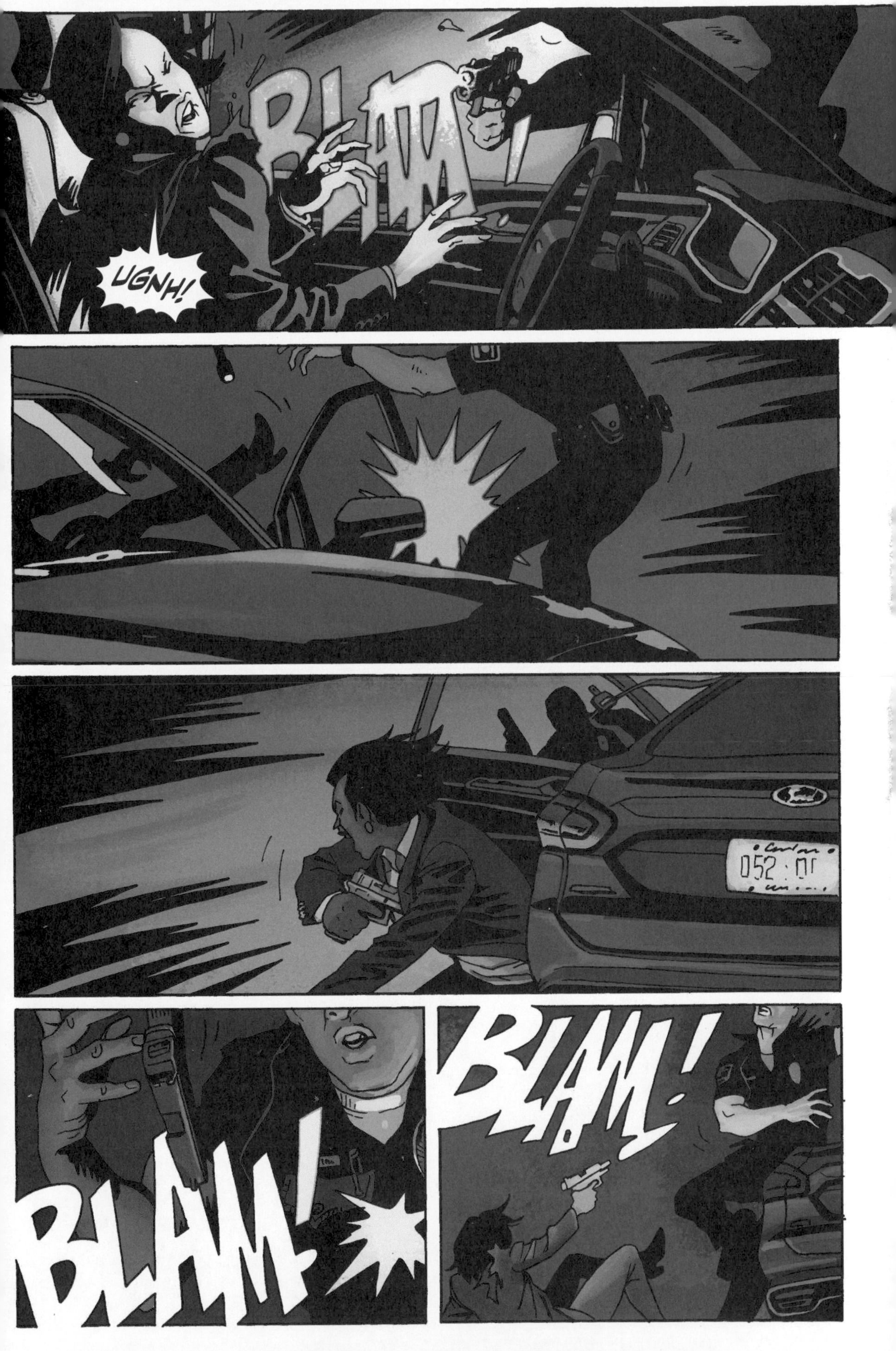
BLAM!
UGNH!
BLAM!
BLAM!

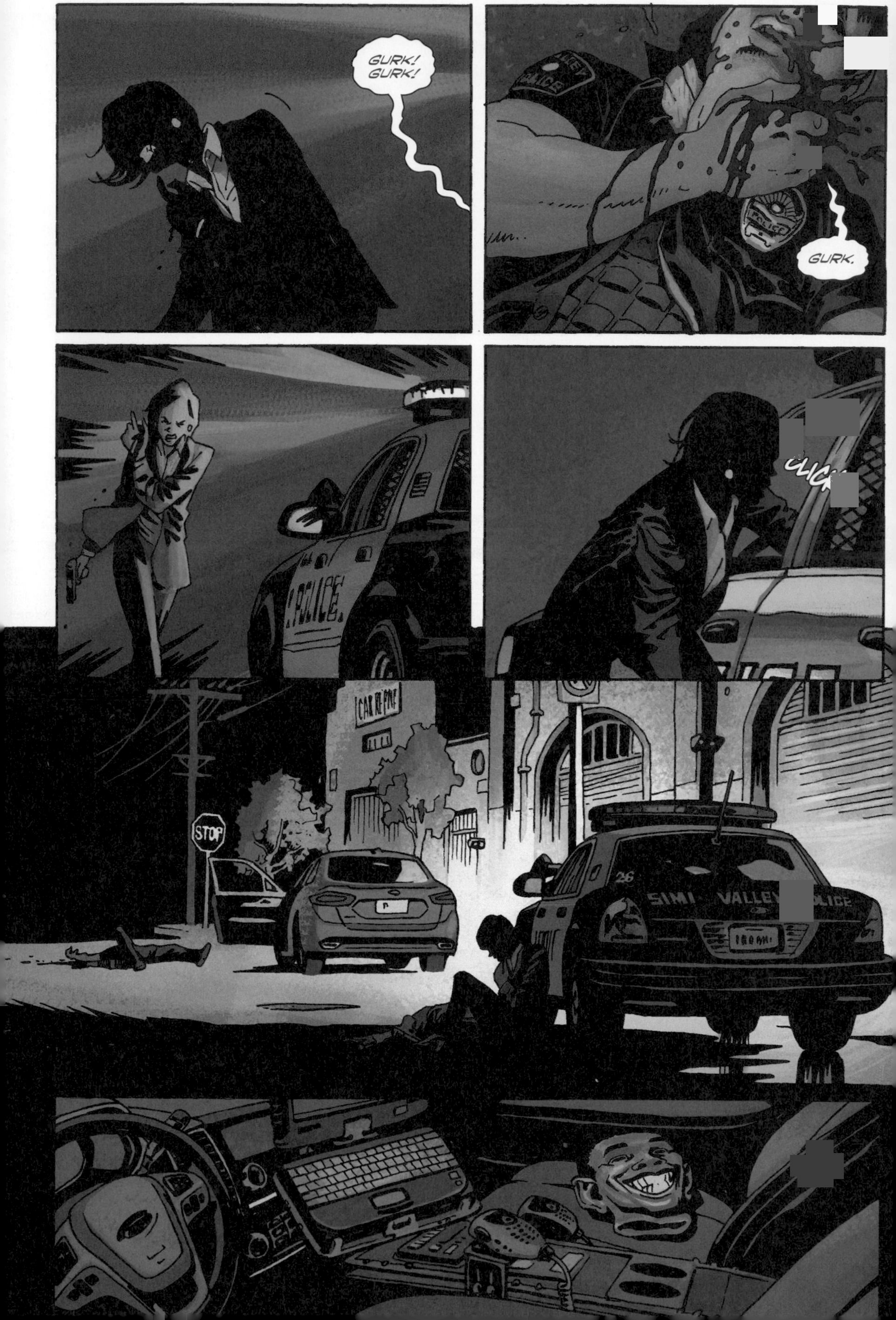
GURK! GURK!
GURK.
POLICE
STOP

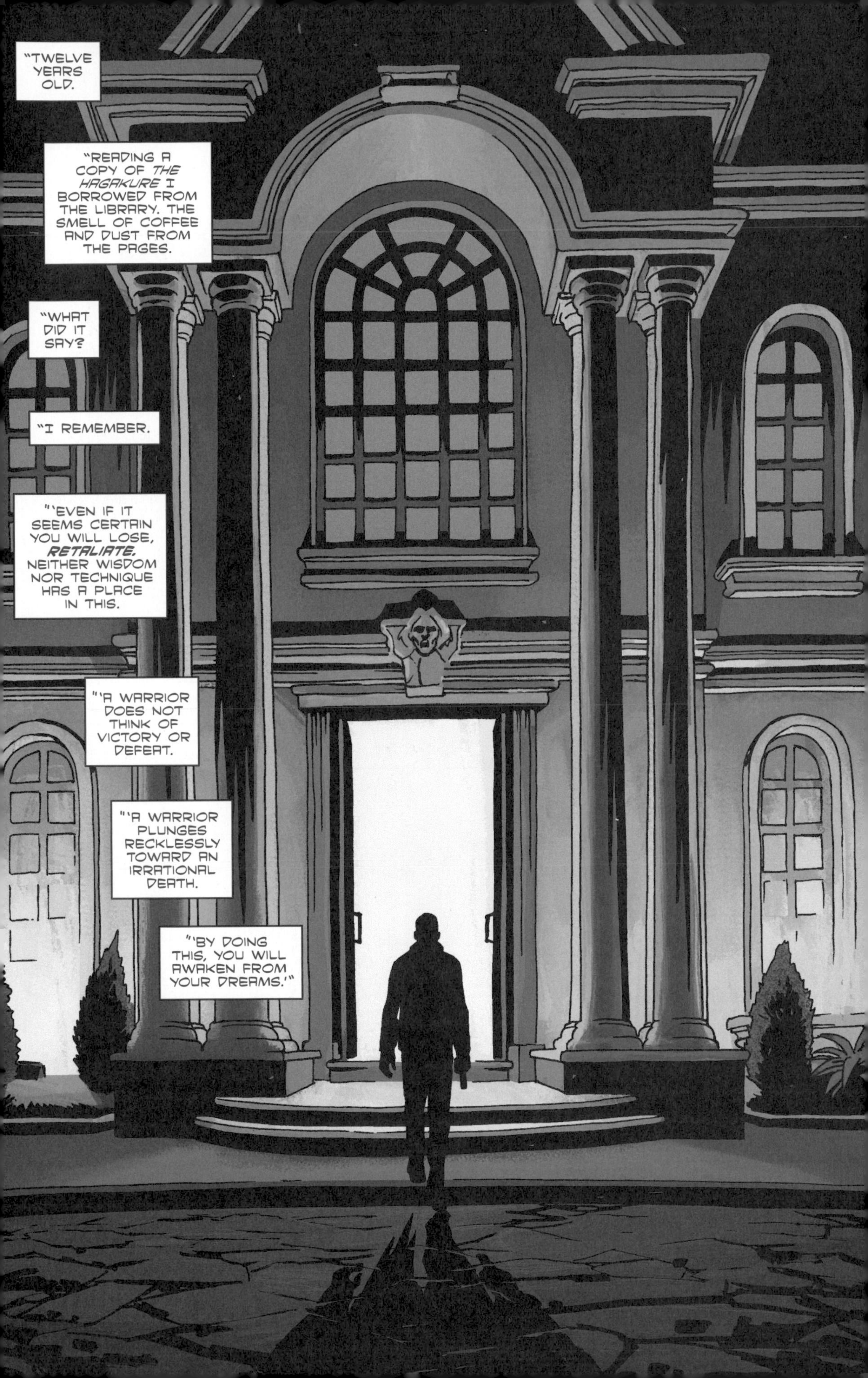
"TWELVE YEARS OLD.
"READING A COPY OF *THE HAGAKURE* I BORROWED FROM THE LIBRARY. THE SMELL OF COFFEE AND DUST FROM THE PAGES.
"WHAT DID IT SAY?
"I REMEMBER.
"'EVEN IF IT SEEMS CERTAIN YOU WILL LOSE, ***RETALIATE.*** NEITHER WISDOM NOR TECHNIQUE HAS A PLACE IN THIS.
"'A WARRIOR DOES NOT THINK OF VICTORY OR DEFEAT.
"'A WARRIOR PLUNGES RECKLESSLY TOWARD AN IRRATIONAL DEATH.
"'BY DOING THIS, YOU WILL AWAKEN FROM YOUR DREAMS.'"

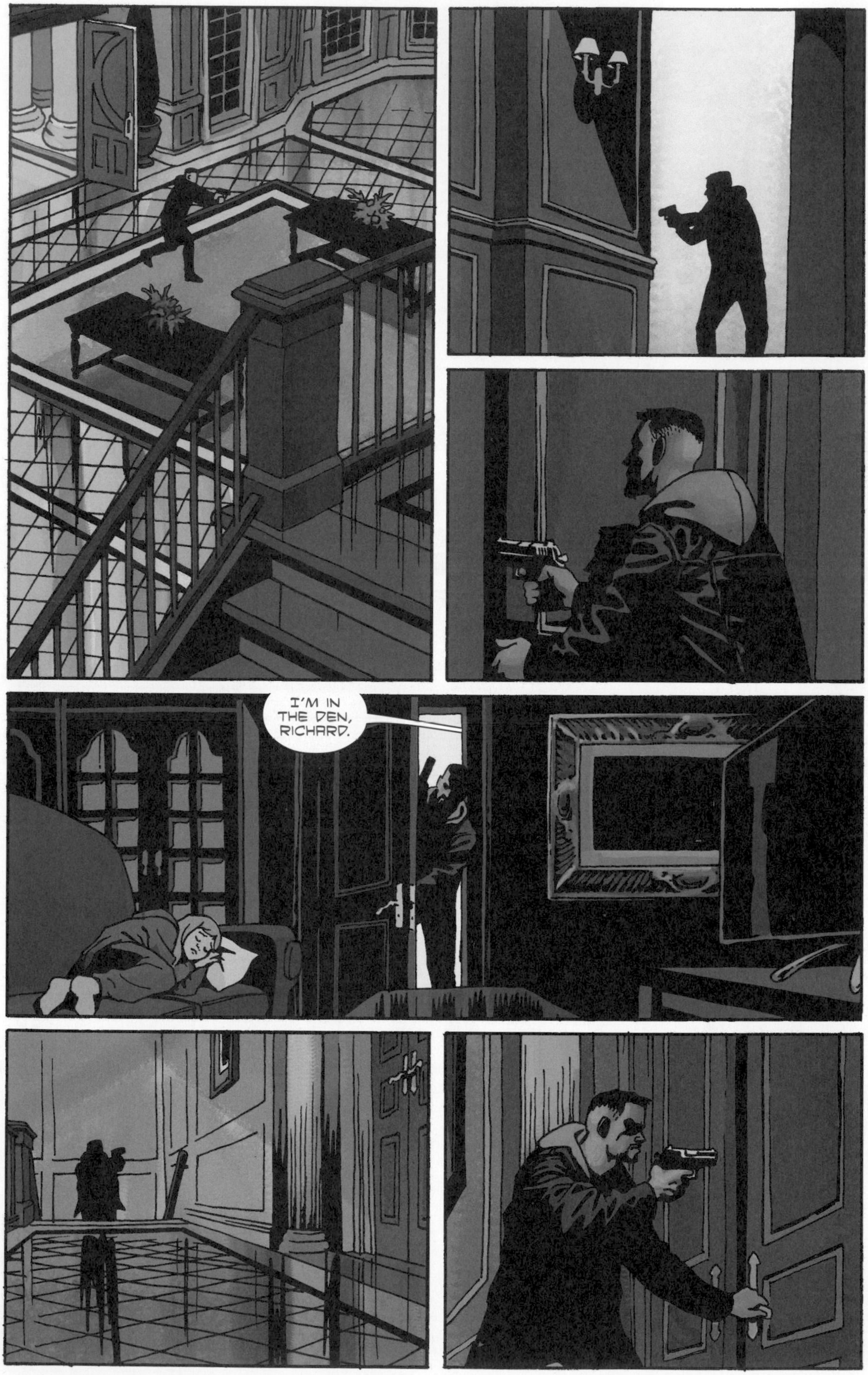
I'M IN THE DEN, RICHARD.

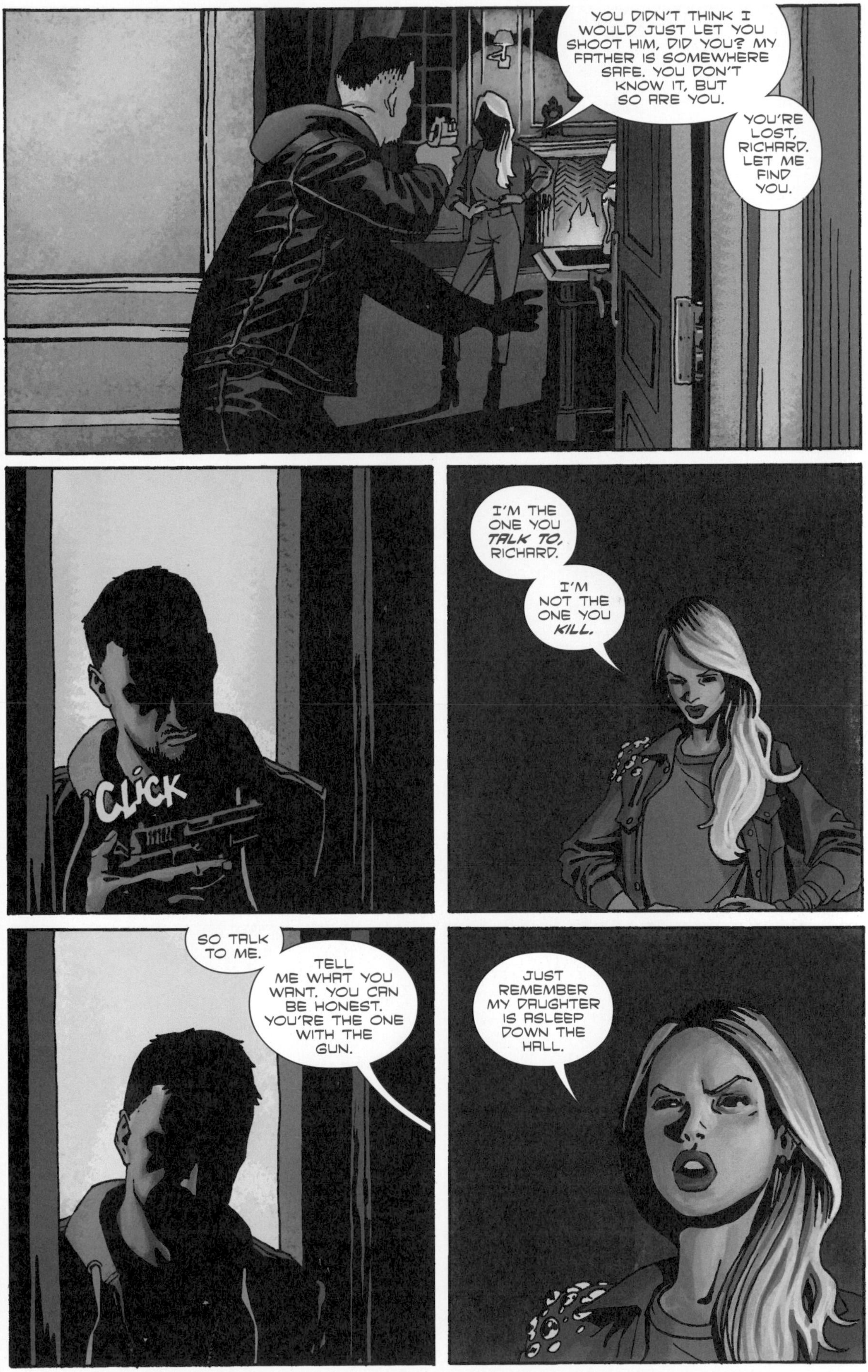
YOU DIDN'T THINK I WOULD JUST LET YOU SHOOT HIM, DID YOU? MY FATHER IS SOMEWHERE SAFE. YOU DON'T KNOW IT, BUT SO ARE YOU.
YOU'RE LOST, RICHARD. LET ME FIND YOU.
CLICK
I'M THE ONE YOU TALK TO, RICHARD.
I'M NOT THE ONE YOU KILL.
SO TALK TO ME.
TELL ME WHAT YOU WANT. YOU CAN BE HONEST. YOU'RE THE ONE WITH THE GUN.
JUST REMEMBER MY DAUGHTER IS ASLEEP DOWN THE HALL.

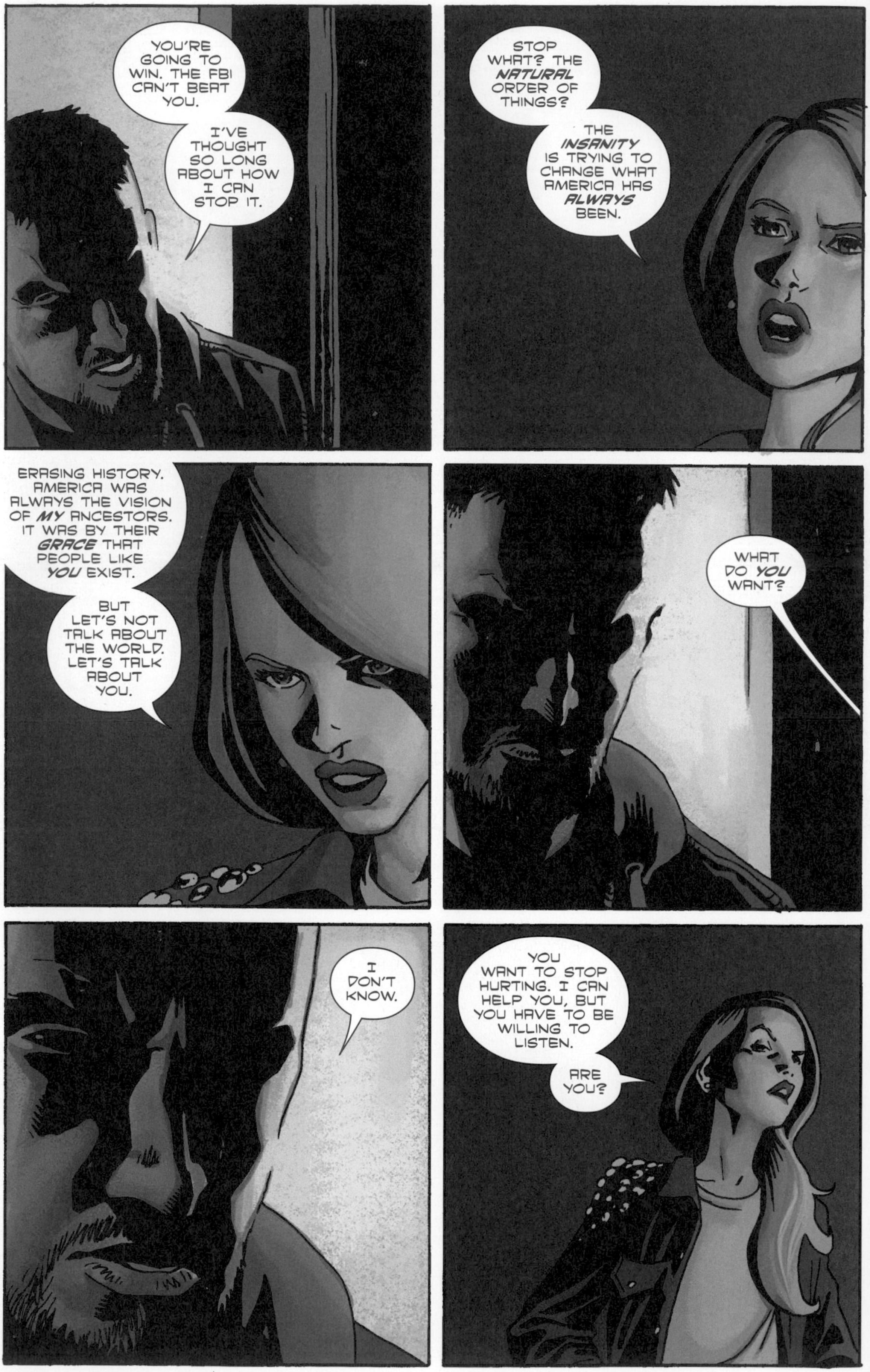
YOU'RE GOING TO WIN. THE FBI CAN'T BEAT YOU.
I'VE THOUGHT SO LONG ABOUT HOW I CAN STOP IT.
STOP WHAT? THE *NATURAL* ORDER OF THINGS?
THE *INSANITY* IS TRYING TO CHANGE WHAT AMERICA HAS *ALWAYS* BEEN.
ERASING HISTORY. AMERICA WAS ALWAYS THE VISION OF *MY* ANCESTORS. IT WAS BY THEIR *GRACE* THAT PEOPLE LIKE *YOU* EXIST.
BUT LET'S NOT TALK ABOUT THE WORLD. LET'S TALK ABOUT YOU.
WHAT DO *YOU* WANT?
I DON'T KNOW.
YOU WANT TO STOP HURTING. I CAN HELP YOU, BUT YOU HAVE TO BE WILLING TO LISTEN.
ARE YOU?

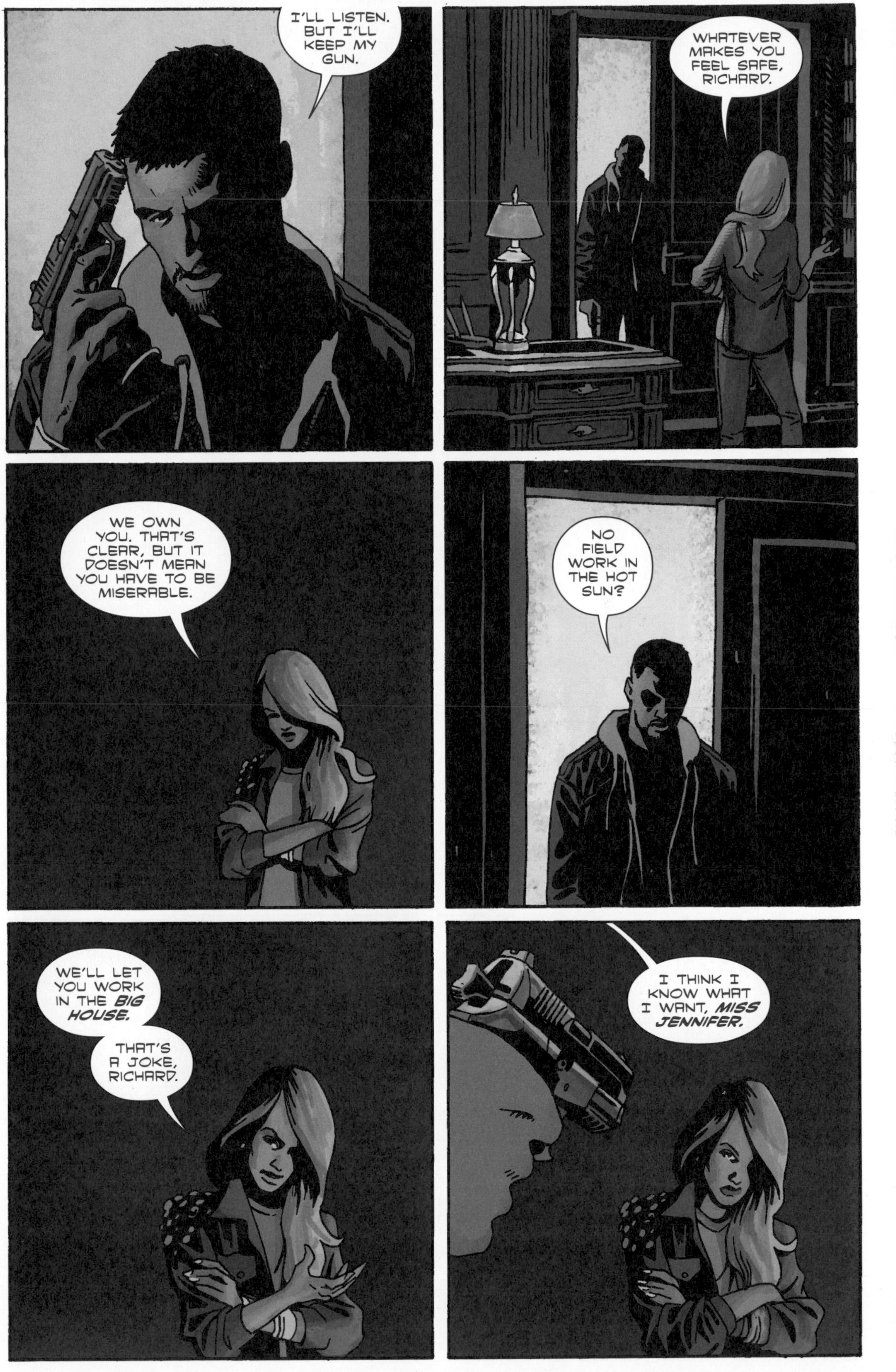
I'LL LISTEN. BUT I'LL KEEP MY GUN.
WHATEVER MAKES YOU FEEL SAFE, RICHARD.
WE OWN YOU. THAT'S CLEAR, BUT IT DOESN'T MEAN YOU HAVE TO BE MISERABLE.
NO FIELD WORK IN THE HOT SUN?
WE'LL LET YOU WORK IN THE *BIG HOUSE.*
THAT'S A JOKE, RICHARD.
I THINK I KNOW WHAT I WANT, *MISS JENNIFER.*

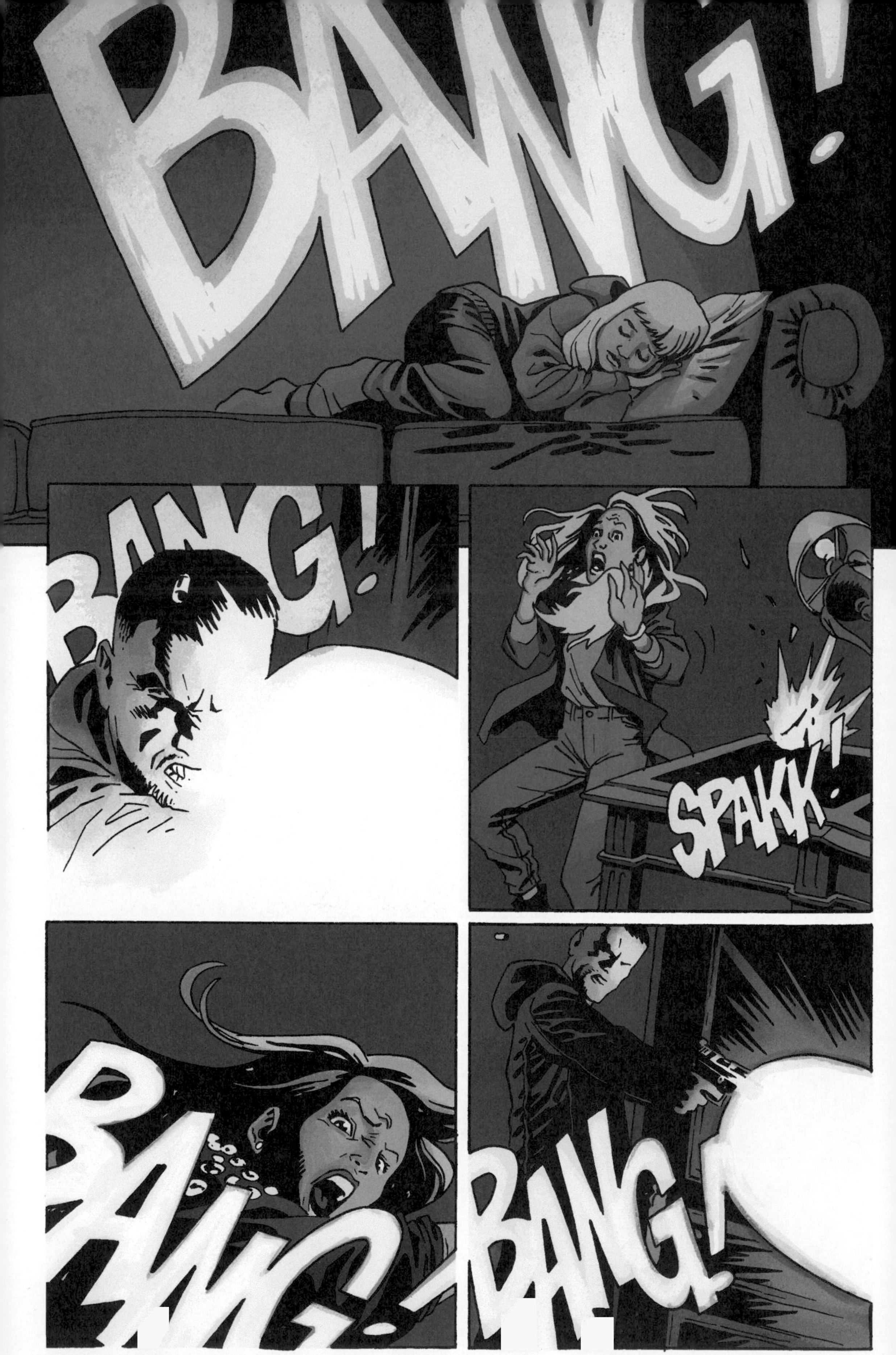
BANG!
BANG!
SPAKK!
BANG!
BANG!

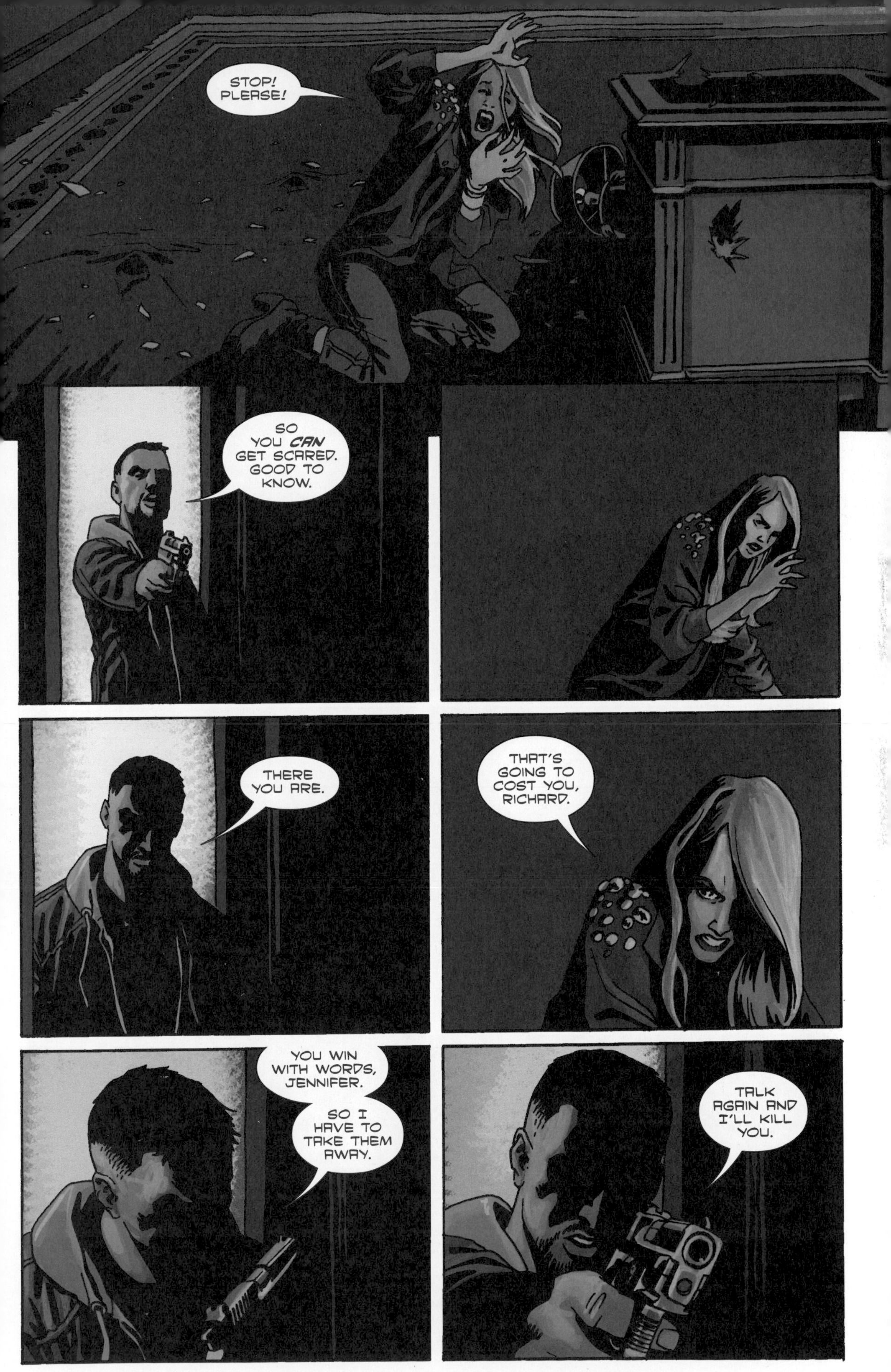
STOP! PLEASE!
SO YOU *CAN* GET SCARED. GOOD TO KNOW.
THERE YOU ARE.
THAT'S GOING TO COST YOU, RICHARD.
YOU WIN WITH WORDS, JENNIFER.
SO I HAVE TO TAKE THEM AWAY.
TALK AGAIN AND I'LL KILL YOU.

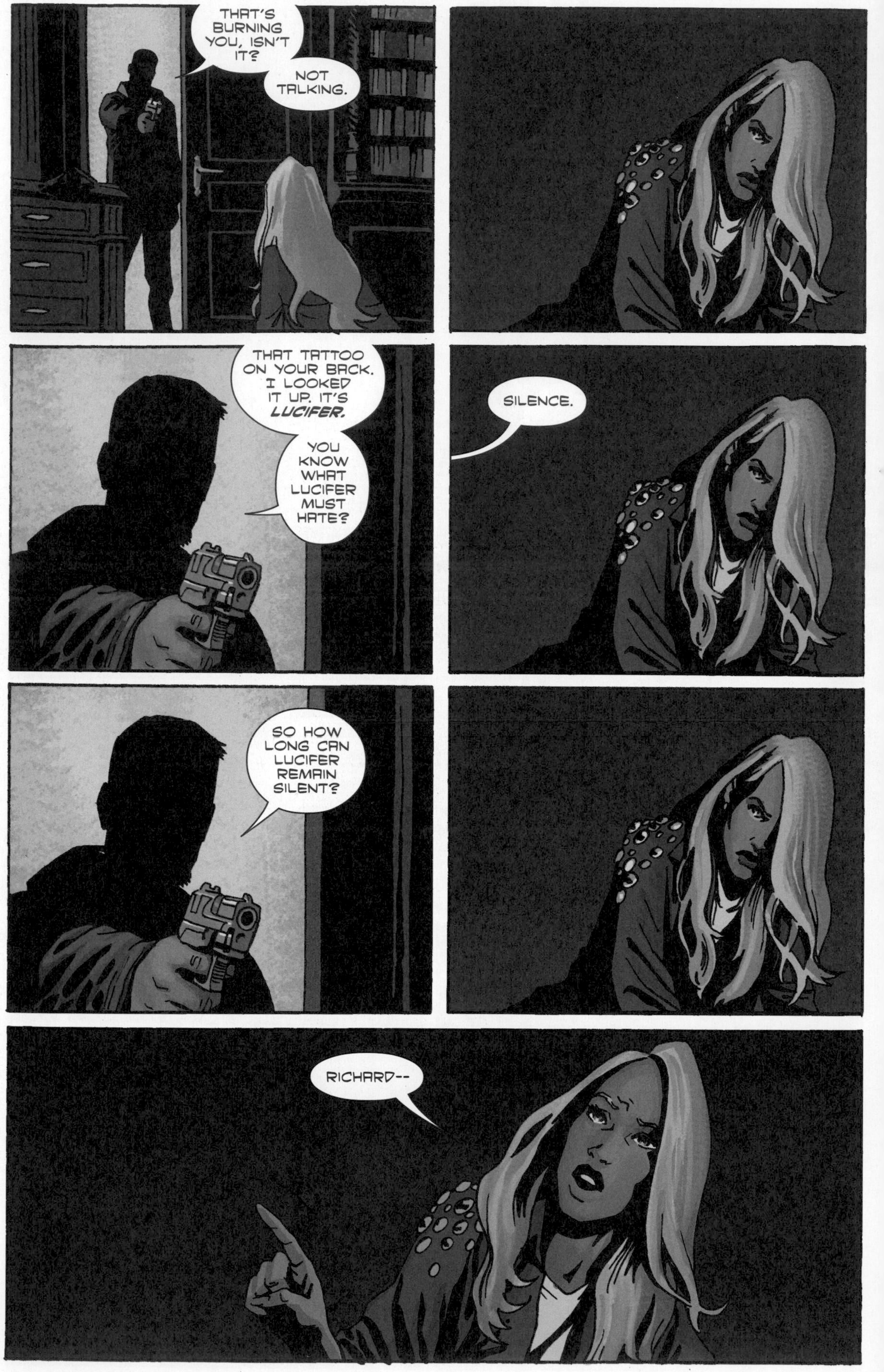
THAT'S BURNING YOU, ISN'T IT?
NOT TALKING.
THAT TATTOO ON YOUR BACK. I LOOKED IT UP. IT'S *LUCIFER.*
YOU KNOW WHAT LUCIFER MUST HATE?
SILENCE.
SO HOW LONG CAN LUCIFER REMAIN SILENT?
RICHARD--

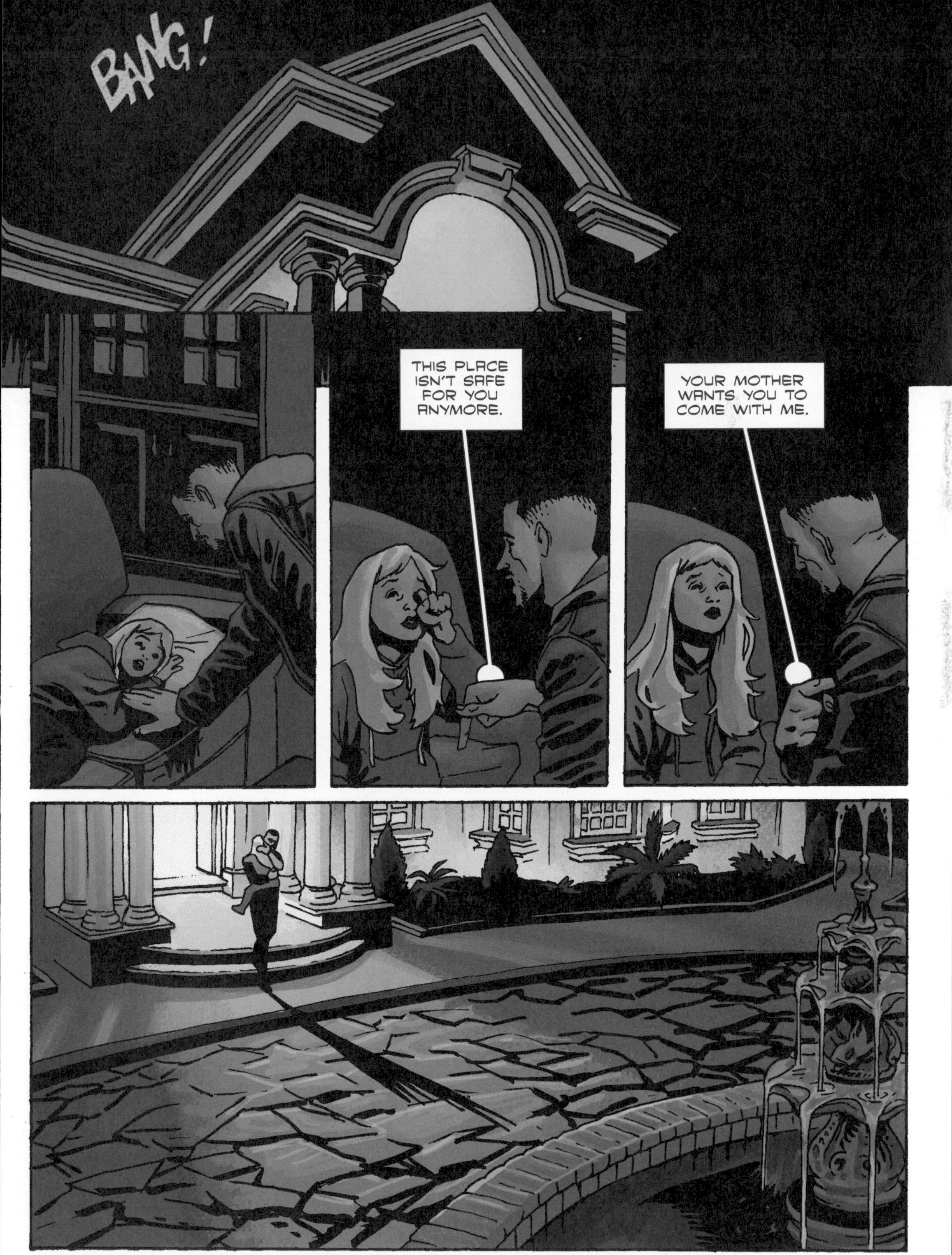
BANG!
THIS PLACE ISN'T SAFE FOR YOU ANYMORE.
YOUR MOTHER WANTS YOU TO COME WITH ME.

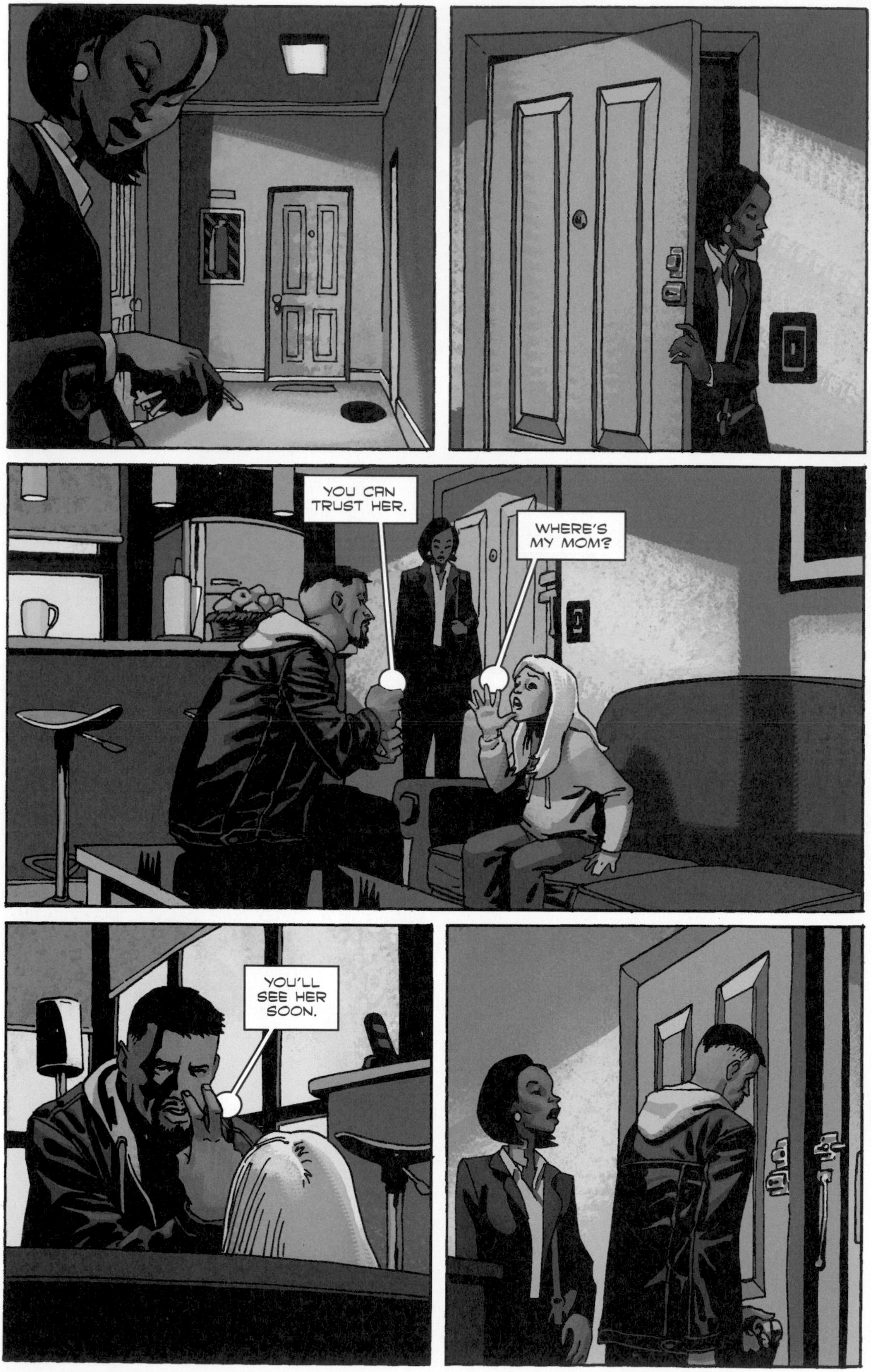
YOU CAN TRUST HER.
WHERE'S MY MOM?
YOU'LL SEE HER SOON.

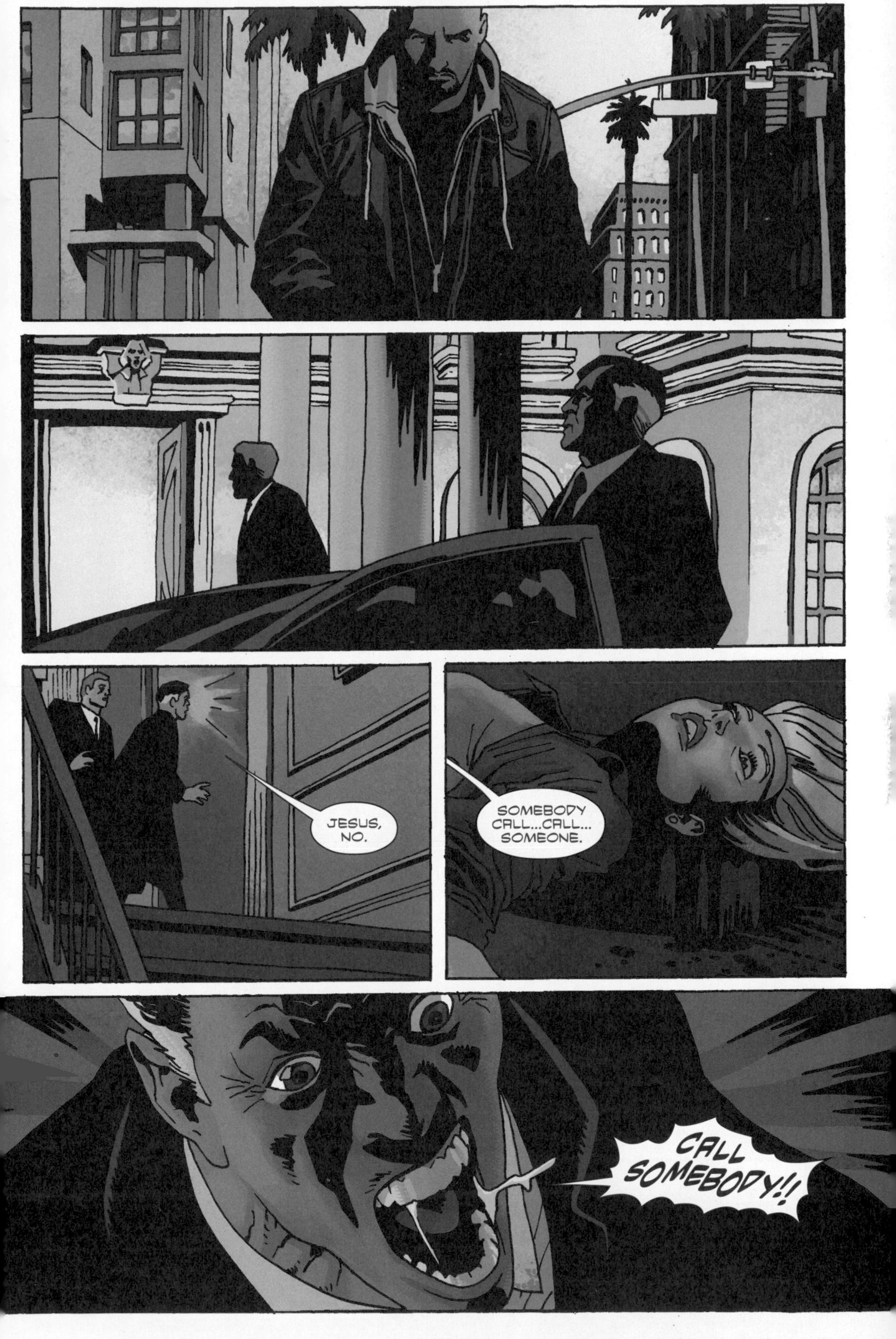
JESUS, NO.
SOMEBODY CALL...CALL... SOMEONE.
CALL SOMEBODY!!

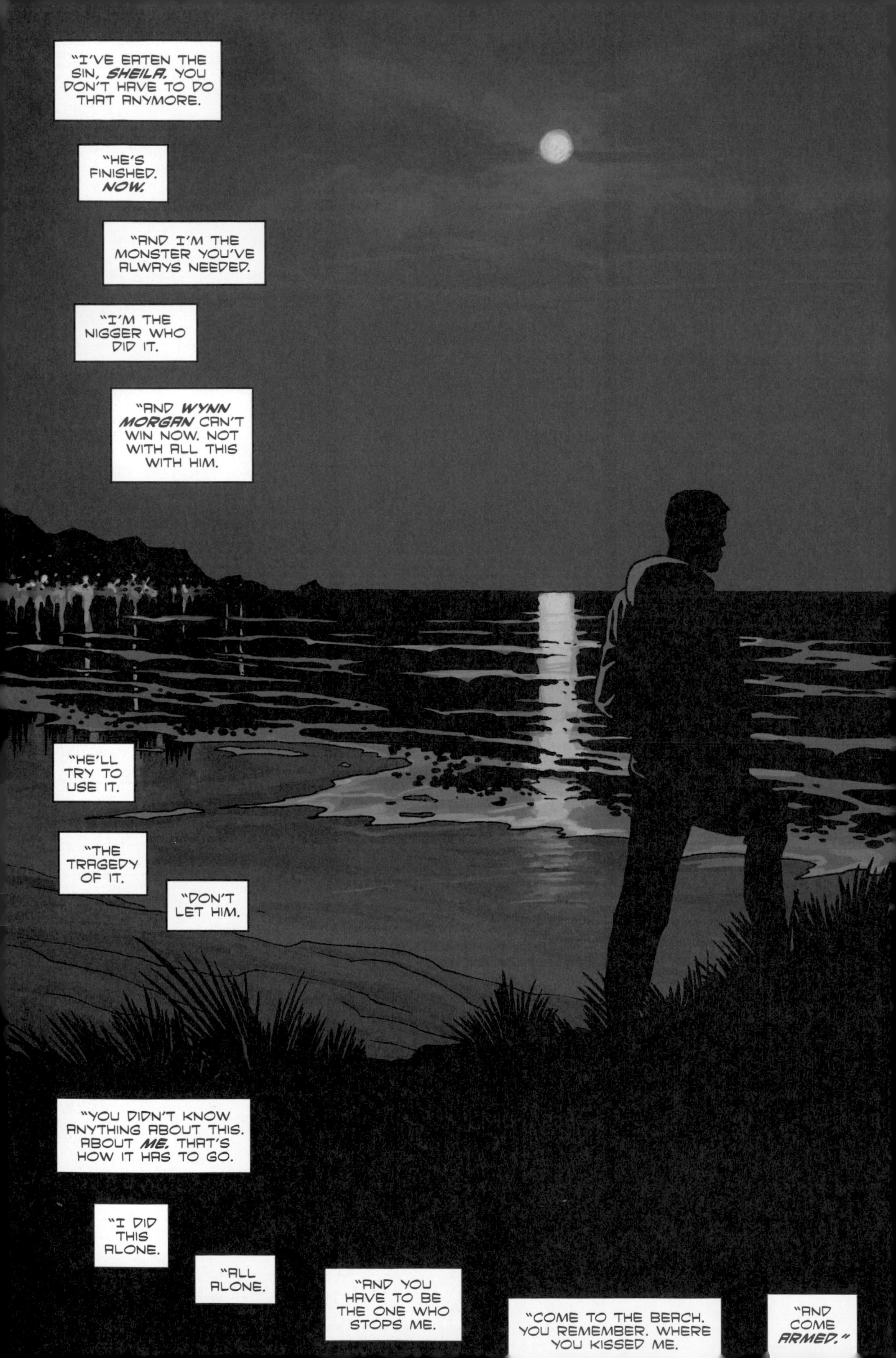
"I'VE EATEN THE SIN, *SHEILA.* YOU DON'T HAVE TO DO THAT ANYMORE.
"HE'S FINISHED. *NOW.*
"AND I'M THE MONSTER YOU'VE ALWAYS NEEDED.
"I'M THE NIGGER WHO DID IT.
"AND *WYNN MORGAN* CAN'T WIN NOW. NOT WITH ALL THIS WITH HIM.
"HE'LL TRY TO USE IT.
"THE TRAGEDY OF IT.
"DON'T LET HIM.
"YOU DIDN'T KNOW ANYTHING ABOUT THIS. ABOUT *ME.* THAT'S HOW IT HAS TO GO.
"I DID THIS ALONE.
"ALL ALONE.
"AND YOU HAVE TO BE THE ONE WHO STOPS ME.
"COME TO THE BEACH. YOU REMEMBER. WHERE YOU KISSED ME.
"AND COME *ARMED.*"

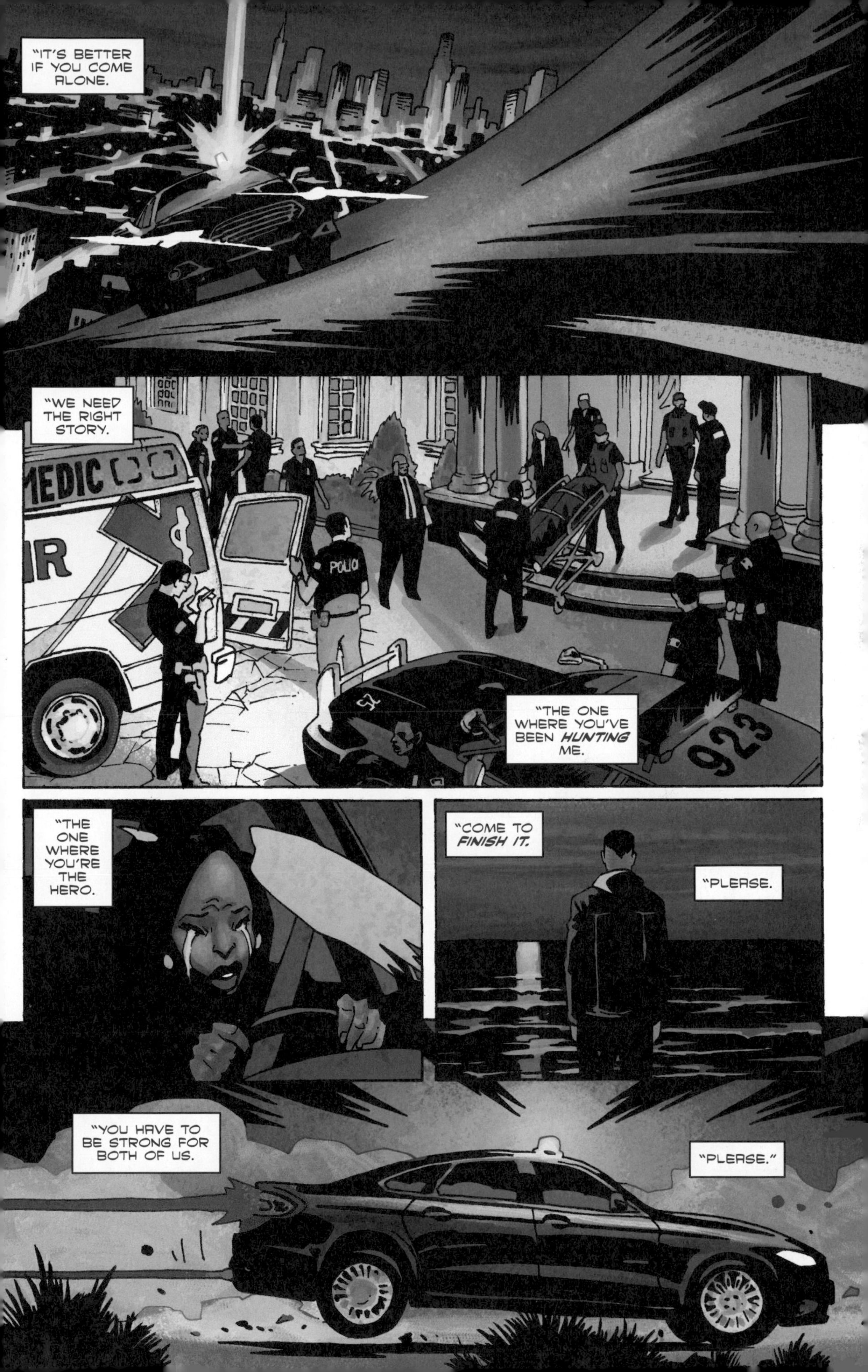
"IT'S BETTER IF YOU COME ALONE.
"WE NEED THE RIGHT STORY.
MEDIC
POLICE
"THE ONE WHERE YOU'VE BEEN *HUNTING* ME.
923
"THE ONE WHERE YOU'RE THE HERO.
"COME TO *FINISH IT.*
"PLEASE.
"YOU HAVE TO BE STRONG FOR BOTH OF US.
"PLEASE."

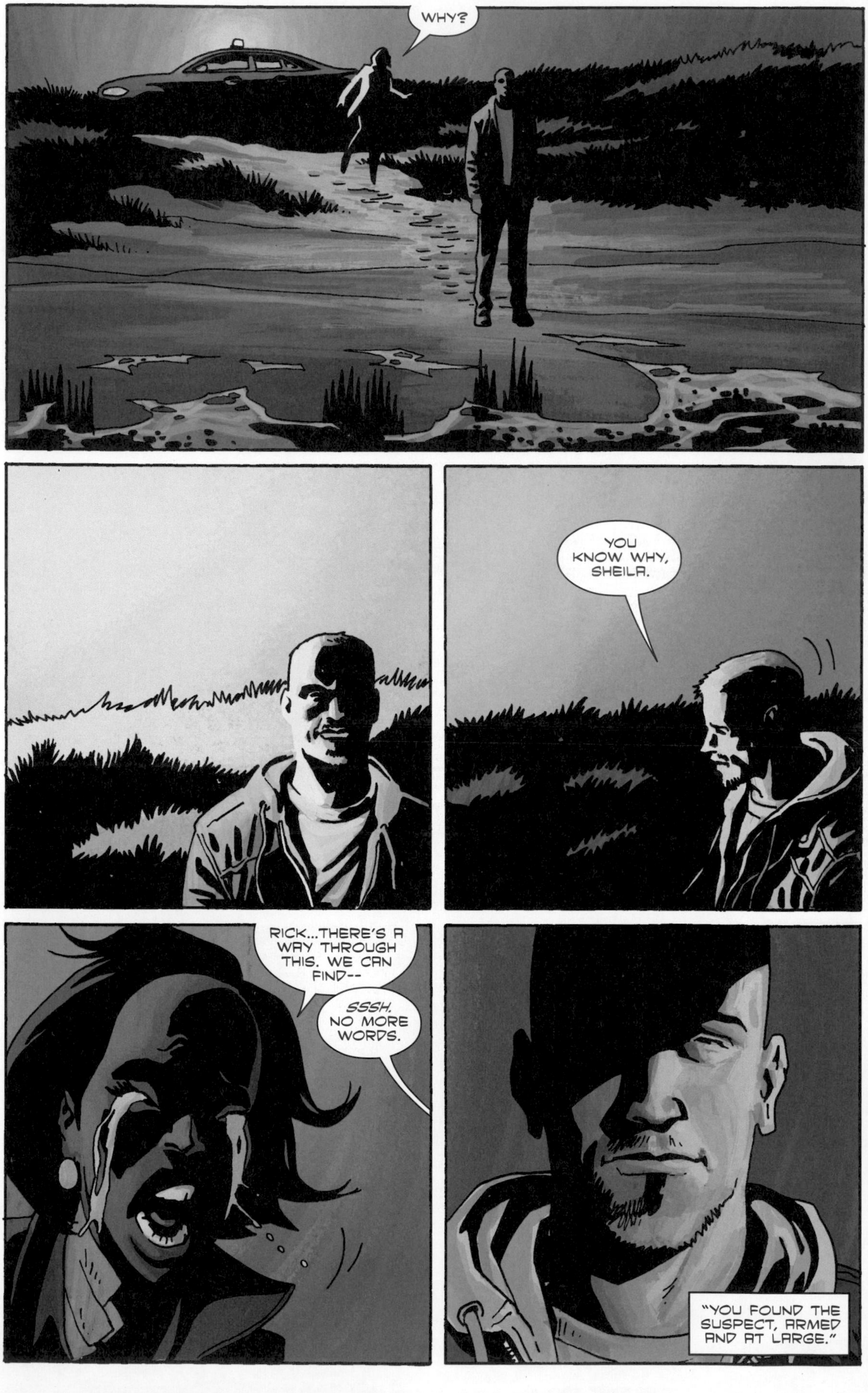
WHY?
YOU KNOW WHY, SHEILA.
RICK...THERE'S A WAY THROUGH THIS. WE CAN FIND--
SSSH. NO MORE WORDS.
"YOU FOUND THE SUSPECT, ARMED AND AT LARGE."

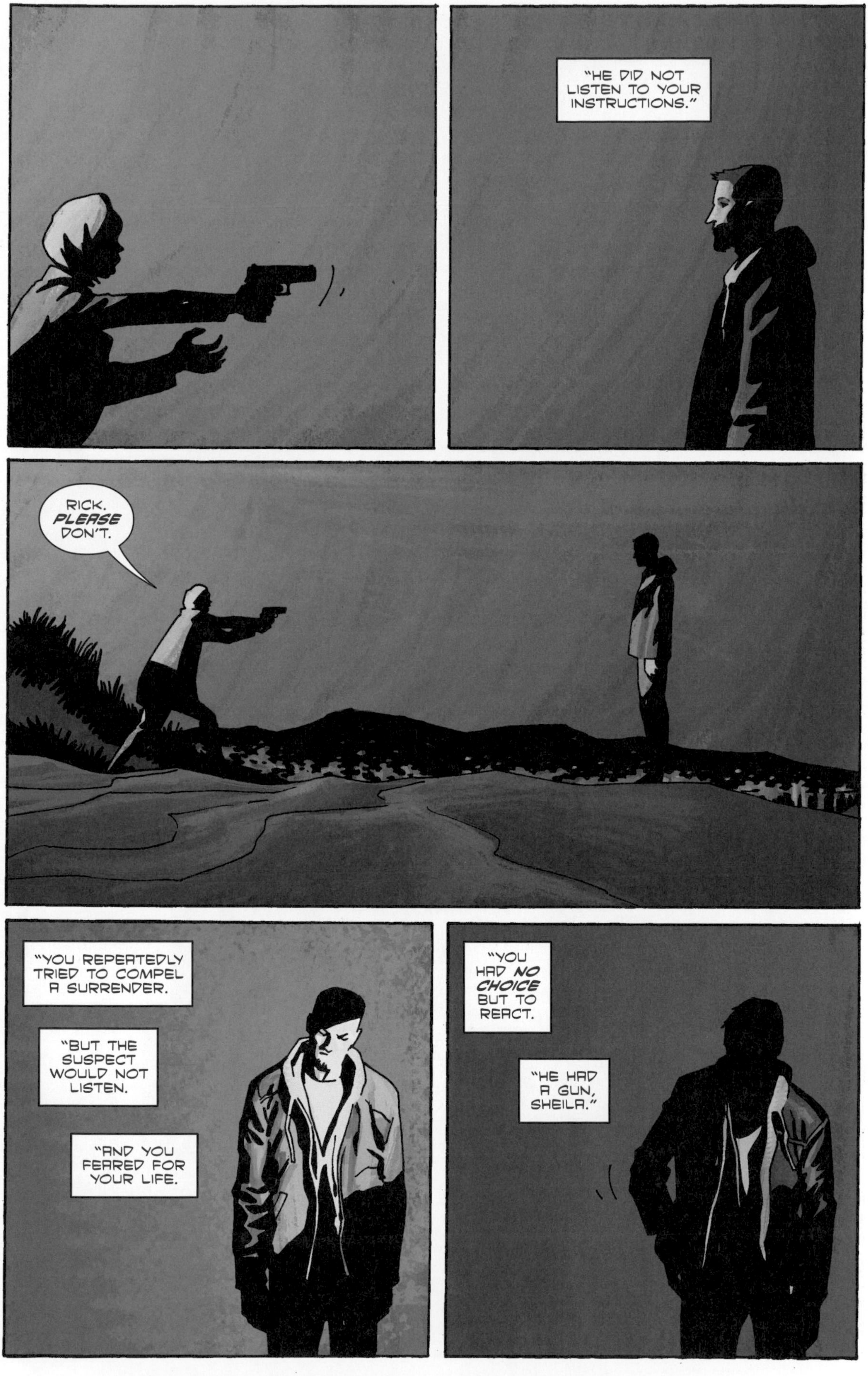
"HE DID NOT LISTEN TO YOUR INSTRUCTIONS."
RICK. *PLEASE* DON'T.
"YOU REPEATEDLY TRIED TO COMPEL A SURRENDER.
"BUT THE SUSPECT WOULD NOT LISTEN.
"AND YOU FEARED FOR YOUR LIFE.
"YOU HAD *NO CHOICE* BUT TO REACT.
"HE HAD A GUN, SHEILA."

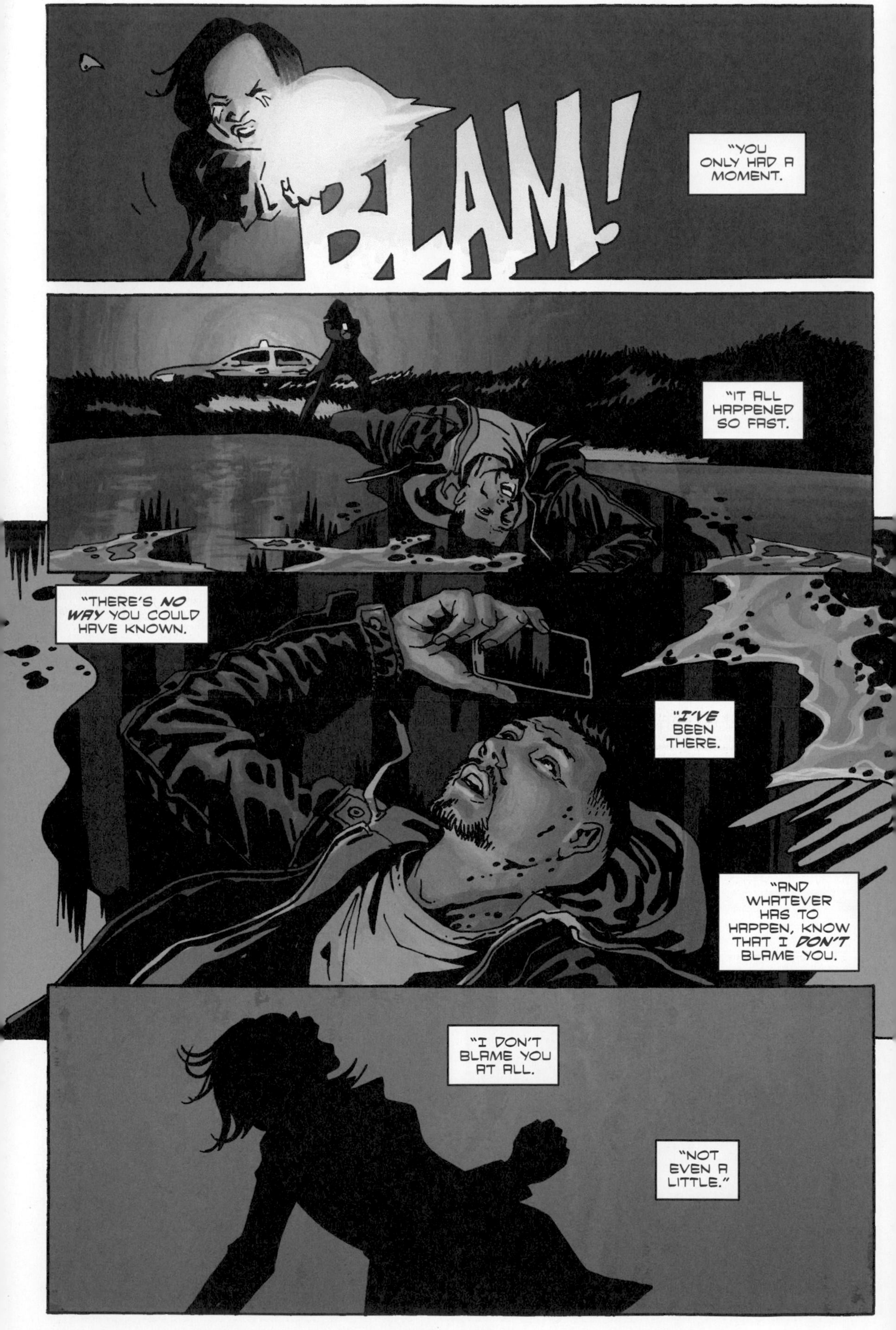
BLAM!
"YOU ONLY HAD A MOMENT.
"IT ALL HAPPENED SO FAST.
"THERE'S *NO WAY* YOU COULD HAVE KNOWN.
"*I'VE* BEEN THERE.
"AND WHATEVER HAS TO HAPPEN, KNOW THAT I *DON'T* BLAME YOU.
"I DON'T BLAME YOU AT ALL.
"NOT EVEN A LITTLE."

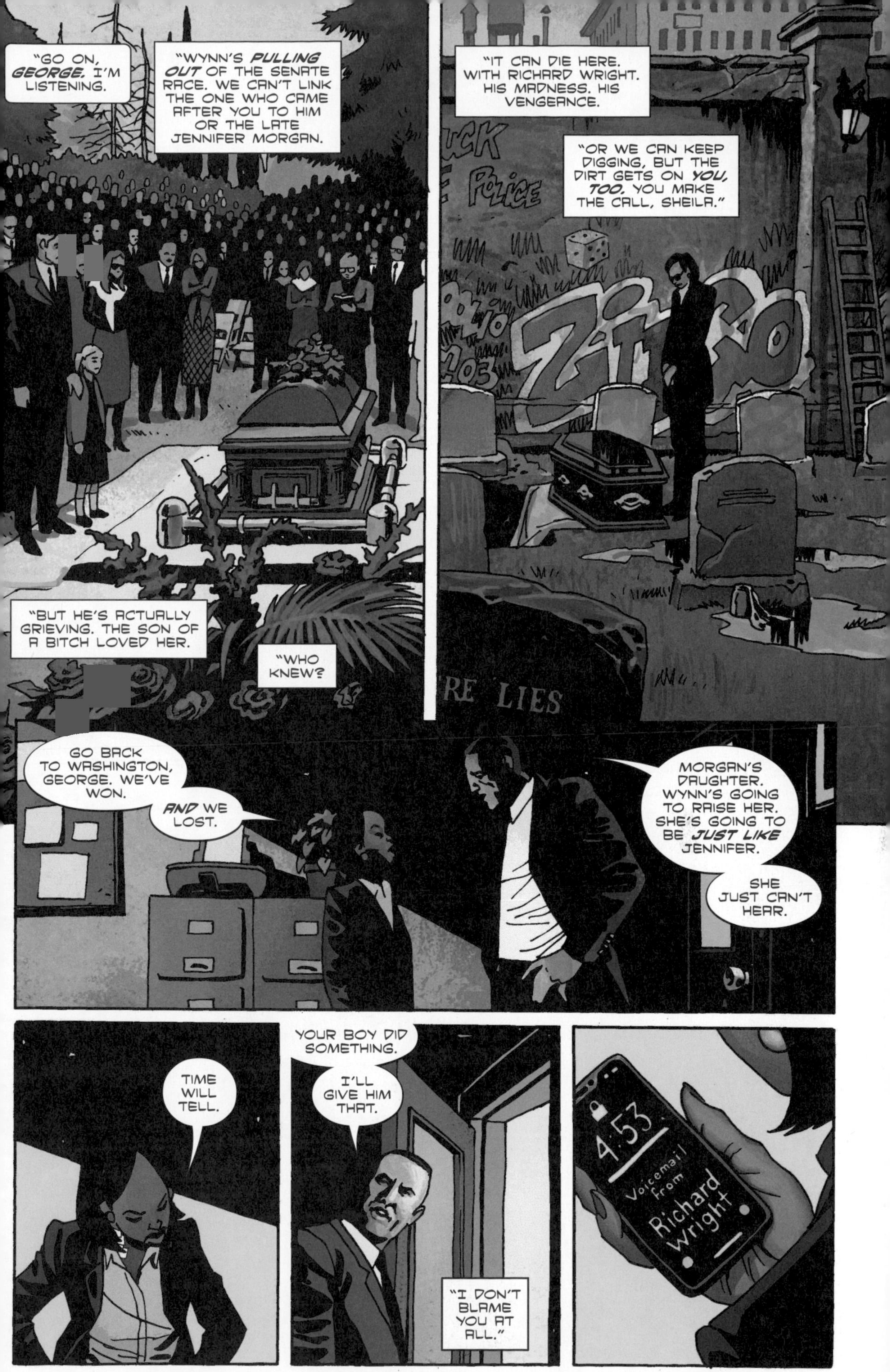
"GO ON, GEORGE. I'M LISTENING.
"WYNN'S PULLING OUT OF THE SENATE RACE. WE CAN'T LINK THE ONE WHO CAME AFTER YOU TO HIM OR THE LATE JENNIFER MORGAN.
"BUT HE'S ACTUALLY GRIEVING. THE SON OF A BITCH LOVED HER.
"WHO KNEW?
"IT CAN DIE HERE. WITH RICHARD WRIGHT. HIS MADNESS. HIS VENGEANCE.
"OR WE CAN KEEP DIGGING, BUT THE DIRT GETS ON YOU, TOO. YOU MAKE THE CALL, SHEILA."
RE LIES
GO BACK TO WASHINGTON, GEORGE. WE'VE WON.
AND WE LOST.
MORGAN'S DAUGHTER. WYNN'S GOING TO RAISE HER. SHE'S GOING TO BE JUST LIKE JENNIFER.
SHE JUST CAN'T HEAR.
TIME WILL TELL.
YOUR BOY DID SOMETHING.
I'LL GIVE HIM THAT.
"I DON'T BLAME YOU AT ALL."
4:53
Voicemail from Richard Wright

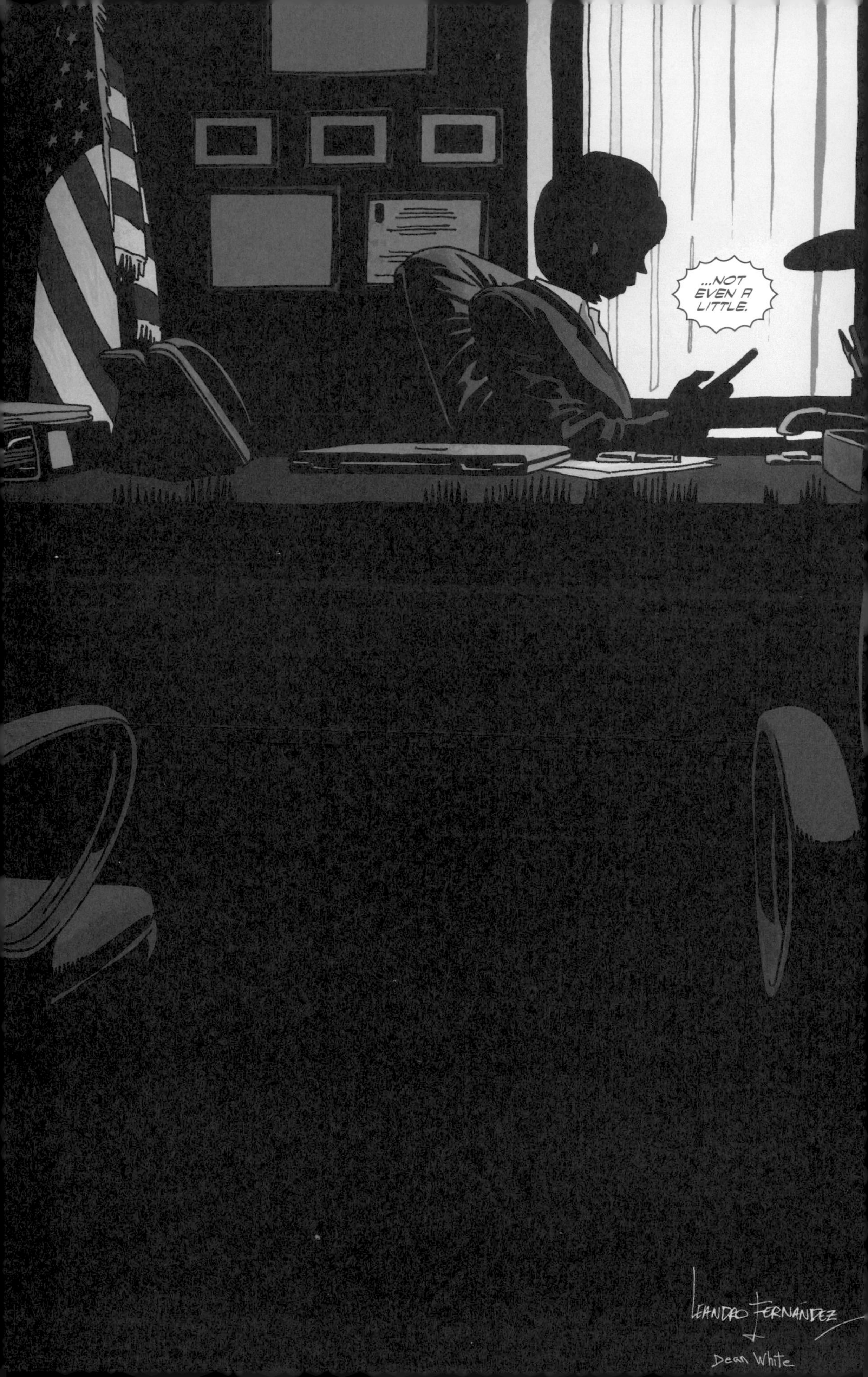
...NOT EVEN A LITTLE.
LEANDRO FERNÁNDEZ
Dean White

Variant cover art for issue #1 by
RAFAEL ALBUQUERQUE and RICO RENZI

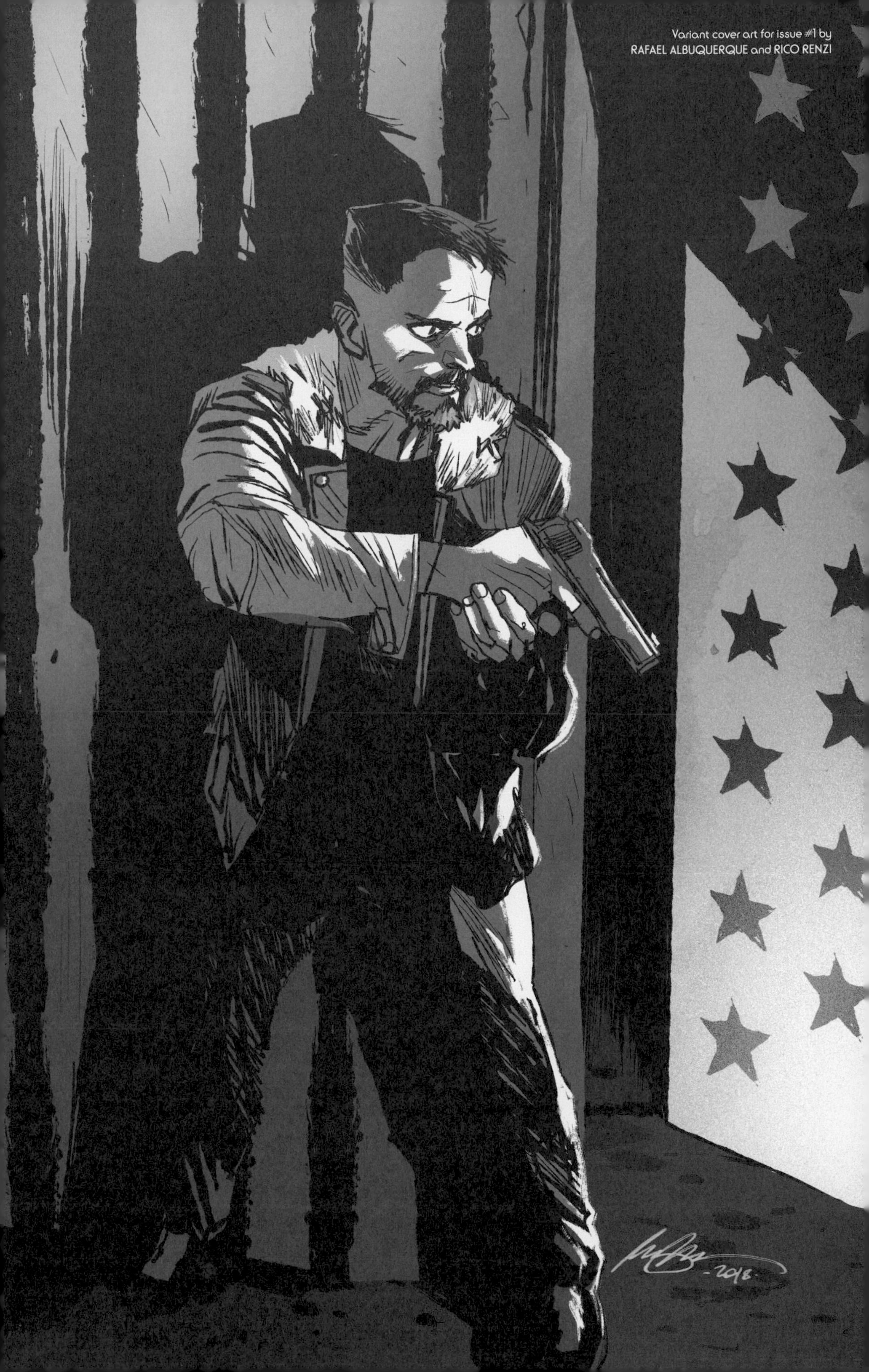

CHARACTER DESIGNS BY LEANDRO FERNANDEZ

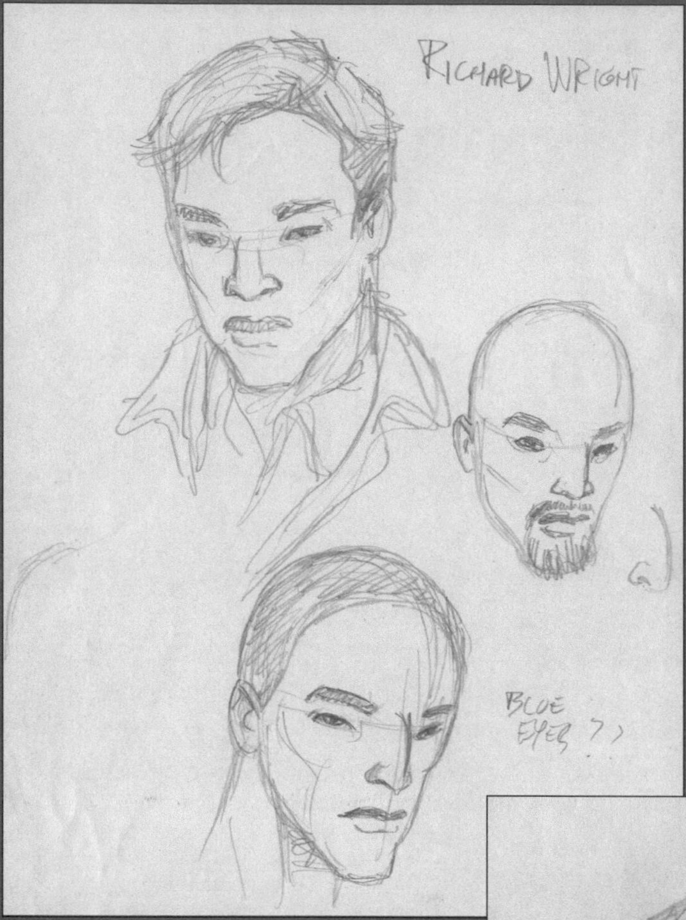
RICHARD WRIGHT
BLUE
EYES ??

Early character designs for Richard Wright

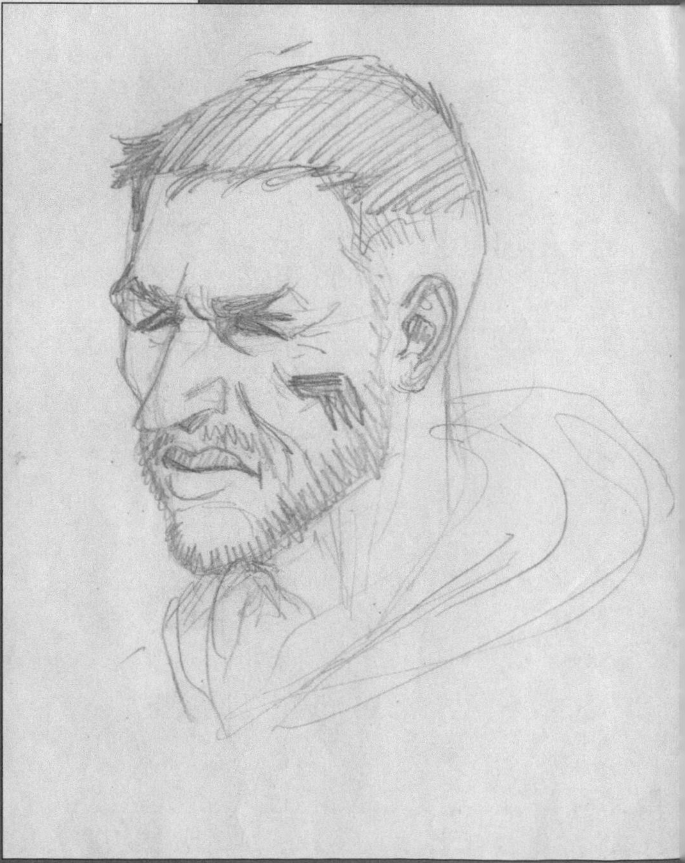

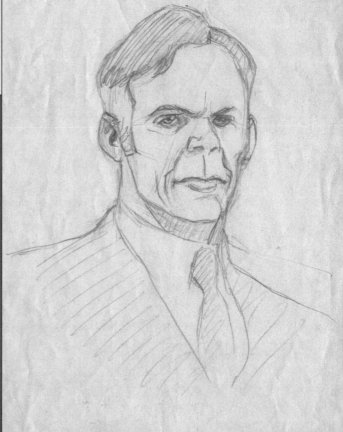

An early sketch and a more finished design for Wynn Morgan

Preliminary designs for Sheila Curry

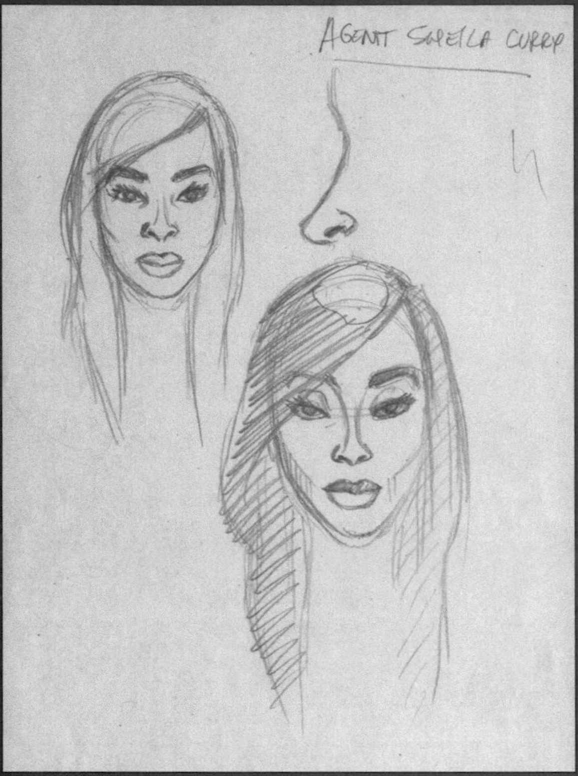
AGENT SHEILA CURRY

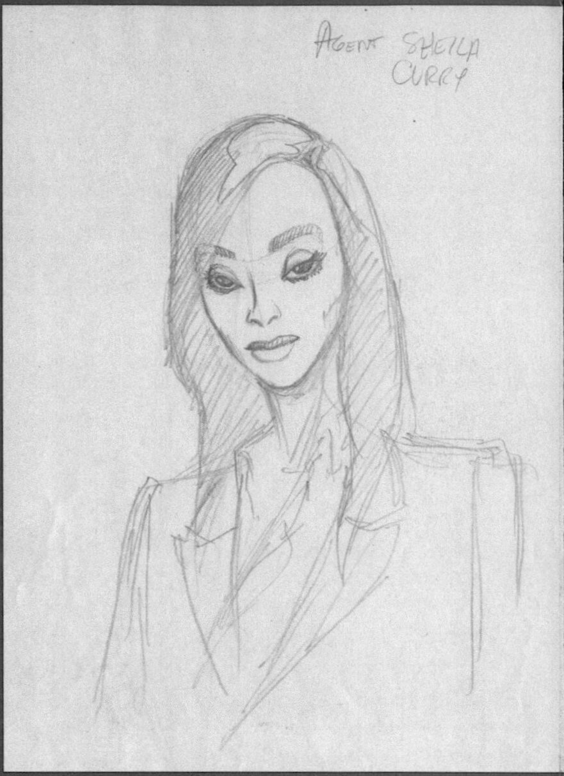
AGENT SHEILA
CURRY

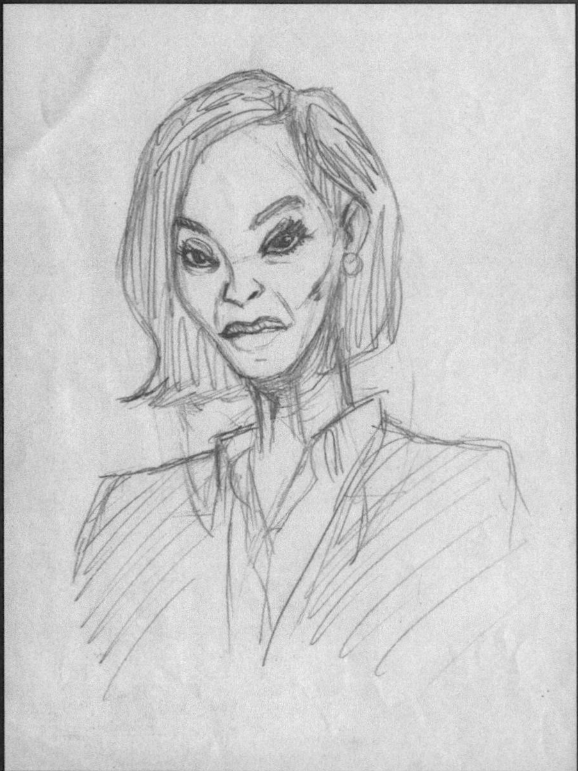

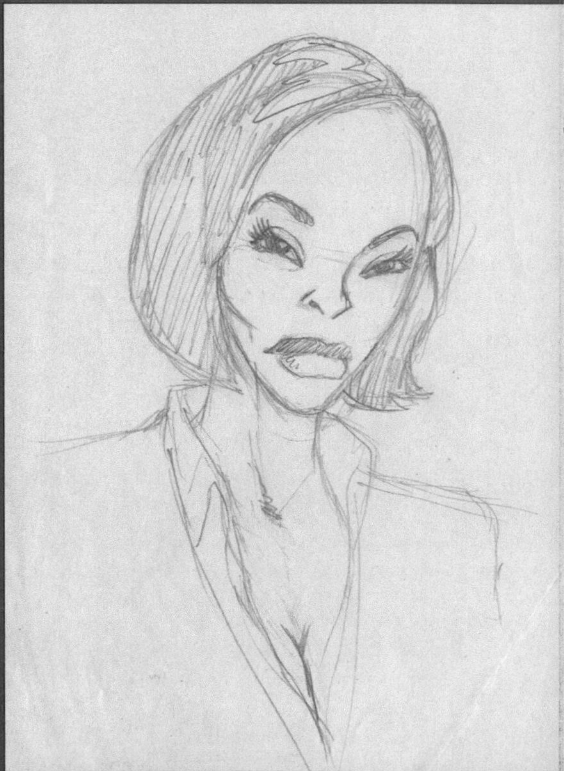